Norihiro Yagi won the 32nd Akatsuka Award for his debut work, *UNDEADMAN*, which appeared in *Monthly Shonen Jump* magazine and produced two sequels. His first serialized manga was his comedy *Angel Densetsu* (Angel Legend), which appeared in *Monthly Shonen Jump* from 1992 to 2000. His epic saga, *Claymore*, is running in *Monthly Jump Square* magazine.

In his spare time, Yagi enjoys things like the Japanese comedic duo Downtown, martial arts, games, driving, and hard rock music, but he doesn't consider these actual hobbies.

CLAYMORE VOL. 24
SHONEN JUMP ADVANCED Manga Edition

STORY AND ART BY
NORIHIRO YAGI

English Adaptation & Translation/John Werry
Touch-up Art & Lettering/Sabrina Heep
Design/Amy Martin
Editor/Megan Bates

Printed in the U.S.A.

Published by VIZ Media, LLC
P.O. Box 77010
San Francisco, CA 94107

10 9 8 7 6 5 4 3 2 1
First printing, May 2014

SHONEN JUMP ADVANCED Manga Edition

Claymore

クレイモア

Vol. 24
Army of the Underworld

Story and Art by **Norihiro Yagi**

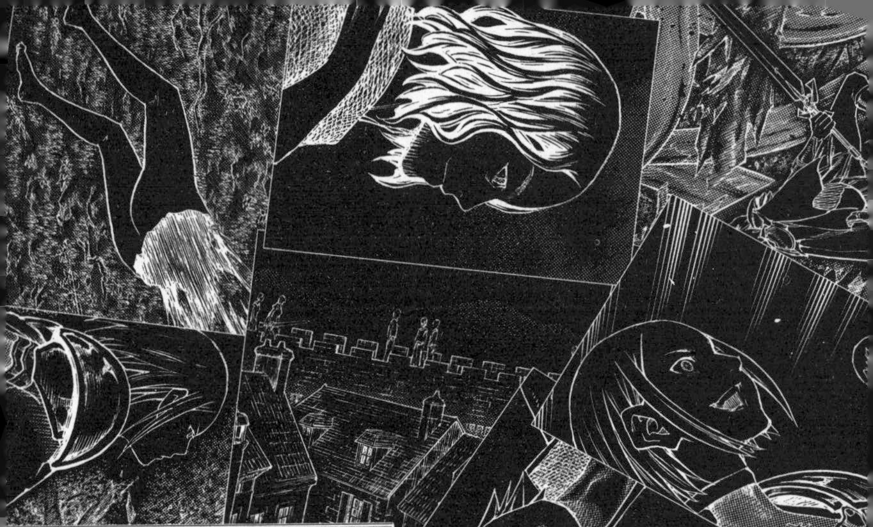

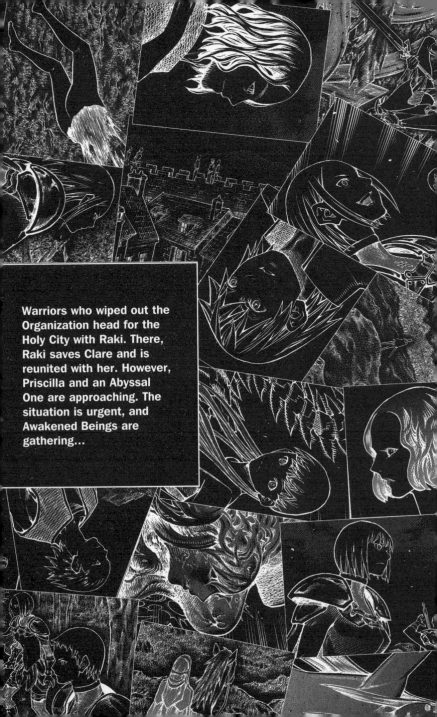

Warriors who wiped out the Organization head for the Holy City with Raki. There, Raki saves Clare and is reunited with her. However, Priscilla and an Abyssal One are approaching. The situation is urgent, and Awakened Beings are gathering...

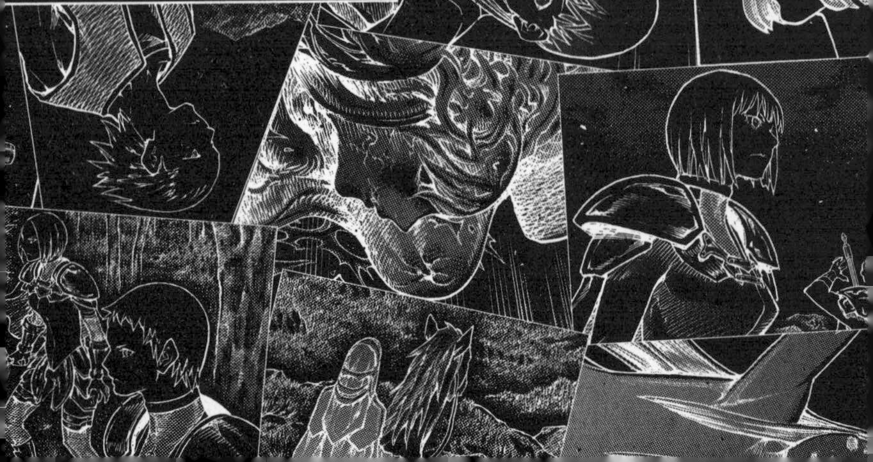

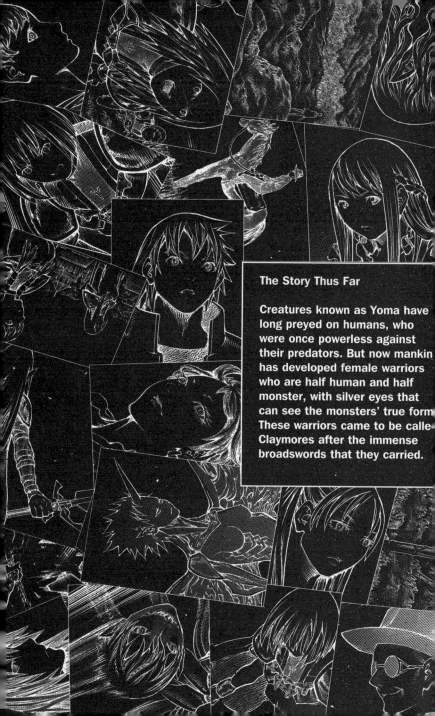

The Story Thus Far

Creatures known as Yoma have long preyed on humans, who were once powerless against their predators. But now mankin has developed female warriors who are half human and half monster, with silver eyes that can see the monsters' true form These warriors came to be calle Claymores after the immense broadswords that they carried.

Claymore

クレイモア

Vol. 24

CONTENTS

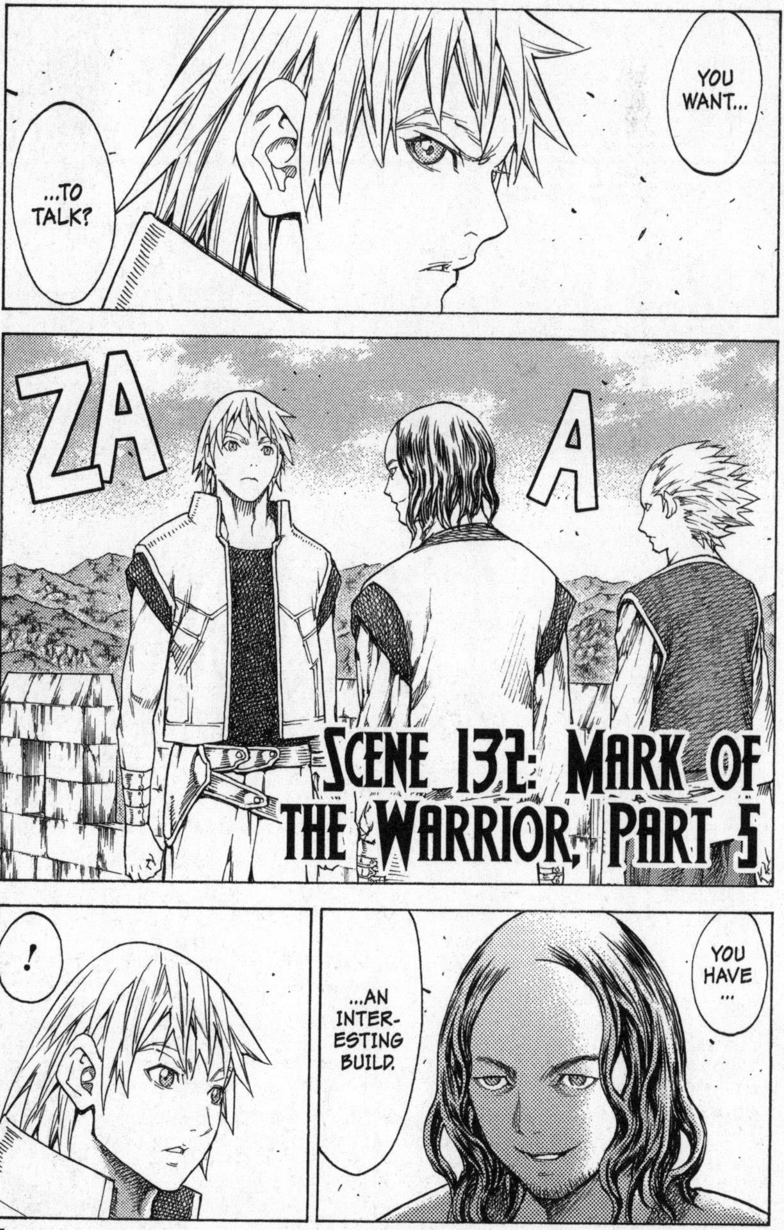
YOU WANT...
...TO TALK?
ZA
A
SCENE 132: MARK OF THE WARRIOR, PART 5
YOU HAVE...
...AN INTER-ESTING BUILD.
!

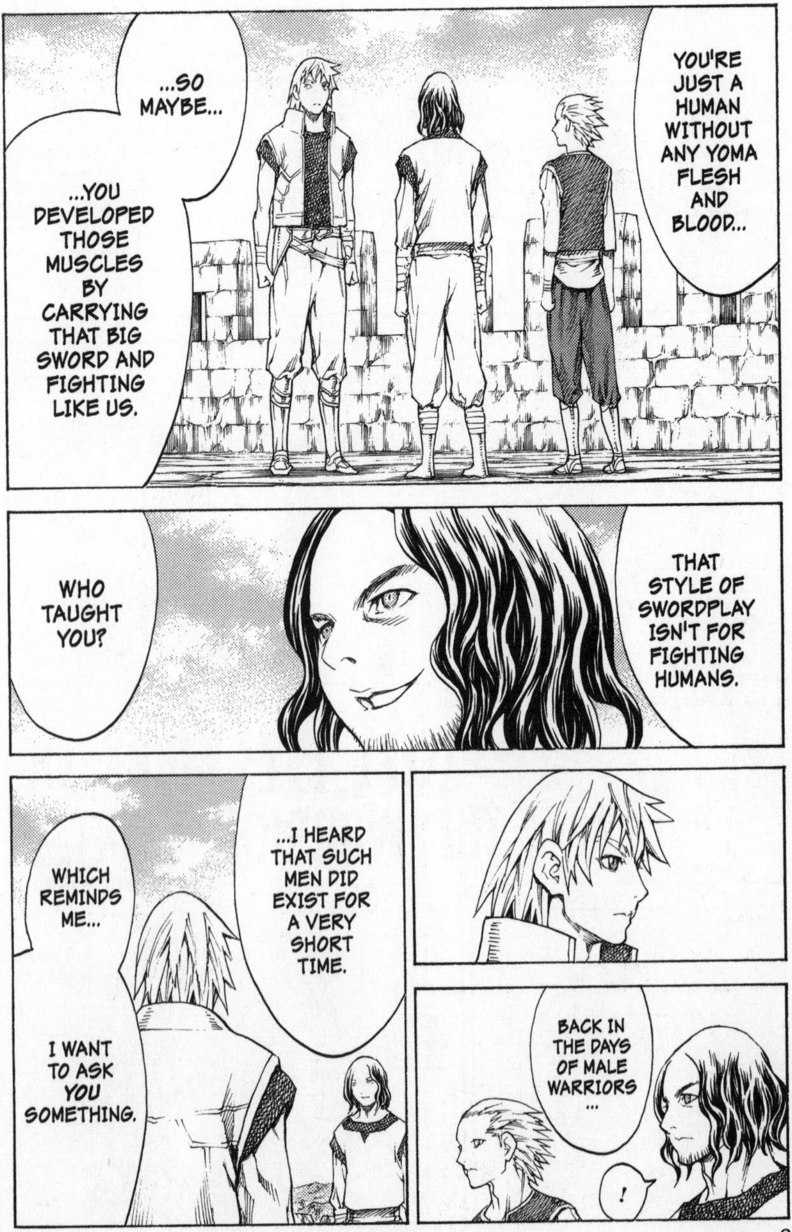
YOU'RE JUST A HUMAN WITHOUT ANY YOMA FLESH AND BLOOD...
...SO MAYBE...
...YOU DEVELOPED THOSE MUSCLES BY CARRYING THAT BIG SWORD AND FIGHTING LIKE US.
THAT STYLE OF SWORDPLAY ISN'T FOR FIGHTING HUMANS.
WHO TAUGHT YOU?
BACK IN THE DAYS OF MALE WARRIORS ...
!
...I HEARD THAT SUCH MEN DID EXIST FOR A VERY SHORT TIME.
WHICH REMINDS ME...
I WANT TO ASK *YOU* SOMETHING.

READ THIS WAY

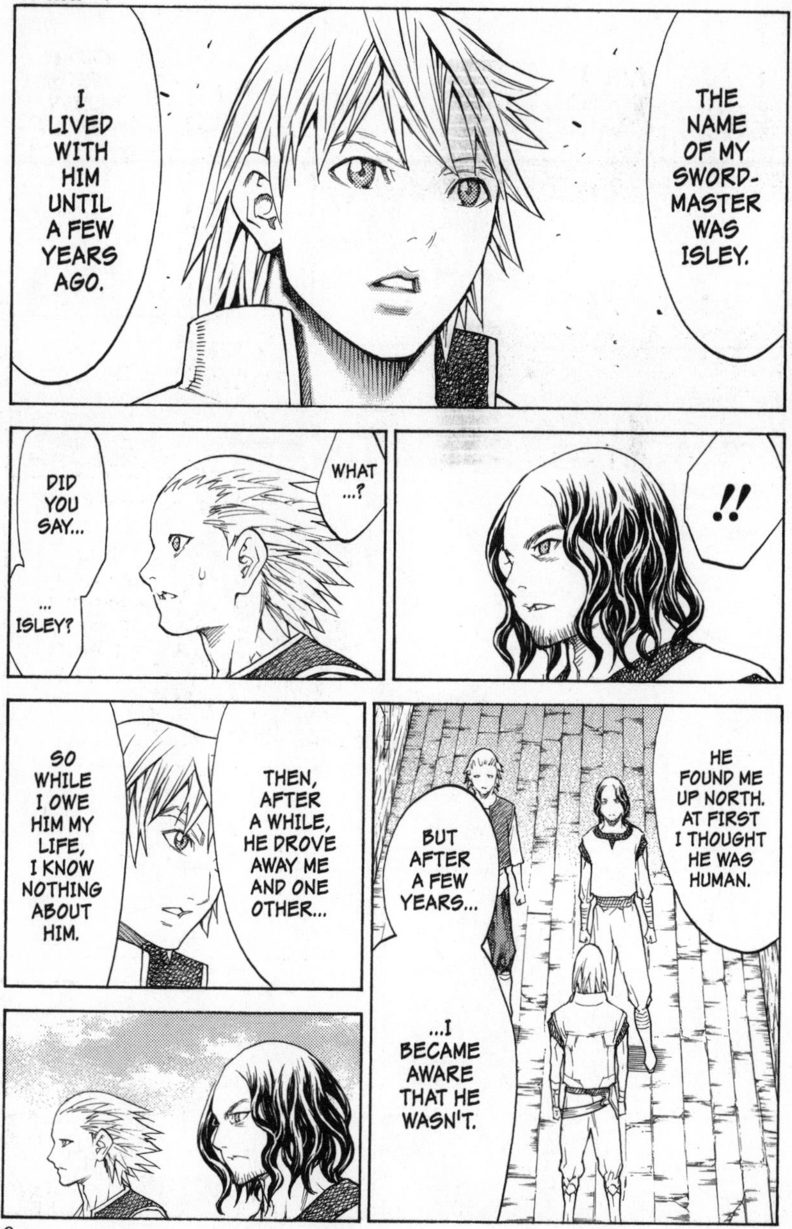

THE NAME OF MY SWORD-MASTER WAS ISLEY.
I LIVED WITH HIM UNTIL A FEW YEARS AGO.
!!
WHAT ...?
DID YOU SAY...
... ISLEY?
HE FOUND ME UP NORTH. AT FIRST I THOUGHT HE WAS HUMAN.
BUT AFTER A FEW YEARS...
...I BECAME AWARE THAT HE WASN'T.
THEN, AFTER A WHILE, HE DROVE AWAY ME AND ONE OTHER...
SO WHILE I OWE HIM MY LIFE, I KNOW NOTHING ABOUT HIM.

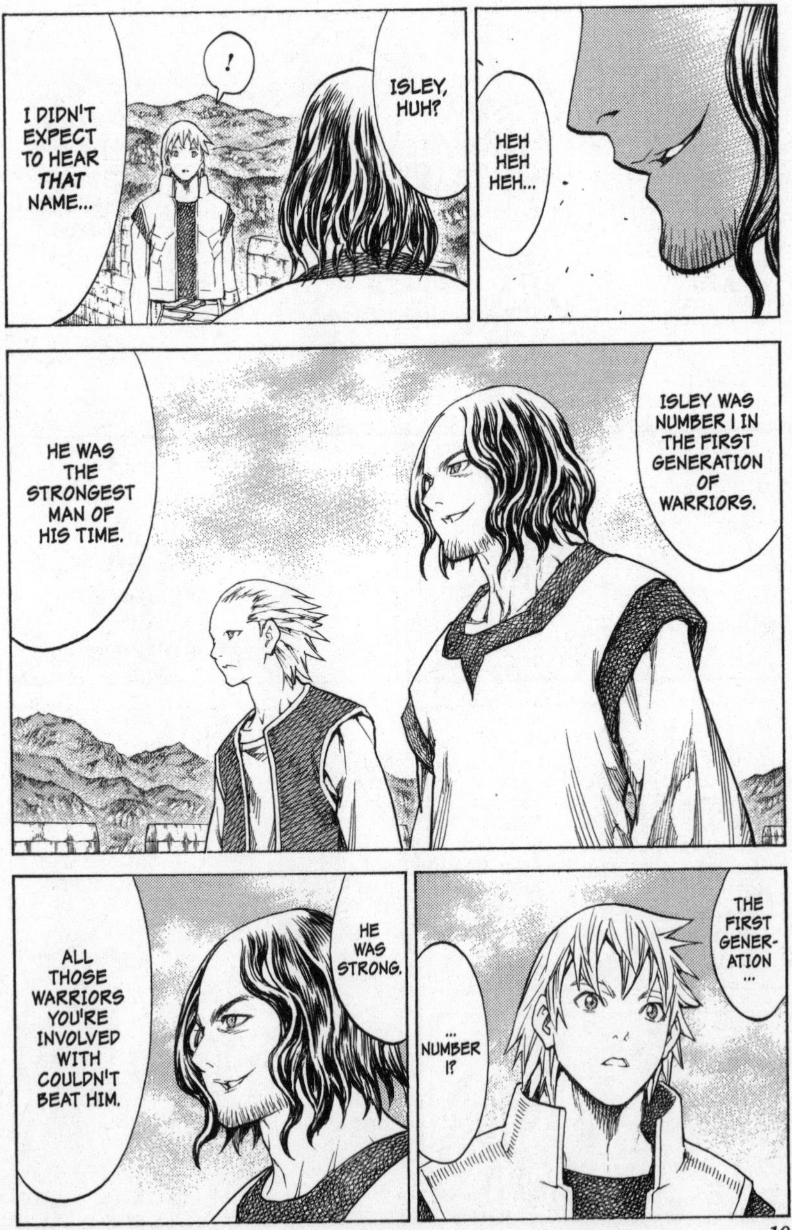
HEH HEH HEH...
ISLEY, HUH?
!
I DIDN'T EXPECT TO HEAR THAT NAME...
ISLEY WAS NUMBER 1 IN THE FIRST GENERATION OF WARRIORS.
HE WAS THE STRONGEST MAN OF HIS TIME.
THE FIRST GENERATION...
...NUMBER 1?
HE WAS STRONG.
ALL THOSE WARRIORS YOU'RE INVOLVED WITH COULDN'T BEAT HIM.

READ THIS WAY

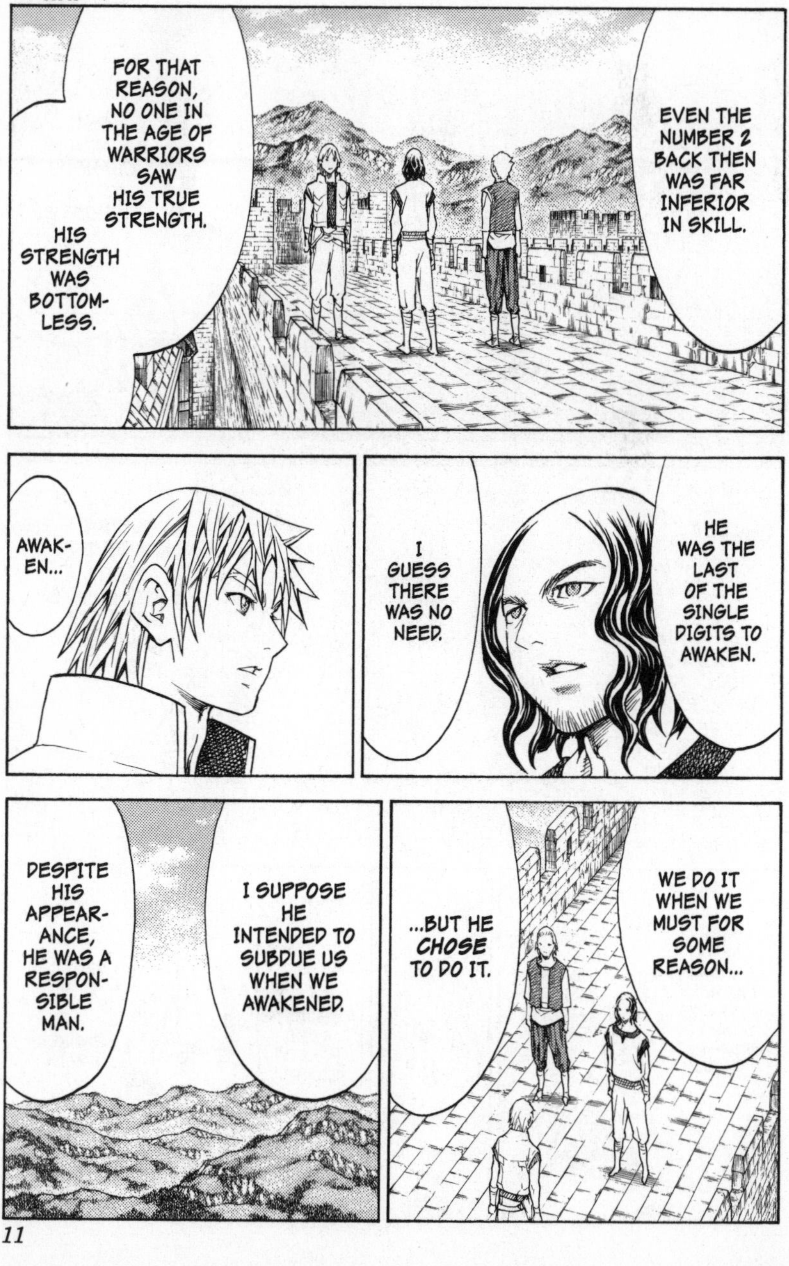
EVEN THE NUMBER 2 BACK THEN WAS FAR INFERIOR IN SKILL.
FOR THAT REASON, NO ONE IN THE AGE OF WARRIORS SAW HIS TRUE STRENGTH.
HIS STRENGTH WAS BOTTOMLESS.
HE WAS THE LAST OF THE SINGLE DIGITS TO AWAKEN.
I GUESS THERE WAS NO NEED.
AWAKEN...
WE DO IT WHEN WE MUST FOR SOME REASON...
...BUT HE *CHOSE* TO DO IT.
I SUPPOSE HE INTENDED TO SUBDUE US WHEN WE AWAKENED.
DESPITE HIS APPEARANCE, HE WAS A RESPONSIBLE MAN.

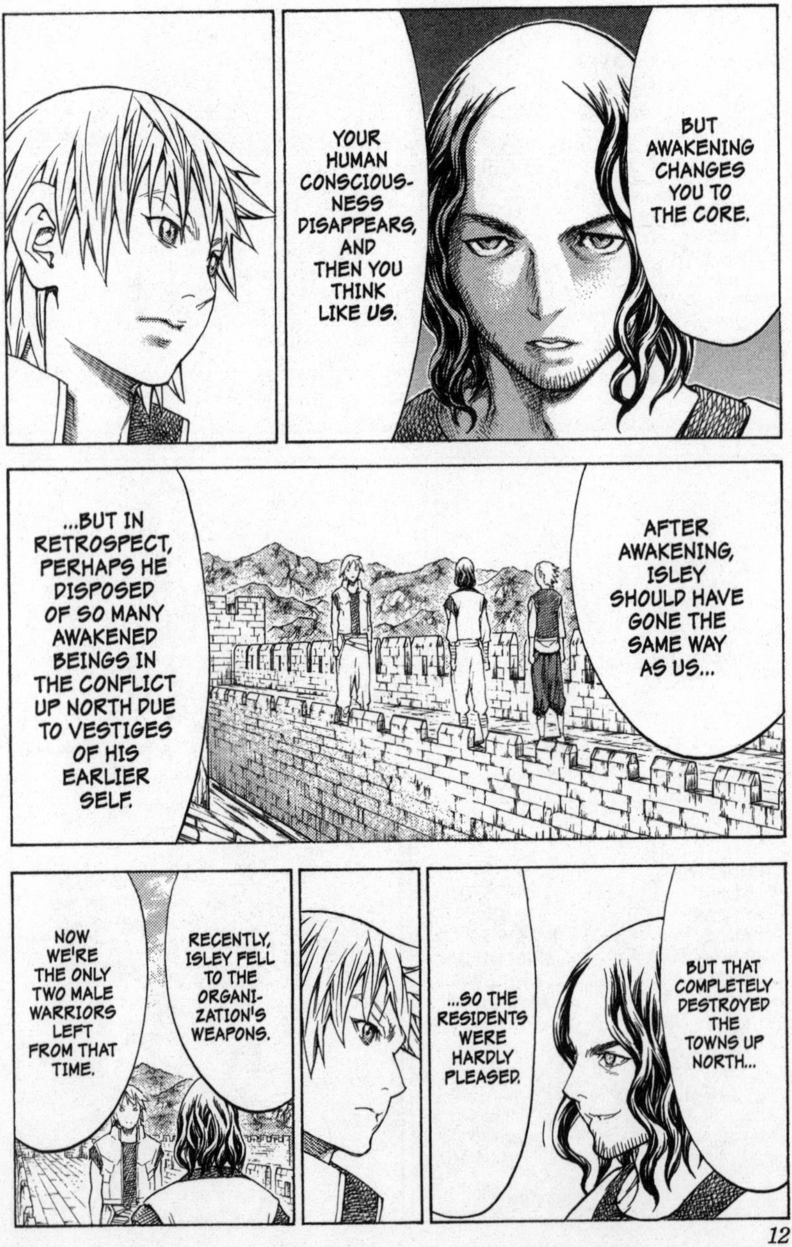
BUT AWAKENING CHANGES YOU TO THE CORE.
YOUR HUMAN CONSCIOUSNESS DISAPPEARS, AND THEN YOU THINK LIKE US.
AFTER AWAKENING, ISLEY SHOULD HAVE GONE THE SAME WAY AS US...
...BUT IN RETROSPECT, PERHAPS HE DISPOSED OF SO MANY AWAKENED BEINGS IN THE CONFLICT UP NORTH DUE TO VESTIGES OF HIS EARLIER SELF.
BUT THAT COMPLETELY DESTROYED THE TOWNS UP NORTH...
...SO THE RESIDENTS WERE HARDLY PLEASED.
RECENTLY, ISLEY FELL TO THE ORGANIZATION'S WEAPONS.
NOW WE'RE THE ONLY TWO MALE WARRIORS LEFT FROM THAT TIME.

READ THIS WAY

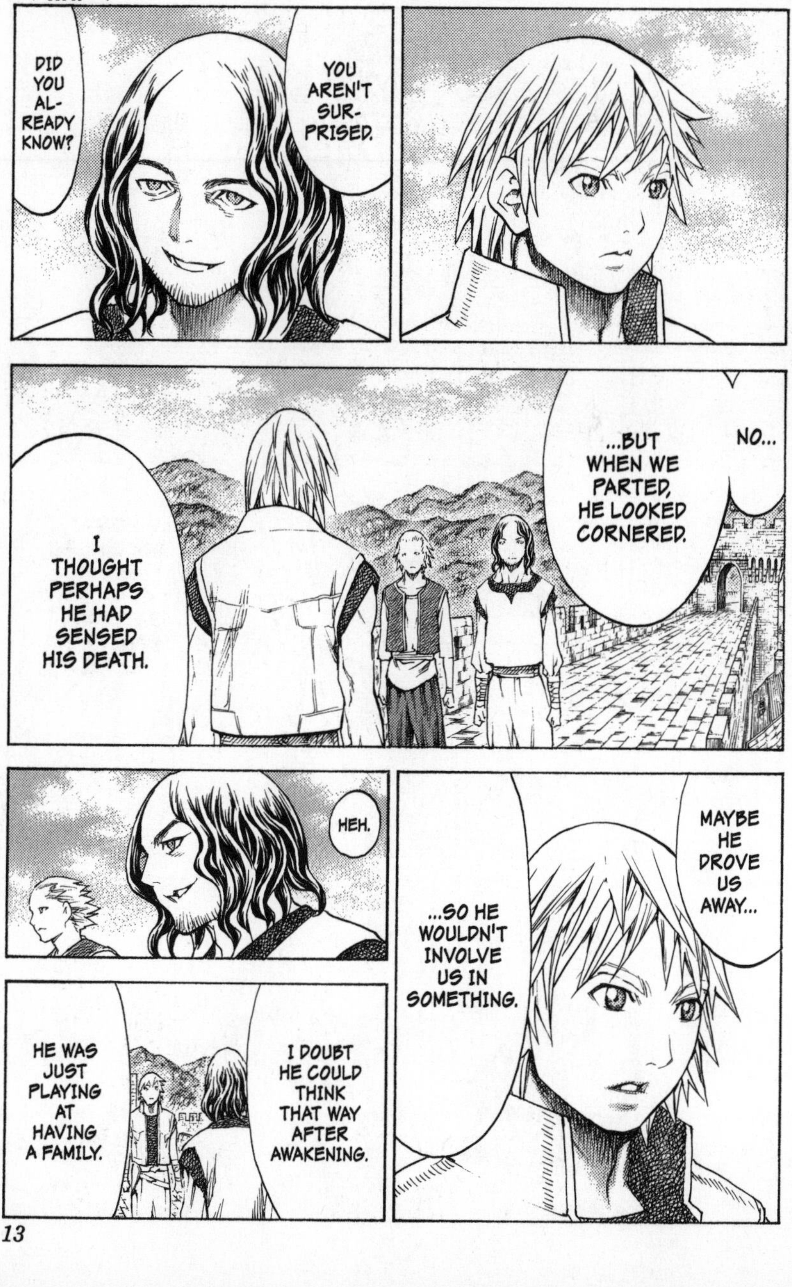

YOU AREN'T SURPRISED.
DID YOU ALREADY KNOW?
NO...
...BUT WHEN WE PARTED, HE LOOKED CORNERED.
I THOUGHT PERHAPS HE HAD SENSED HIS DEATH.
MAYBE HE DROVE US AWAY...
...SO HE WOULDN'T INVOLVE US IN SOMETHING.
HEH.
I DOUBT HE COULD THINK THAT WAY AFTER AWAKENING.
HE WAS JUST PLAYING AT HAVING A FAMILY.

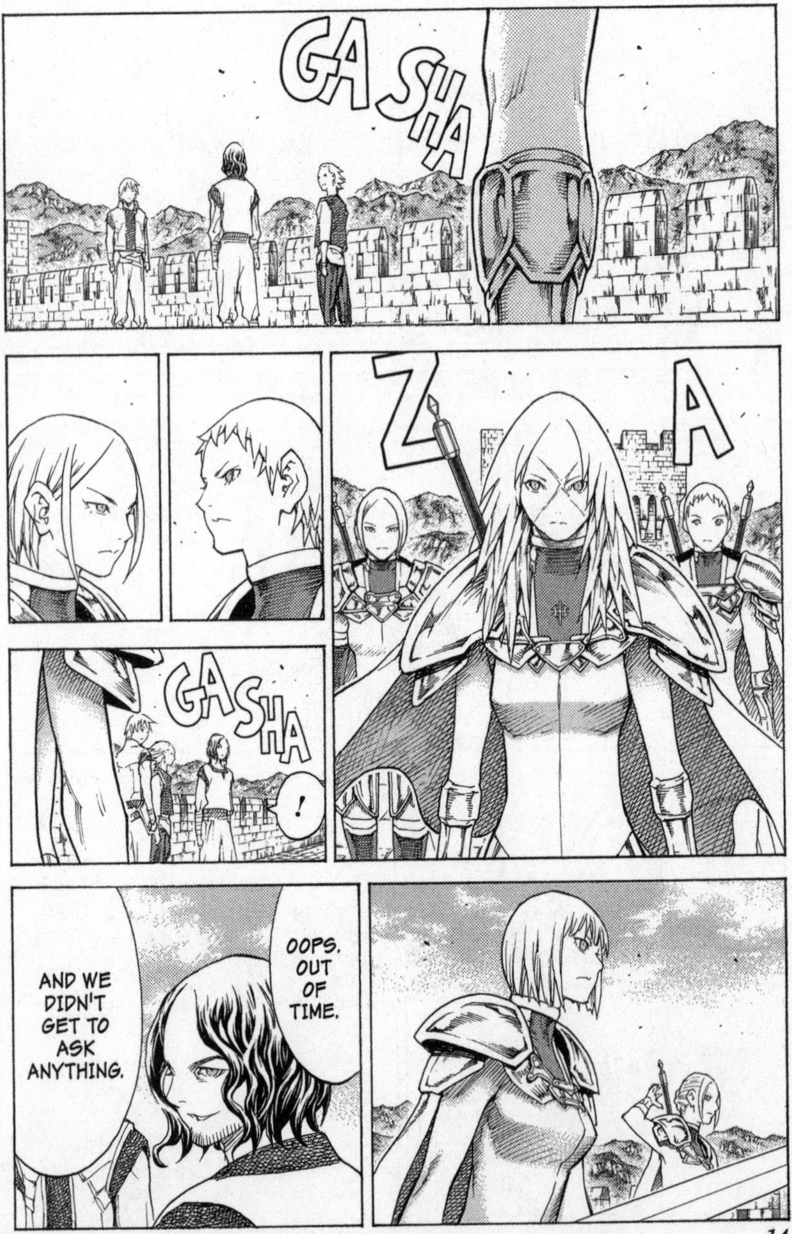
GASHA
ZA
GASHA
!
OOPS. OUT OF TIME.
AND WE DIDN'T GET TO ASK ANYTHING.

READ THIS WAY

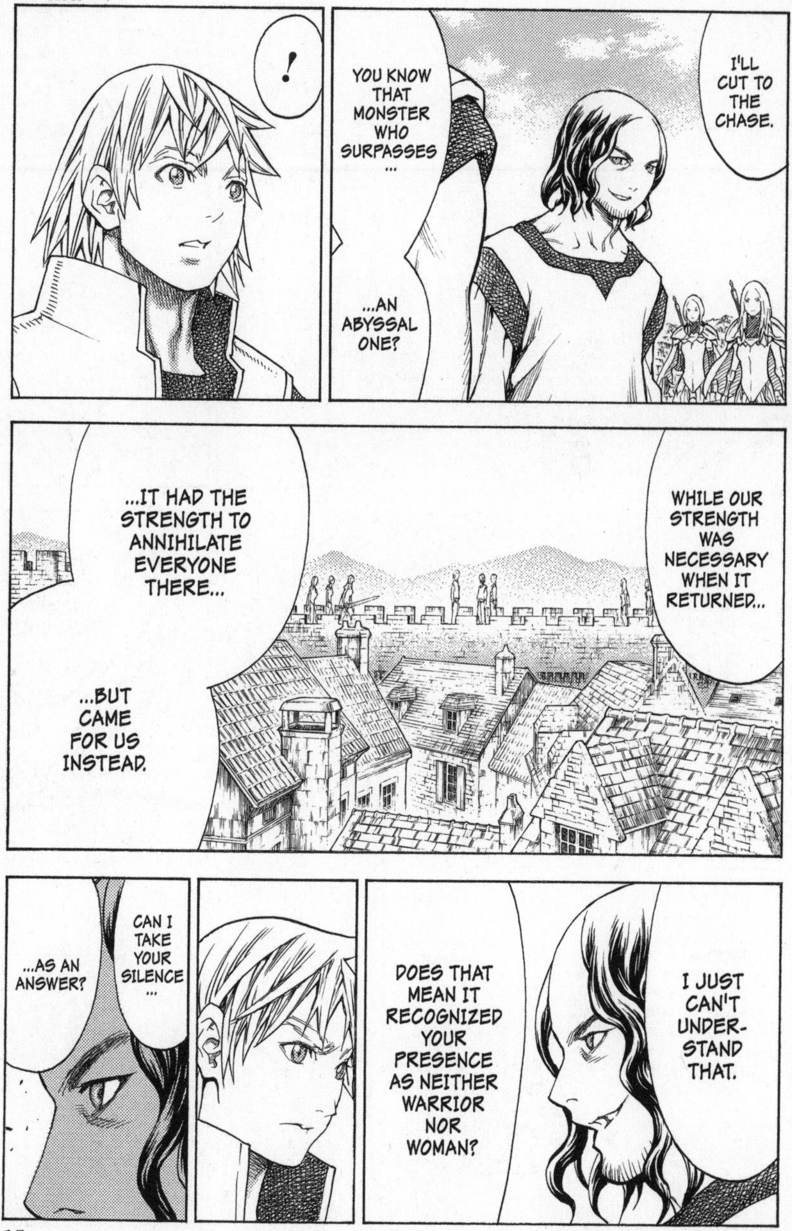

I'LL CUT TO THE CHASE.
YOU KNOW THAT MONSTER WHO SURPASSES...
...AN ABYSSAL ONE?
!
WHILE OUR STRENGTH WAS NECESSARY WHEN IT RETURNED...
...IT HAD THE STRENGTH TO ANNIHILATE EVERYONE THERE...
...BUT CAME FOR US INSTEAD.
I JUST CAN'T UNDER-STAND THAT.
DOES THAT MEAN IT RECOGNIZED YOUR PRESENCE AS NEITHER WARRIOR NOR WOMAN?
CAN I TAKE YOUR SILENCE...
...AS AN ANSWER?

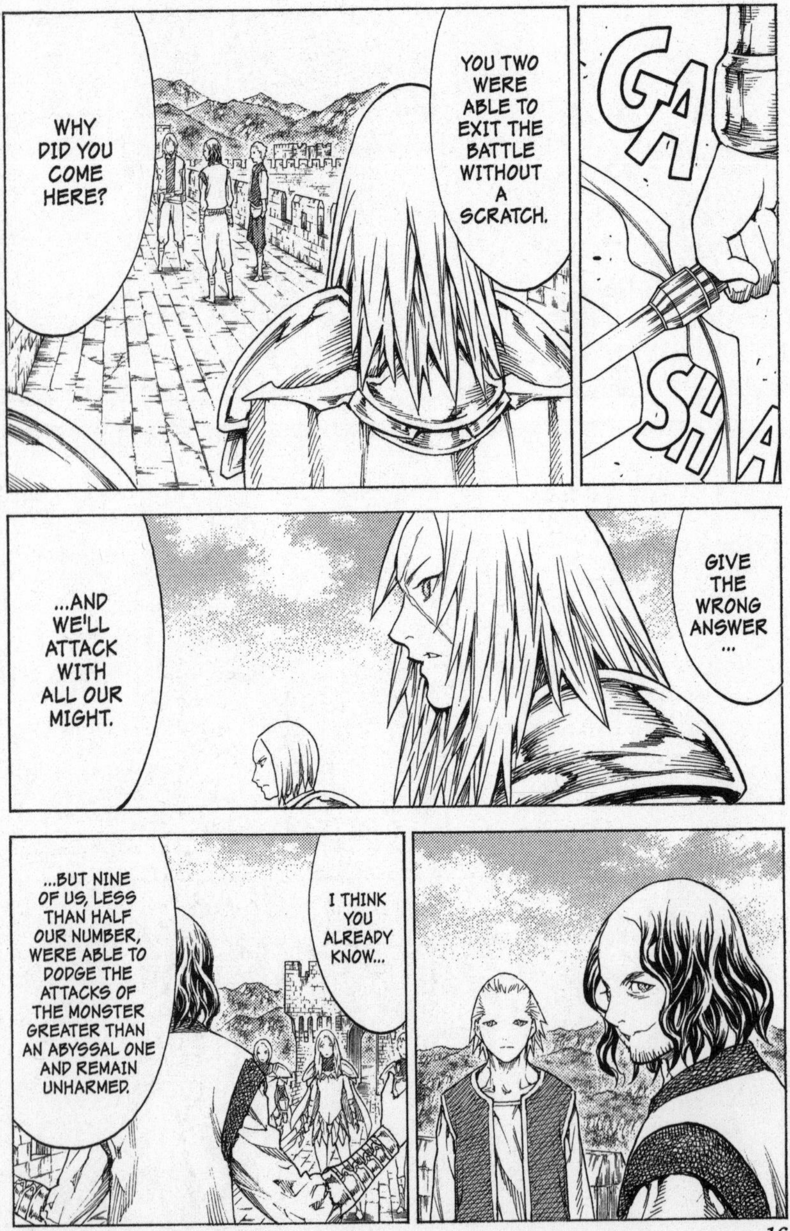
GA
SHA
YOU TWO WERE ABLE TO EXIT THE BATTLE WITHOUT A SCRATCH.
WHY DID YOU COME HERE?
GIVE THE WRONG ANSWER...
...AND WE'LL ATTACK WITH ALL OUR MIGHT.
I THINK YOU ALREADY KNOW...
...BUT NINE OF US, LESS THAN HALF OUR NUMBER, WERE ABLE TO DODGE THE ATTACKS OF THE MONSTER GREATER THAN AN ABYSSAL ONE AND REMAIN UNHARMED.

READ THIS WAY

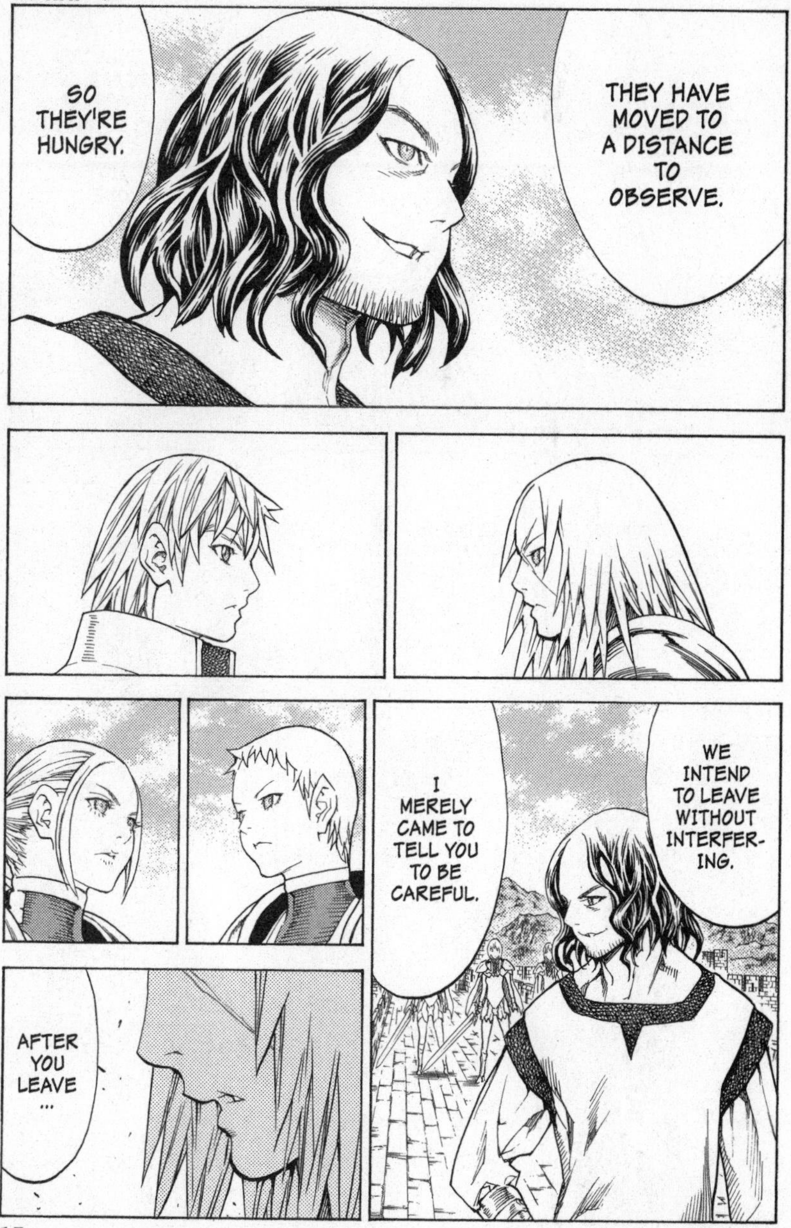
THEY HAVE MOVED TO A DISTANCE TO OBSERVE.
SO THEY'RE HUNGRY.
WE INTEND TO LEAVE WITHOUT INTERFER-ING.
I MERELY CAME TO TELL YOU TO BE CAREFUL.
AFTER YOU LEAVE ...

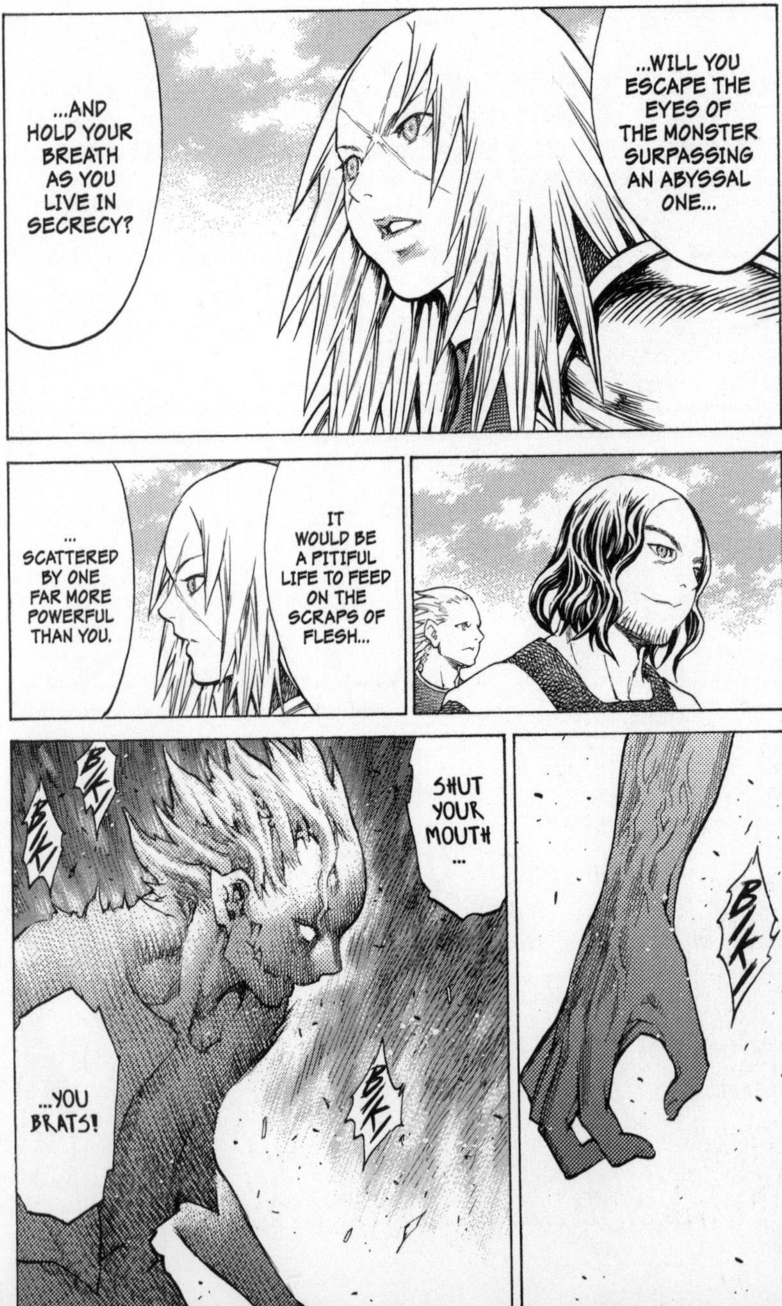
...WILL YOU ESCAPE THE EYES OF THE MONSTER SURPASSING AN ABYSSAL ONE...
...AND HOLD YOUR BREATH AS YOU LIVE IN SECRECY?
IT WOULD BE A PITIFUL LIFE TO FEED ON THE SCRAPS OF FLESH...
...SCATTERED BY ONE FAR MORE POWERFUL THAN YOU.
BIKI
BIKI
BIKI
SHUT YOUR MOUTH...
BIKI
...YOU BRATS!

READ THIS WAY

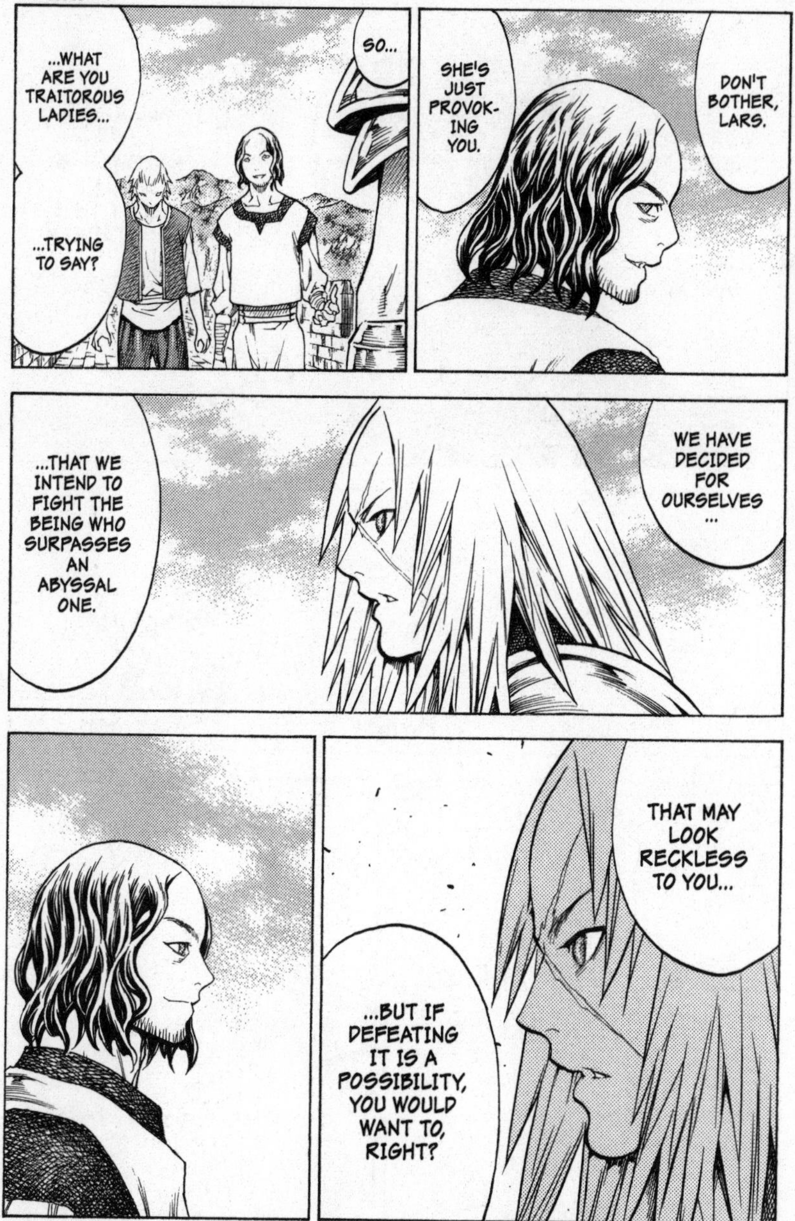
DON'T BOTHER, LARS.
SHE'S JUST PROVOK-ING YOU.
SO...
...WHAT ARE YOU TRAITOROUS LADIES...
...TRYING TO SAY?
WE HAVE DECIDED FOR OURSELVES...
...THAT WE INTEND TO FIGHT THE BEING WHO SURPASSES AN ABYSSAL ONE.
THAT MAY LOOK RECKLESS TO YOU...
...BUT IF DEFEATING IT IS A POSSIBILITY, YOU WOULD WANT TO, RIGHT?

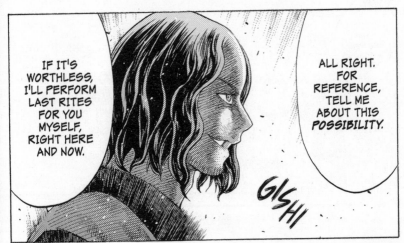

ALL RIGHT. FOR REFERENCE, TELL ME ABOUT THIS POSSIBILITY.
IF IT'S WORTHLESS, I'LL PERFORM LAST RITES FOR YOU MYSELF, RIGHT HERE AND NOW.
GISHI
BIRI
!
UNGH ...
BIRI
BIRI
BIRI
BIRI
BIRI

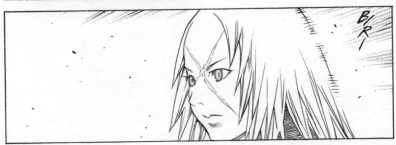

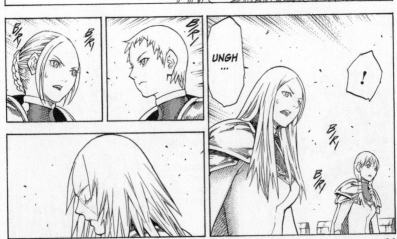

READ THIS WAY

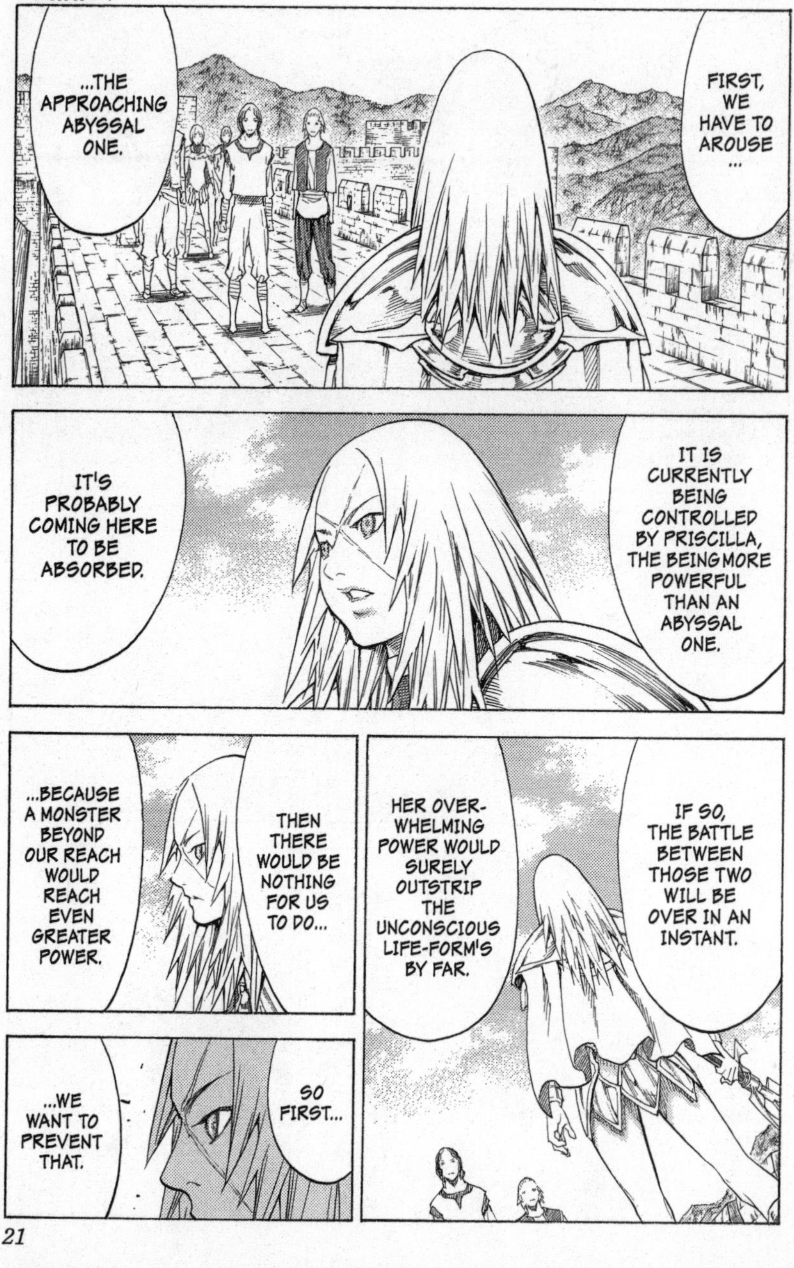
FIRST, WE HAVE TO AROUSE ...
...THE APPROACHING ABYSSAL ONE.
IT IS CURRENTLY BEING CONTROLLED BY PRISCILLA, THE BEING MORE POWERFUL THAN AN ABYSSAL ONE.
IT'S PROBABLY COMING HERE TO BE ABSORBED.
IF SO, THE BATTLE BETWEEN THOSE TWO WILL BE OVER IN AN INSTANT.
HER OVER-WHELMING POWER WOULD SURELY OUTSTRIP THE UNCONSCIOUS LIFE-FORM'S BY FAR.
THEN THERE WOULD BE NOTHING FOR US TO DO...
...BECAUSE A MONSTER BEYOND OUR REACH WOULD REACH EVEN GREATER POWER.
SO FIRST...
...WE WANT TO PREVENT THAT.

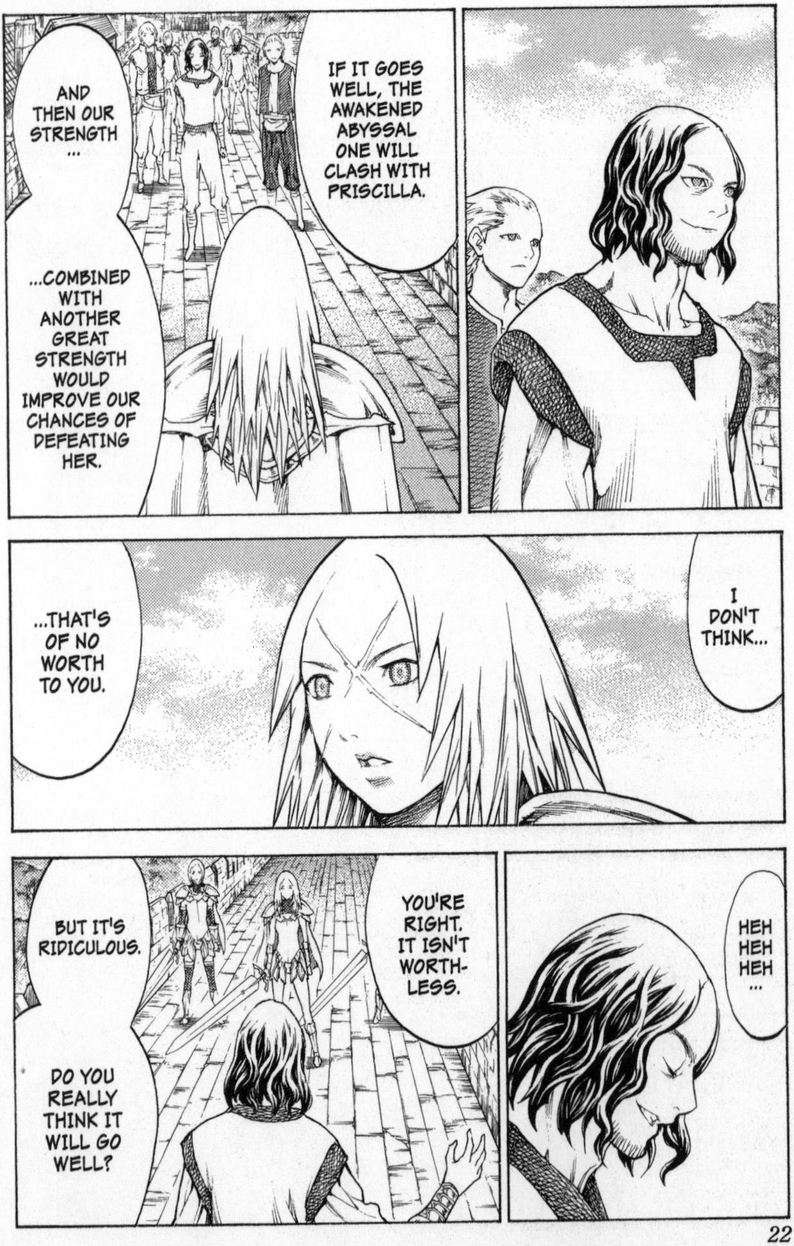
IF IT GOES WELL, THE AWAKENED ABYSSAL ONE WILL CLASH WITH PRISCILLA.
AND THEN OUR STRENGTH ...
...COMBINED WITH ANOTHER GREAT STRENGTH WOULD IMPROVE OUR CHANCES OF DEFEATING HER.
I DON'T THINK...
...THAT'S OF NO WORTH TO YOU.
HEH HEH HEH ...
YOU'RE RIGHT. IT ISN'T WORTH-LESS.
BUT IT'S RIDICULOUS.
DO YOU REALLY THINK IT WILL GO WELL?

READ THIS WAY

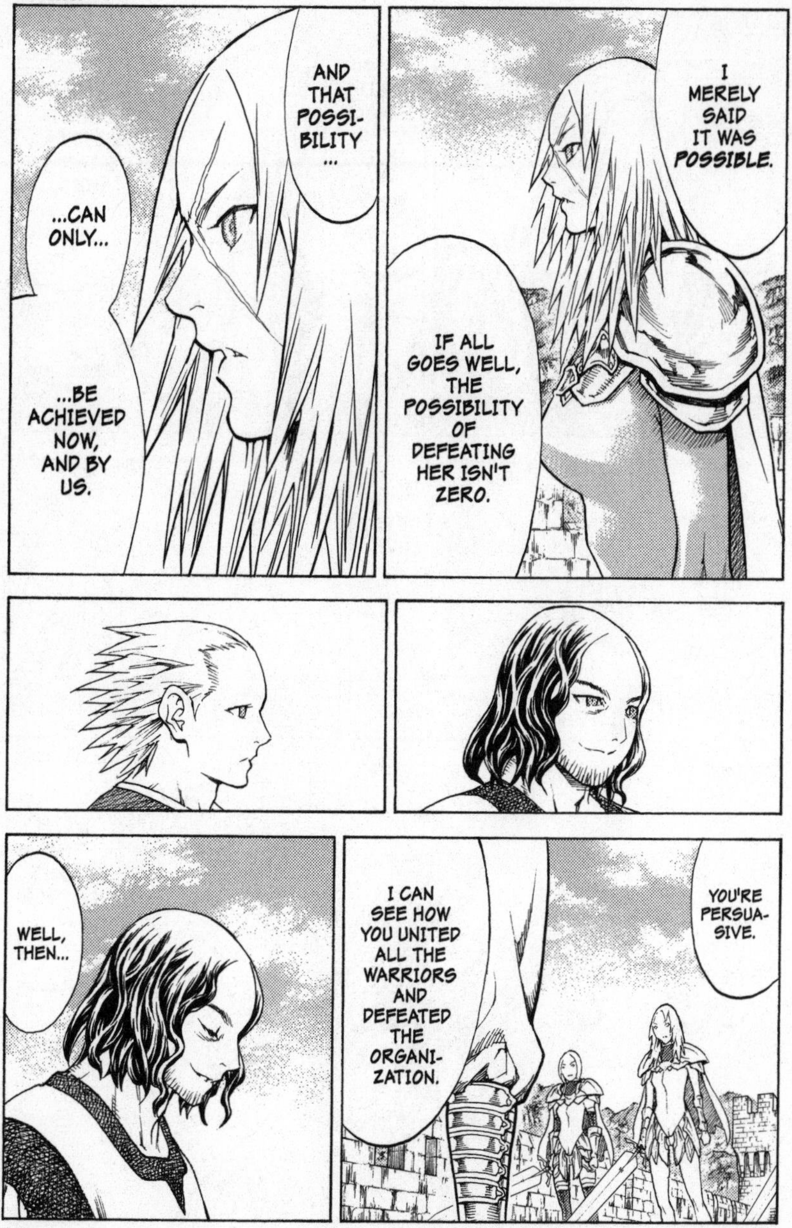
I MERELY SAID IT WAS POSSIBLE.
IF ALL GOES WELL, THE POSSIBILITY OF DEFEATING HER ISN'T ZERO.
AND THAT POSSIBILITY...
...CAN ONLY...
...BE ACHIEVED NOW, AND BY US.
YOU'RE PERSUASIVE.
I CAN SEE HOW YOU UNITED ALL THE WARRIORS AND DEFEATED THE ORGANIZATION.
WELL, THEN...

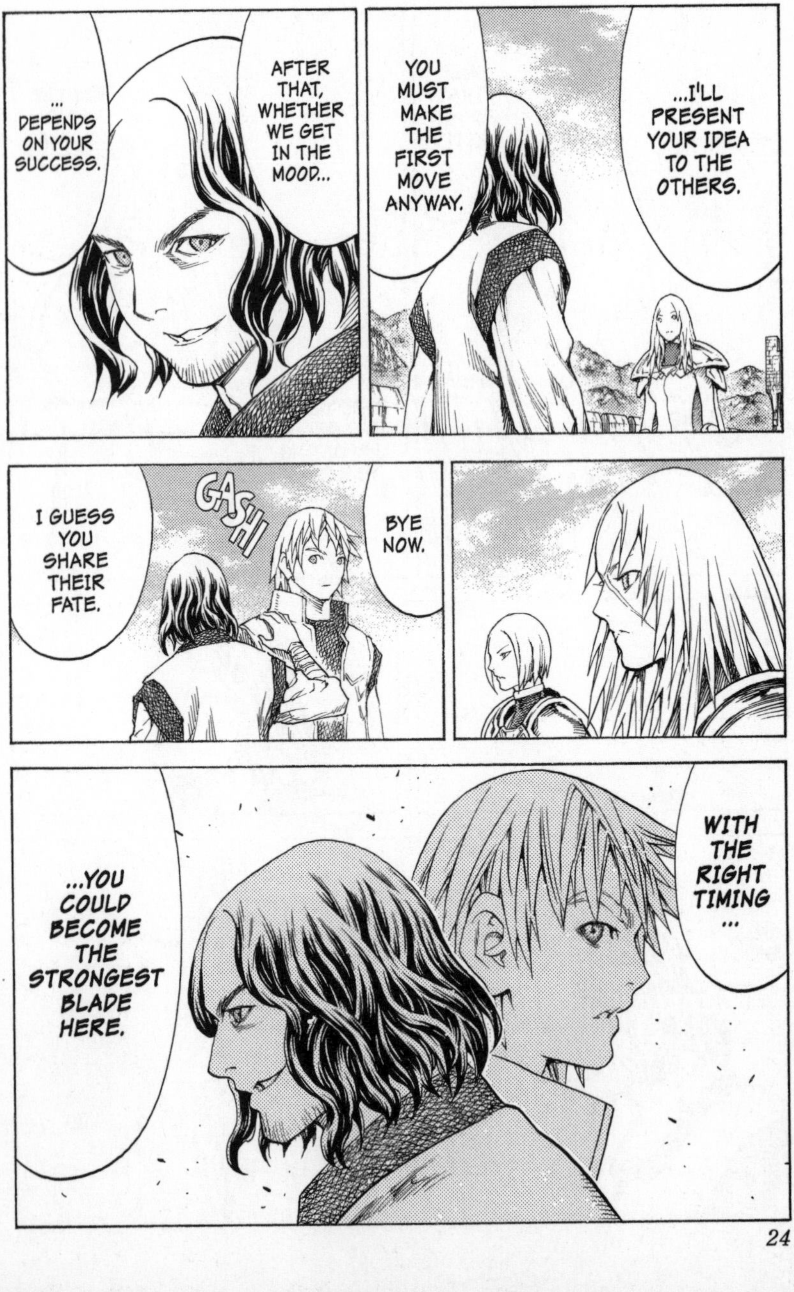
...I'LL PRESENT YOUR IDEA TO THE OTHERS.
YOU MUST MAKE THE FIRST MOVE ANYWAY.
AFTER THAT, WHETHER WE GET IN THE MOOD...
... DEPENDS ON YOUR SUCCESS.
BYE NOW.
GASHI
I GUESS YOU SHARE THEIR FATE.
WITH THE RIGHT TIMING ...
...YOU COULD BECOME THE STRONGEST BLADE HERE.

READ THIS WAY

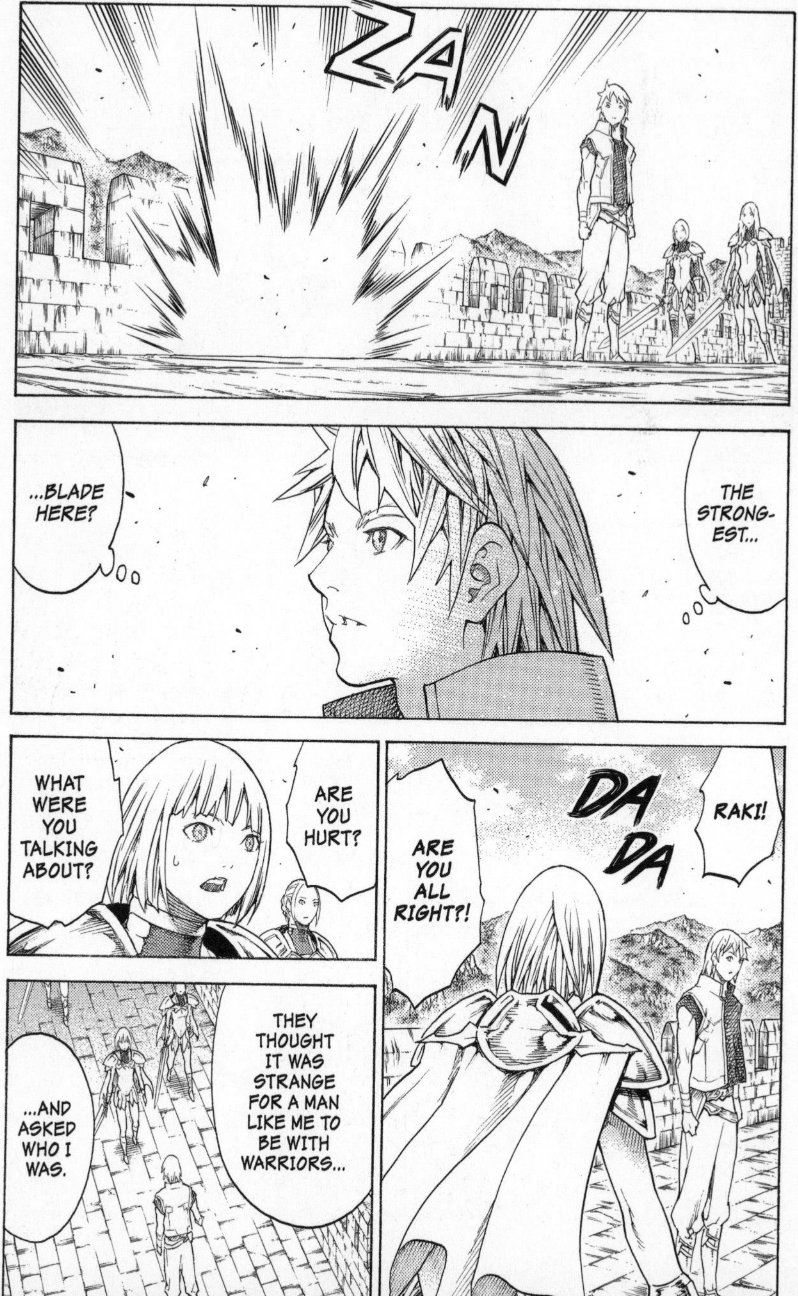
ZAN
THE STRONGEST...
...BLADE HERE?
DA DA
RAKI!
ARE YOU ALL RIGHT?!
ARE YOU HURT?
WHAT WERE YOU TALKING ABOUT?
THEY THOUGHT IT WAS STRANGE FOR A MAN LIKE ME TO BE WITH WARRIORS...
...AND ASKED WHO I WAS.

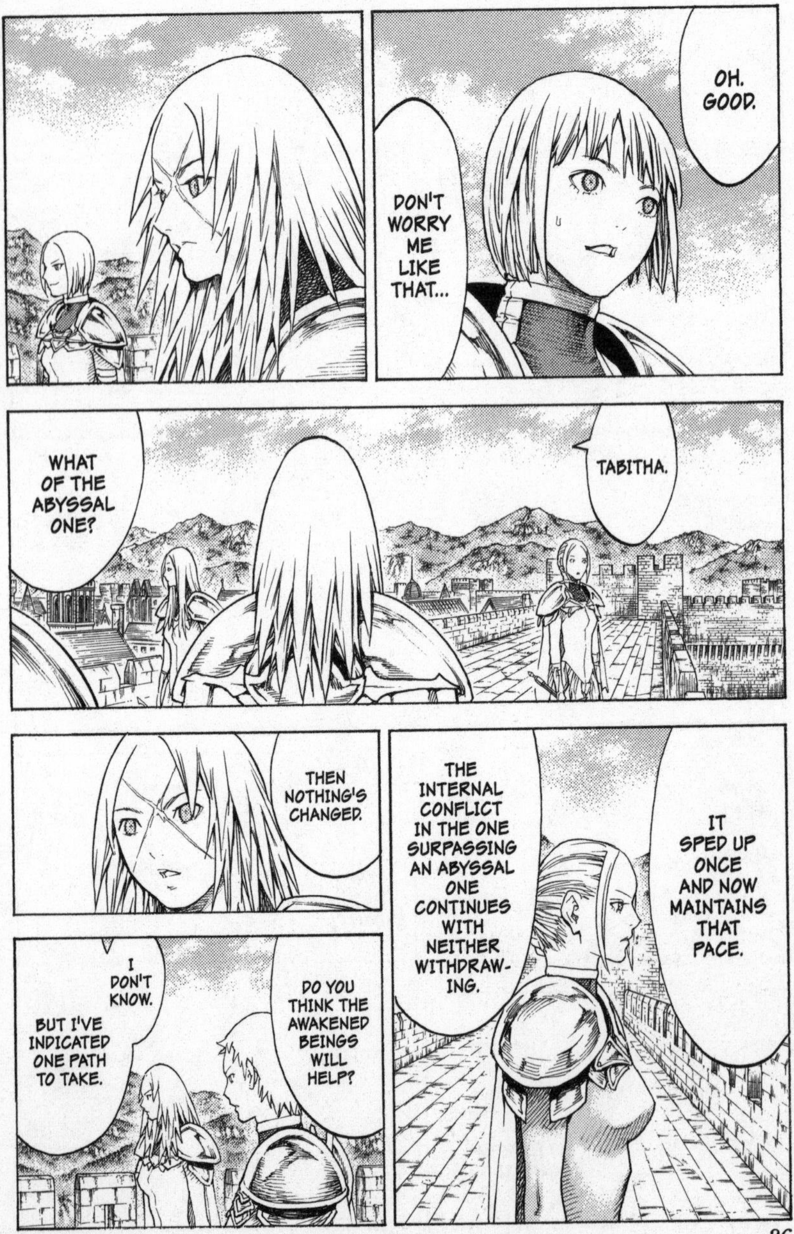
OH. GOOD.
DON'T WORRY ME LIKE THAT...
TABITHA.
WHAT OF THE ABYSSAL ONE?
IT SPED UP ONCE AND NOW MAINTAINS THAT PACE.
THE INTERNAL CONFLICT IN THE ONE SURPASSING AN ABYSSAL ONE CONTINUES WITH NEITHER WITHDRAW-ING.
THEN NOTHING'S CHANGED.
DO YOU THINK THE AWAKENED BEINGS WILL HELP?
I DON'T KNOW.
BUT I'VE INDICATED ONE PATH TO TAKE.

READ THIS WAY

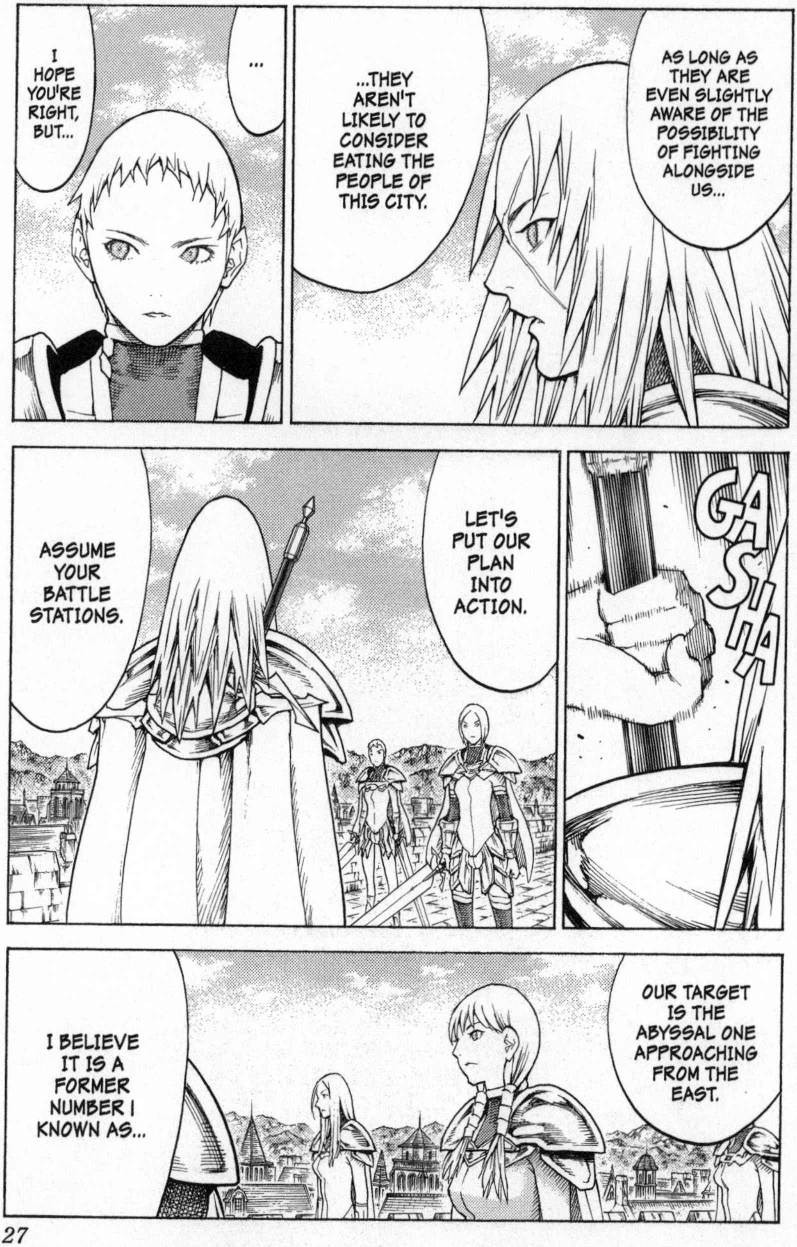
AS LONG AS THEY ARE EVEN SLIGHTLY AWARE OF THE POSSIBILITY OF FIGHTING ALONGSIDE US...
...THEY AREN'T LIKELY TO CONSIDER EATING THE PEOPLE OF THIS CITY.
...
I HOPE YOU'RE RIGHT, BUT...
GASHA
LET'S PUT OUR PLAN INTO ACTION.
ASSUME YOUR BATTLE STATIONS.
OUR TARGET IS THE ABYSSAL ONE APPROACHING FROM THE EAST.
I BELIEVE IT IS A FORMER NUMBER I KNOWN AS...

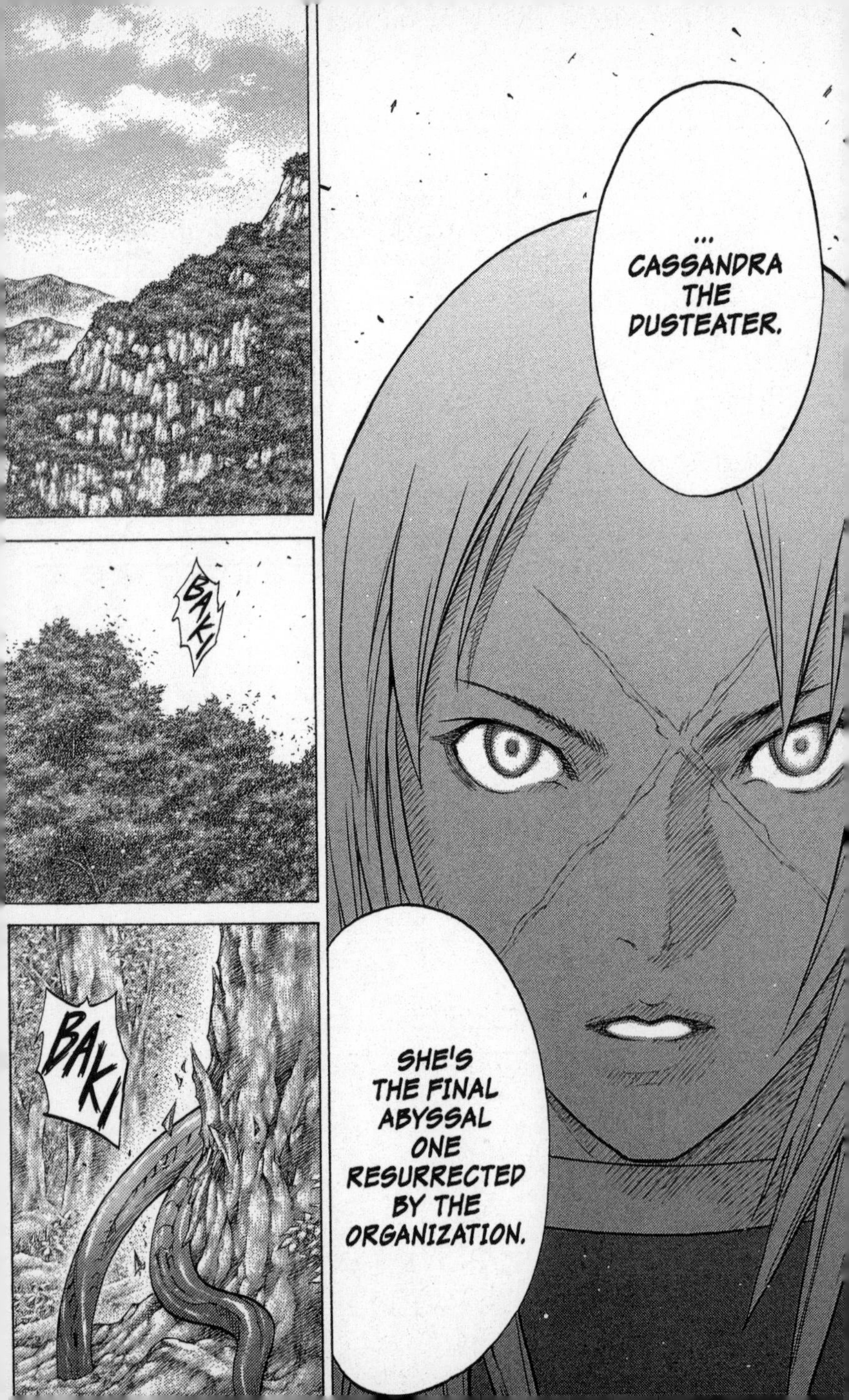
... CASSANDRA THE DUSTEATER.
SHE'S THE FINAL ABYSSAL ONE RESURRECTED BY THE ORGANIZATION.
BAKI
BAKI

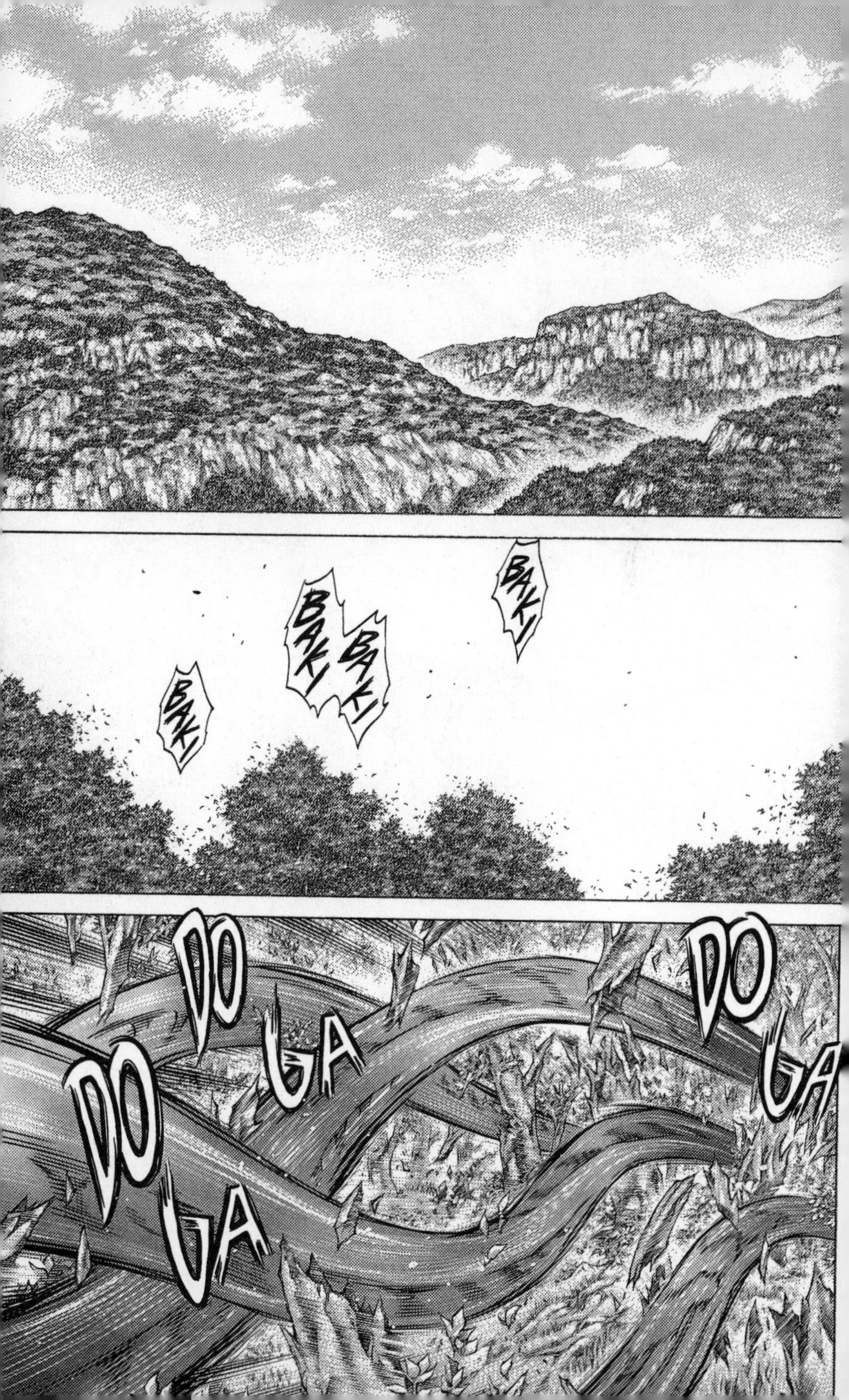
BAKI
BAKI
BAKI
BAKI
DO
GA
DO
GA
DO
GA

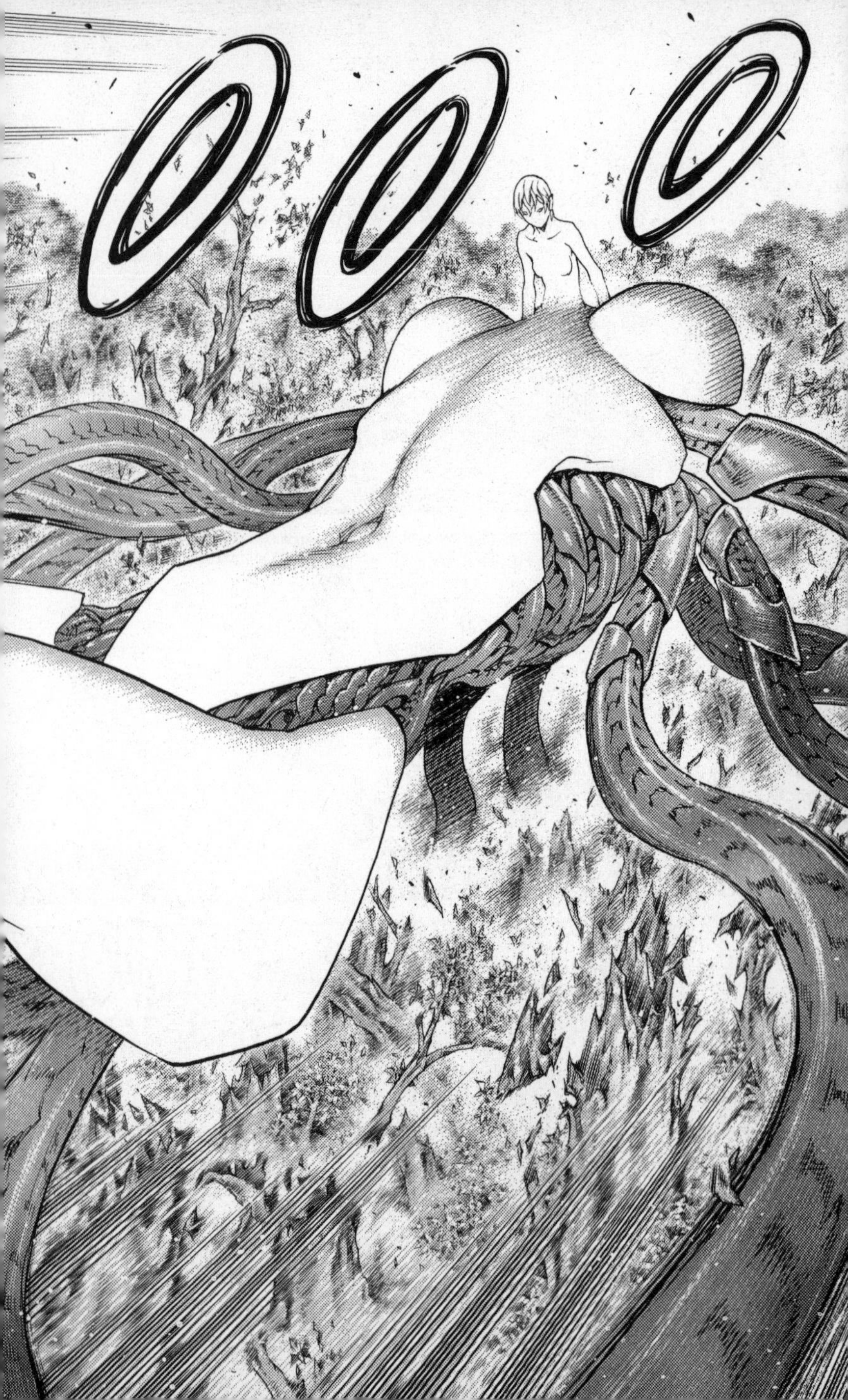

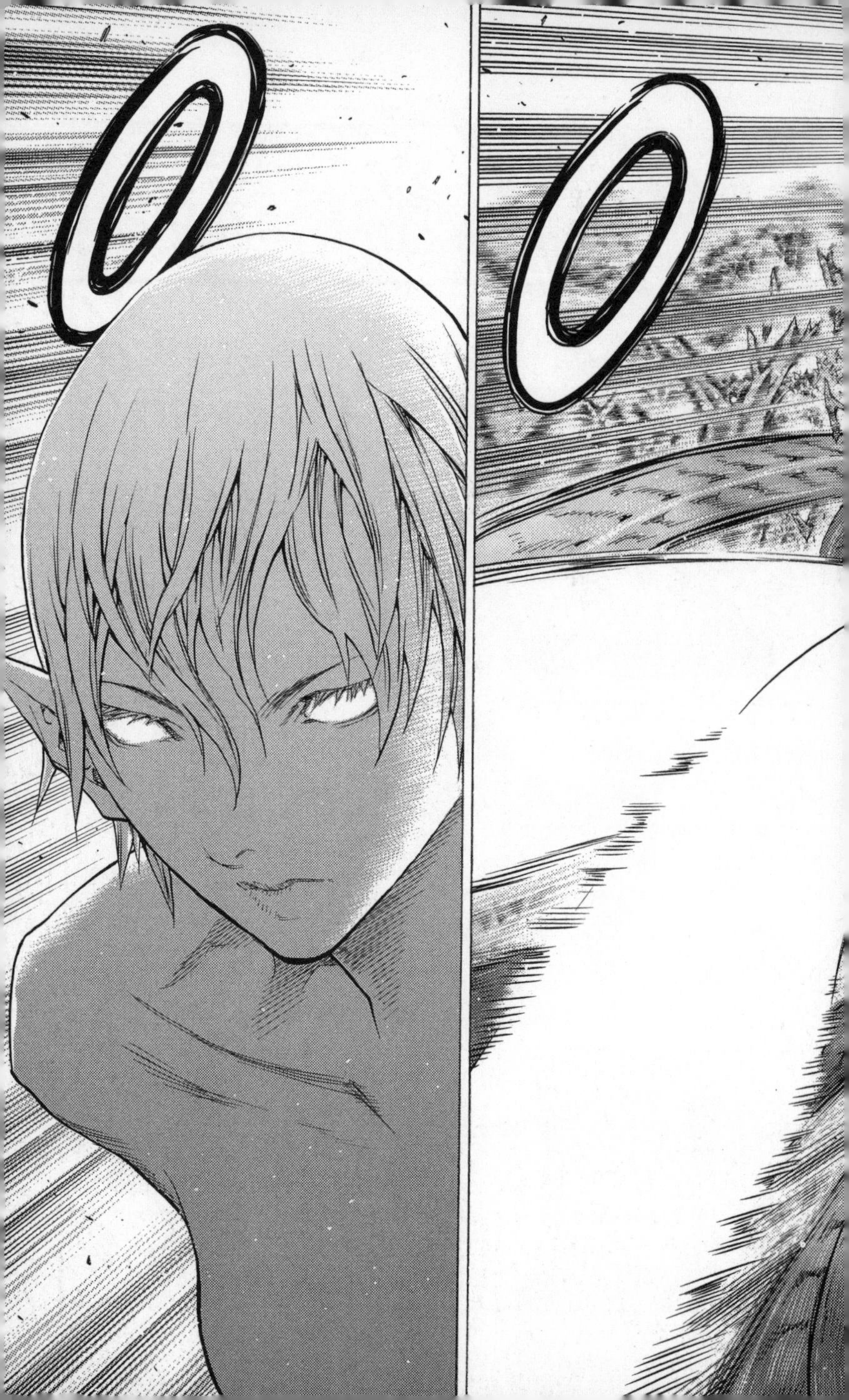

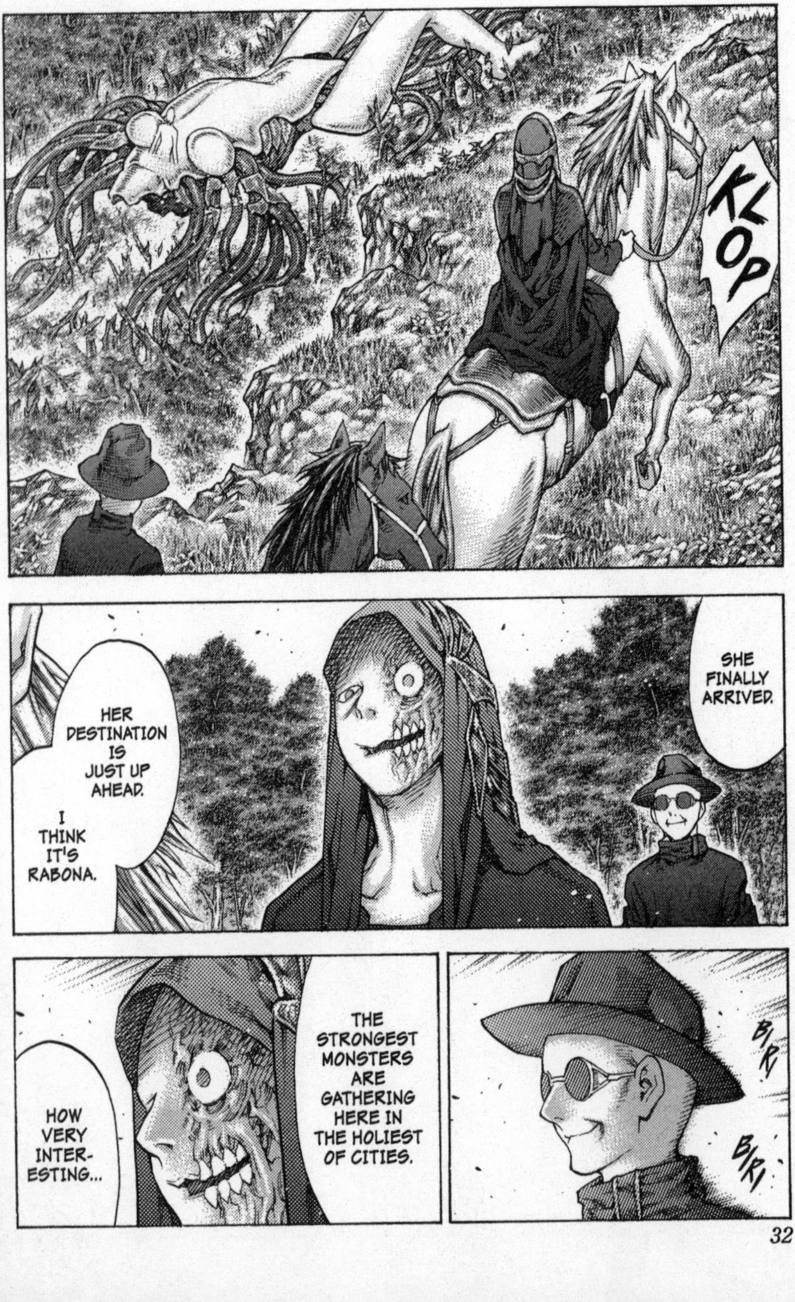
KLOP
SHE FINALLY ARRIVED.
HER DESTINATION IS JUST UP AHEAD.
I THINK IT'S RABONA.
BIRI
BIRI
THE STRONGEST MONSTERS ARE GATHERING HERE IN THE HOLIEST OF CITIES.
HOW VERY INTER-ESTING...

READ THIS WAY

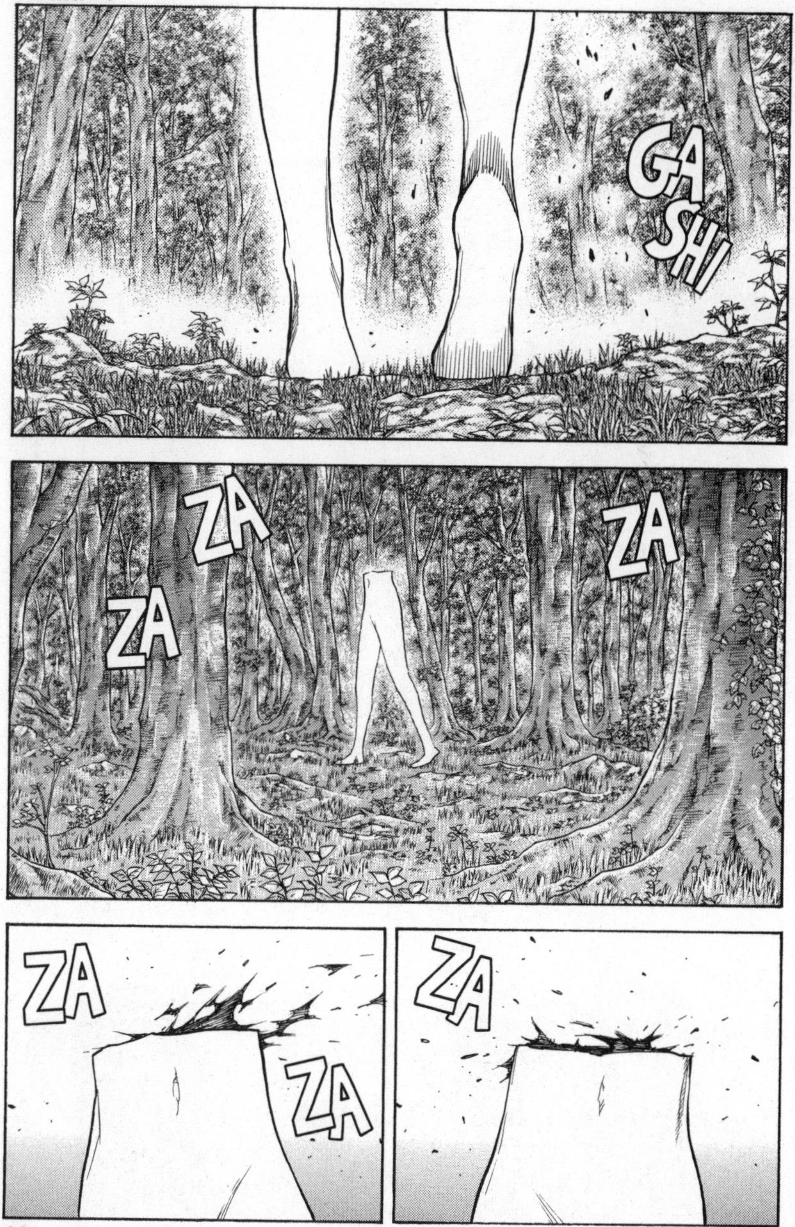
GASHI
ZA
ZA
ZA
ZA
ZA
ZA

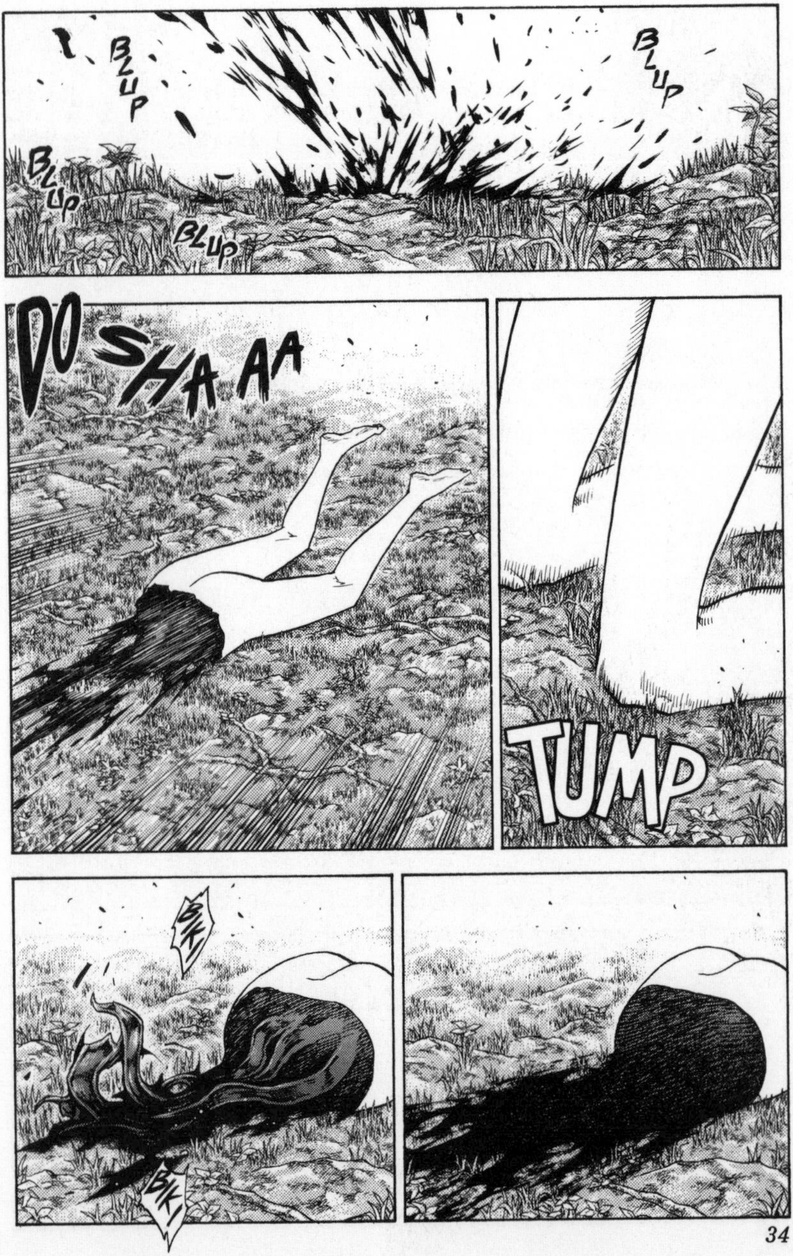
BLUP
BLUP
BLUP
BLUP
TUMP
DOSHAAA
BIKI
BIKI

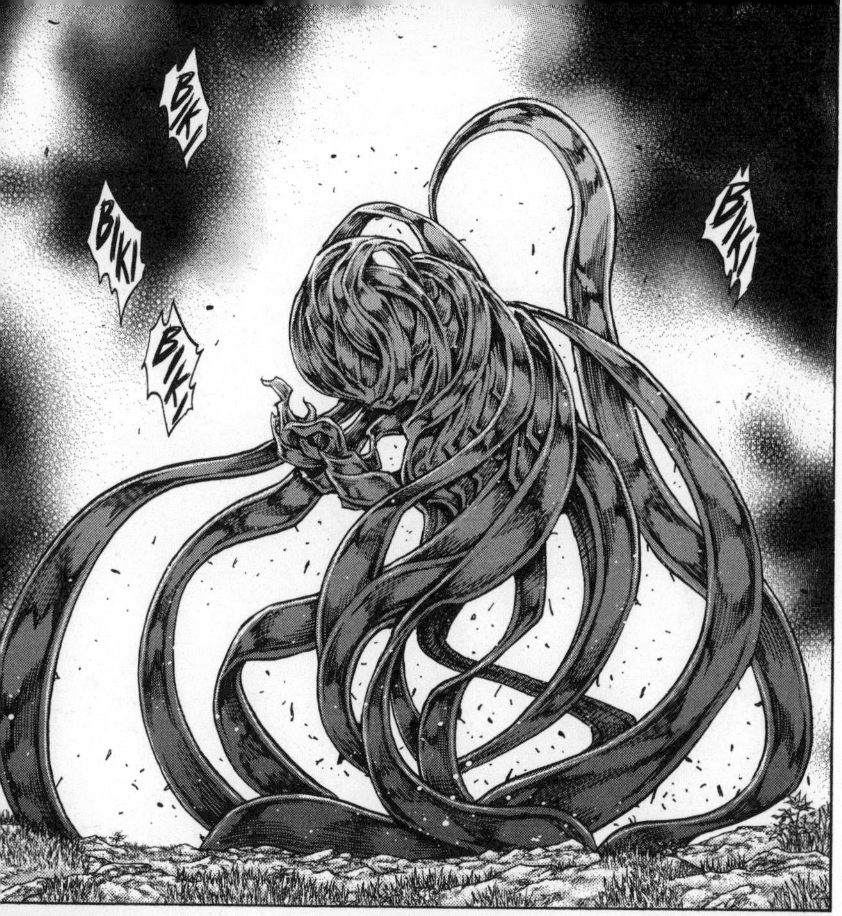
BIKI
BIKI
BIKI
BIKI

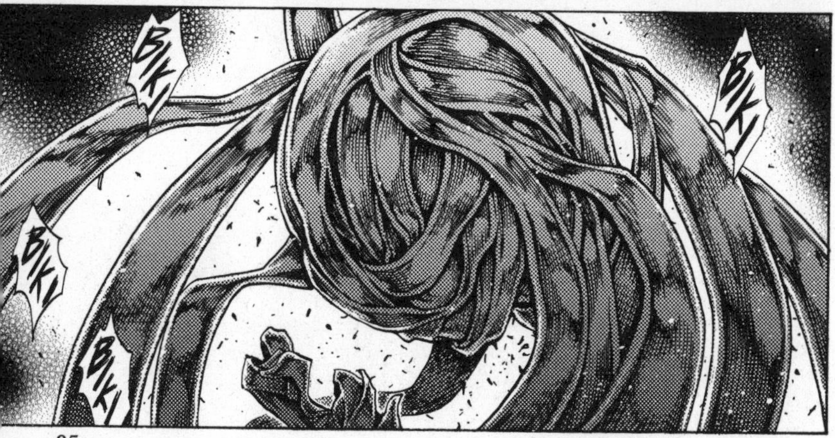
BIKI
BIKI
BIKI
BIKI

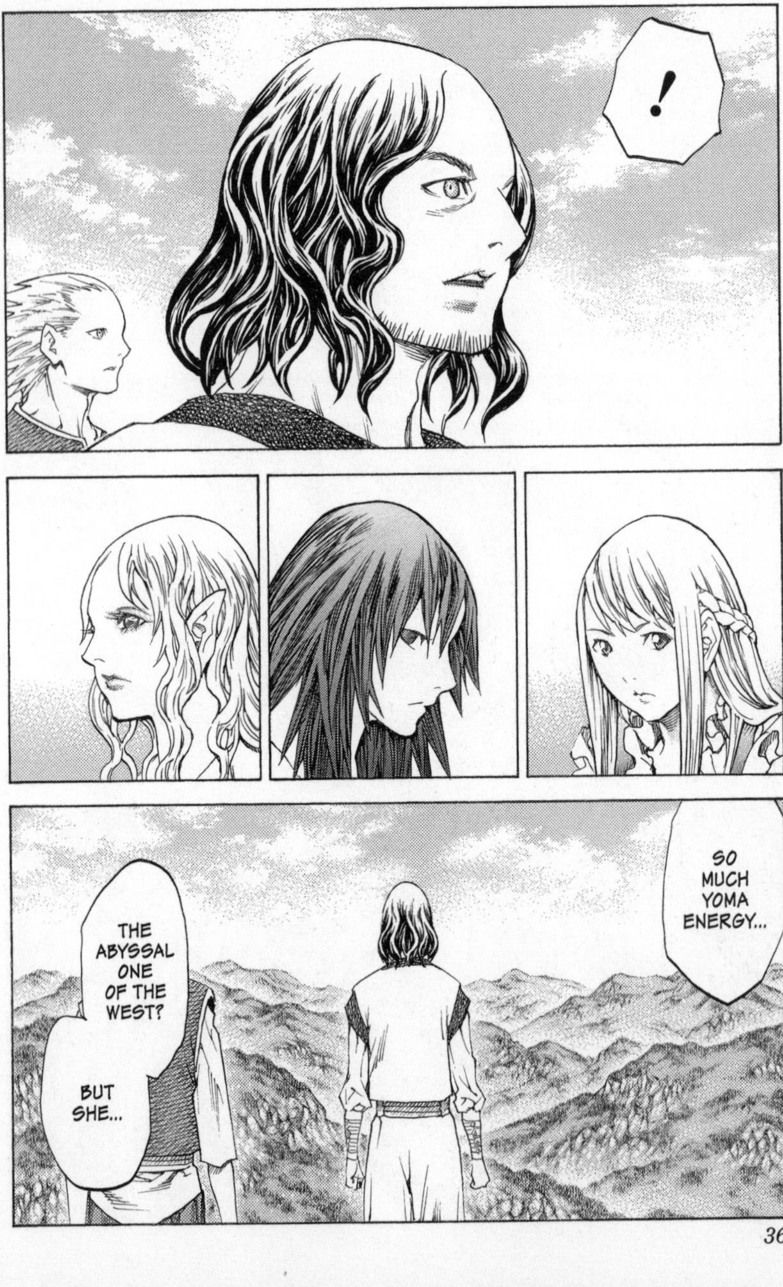
!
SO MUCH YOMA ENERGY...
THE ABYSSAL ONE OF THE WEST?
BUT SHE...

READ THIS WAY

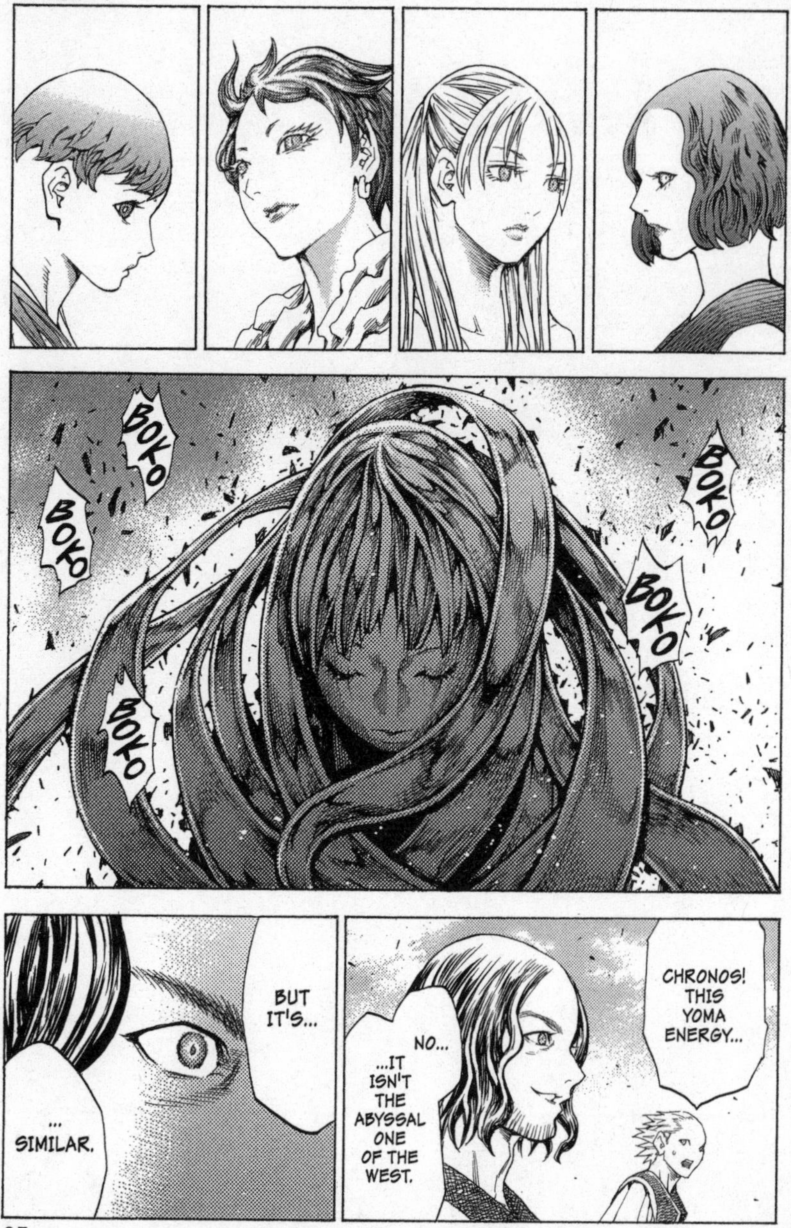
BOKO
BOKO
BOKO
BOKO
BOKO
CHRONOS! THIS YOMA ENERGY...
NO...
...IT ISN'T THE ABYSSAL ONE OF THE WEST.
BUT IT'S...
... SIMILAR.

クレイモア
Claymore

Scene 133: Army of the Underworld, Part 1

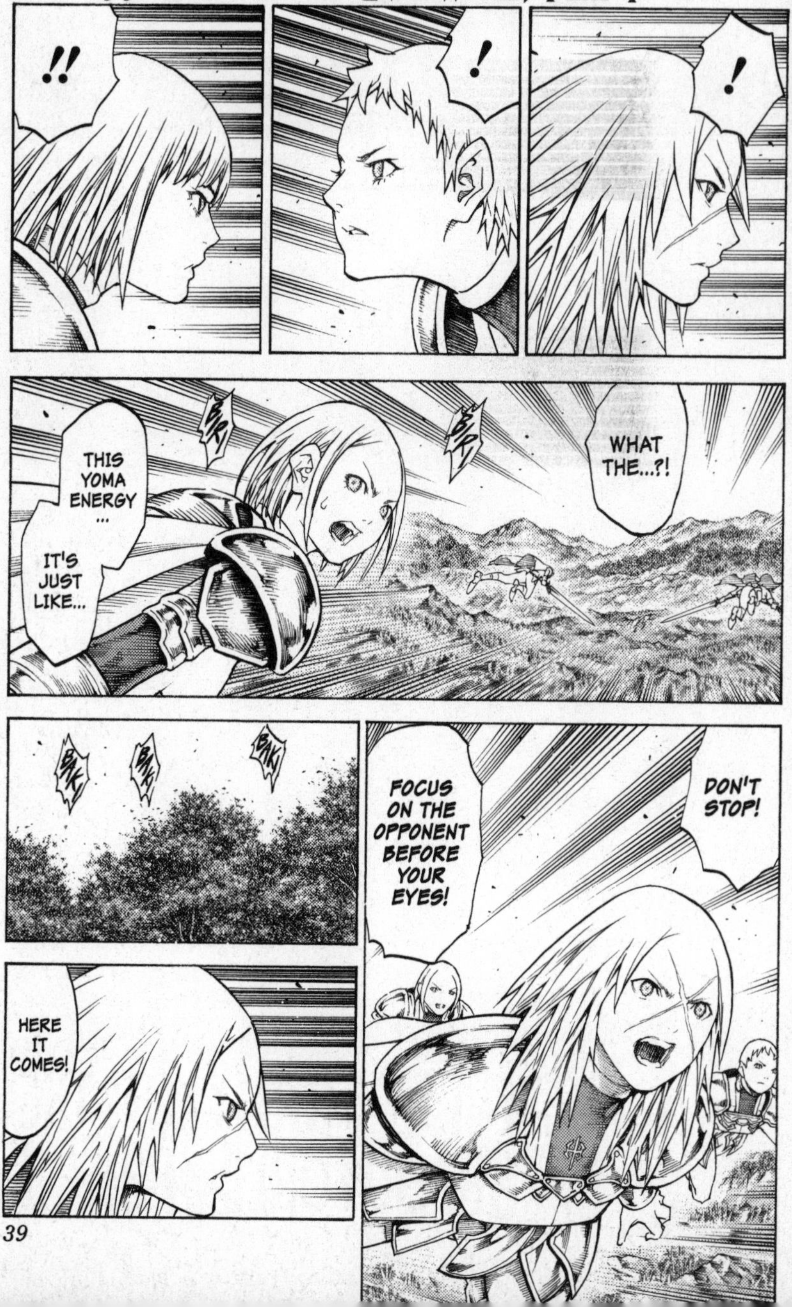
!
!
!!
BIRI
BIRI
WHAT THE...?!
THIS YOMA ENERGY ...
IT'S JUST LIKE...
DON'T STOP!
FOCUS ON THE OPPONENT BEFORE YOUR EYES!
BAKI
BAKI
BAKI
HERE IT COMES!

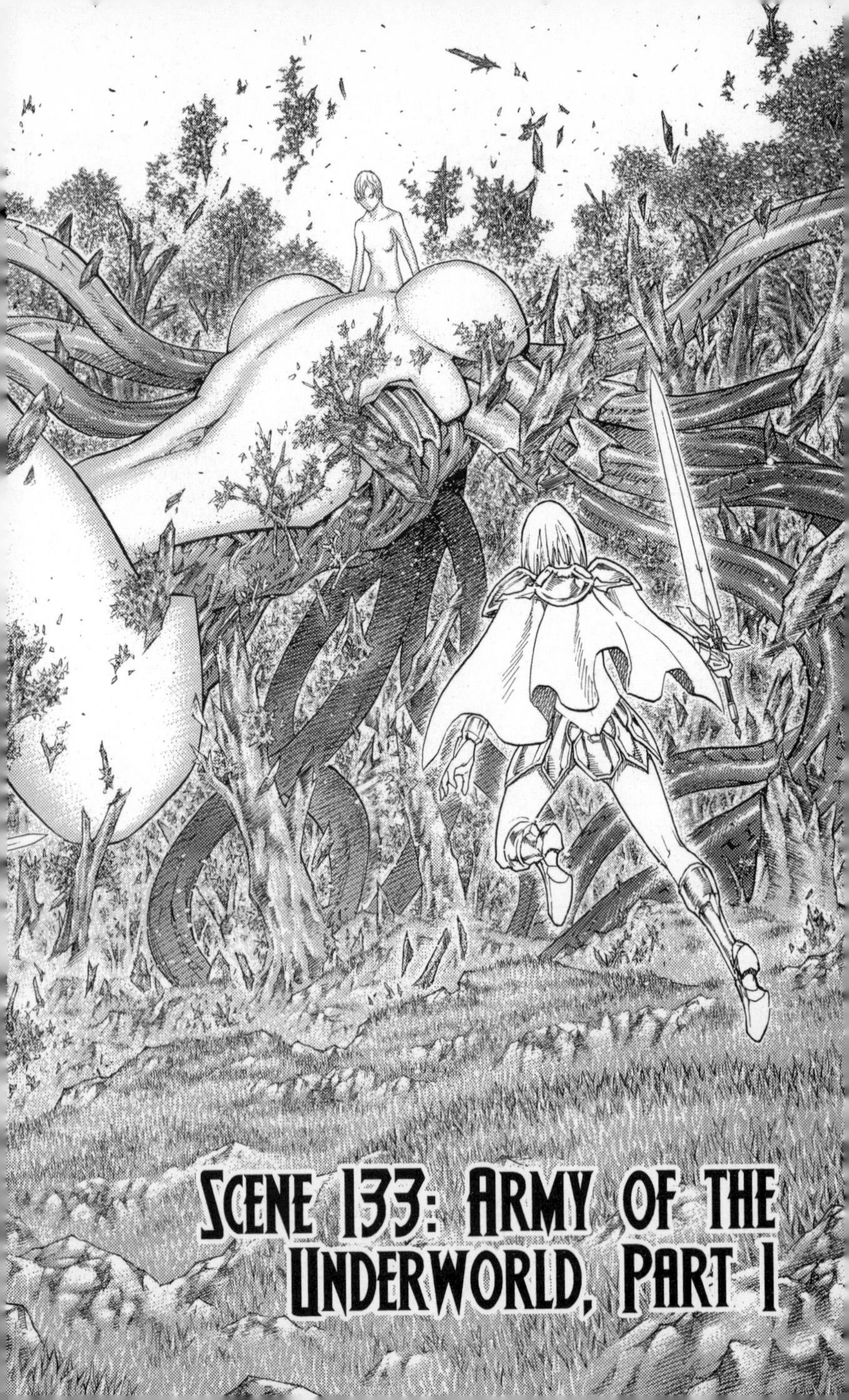
SCENE 133: ARMY OF THE UNDERWORLD, PART 1

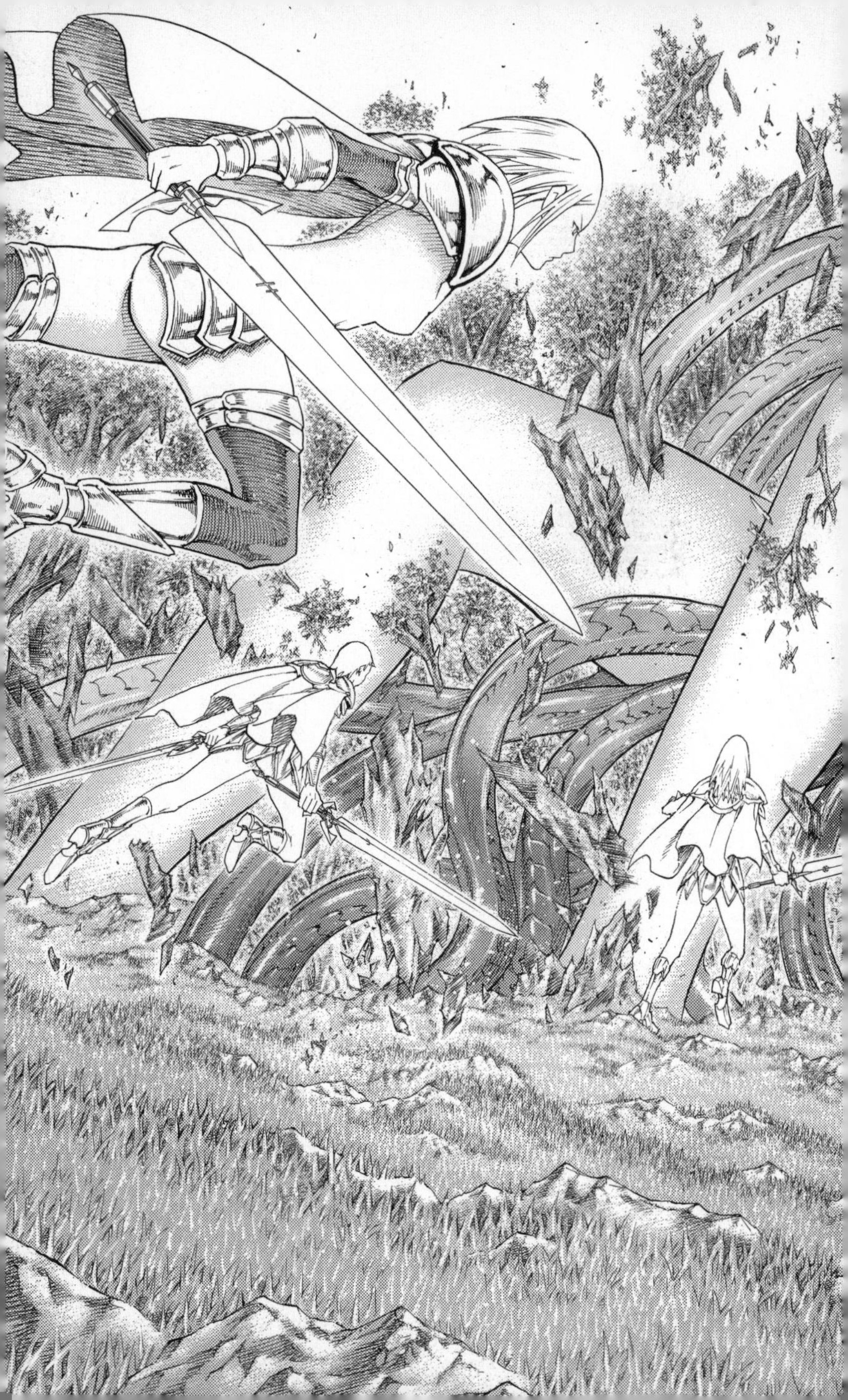

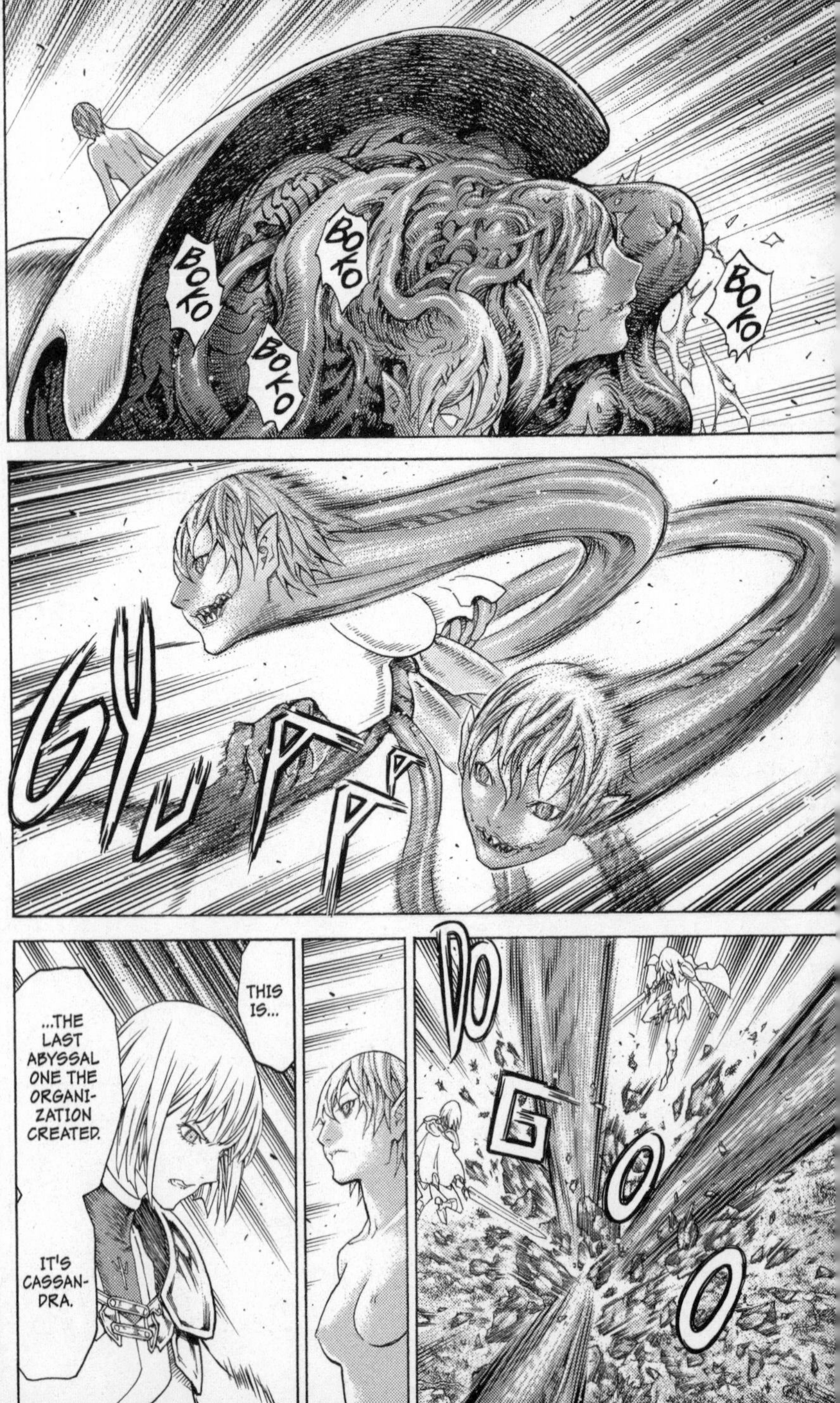
BOKO
BOKO
BOKO
BOKO
GYUPPP
DOGOOO
THIS IS...
...THE LAST ABYSSAL ONE THE ORGANI-ZATION CREATED.
IT'S CASSAN-DRA.

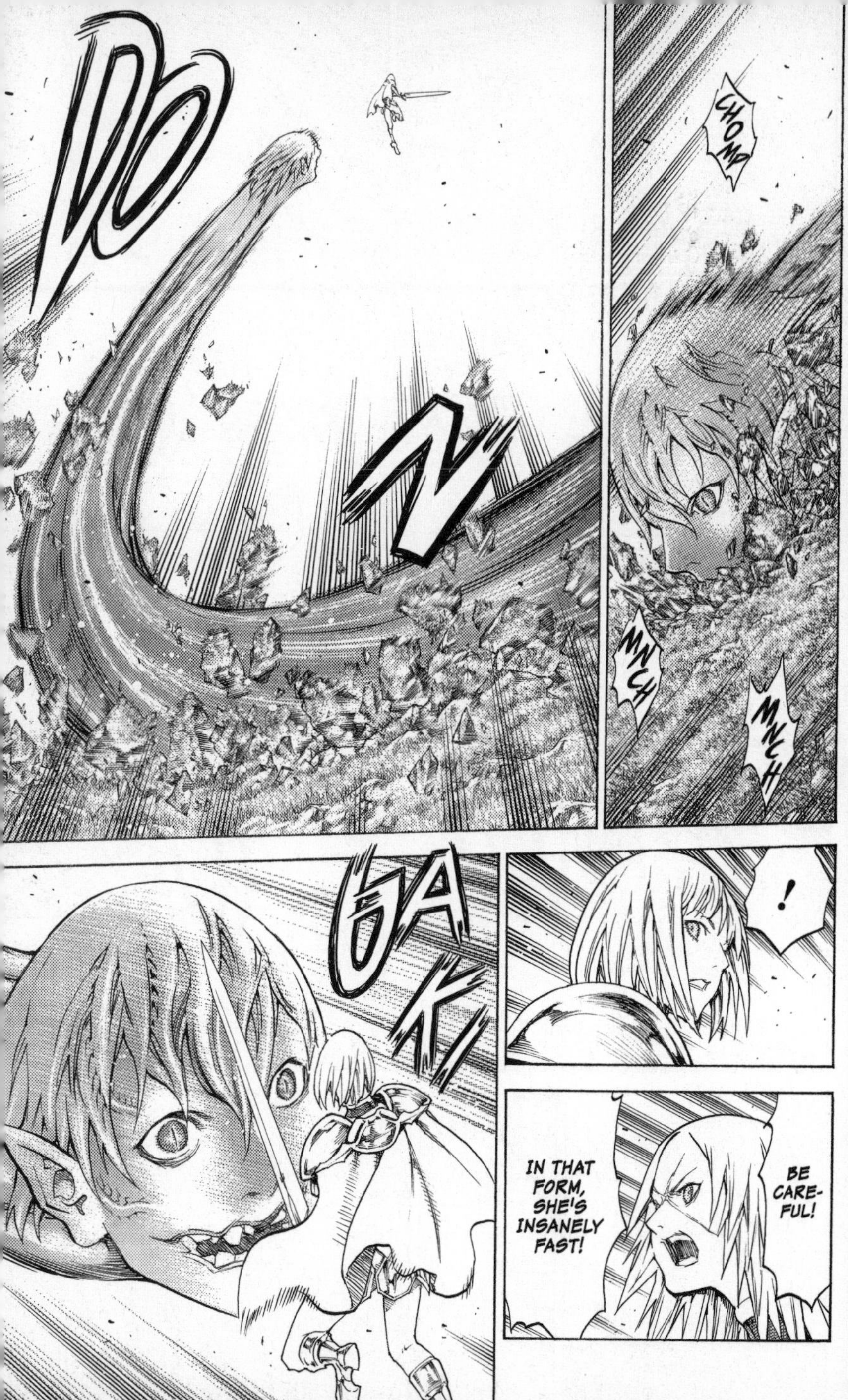
CHOMP
MNCH
MNCH
DO
N
!
BE CARE-FUL!
IN THAT FORM, SHE'S INSANELY FAST!
GAKI

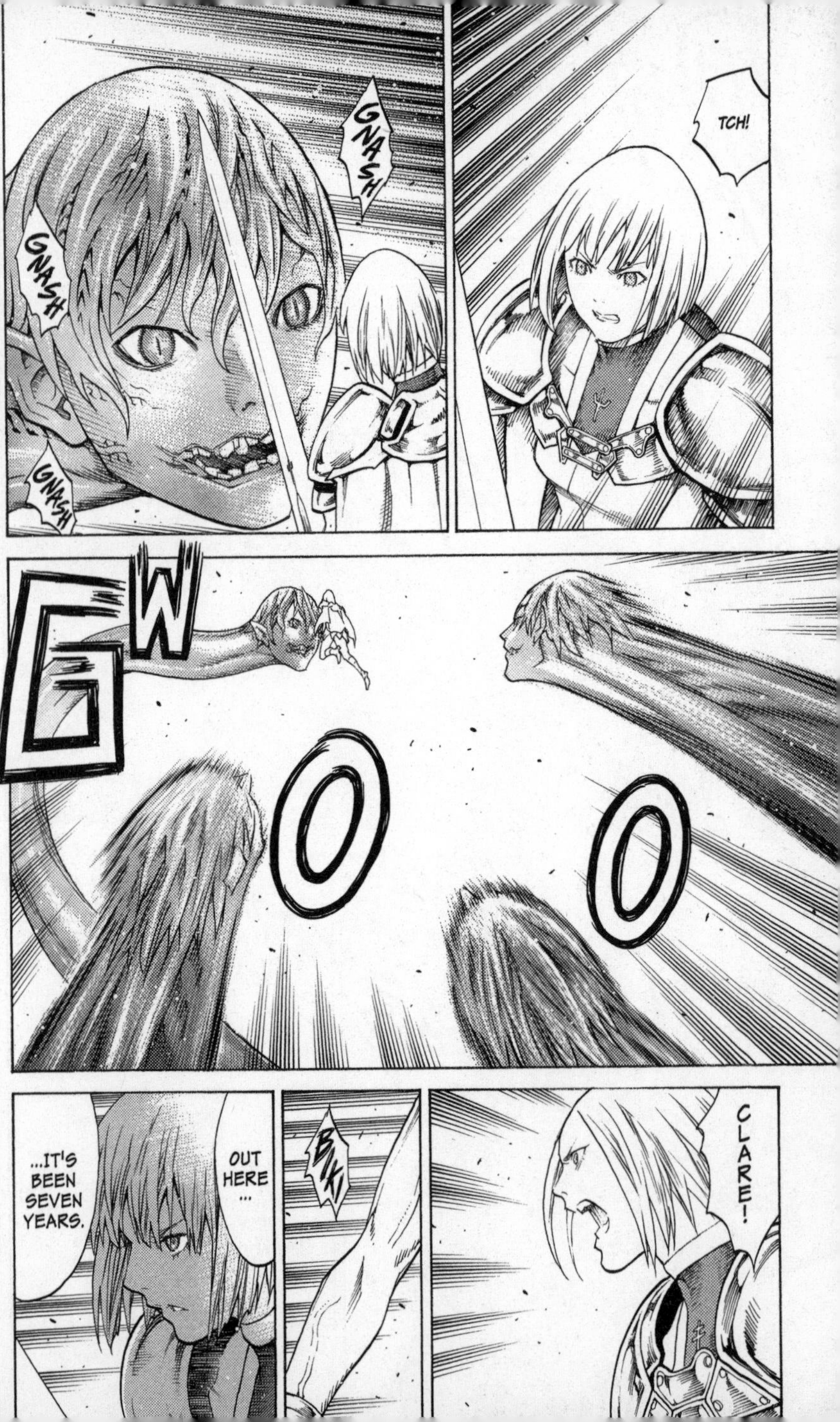
TCH!
GNASH
GNASH
GNASH
GWOO
CLARE!
BAKI!
OUT HERE...
...IT'S BEEN SEVEN YEARS.

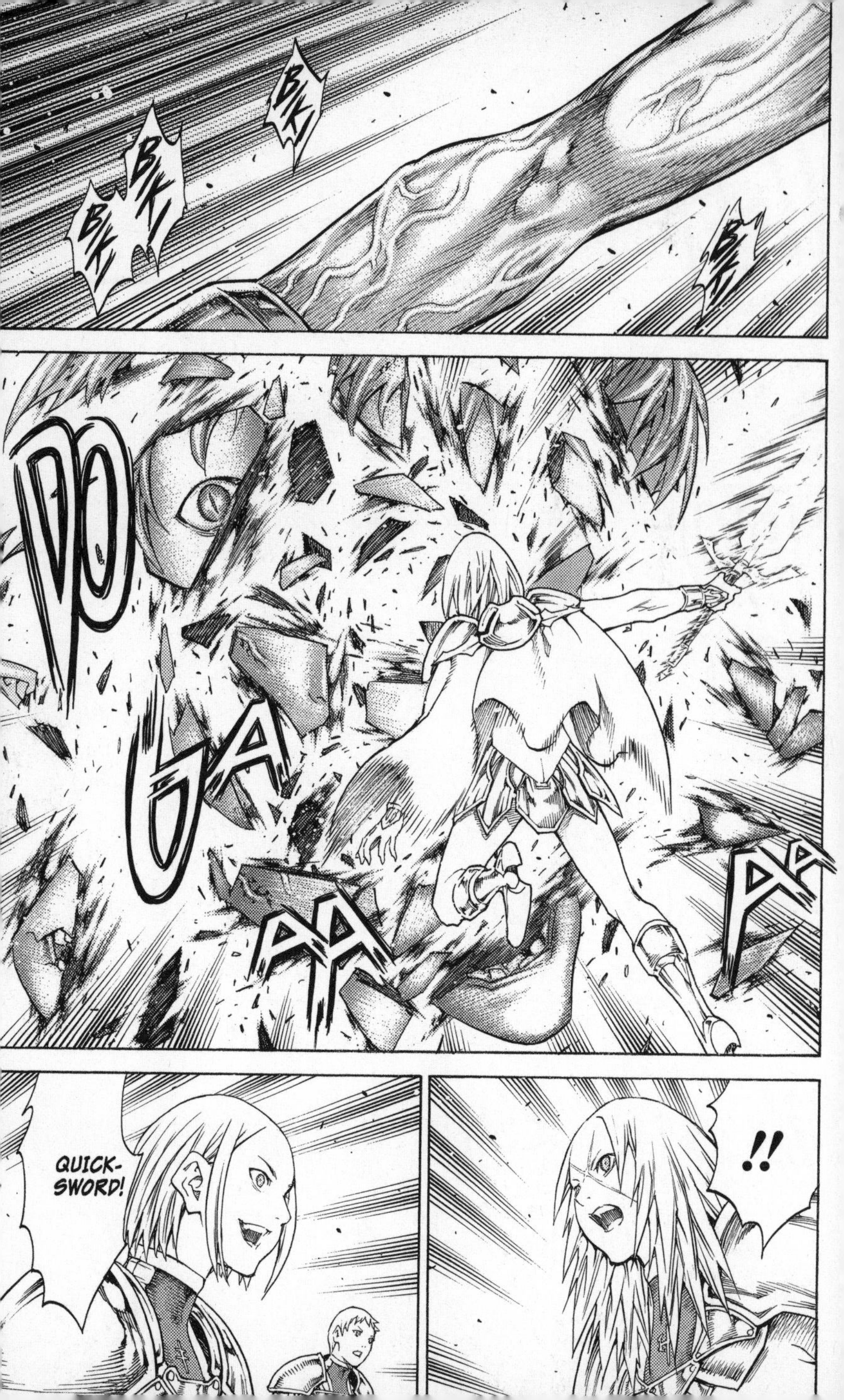
BKI
BKI
BKI
BKI
DOGA
AA
AA
!!
QUICK-SWORD!

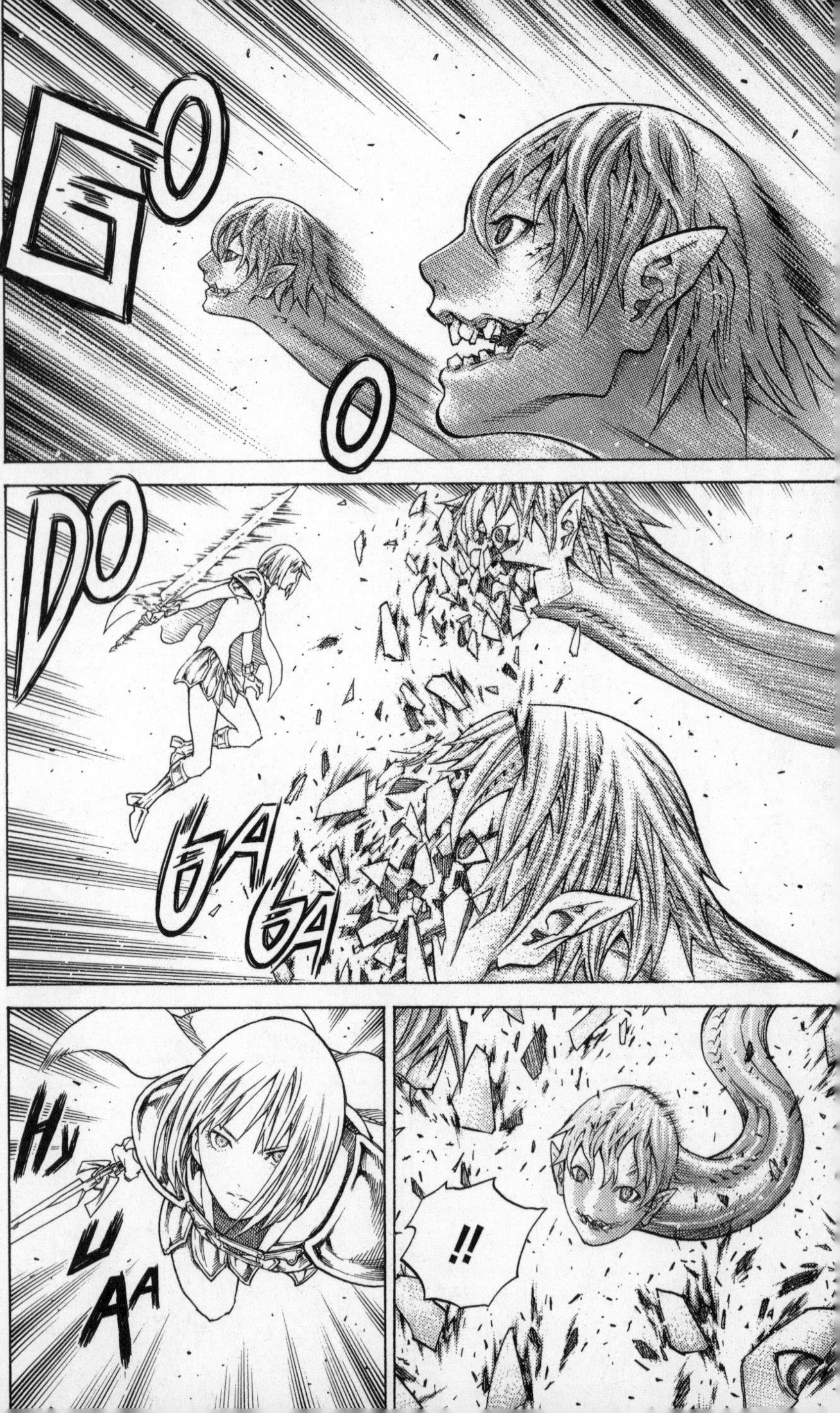
GOOO
DO
GA GA
!!
HYUAA

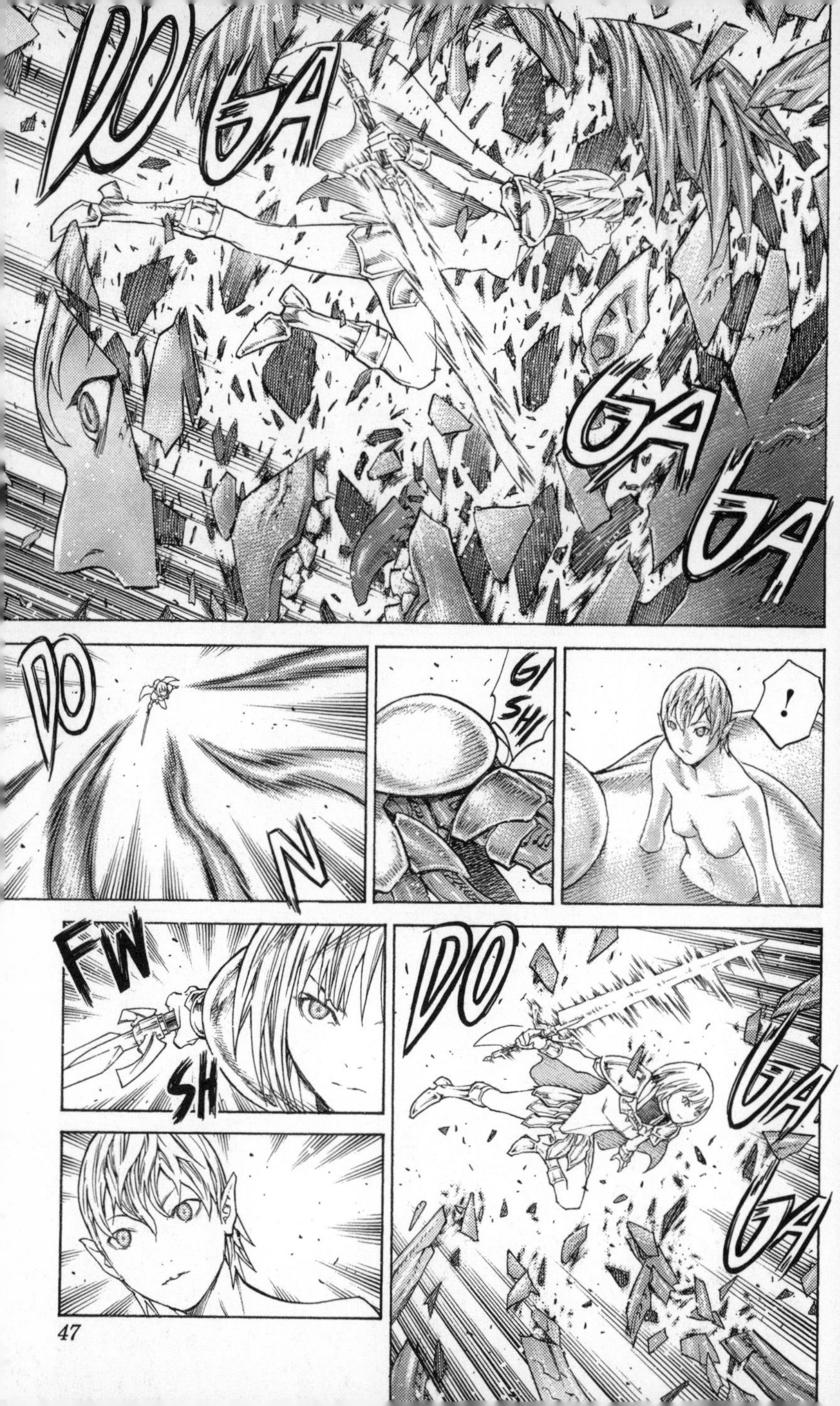
DO GA
GA GA
!
GI SHI
DO
N
DO
GA GA
FW
SH

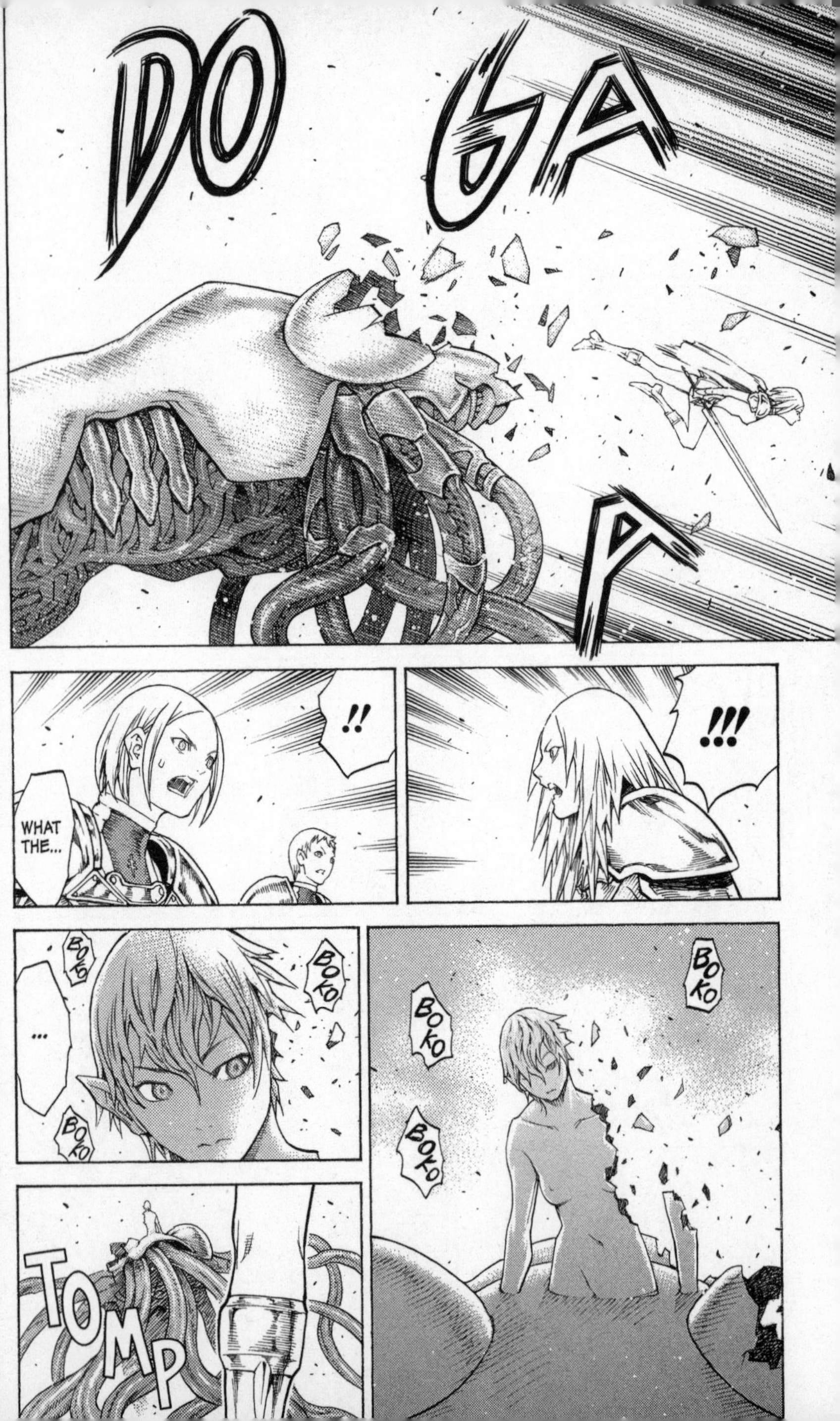
DOGA
A
!!!
!!
WHAT THE...
BOKO
BOKO
BOKO
BOKO
...
BOKO
BOKO
BOKO
TOMP

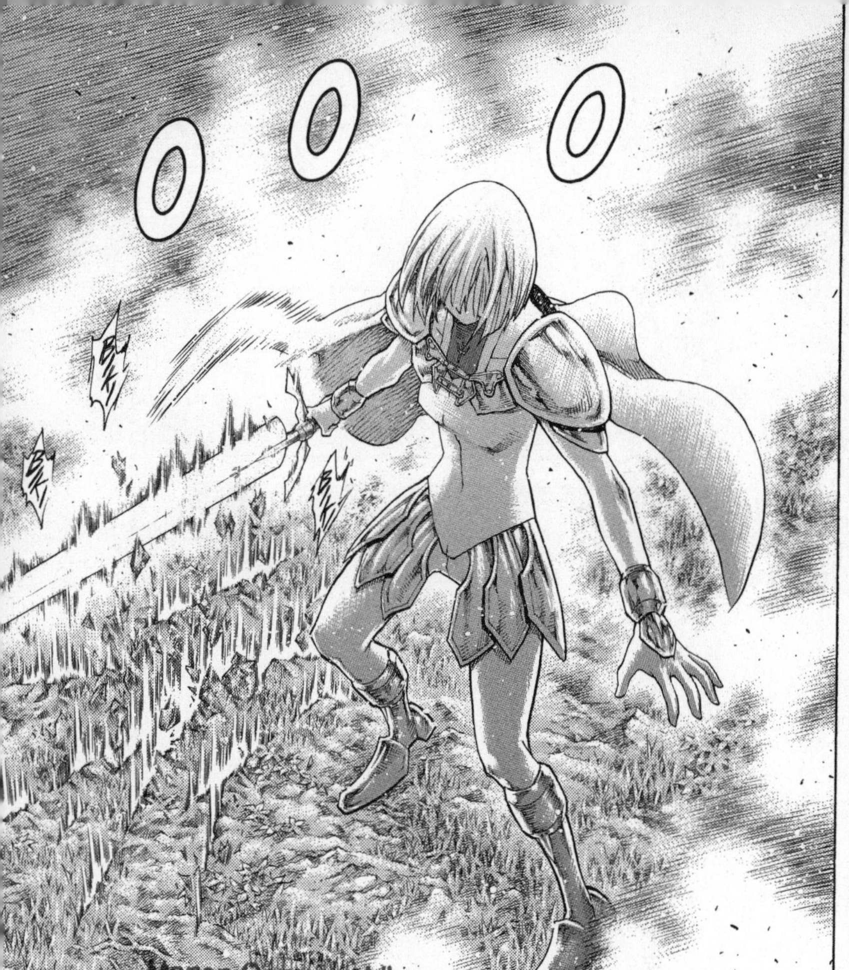
OOO
BIKI
BIKI
BIKI

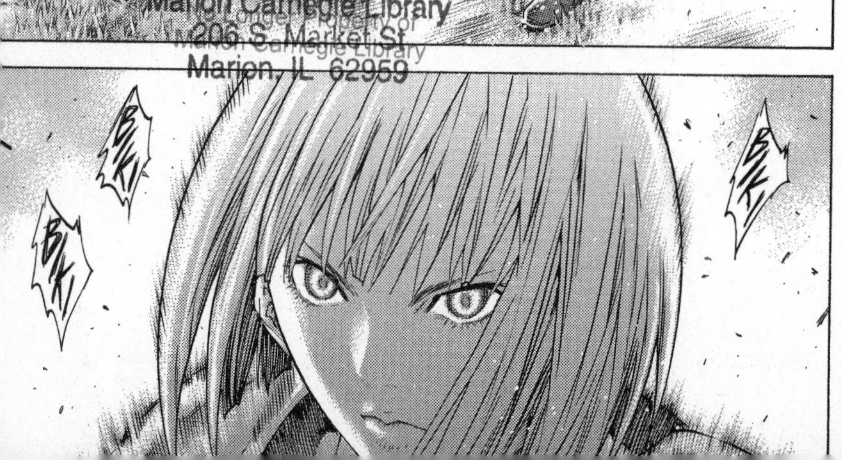
BIKI
BIKI
BIKI

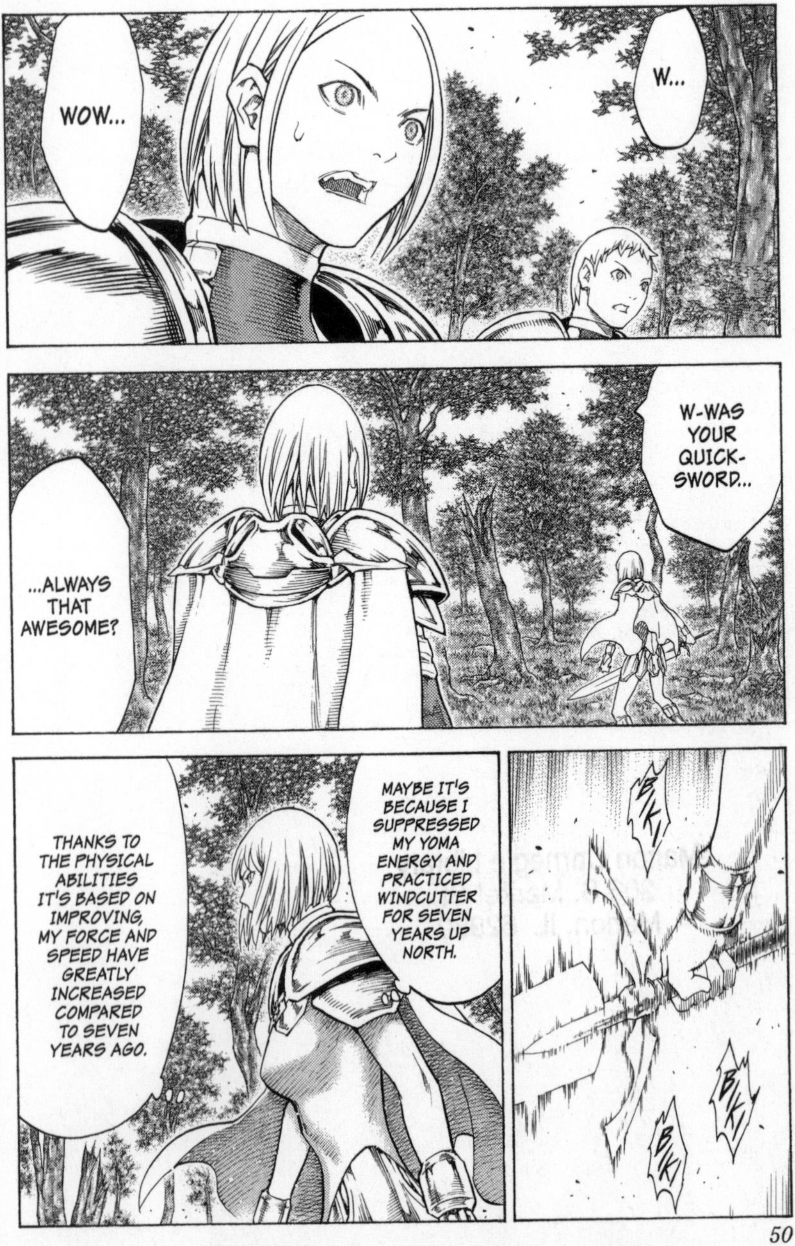
W...
WOW...
W-WAS YOUR QUICK-SWORD...
...ALWAYS THAT AWESOME?
BIKI
BIKI
BIKI
MAYBE IT'S BECAUSE I SUPPRESSED MY YOMA ENERGY AND PRACTICED WINDCUTTER FOR SEVEN YEARS UP NORTH.
THANKS TO THE PHYSICAL ABILITIES IT'S BASED ON IMPROVING, MY FORCE AND SPEED HAVE GREATLY INCREASED COMPARED TO SEVEN YEARS AGO.

READ THIS WAY

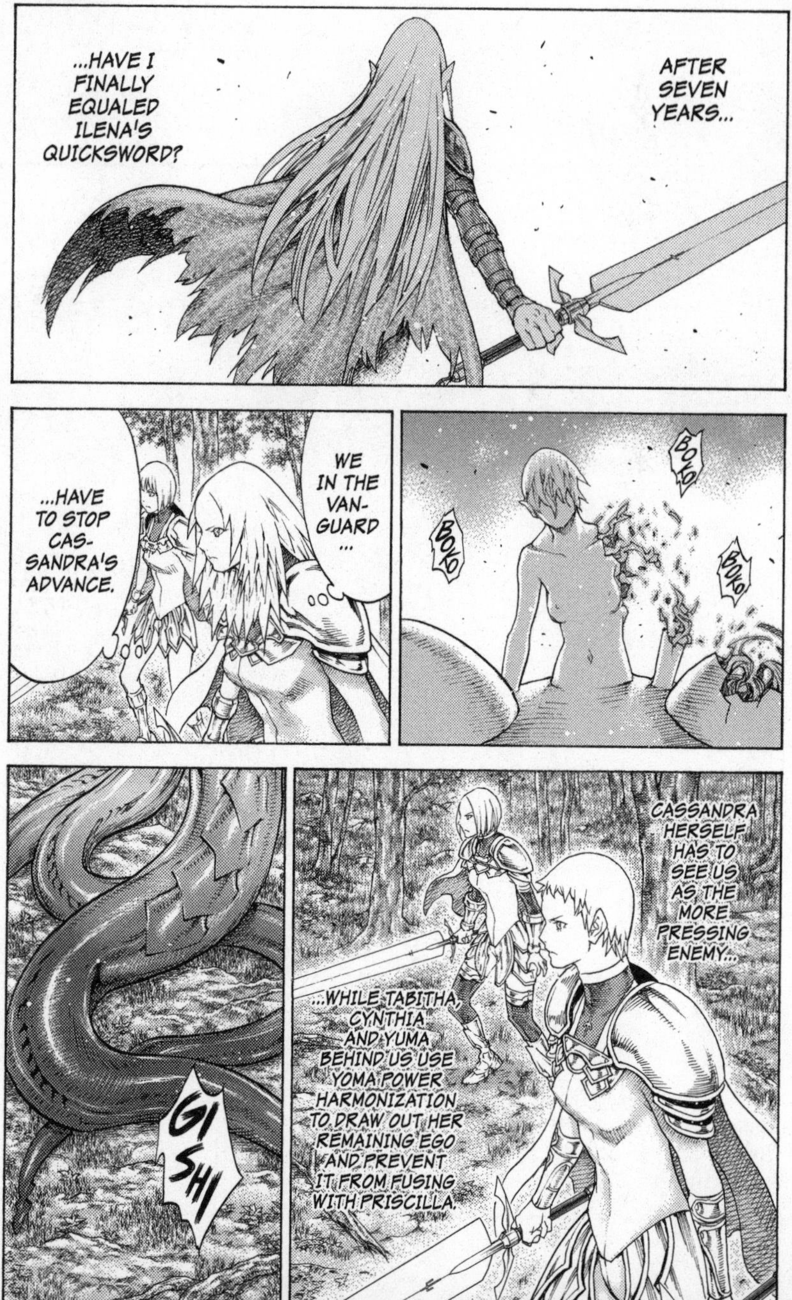
AFTER SEVEN YEARS...
...HAVE I FINALLY EQUALED ILENA'S QUICKSWORD?
BOKO
BOKO
BOKO
WE IN THE VAN-GUARD ...
...HAVE TO STOP CAS-SANDRA'S ADVANCE.
CASSANDRA HERSELF HAS TO SEE US AS THE MORE PRESSING ENEMY...
...WHILE TABITHA, CYNTHIA AND YUMA BEHIND US USE YOMA POWER HARMONIZATION TO DRAW OUT HER REMAINING EGO AND PREVENT IT FROM FUSING WITH PRISCILLA.
GI SHI

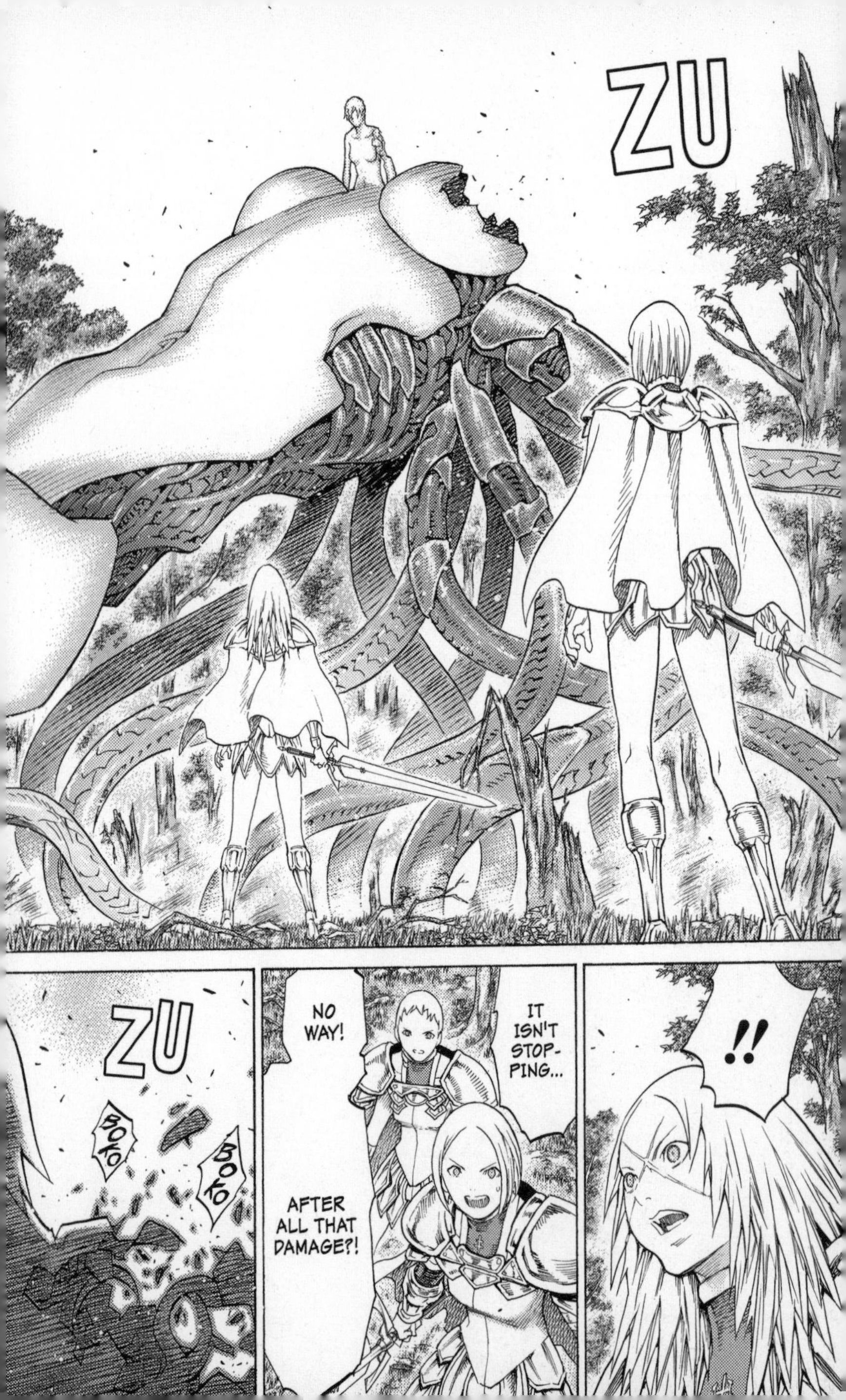
ZU
!!
IT ISN'T STOP-PING...
NO WAY!
AFTER ALL THAT DAMAGE?!
ZU
BOKO
BOKO

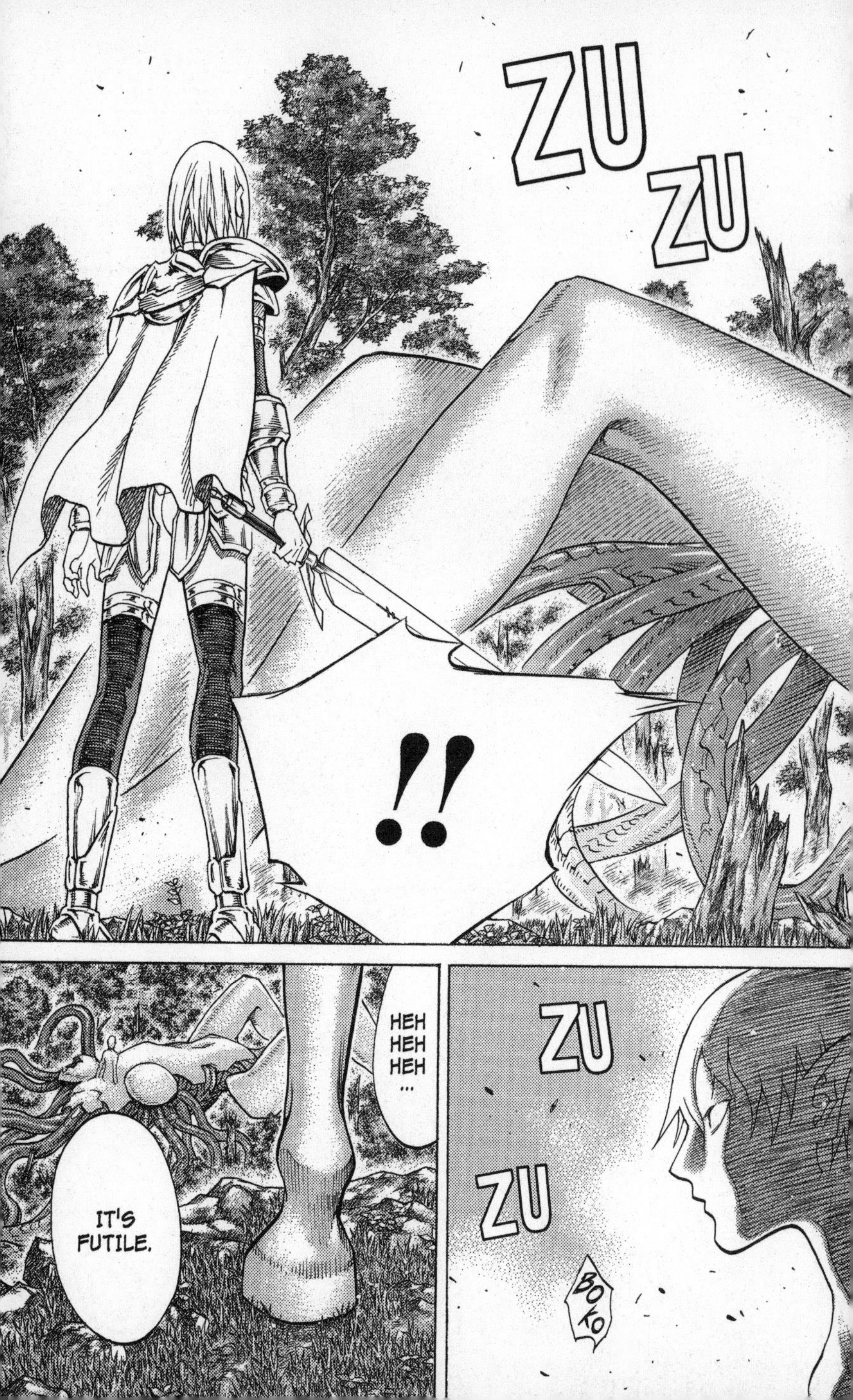
ZU ZU
!!
ZU
ZU
BOKO
HEH HEH HEH ...
IT'S FUTILE.

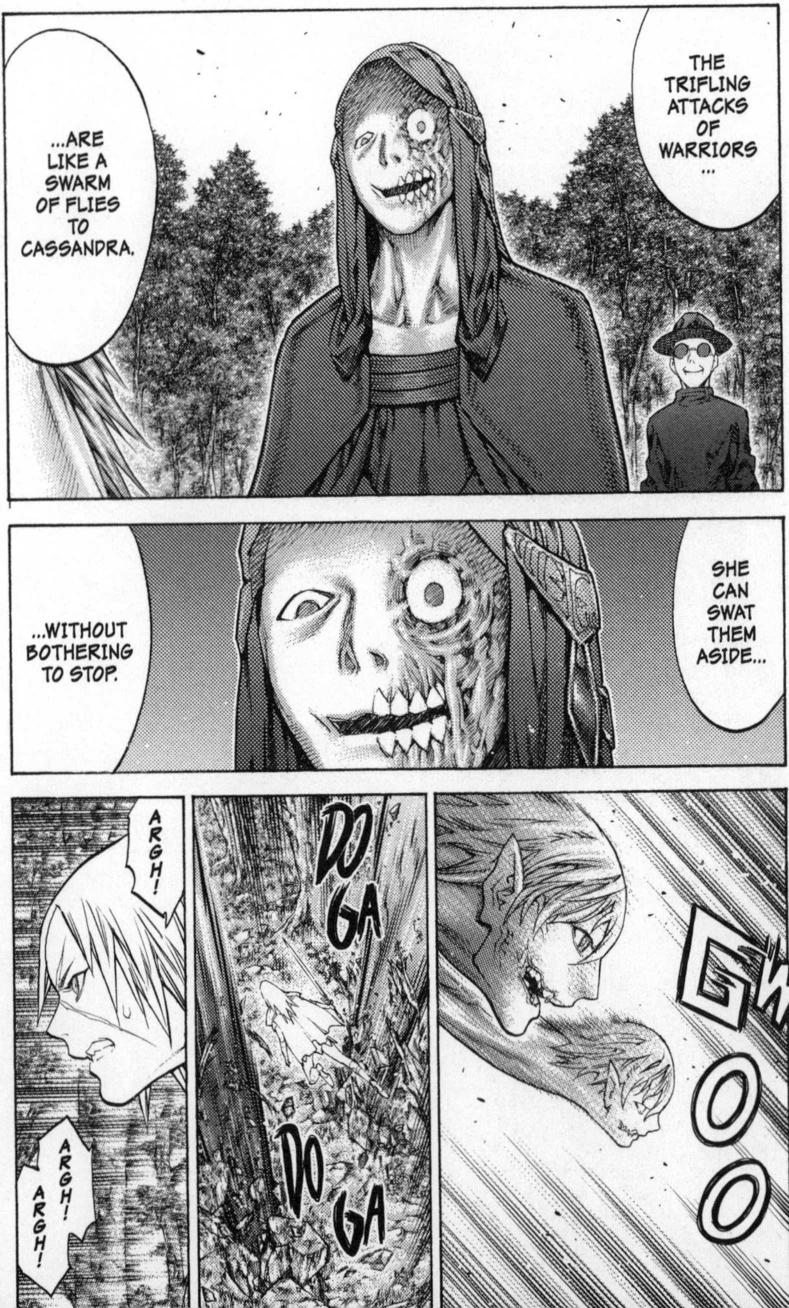
THE TRIFLING ATTACKS OF WARRIORS...
...ARE LIKE A SWARM OF FLIES TO CASSANDRA.
SHE CAN SWAT THEM ASIDE...
...WITHOUT BOTHERING TO STOP.
GWOOO
DOGA
DOGA
ARGH!
ARGH!
ARGH!

READ THIS WAY

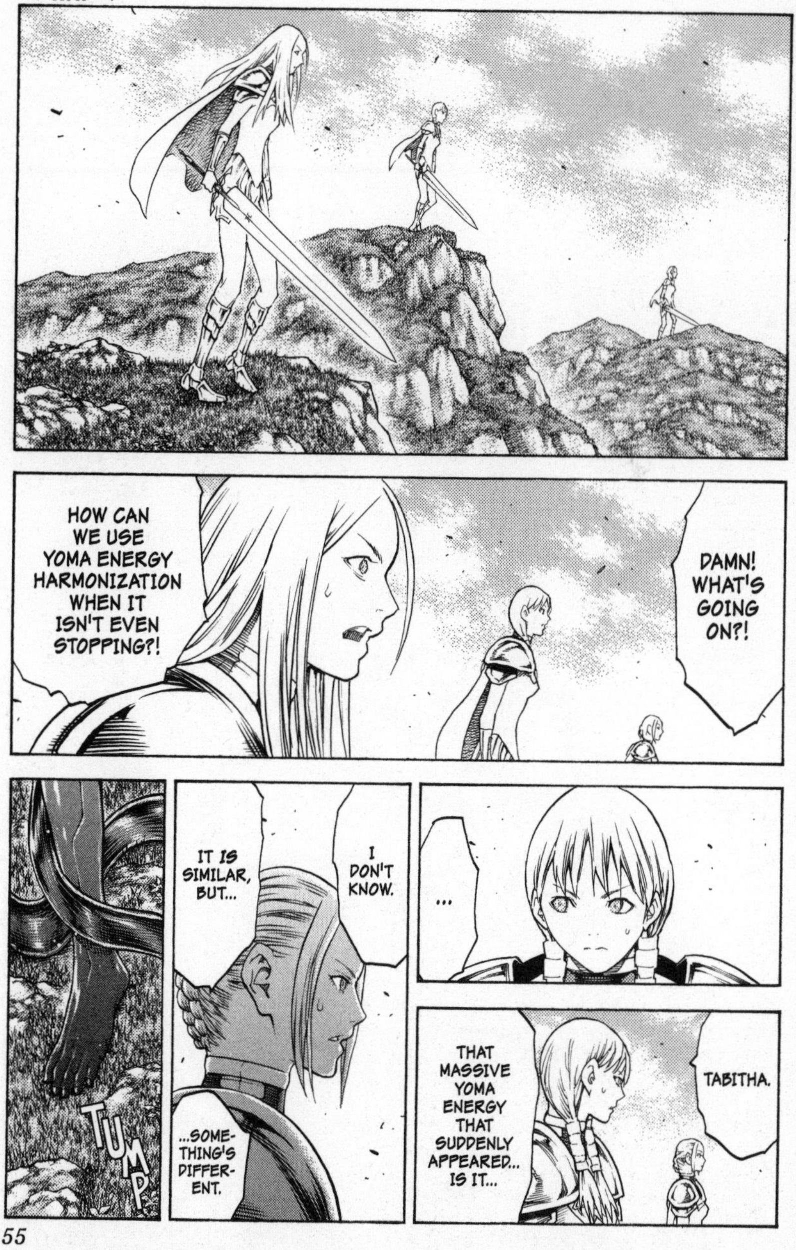
DAMN! WHAT'S GOING ON?!
HOW CAN WE USE YOMA ENERGY HARMONIZATION WHEN IT ISN'T EVEN STOPPING?!
...
TABITHA.
THAT MASSIVE YOMA ENERGY THAT SUDDENLY APPEARED... IS IT...
I DON'T KNOW.
IT IS SIMILAR, BUT...
...SOMETHING'S DIFFERENT.
TUMP

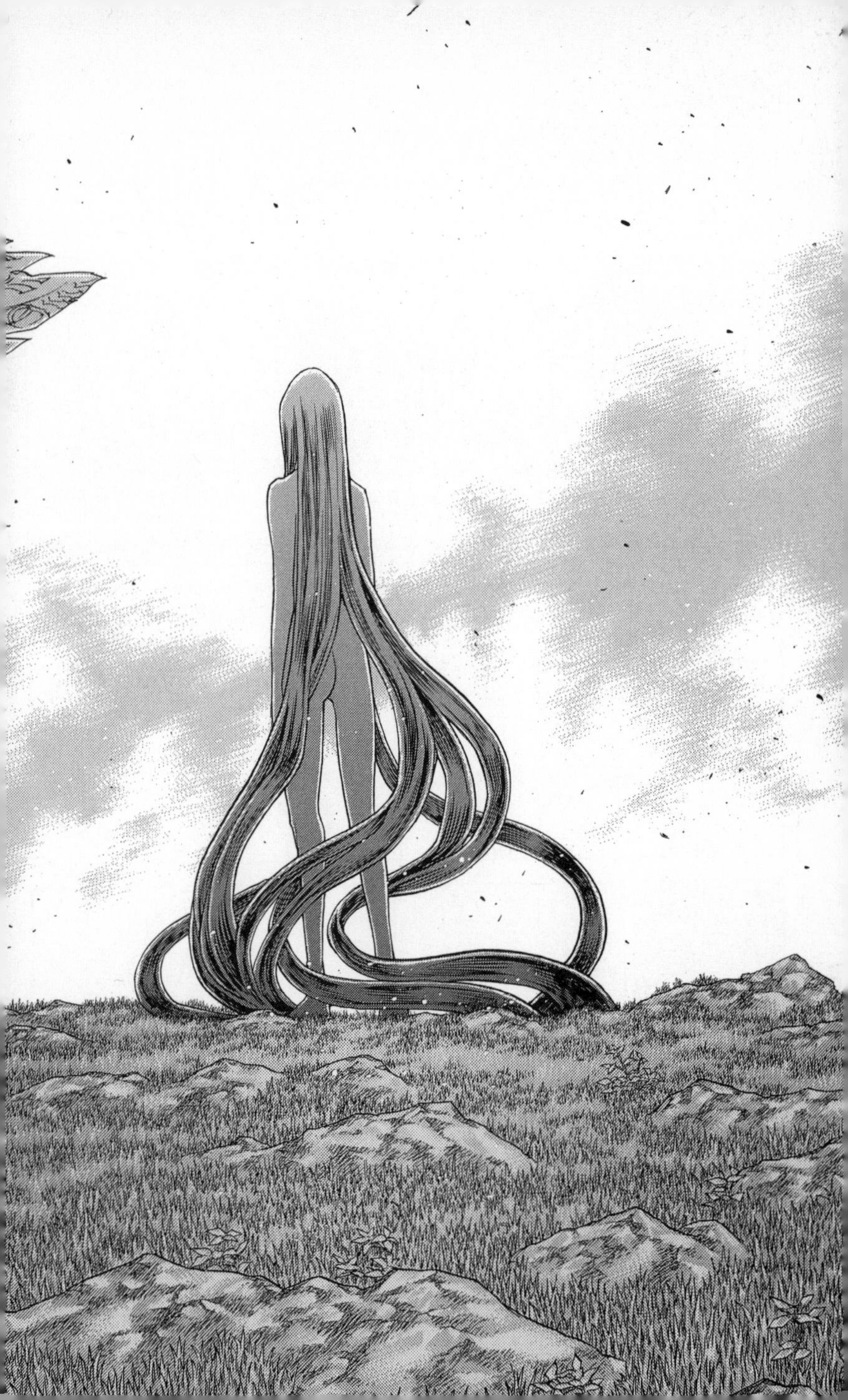

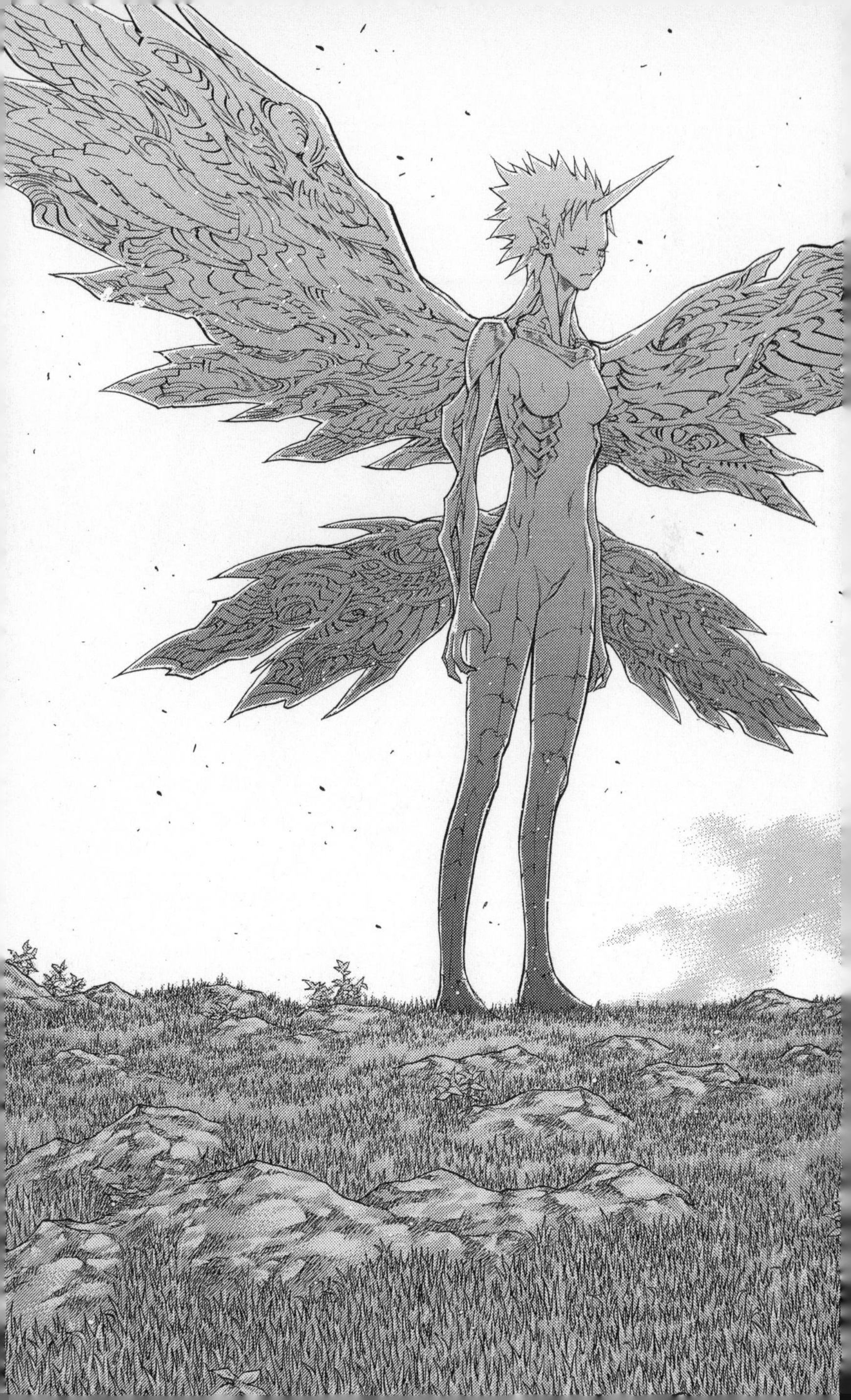

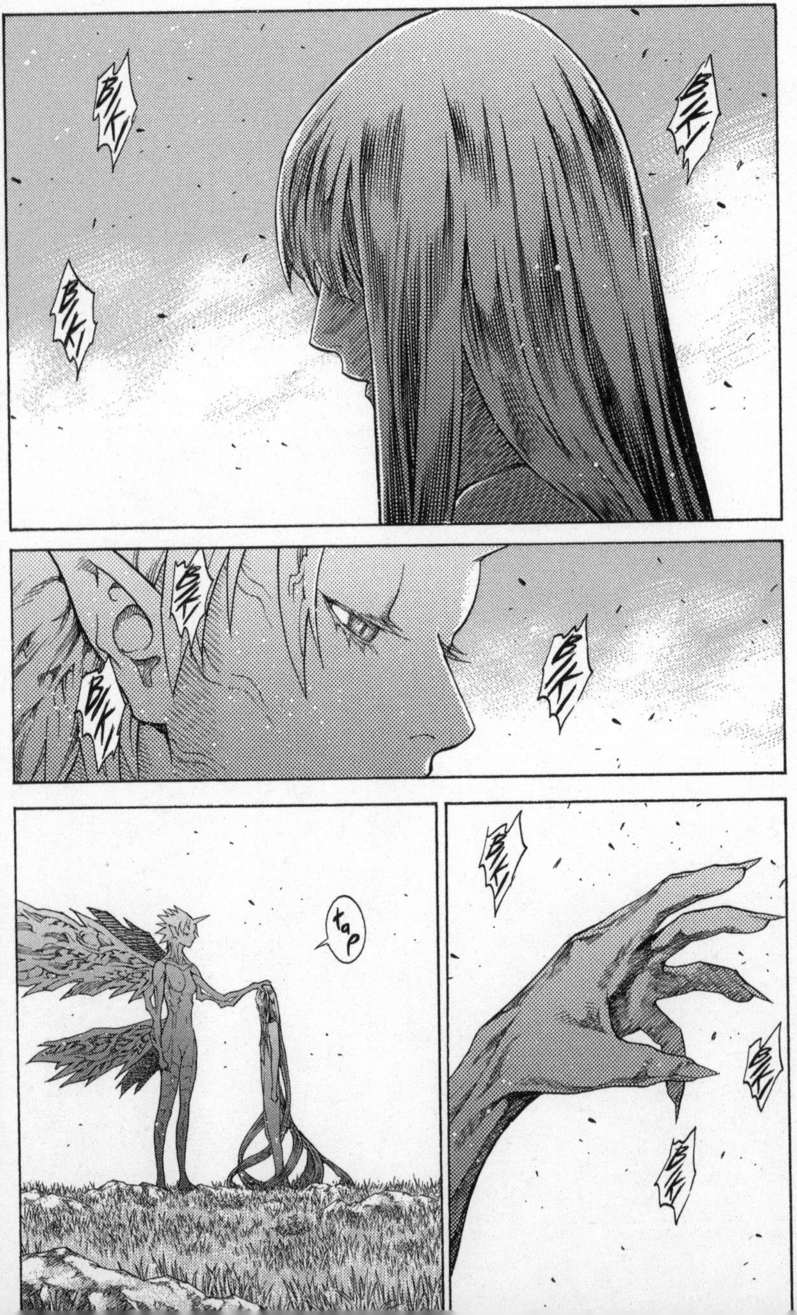
BIKI
BIKI
BIKI
BIKI
BIKI
BIKI
BIKI
BIKI
BIKI
tap

READ THIS WAY

BIKI
BIKI
BIKI
KRNCH
BIKI
BIKI
BIKI
BIKI
BIKI
BIKI
BIKI
BIKI
BIKI
GASH
BIKI
BIKI
BIKI

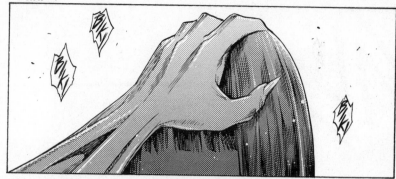

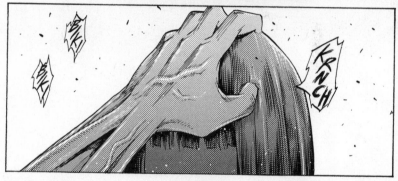

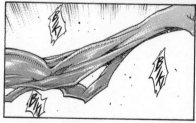

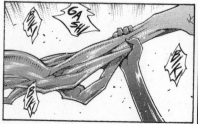

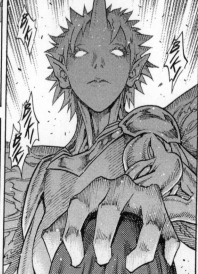

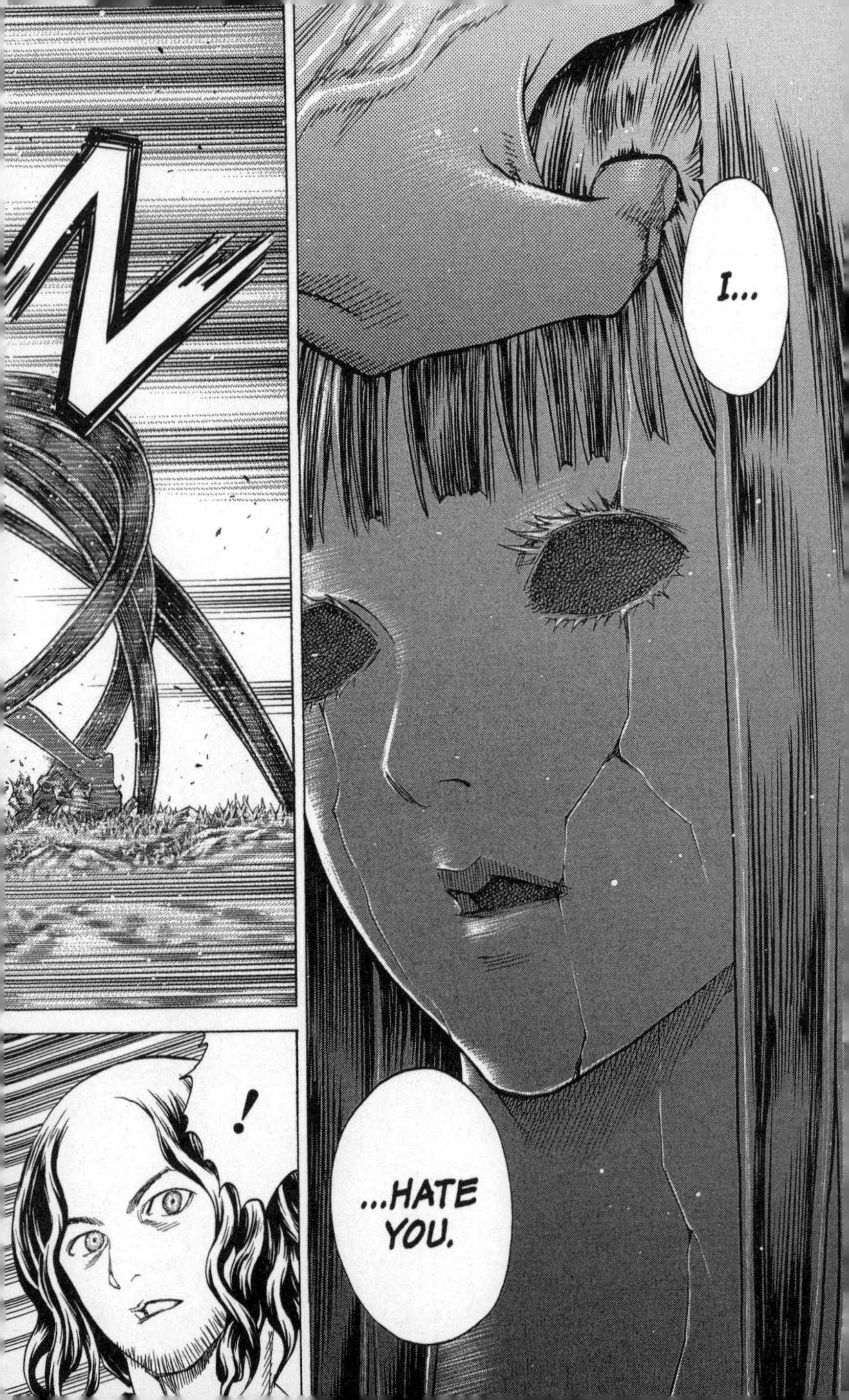
I...
...HATE YOU.
!

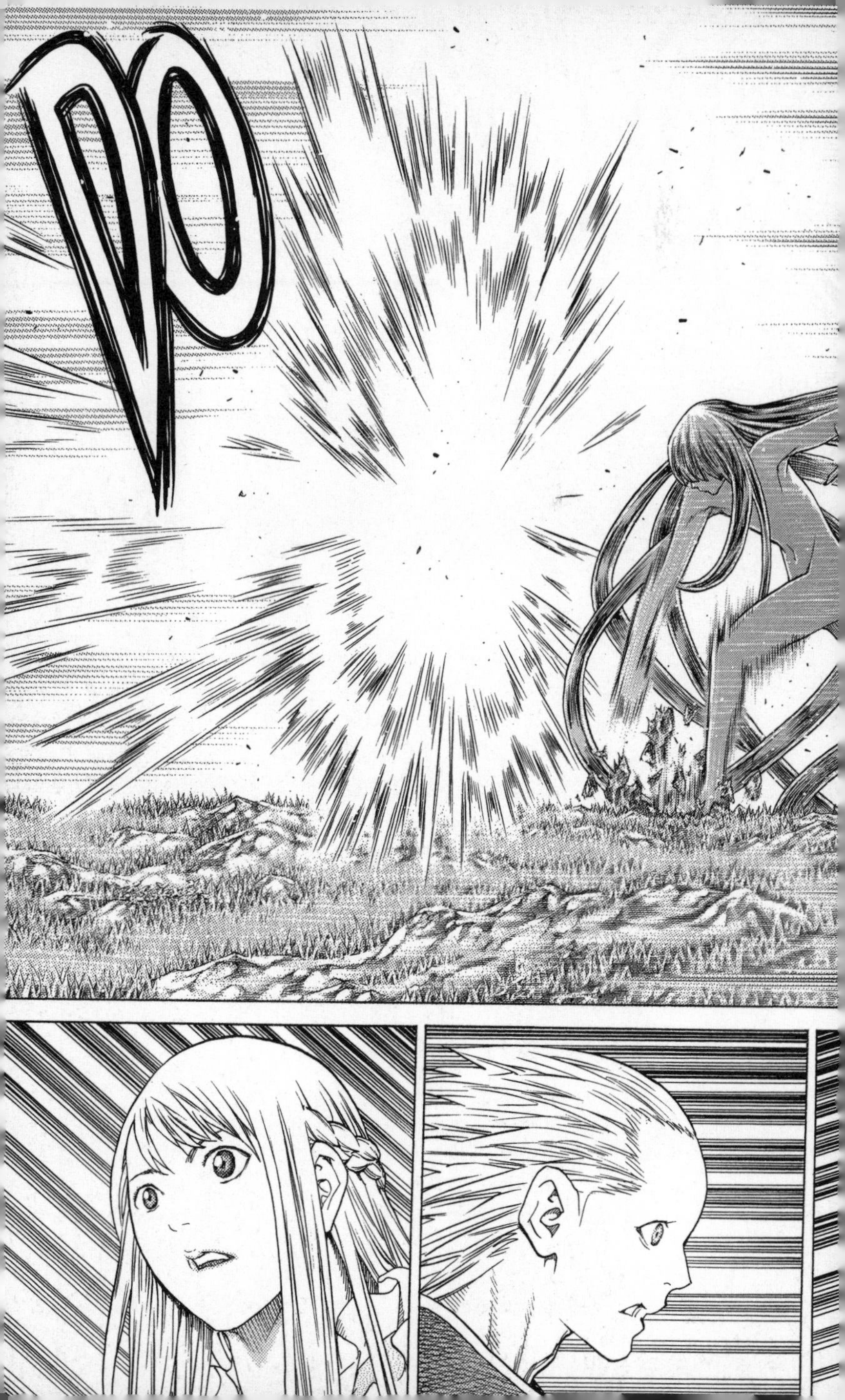

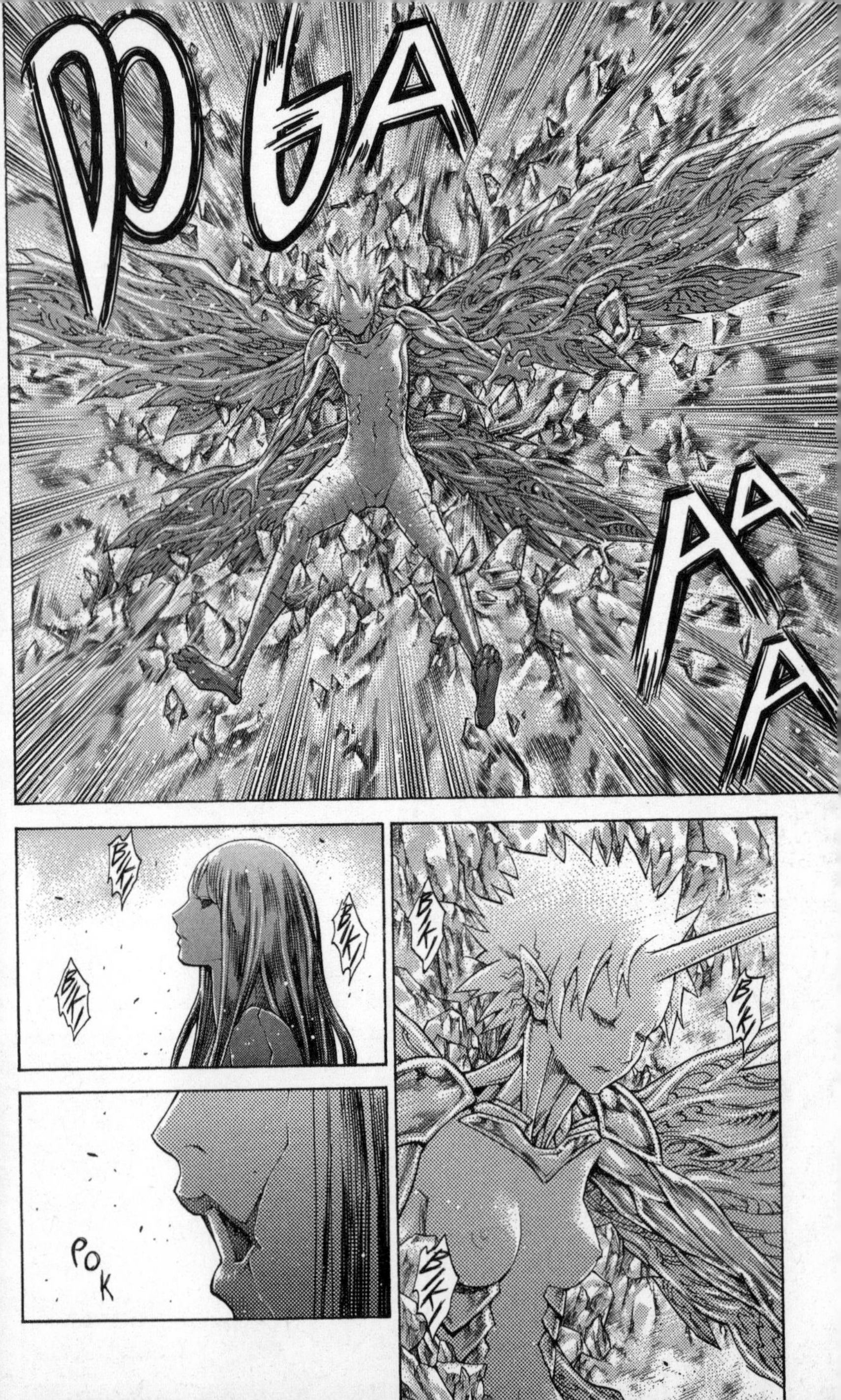
DOGA
AAAA
BIKI
BIKI
BIKI
BIKI
BIKI
BIKI
POK

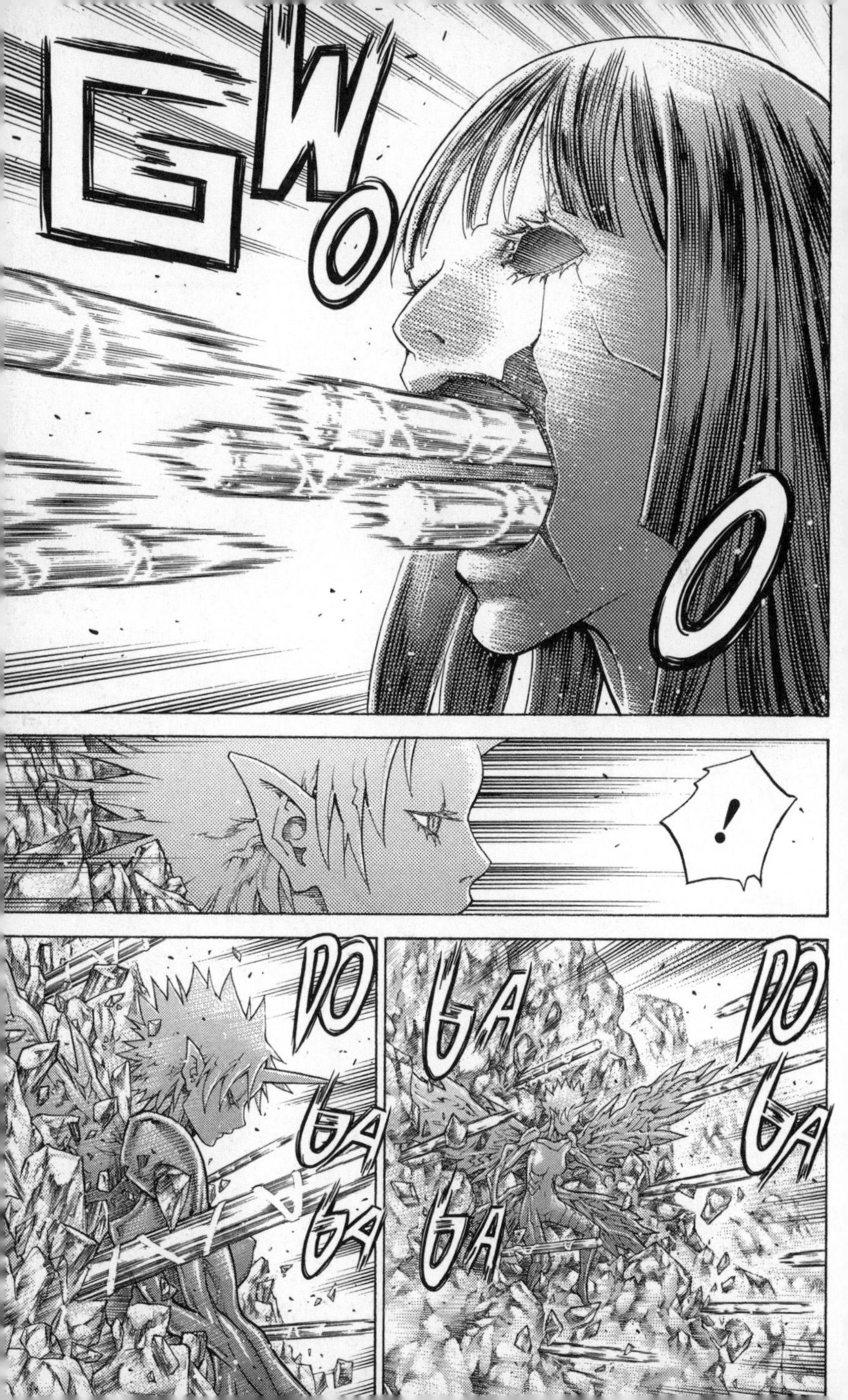
GWOO
!
DO
GA
GA
GA
DO
GA
GA

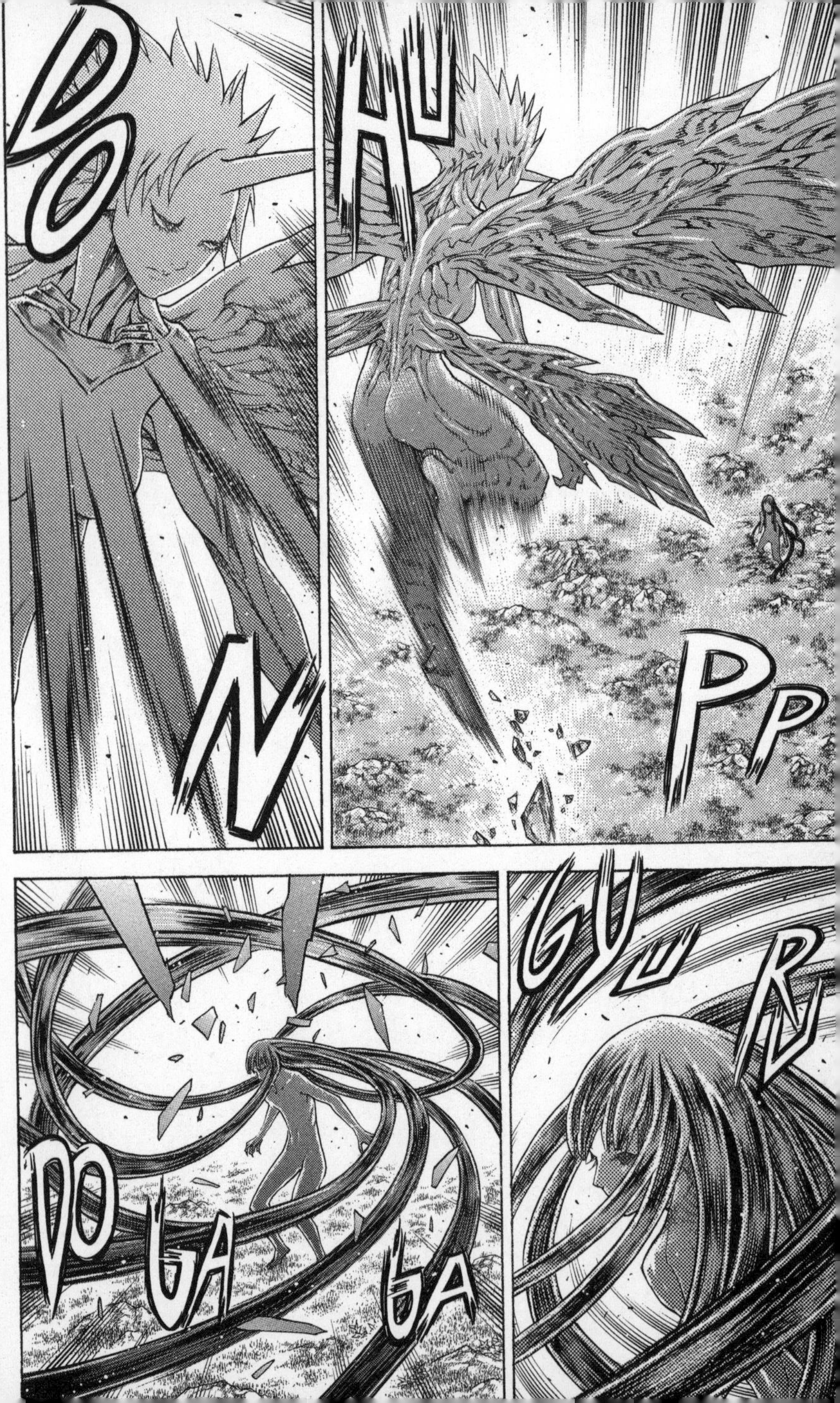
HU
PP
DO
N
GYU
RU
DO
GA
GA

READ THIS WAY

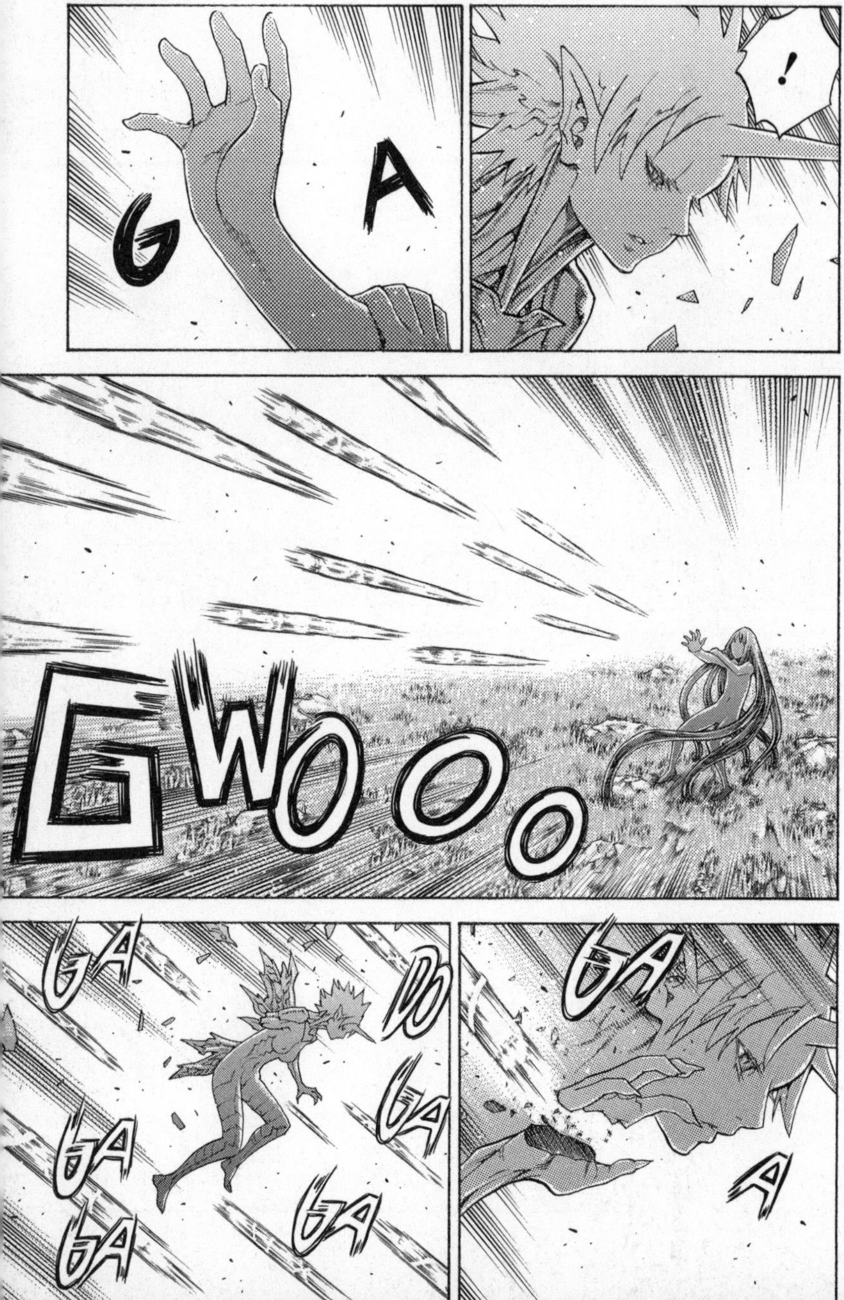
!
GA
GWOOOO
GA
A
DO
GA
GA
GA
GA
GA
GA

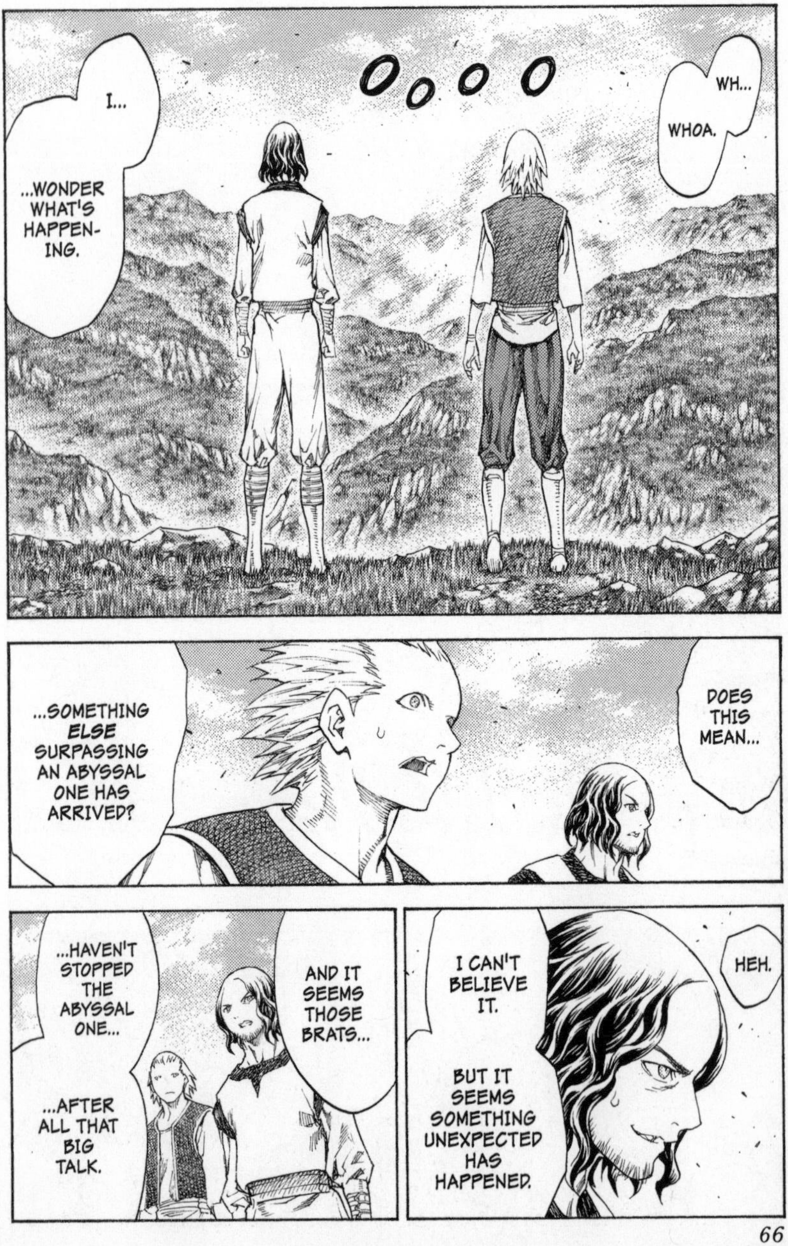
WH... WHOA.
OOOO
I... ...WONDER WHAT'S HAPPENING.
DOES THIS MEAN...
...SOMETHING ELSE SURPASSING AN ABYSSAL ONE HAS ARRIVED?
HEH.
I CAN'T BELIEVE IT.
BUT IT SEEMS SOMETHING UNEXPECTED HAS HAPPENED.
AND IT SEEMS THOSE BRATS...
...HAVEN'T STOPPED THE ABYSSAL ONE...
...AFTER ALL THAT BIG TALK.

READ THIS WAY

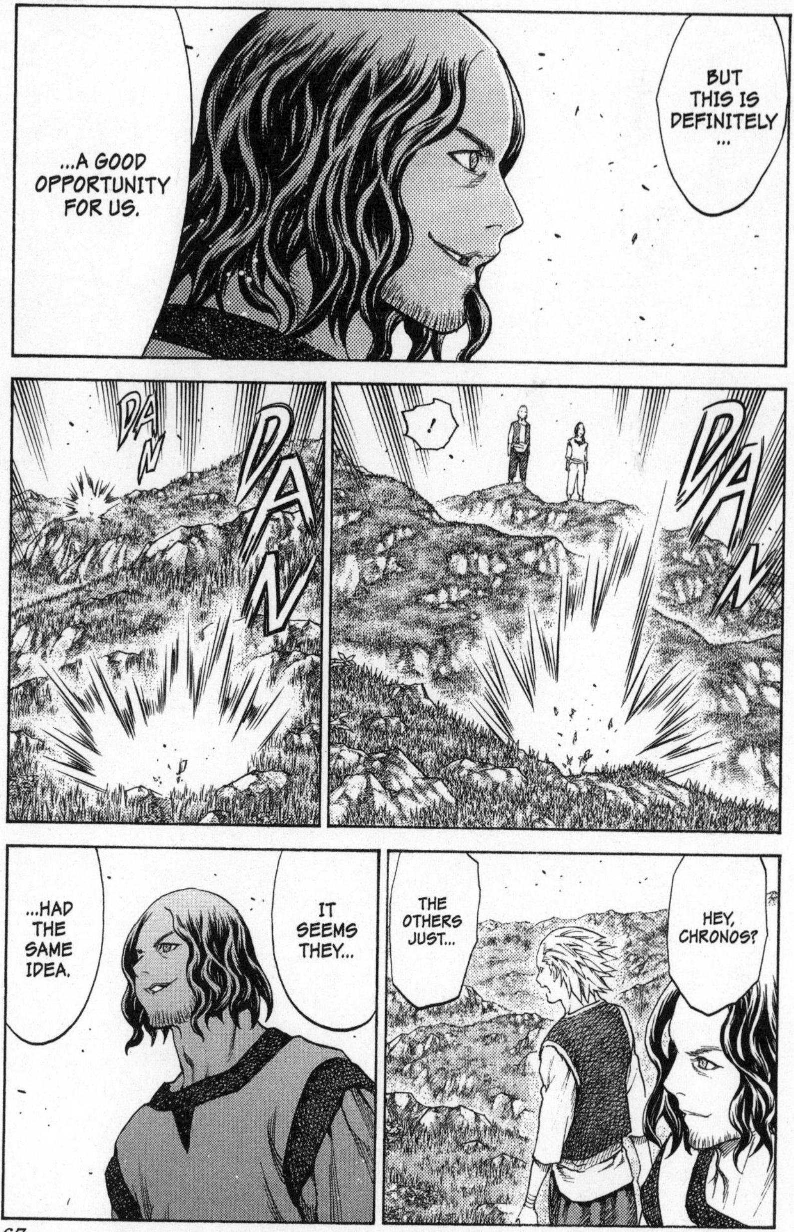

BUT THIS IS DEFINITELY ...
...A GOOD OPPORTUNITY FOR US.
!
DAN
DAN
DAN
HEY, CHRONOS?
THE OTHERS JUST...
IT SEEMS THEY...
...HAD THE SAME IDEA.

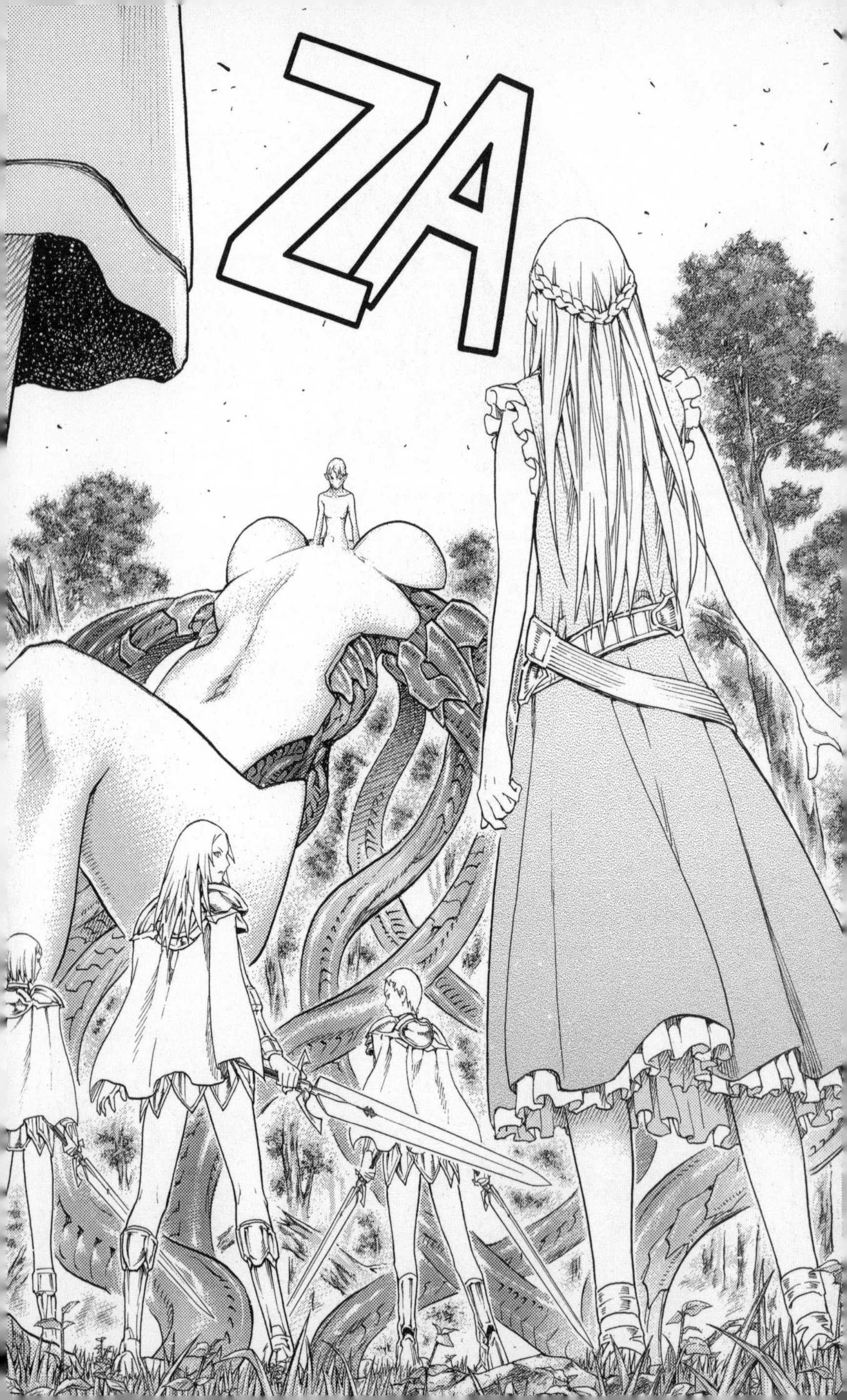
ZA

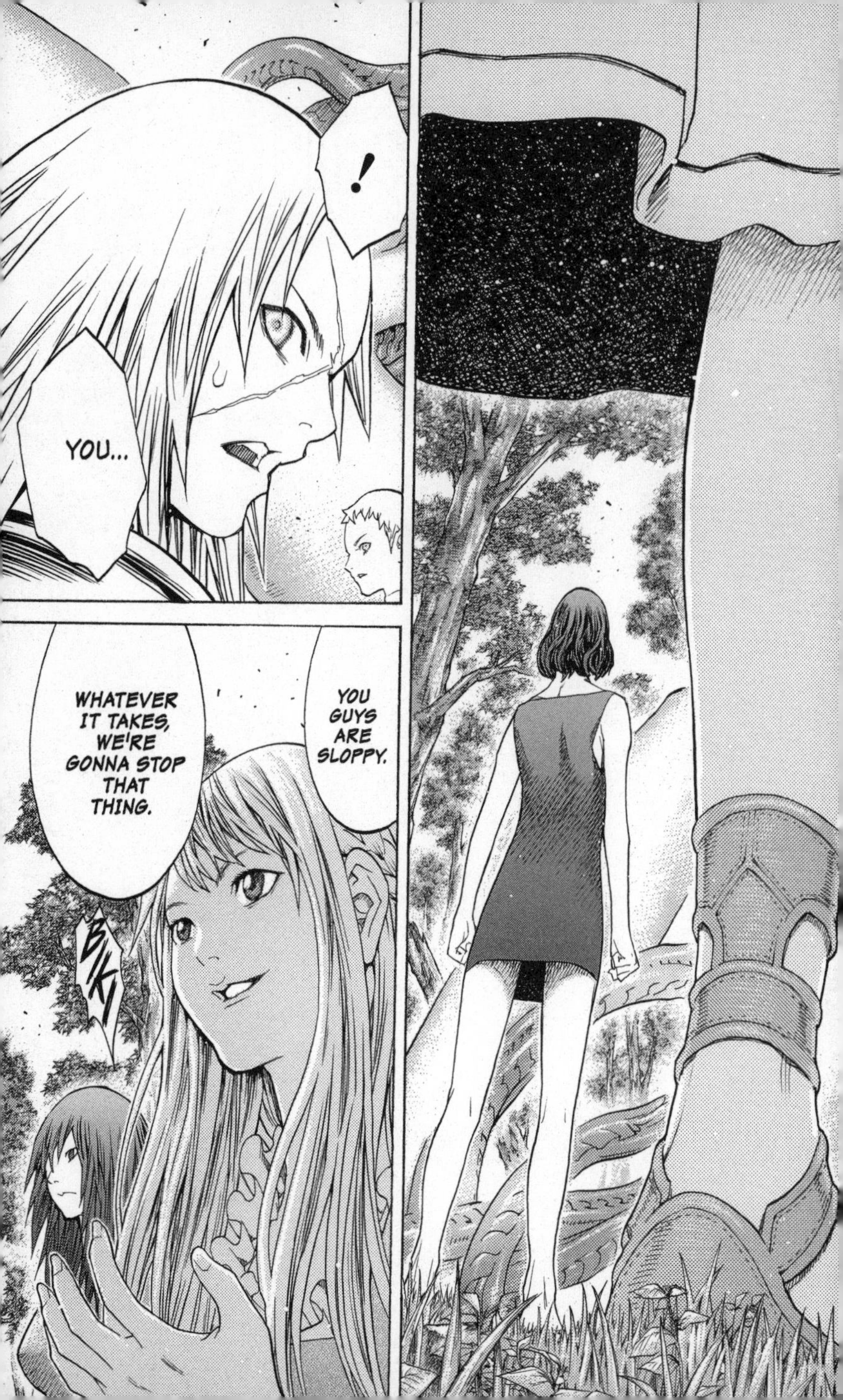
!
YOU...
YOU GUYS ARE SLOPPY.
WHATEVER IT TAKES, WE'RE GONNA STOP THAT THING.
BIKI

Scene 134: Army of the Underworld, Part 2

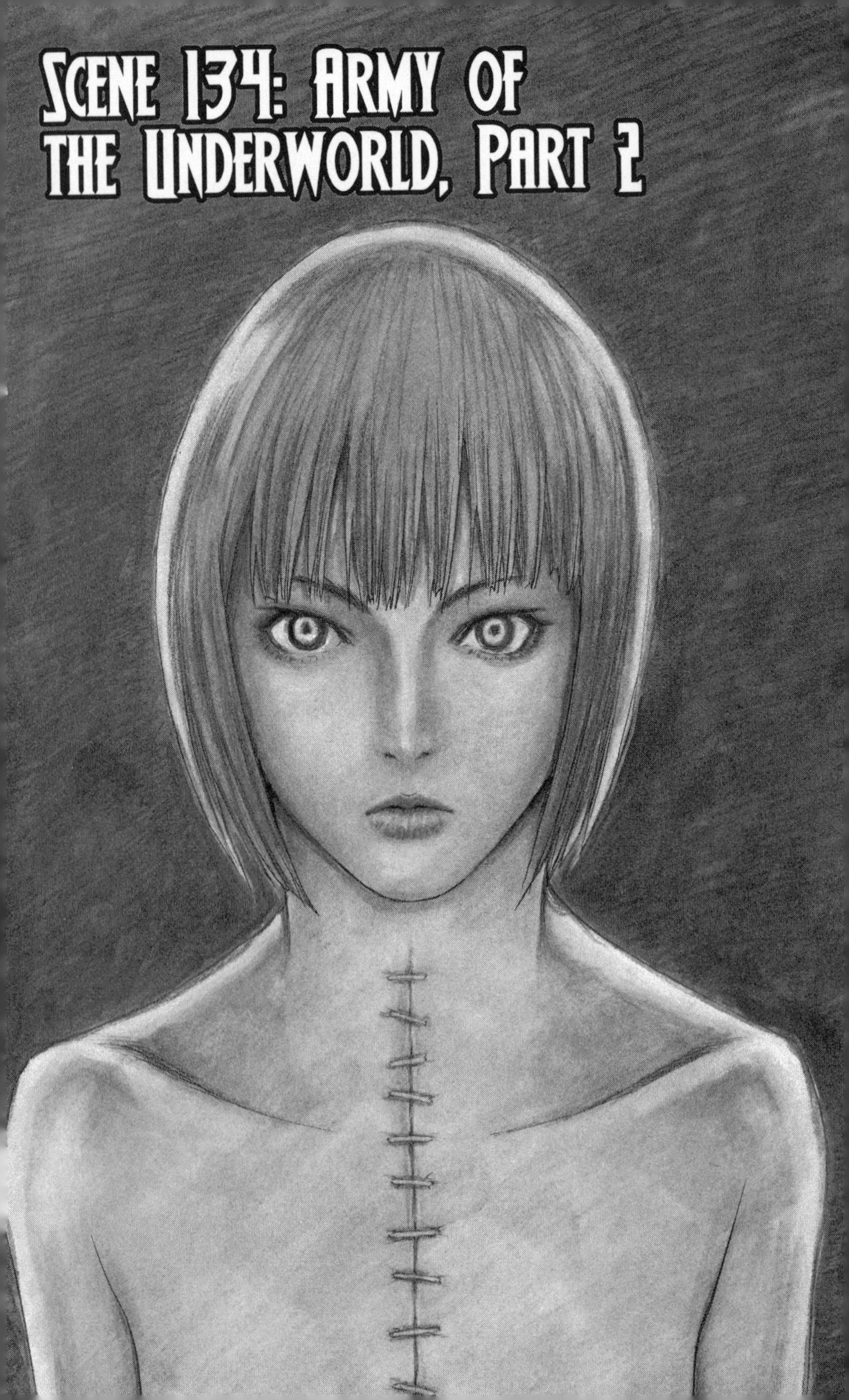

READ THIS WAY

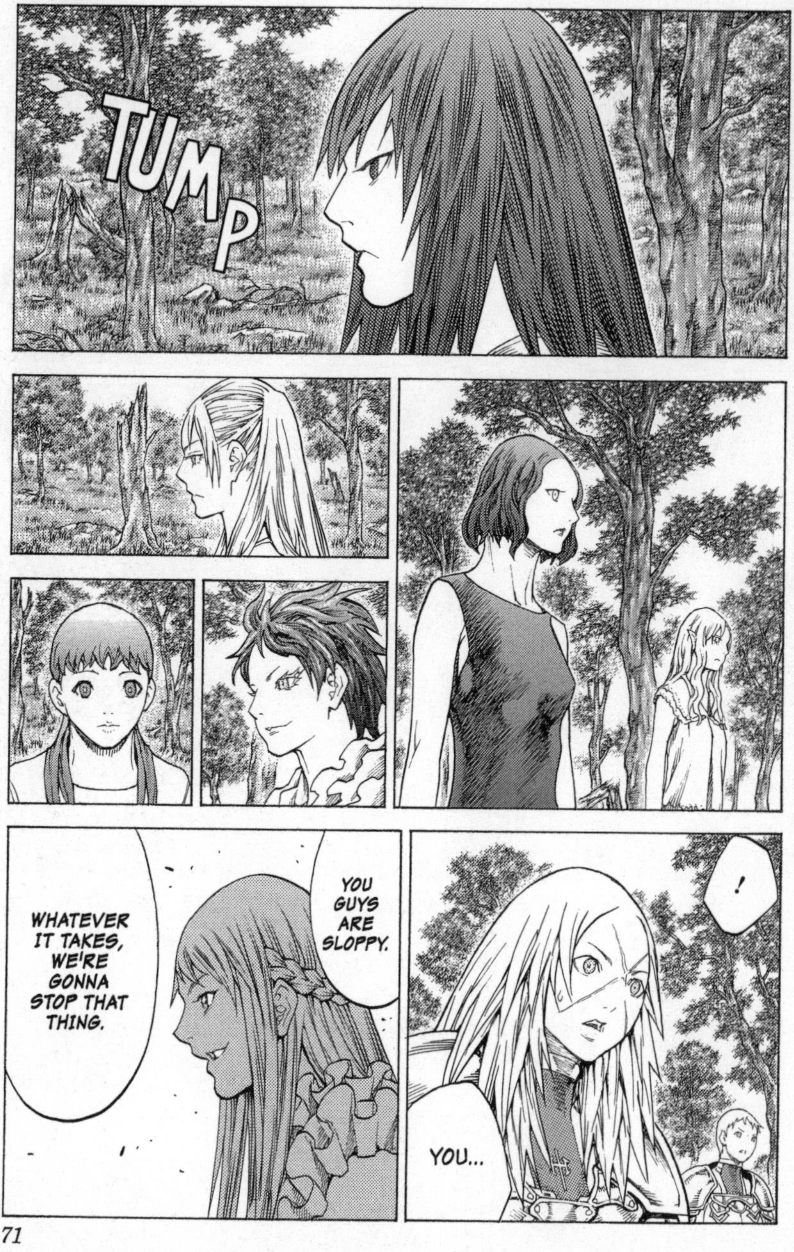
TUMP
!
YOU...
YOU GUYS ARE SLOPPY.
WHATEVER IT TAKES, WE'RE GONNA STOP THAT THING.

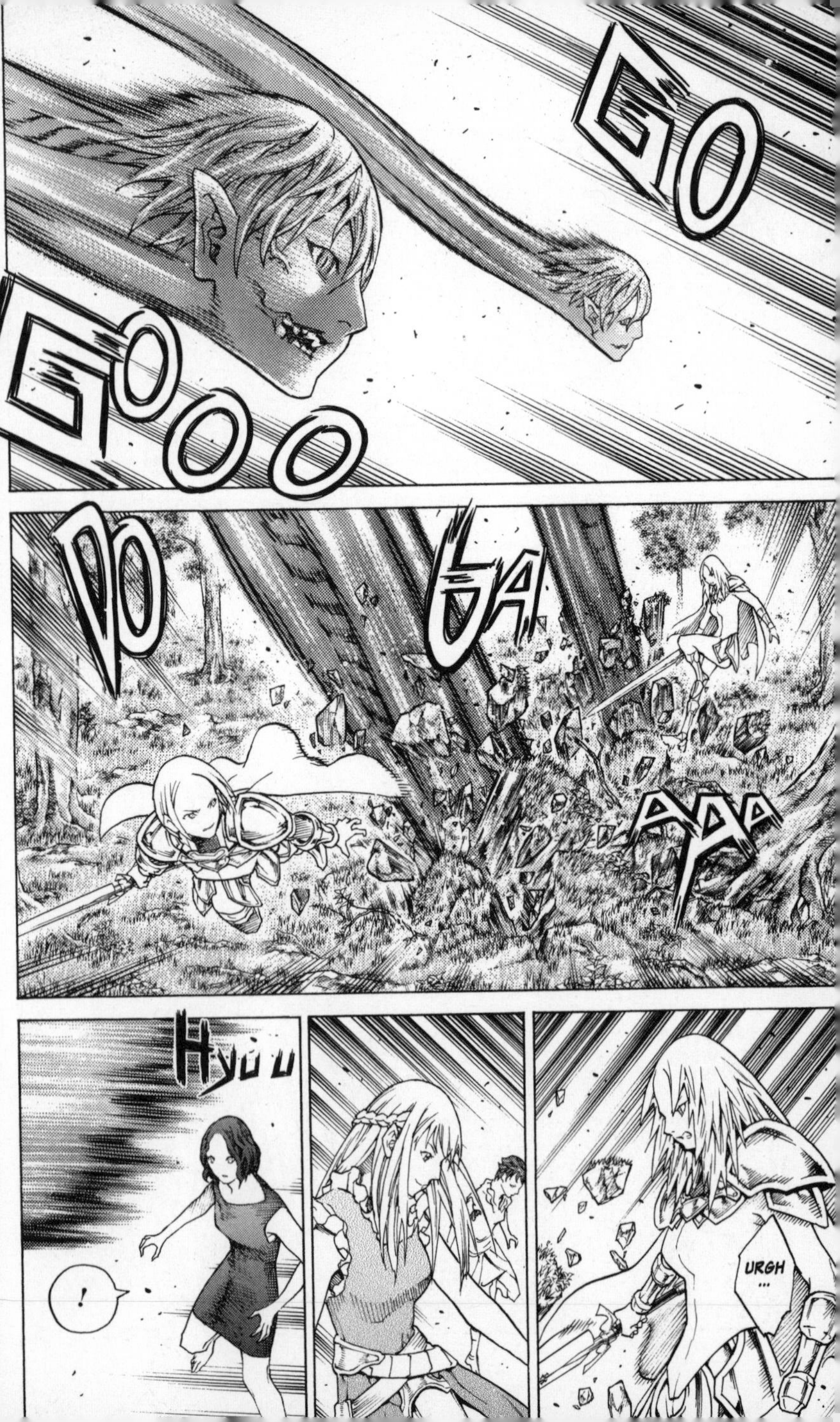
GO
GOOOO
DO
GA
AAA
URGH …
Hyuu
!

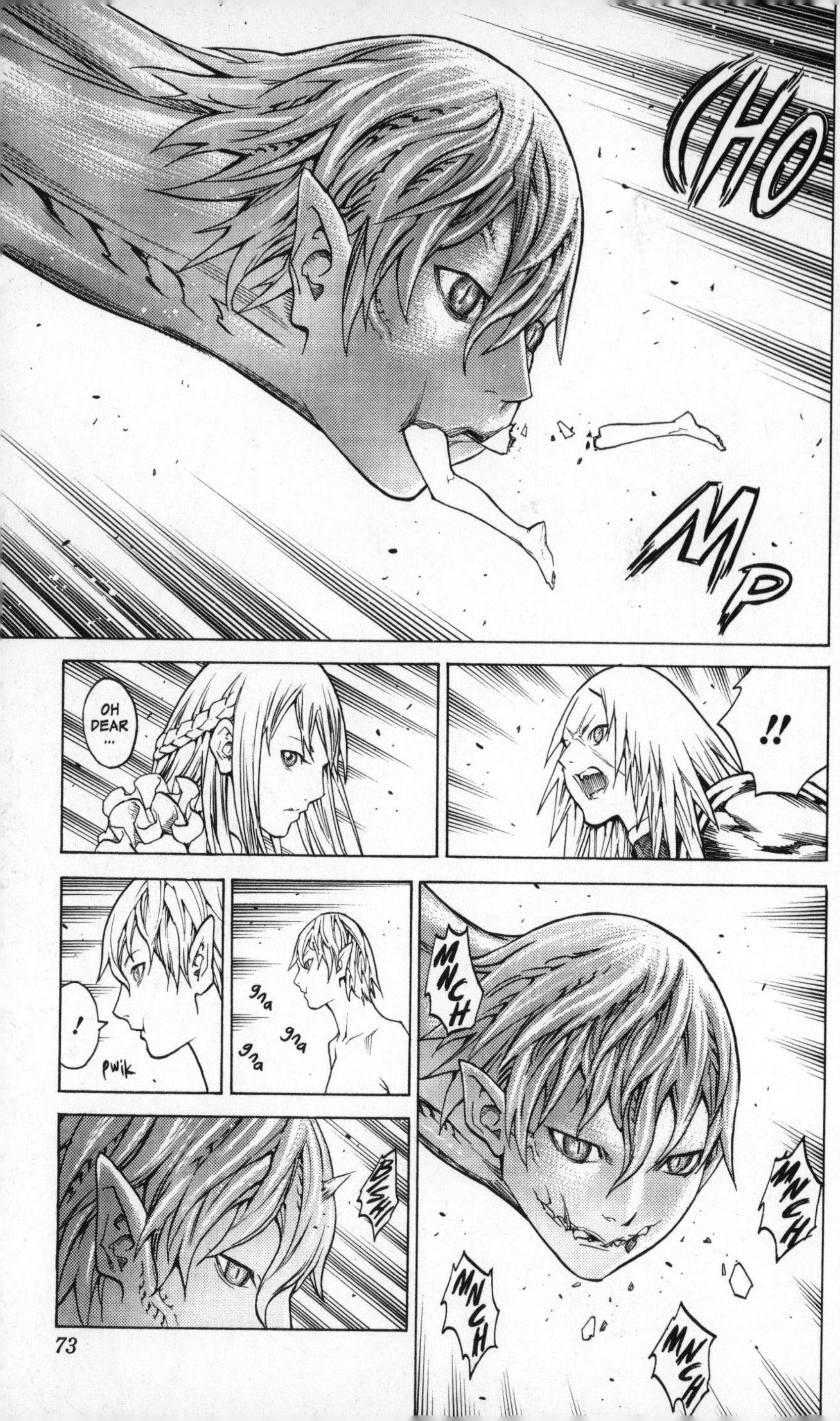
CHOMP
!!
OH DEAR ...
MNCH
MNCH
MNCH
MNCH
gna
gna
gna
!
pwik
BISH!

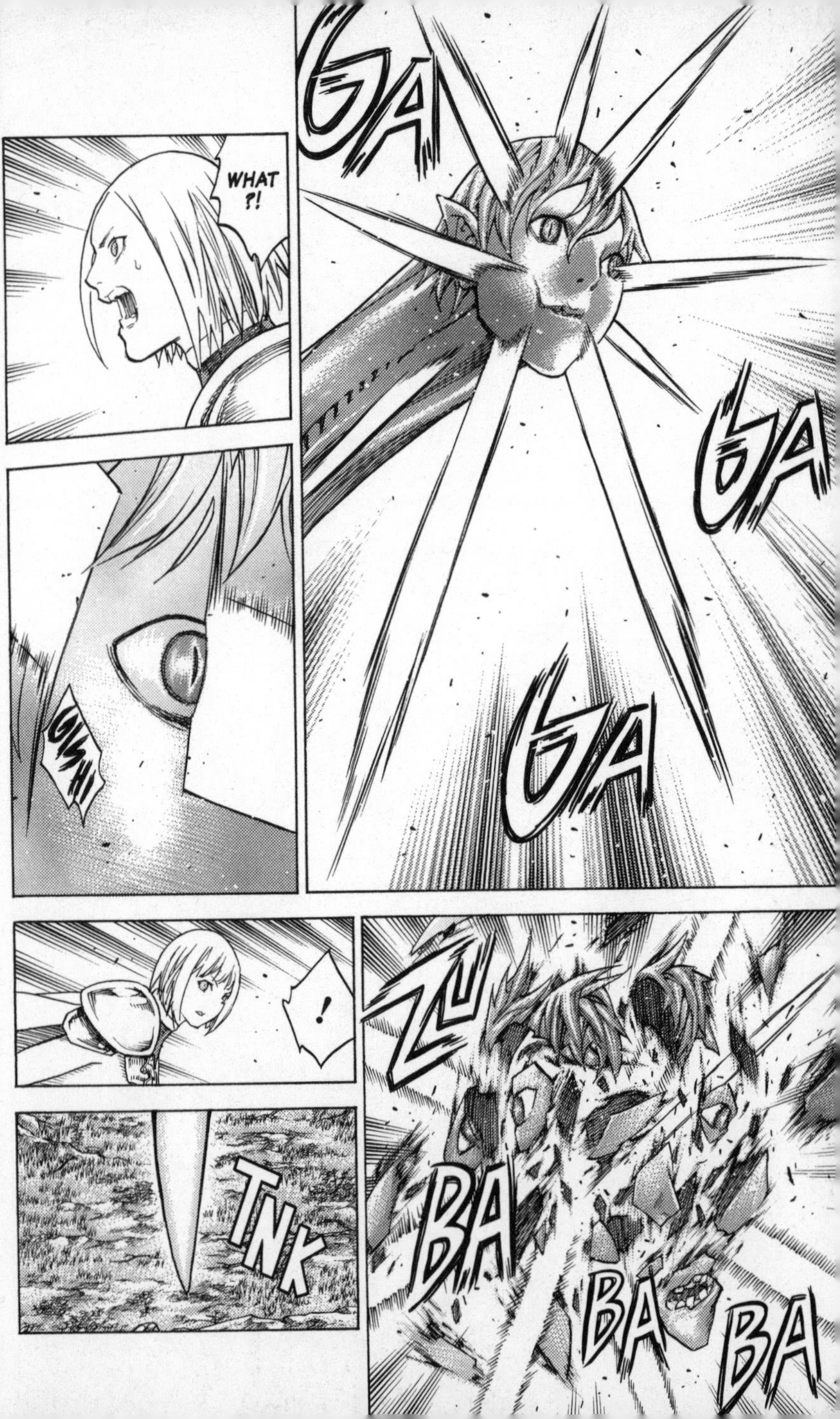
GA
GA
GA
WHAT ?!
GISHI
ZU
BA
BA
BA
!
TNK

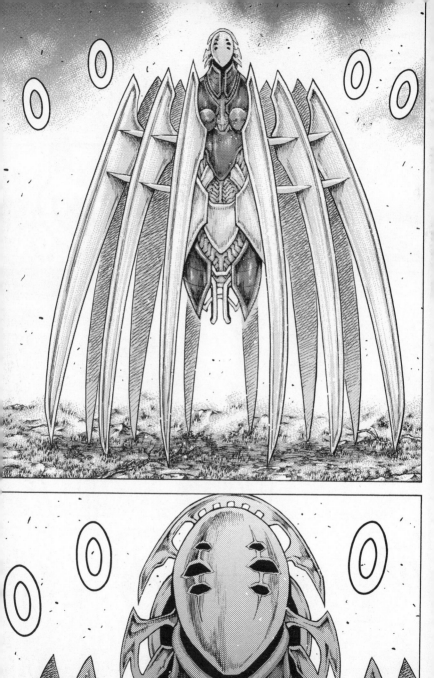

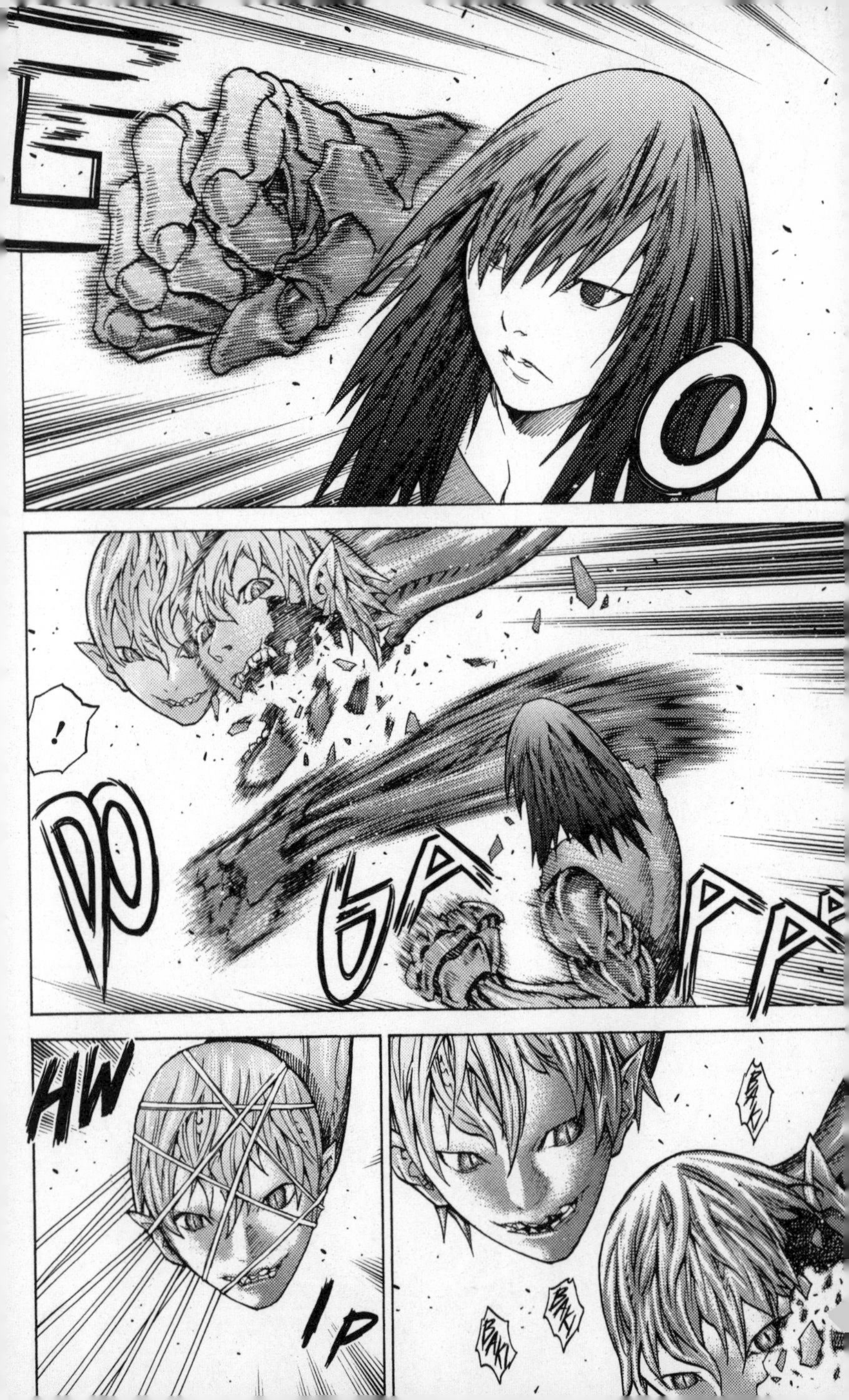
!
DOBAPP
BAKI
BAKI
BAKI
HWIP

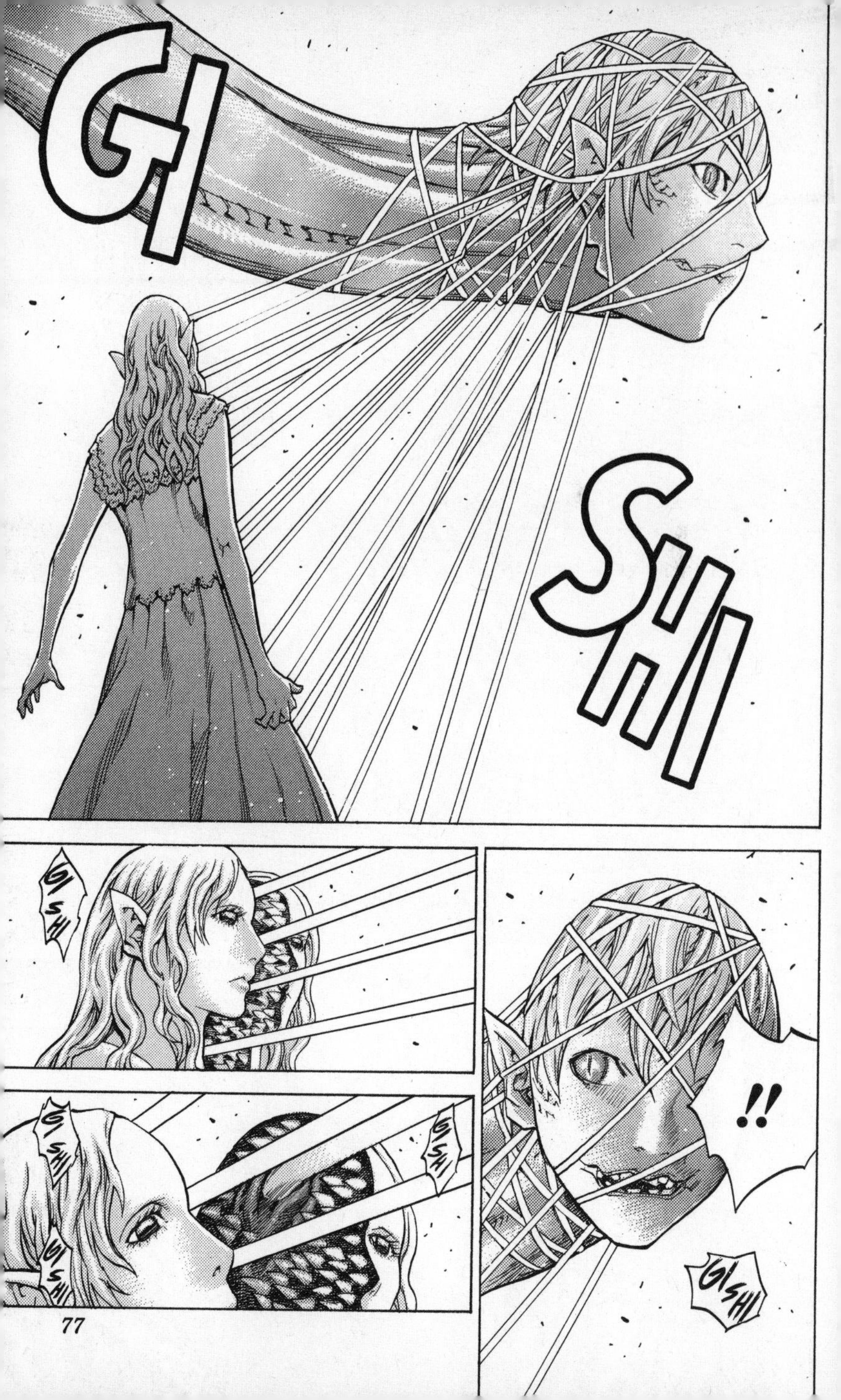
GI
SHI
!!
GI SHI
GI SHI
GI SHI
GI SHI
GI SHI

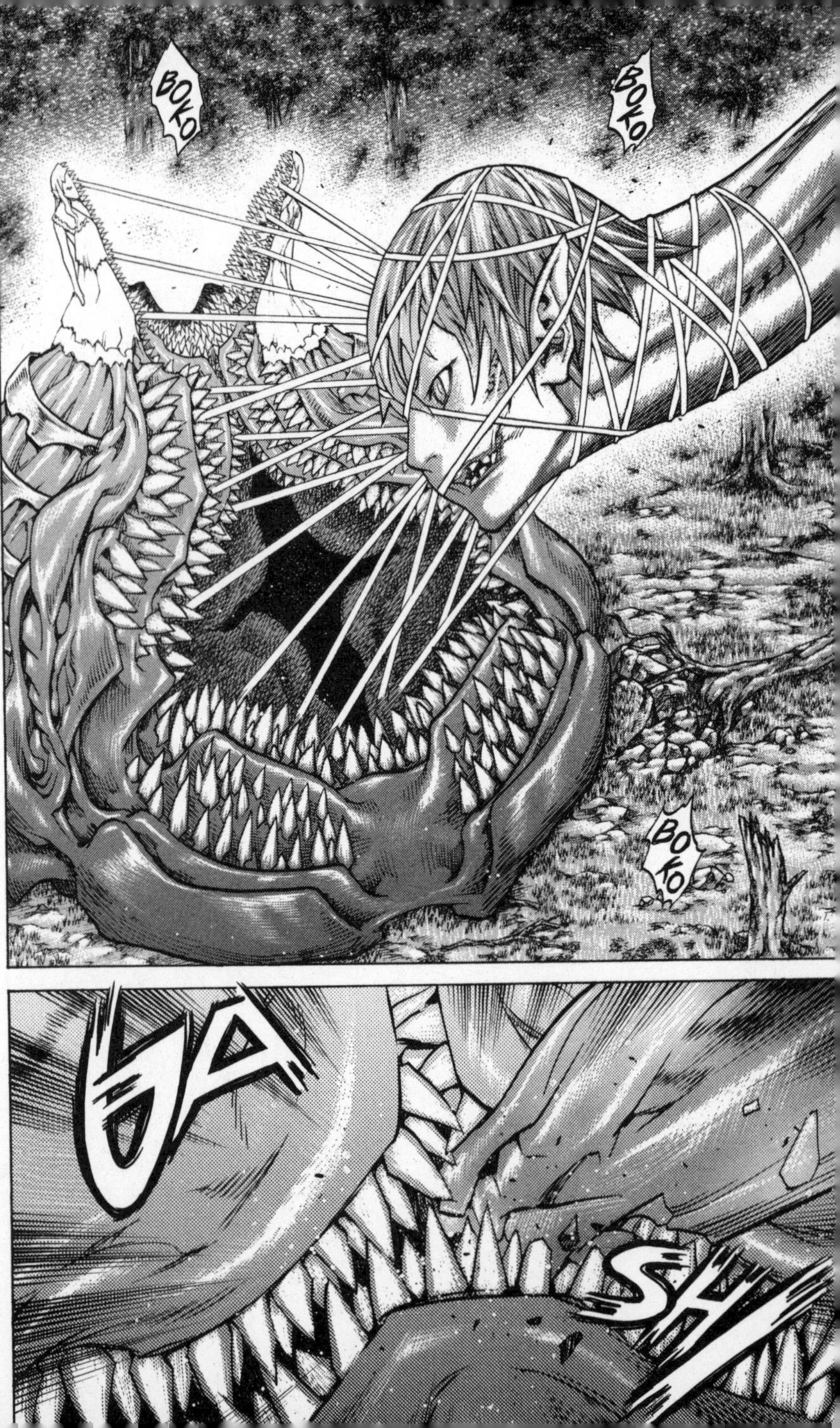
BOKO
BOKO
BOKO
GA
SH

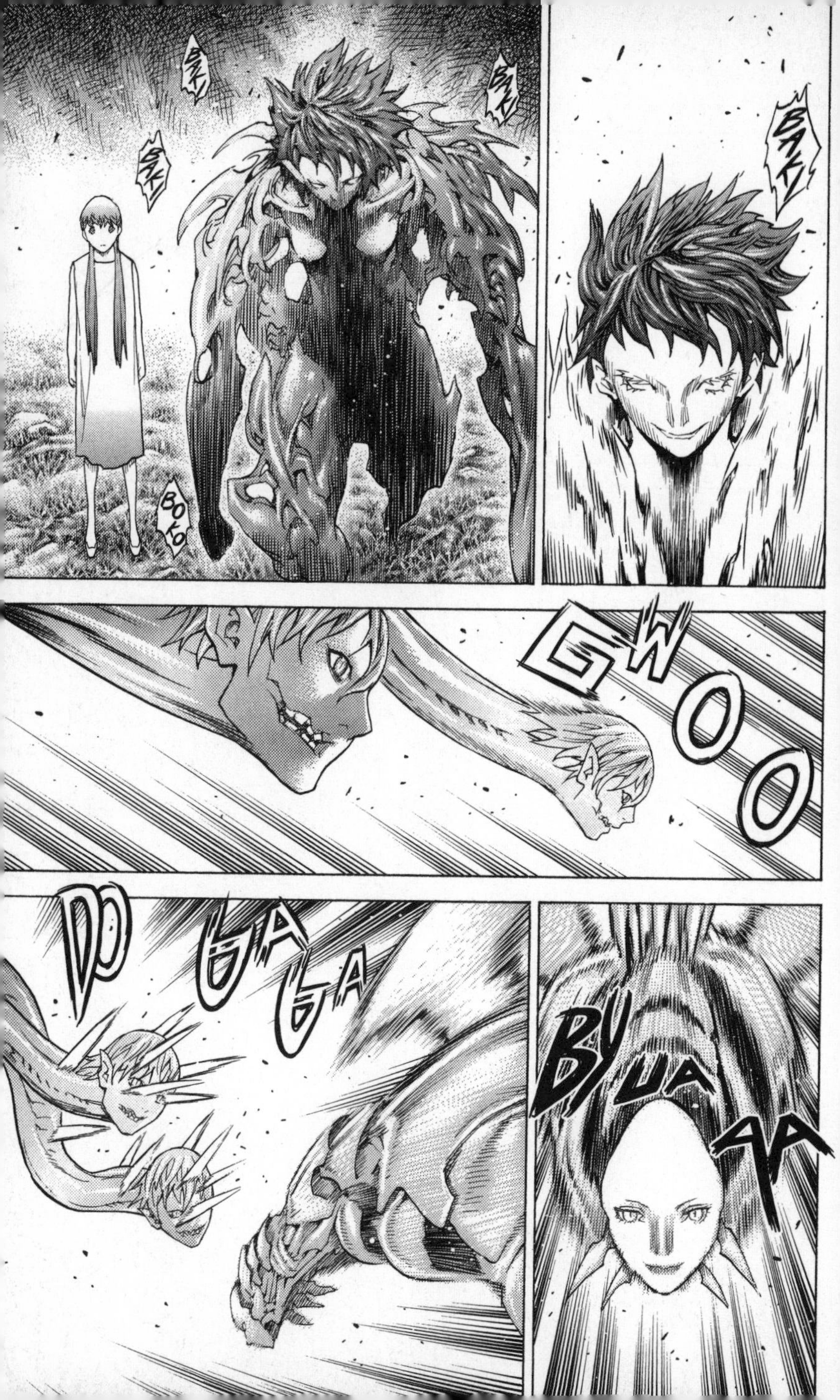
BAKI
BAKI
BAKI
BAKI
BOKO
GWOOO
BYUAAA
DOGAGA

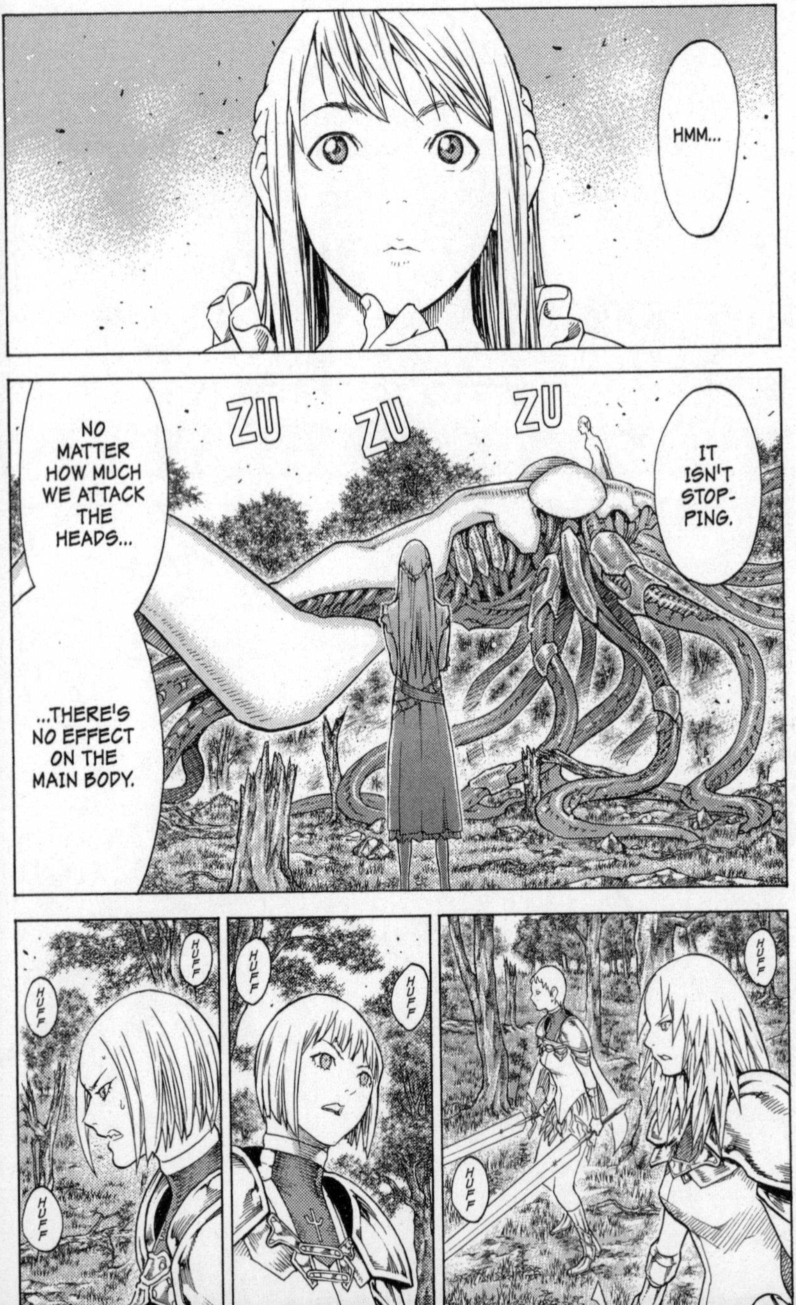
HMM...
IT ISN'T STOP-PING.
ZU
ZU
ZU
NO MATTER HOW MUCH WE ATTACK THE HEADS...
...THERE'S NO EFFECT ON THE MAIN BODY.
HUFF
HUFF
HUFF
HUFF
HUFF
HUFF

READ THIS WAY

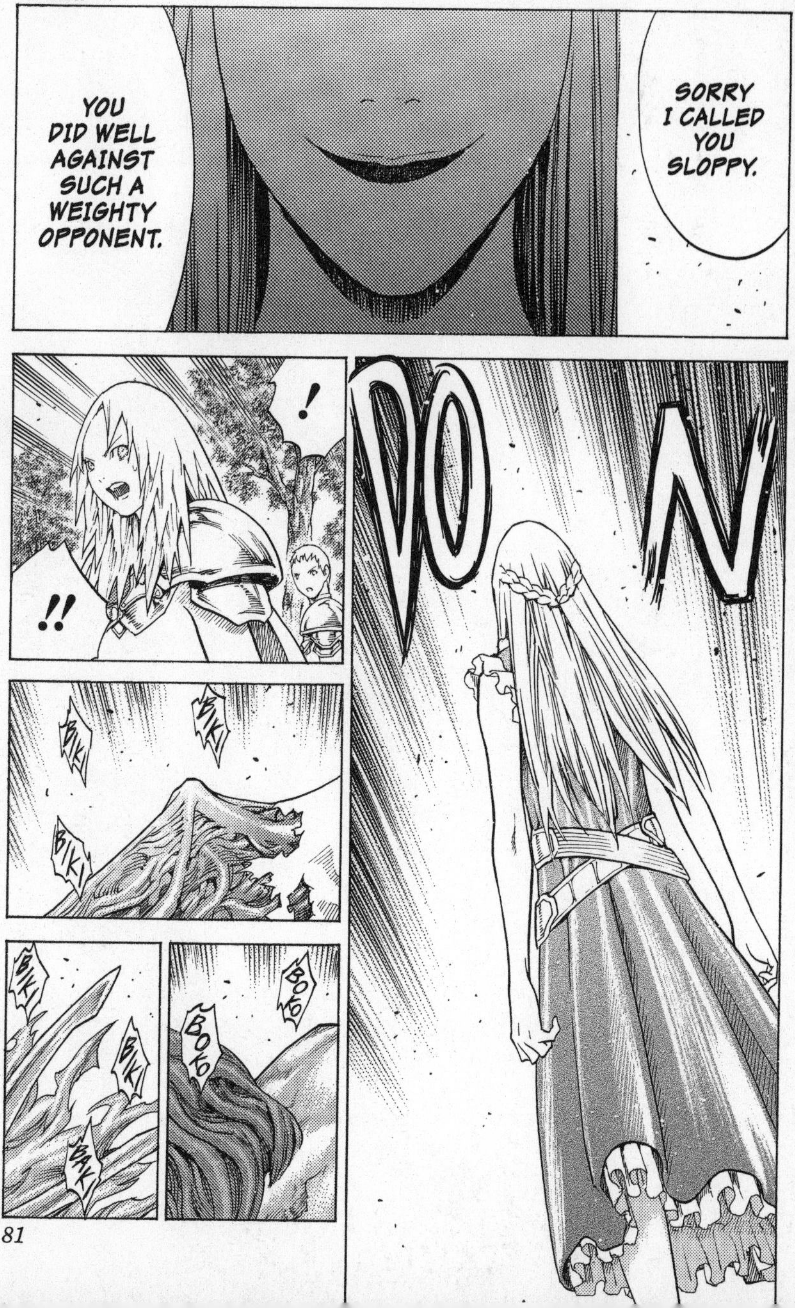

SORRY I CALLED YOU SLOPPY.
YOU DID WELL AGAINST SUCH A WEIGHTY OPPONENT.
DOON
!
!!
BIKI
BIKI
BIKI
BOKO
BOKO
BIKI
BIKI
BAKI

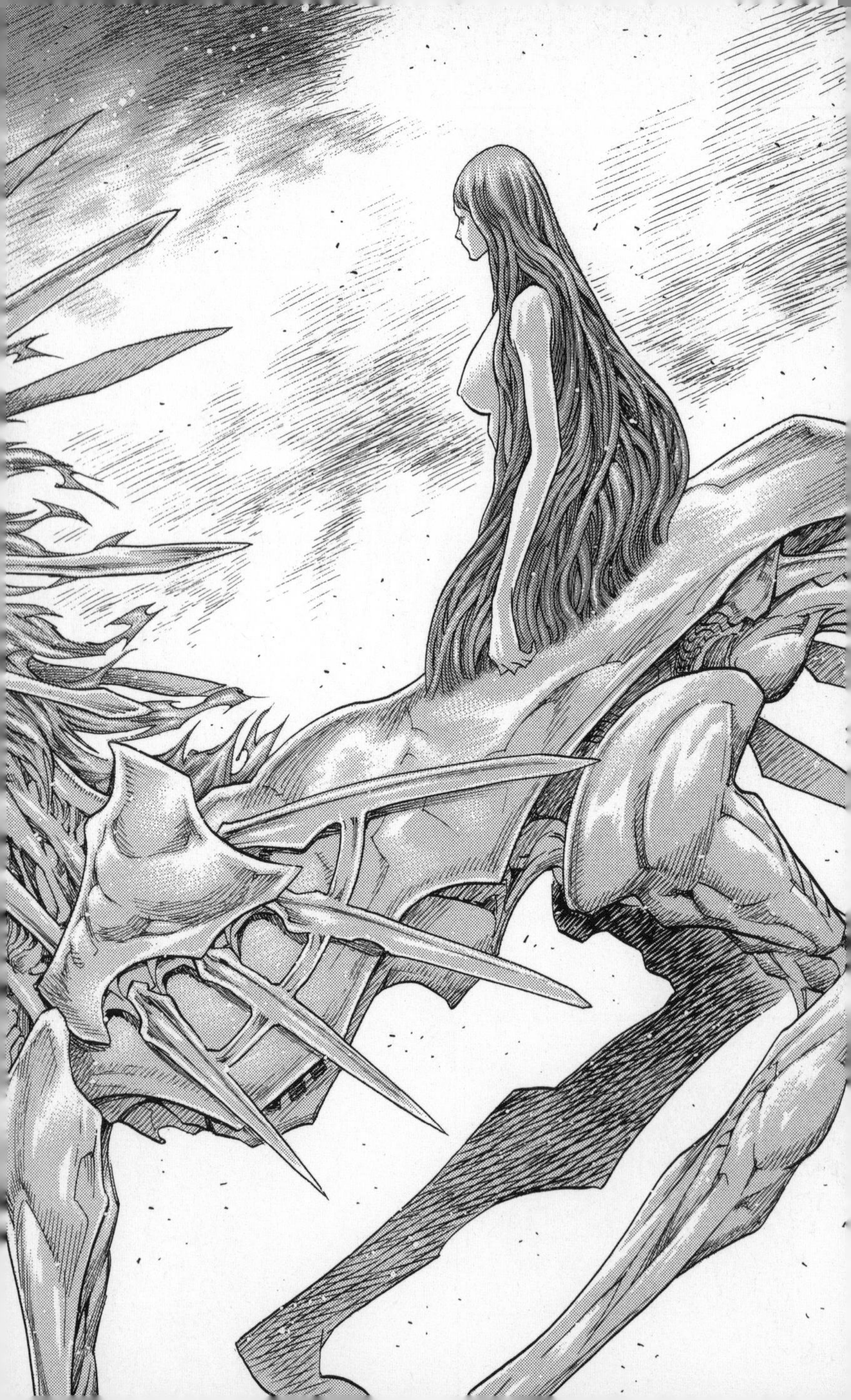

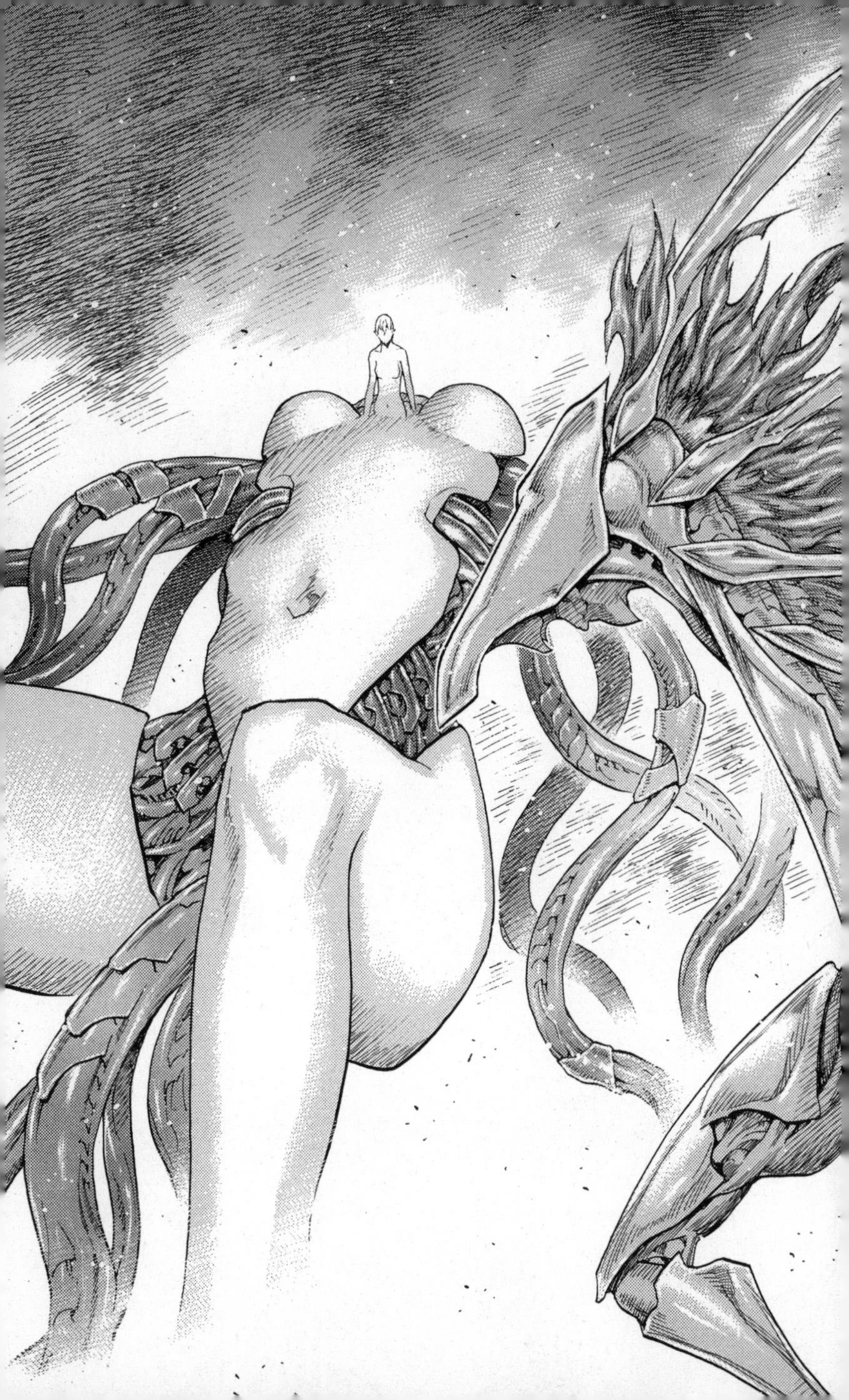

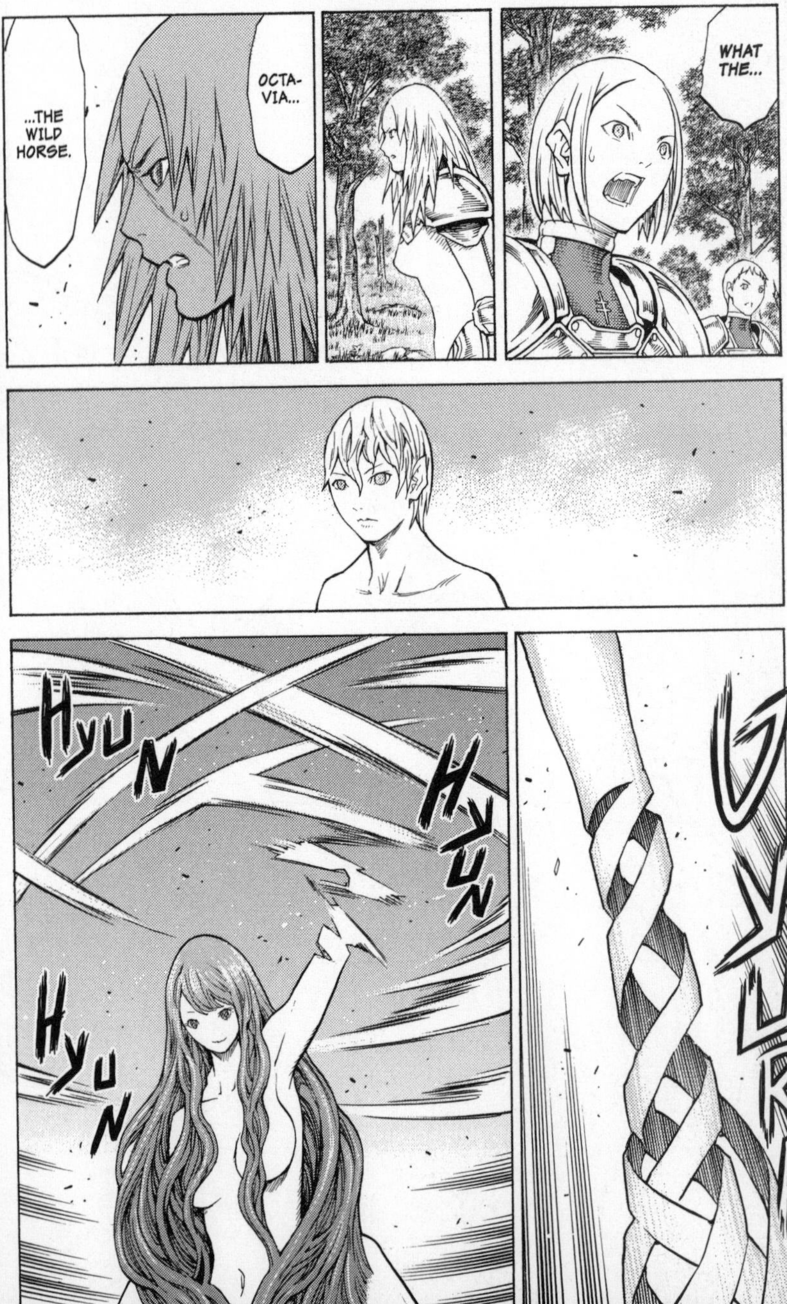
WHAT THE...
OCTA-VIA...
...THE WILD HORSE.
GYURA
HYUN
HYUN
HYUN

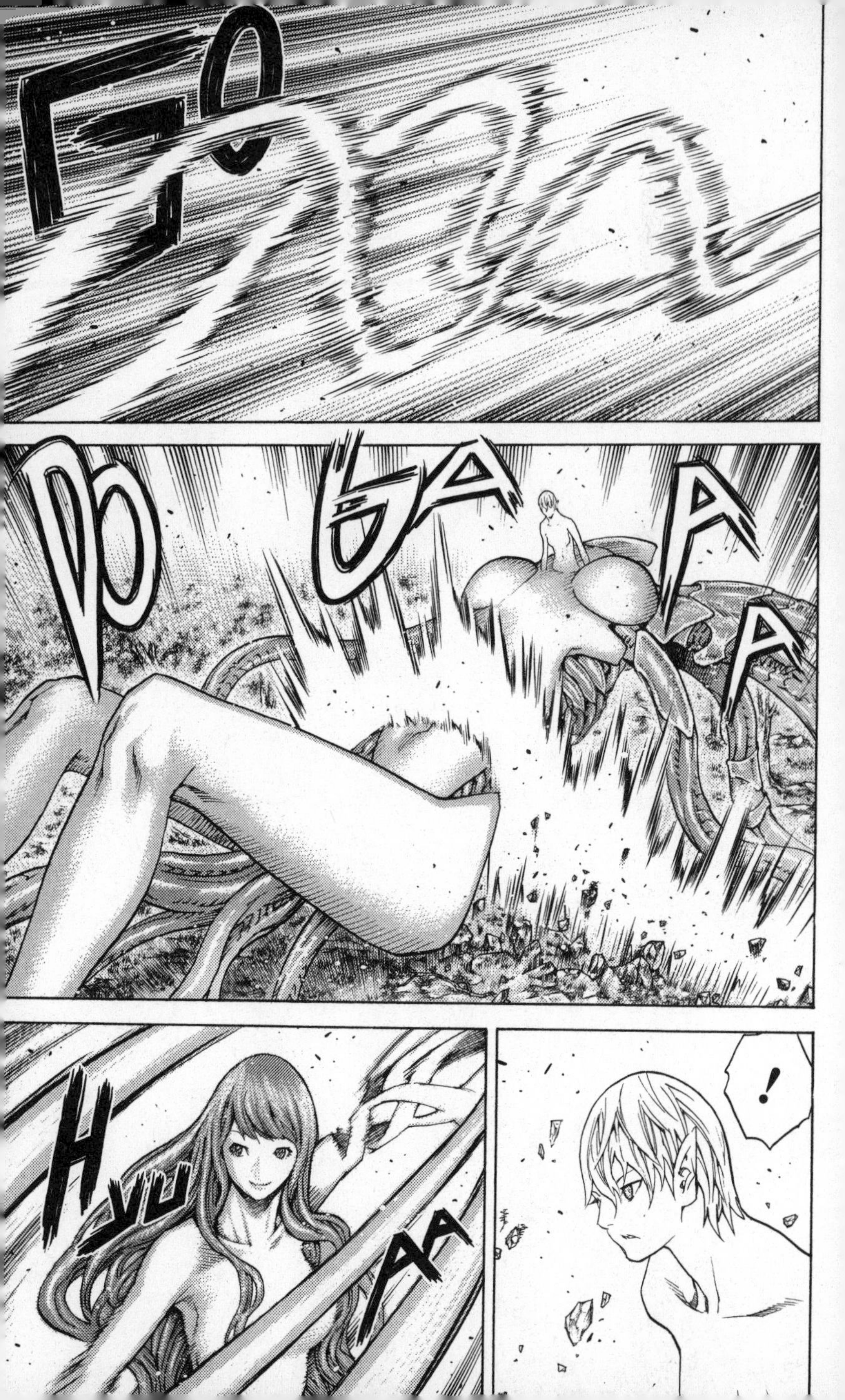
DOBAAA
!
HYUAA

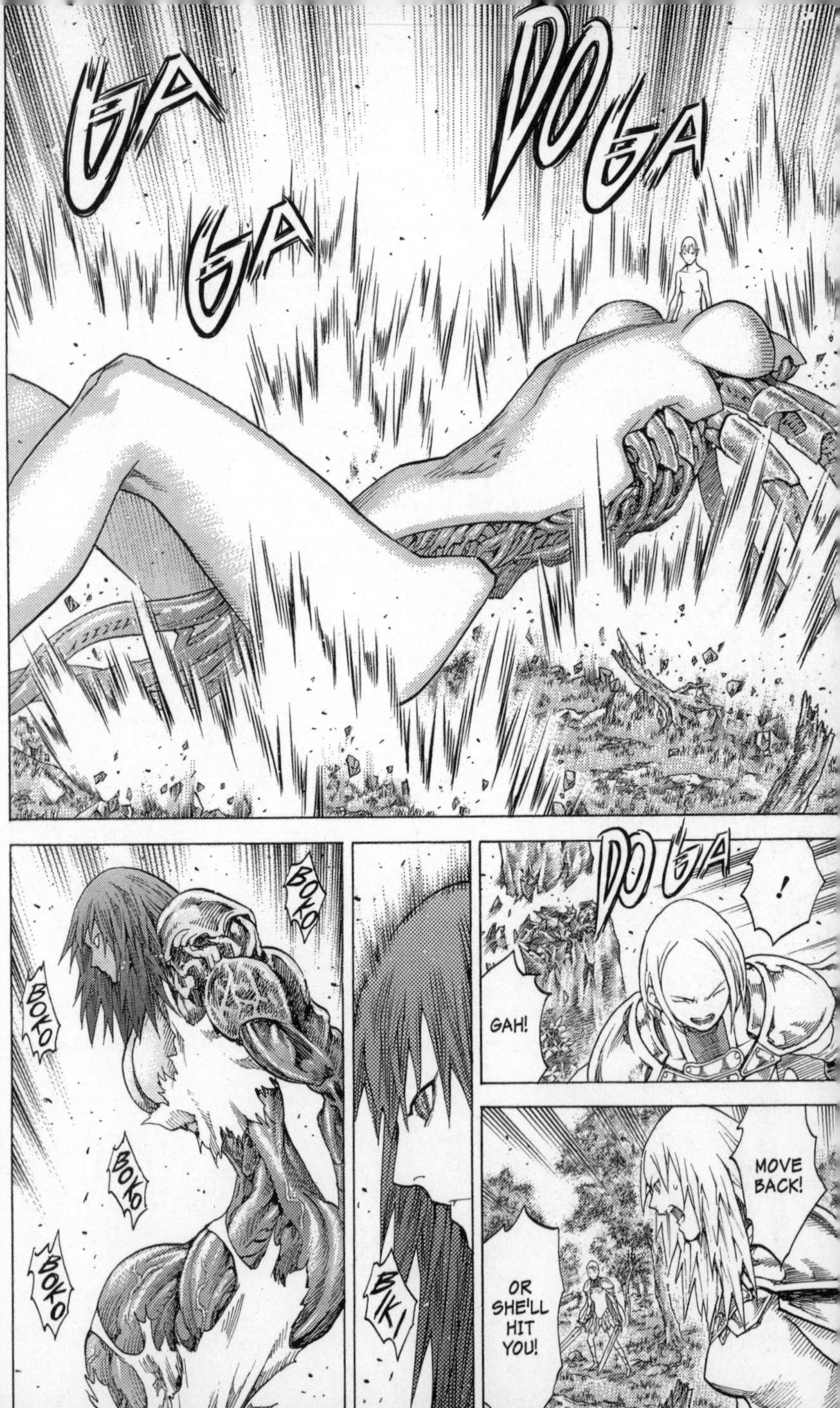
DOGA
GA
GA
DOGA
!
GAH!
MOVE BACK!
OR SHE'LL HIT YOU!
BIKI
BOKO
BOKO
BOKO
BOKO

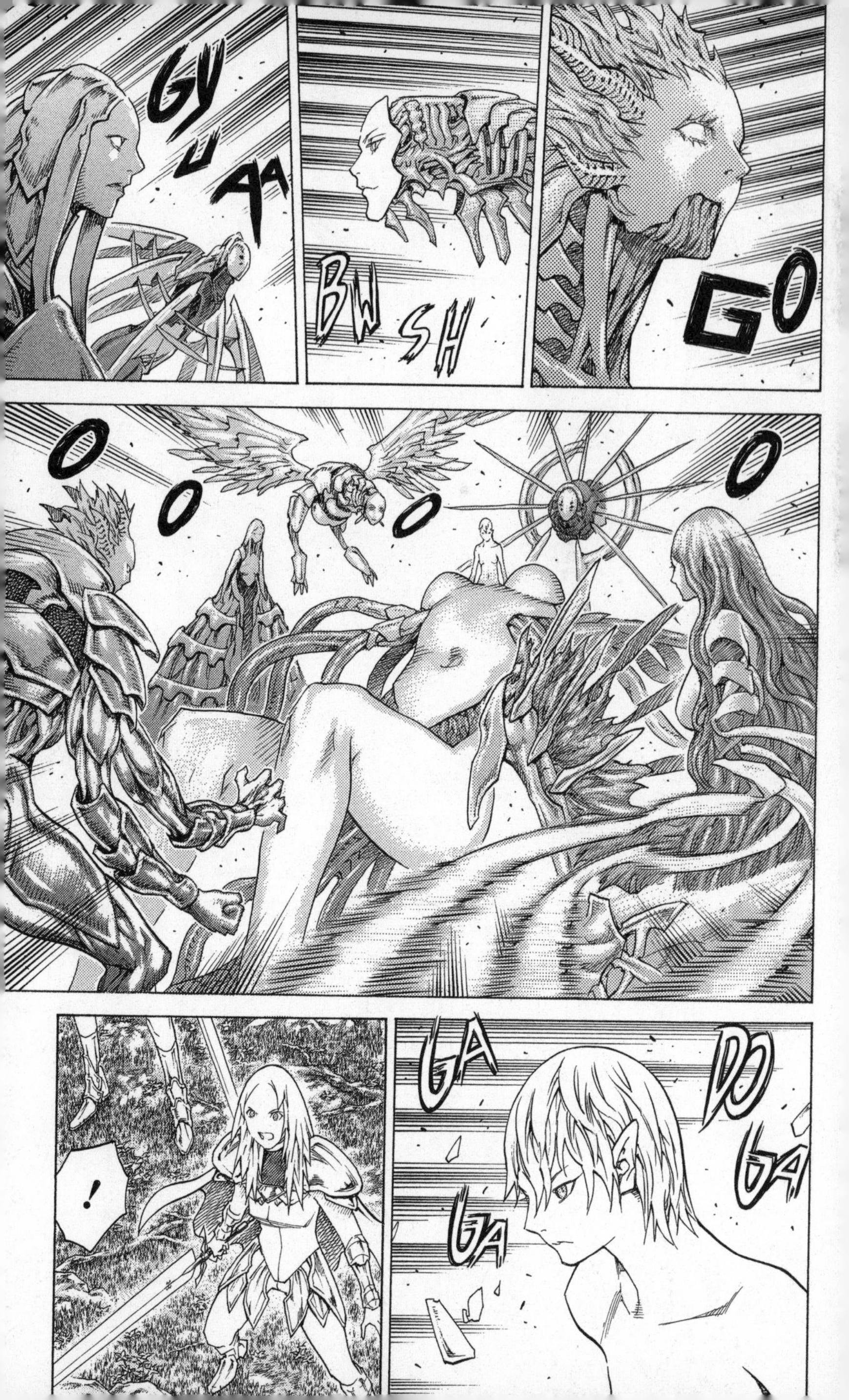
GO
BWSH
GYUAA
OOOO
DOGA
GA
GA
!

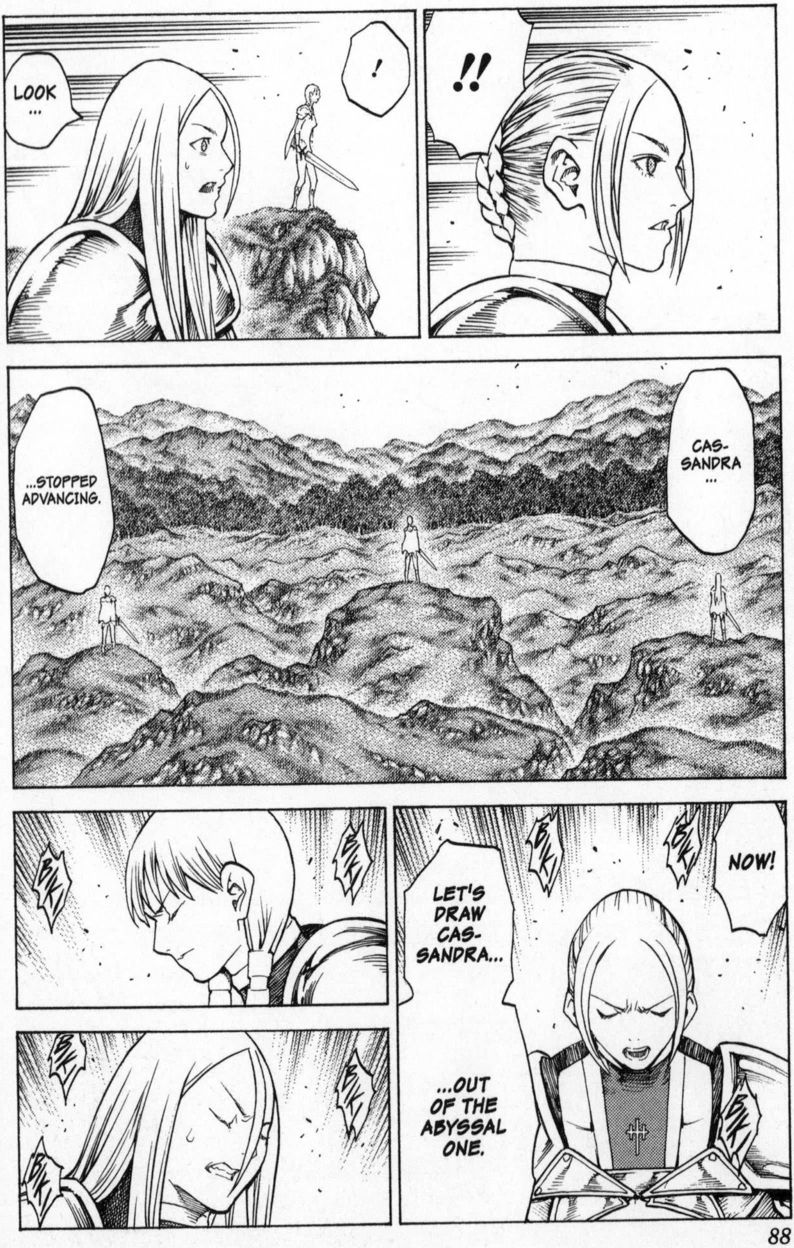
!!
!
LOOK ...
CAS-SANDRA ...
...STOPPED ADVANCING.
NOW!
BIK!
BIK!
LET'S DRAW CAS-SANDRA...
...OUT OF THE ABYSSAL ONE.
BIK!
BIK!
BIK!
BIK!
BIK!
BIK!

READ THIS WAY

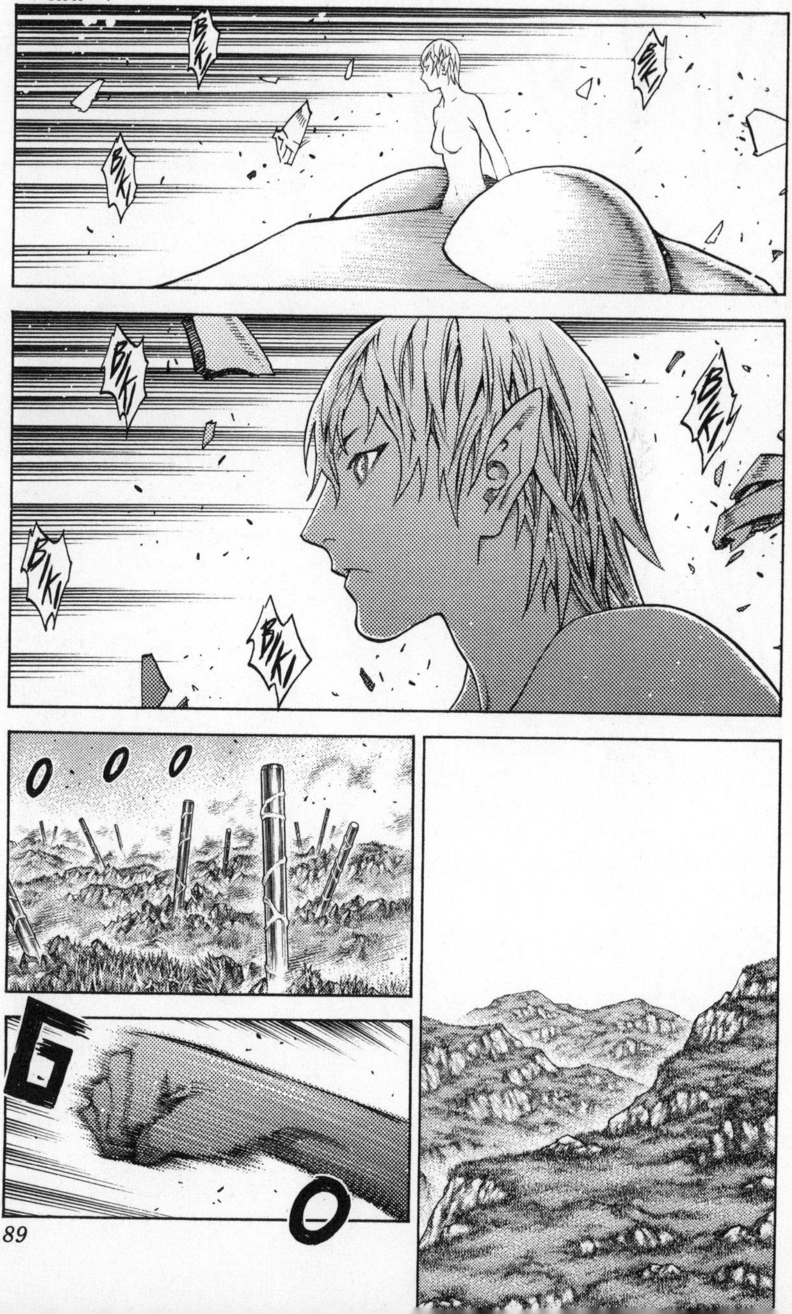
BIKI
BIKI
BIKI
BIKI
BIKI
BIKI
BIKI
BIKI
OOO
GO
O

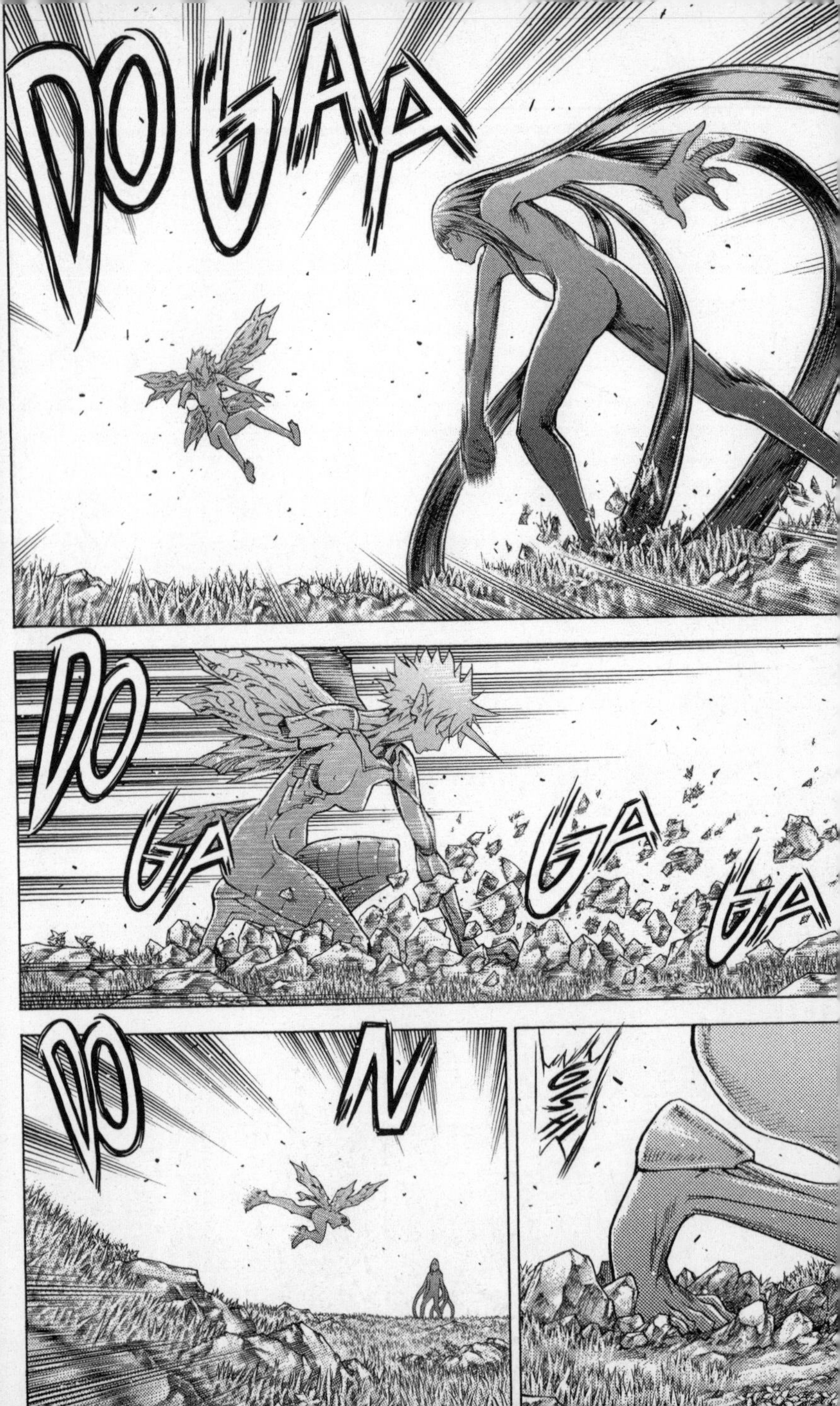
DOGAA
DO GA GA GA
WOSH
DO N

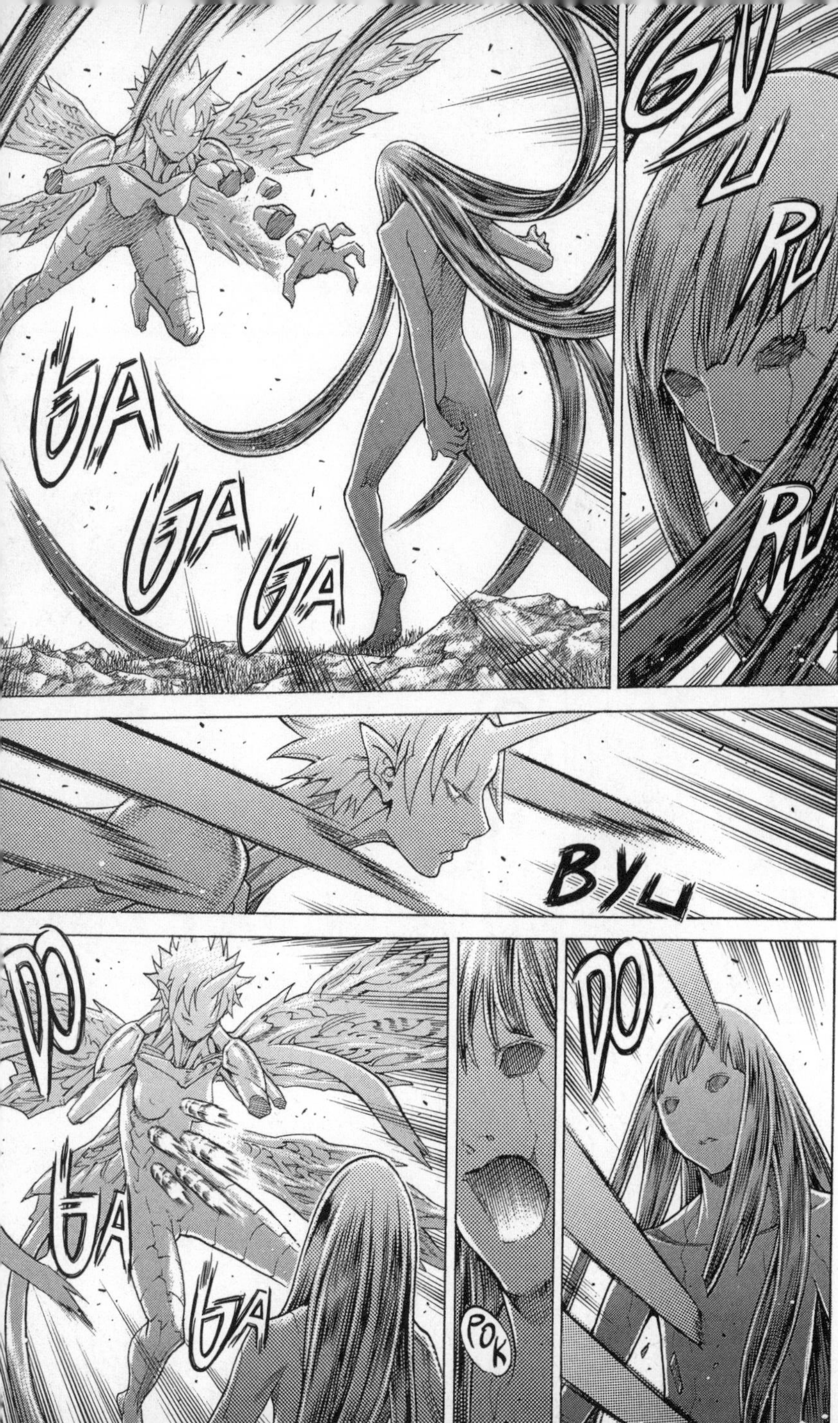
GYU RU RU
GA GA GA
BYU
DO
POK
DO
GA GA

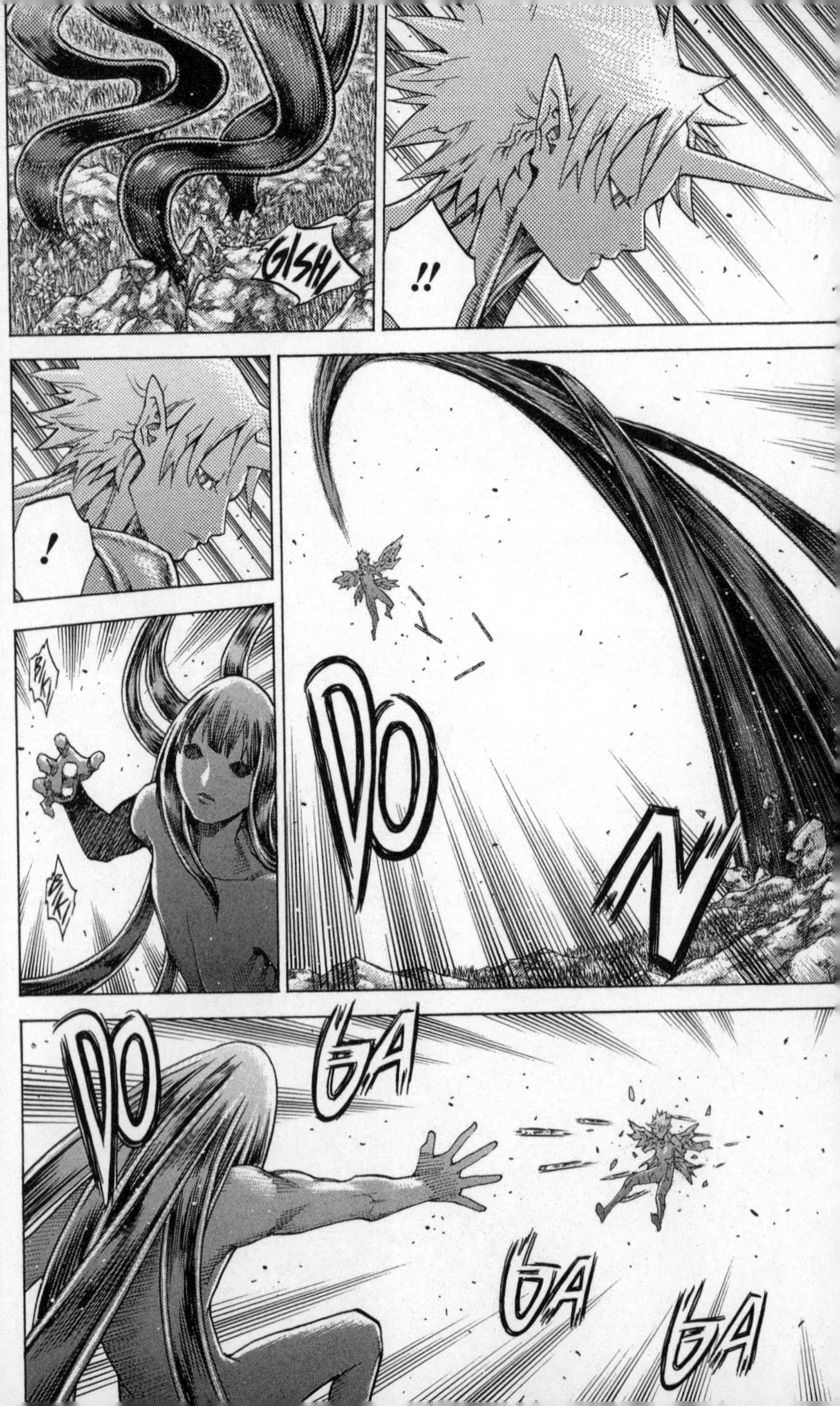
!!
GISHI
DO
N
!
BIKI
BIKI
DO
GA
GA
GA

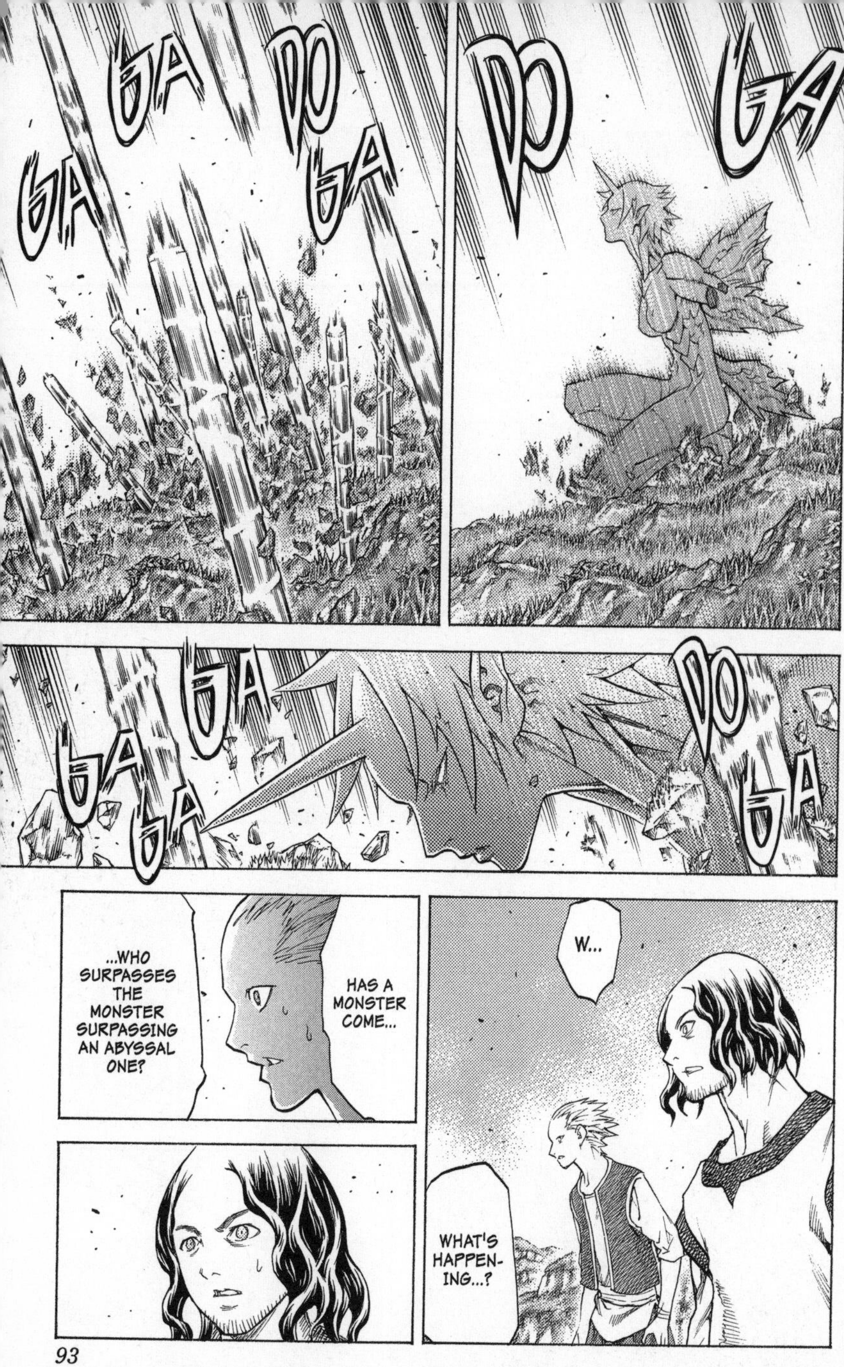
DO
GA
GA
GA
DO
GA
DO
GA
GA
GA
GA
GA
W...
WHAT'S HAPPENING...?
HAS A MONSTER COME...
...WHO SURPASSES THE MONSTER SURPASSING AN ABYSSAL ONE?

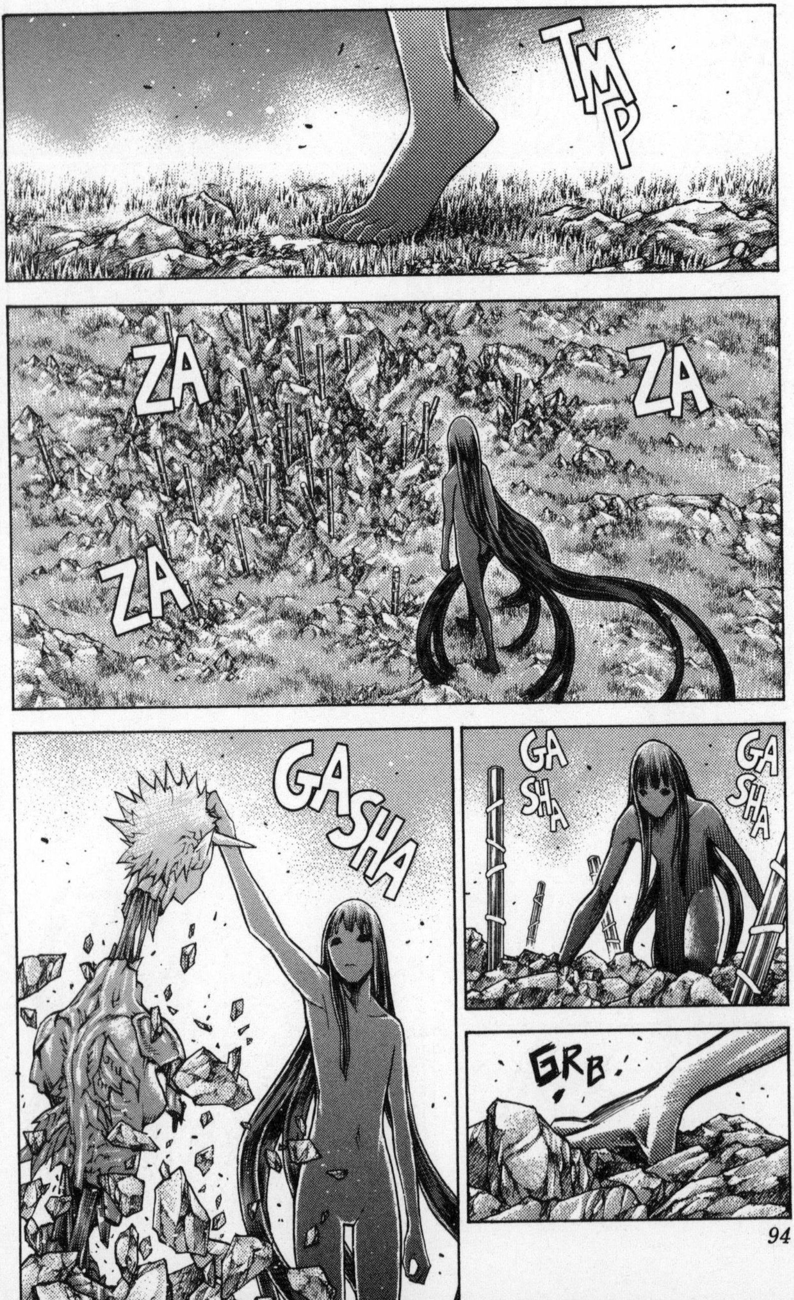
TMP
ZA
ZA
ZA
GA SHA
GA SHA
GRB
GASHA

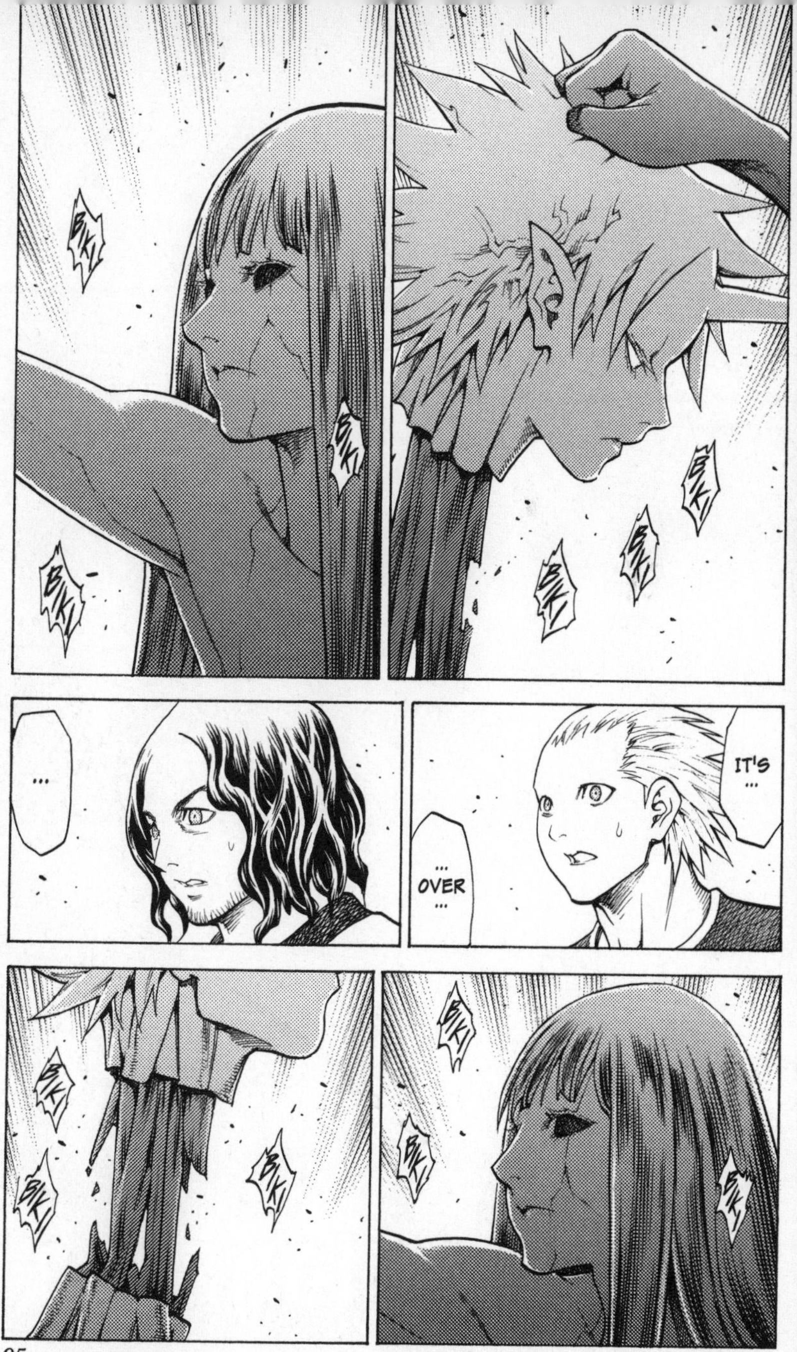
BIKI
BIKI
BIKI
BIKI
BIKI
BIKI
IT'S ...
... OVER ...
...
BIKI
BIKI
BIKI
BIKI
BIKI
BIKI

クレイモア
Claymore

Scene 135: Army of the Underworld, Part 3

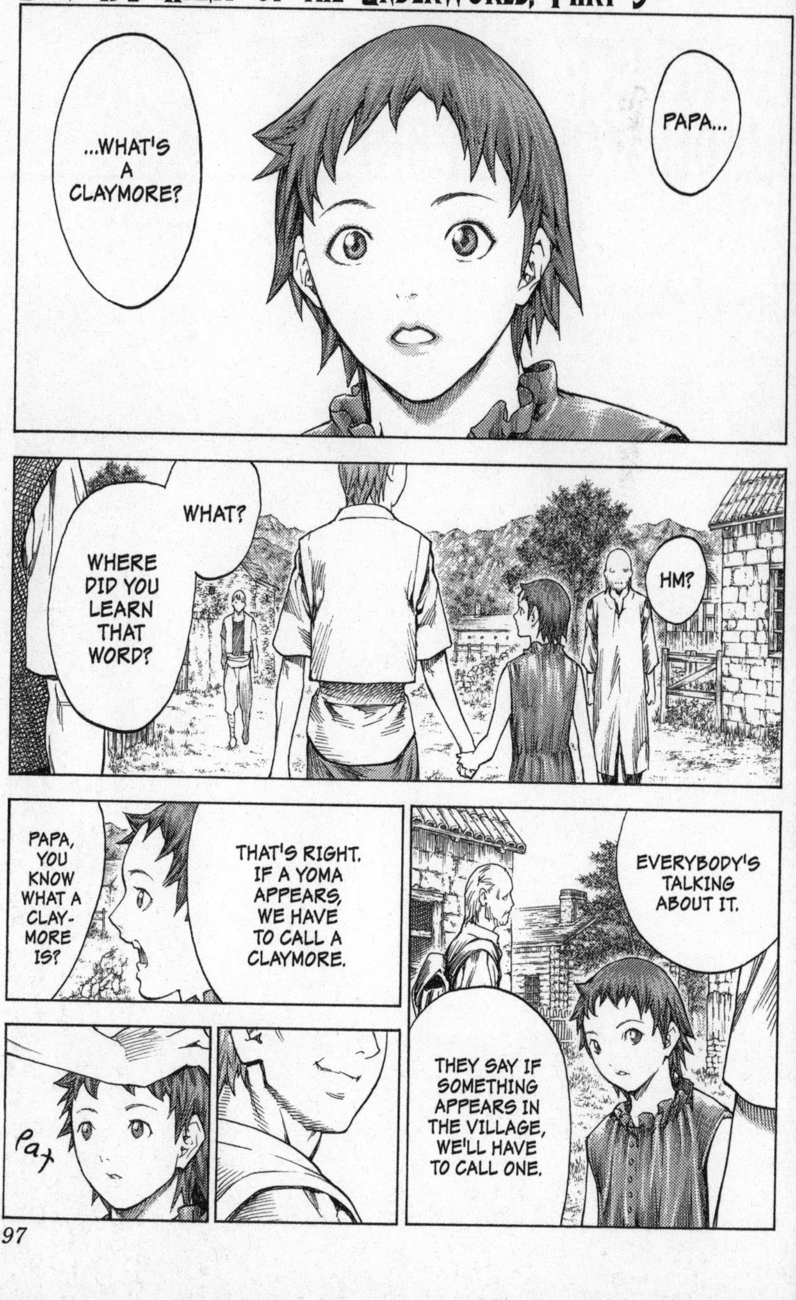
PAPA...
...WHAT'S A CLAYMORE?
HM?
WHAT?
WHERE DID YOU LEARN THAT WORD?
EVERYBODY'S TALKING ABOUT IT.
THEY SAY IF SOMETHING APPEARS IN THE VILLAGE, WE'LL HAVE TO CALL ONE.
THAT'S RIGHT. IF A YOMA APPEARS, WE HAVE TO CALL A CLAYMORE.
PAPA, YOU KNOW WHAT A CLAY-MORE IS?
Pat

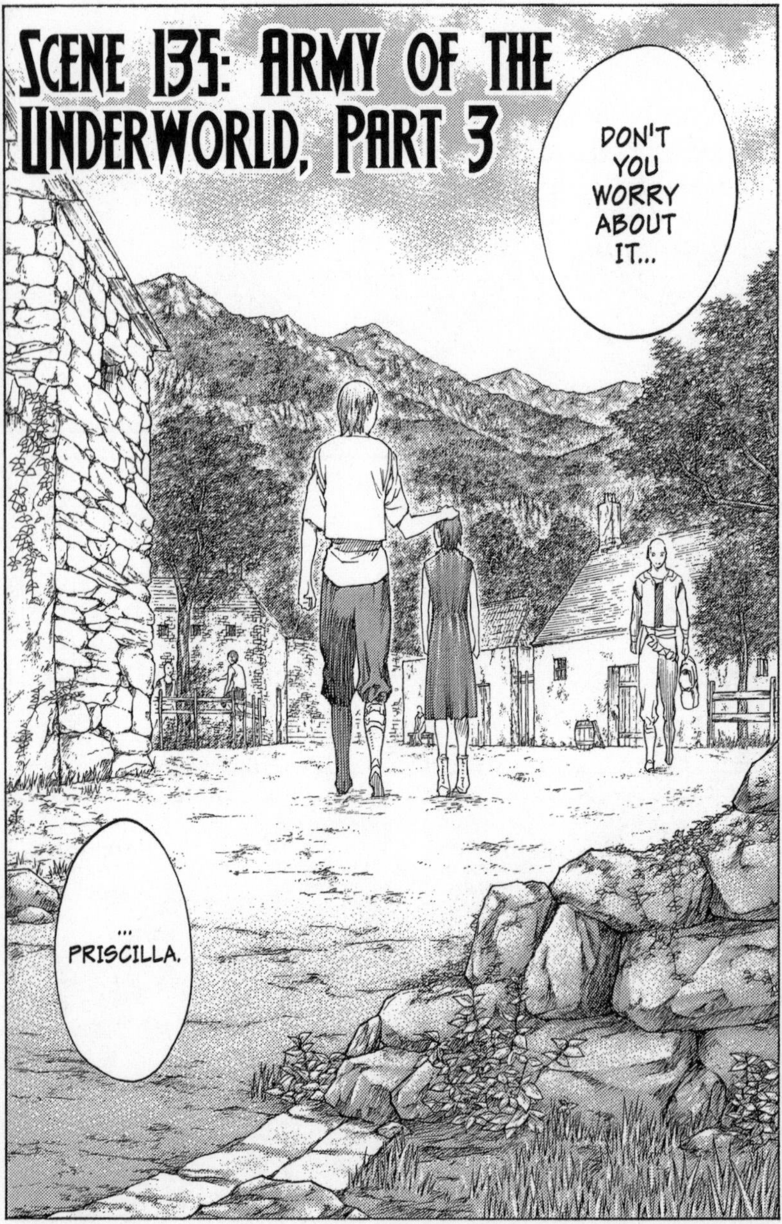
SCENE 135: ARMY OF THE UNDERWORLD, PART 3
DON'T YOU WORRY ABOUT IT...
... PRISCILLA.

READ THIS WAY

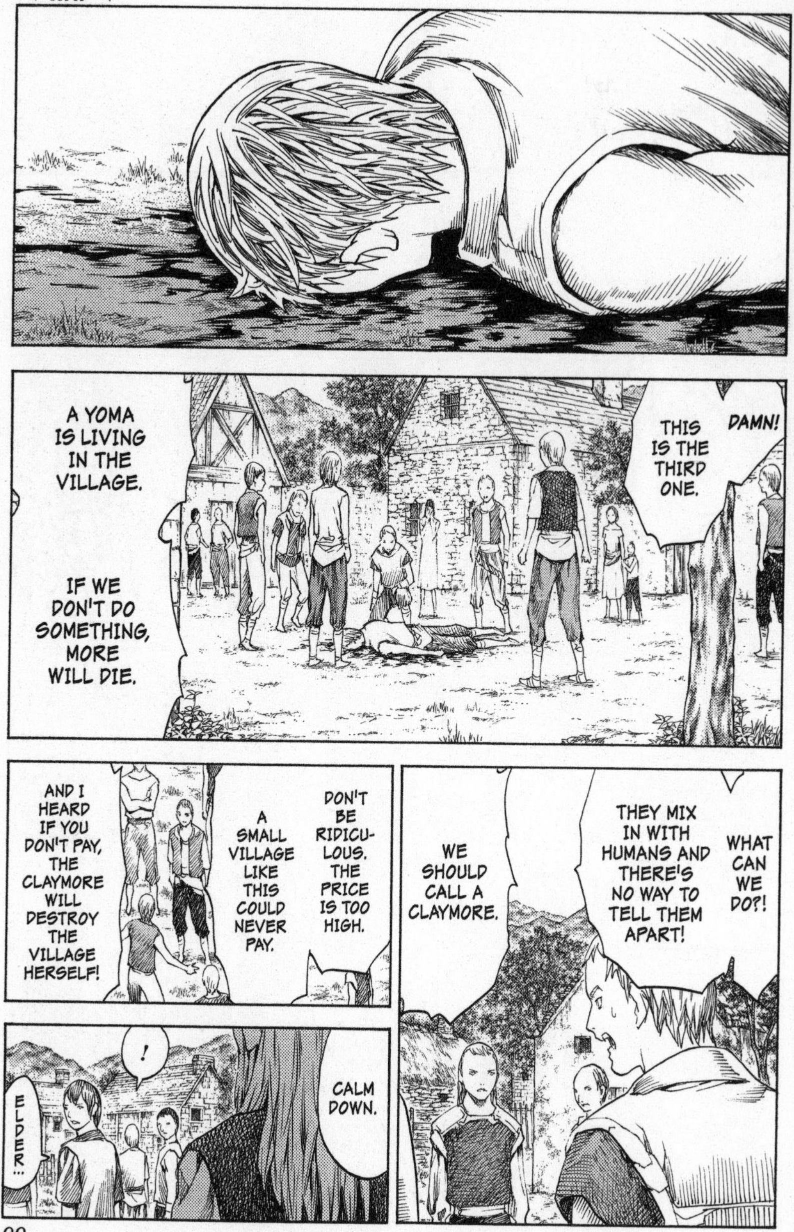
DAMN!
THIS IS THE THIRD ONE.
A YOMA IS LIVING IN THE VILLAGE.
IF WE DON'T DO SOMETHING, MORE WILL DIE.
WHAT CAN WE DO?!
THEY MIX IN WITH HUMANS AND THERE'S NO WAY TO TELL THEM APART!
WE SHOULD CALL A CLAYMORE.
DON'T BE RIDICULOUS. THE PRICE IS TOO HIGH.
A SMALL VILLAGE LIKE THIS COULD NEVER PAY.
AND I HEARD IF YOU DON'T PAY, THE CLAYMORE WILL DESTROY THE VILLAGE HERSELF!
CALM DOWN.
!
ELDER...

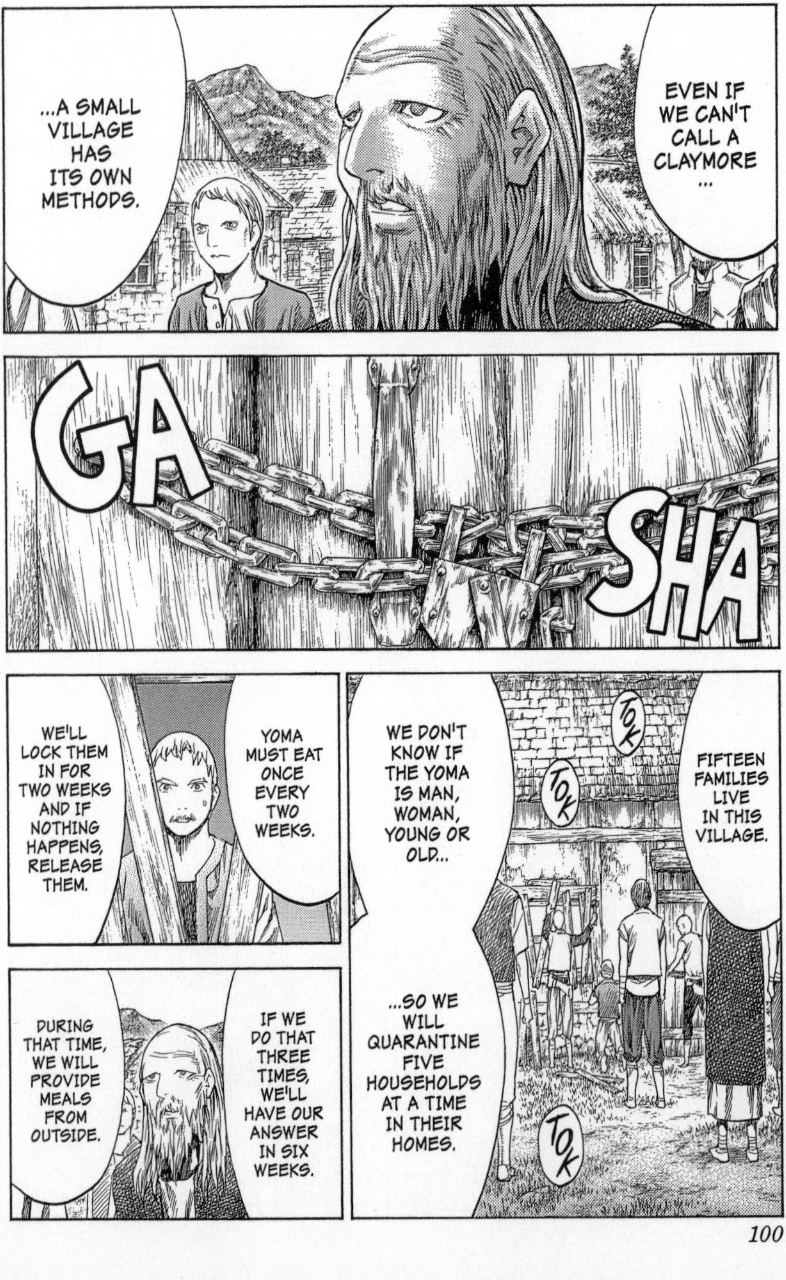
EVEN IF WE CAN'T CALL A CLAYMORE...
...A SMALL VILLAGE HAS ITS OWN METHODS.
GA
SHA
TOK
FIFTEEN FAMILIES LIVE IN THIS VILLAGE.
TOK
WE DON'T KNOW IF THE YOMA IS MAN, WOMAN, YOUNG OR OLD...
...SO WE WILL QUARANTINE FIVE HOUSEHOLDS AT A TIME IN THEIR HOMES.
TOK
YOMA MUST EAT ONCE EVERY TWO WEEKS.
WE'LL LOCK THEM IN FOR TWO WEEKS AND IF NOTHING HAPPENS, RELEASE THEM.
IF WE DO THAT THREE TIMES, WE'LL HAVE OUR ANSWER IN SIX WEEKS.
DURING THAT TIME, WE WILL PROVIDE MEALS FROM OUTSIDE.

READ THIS WAY

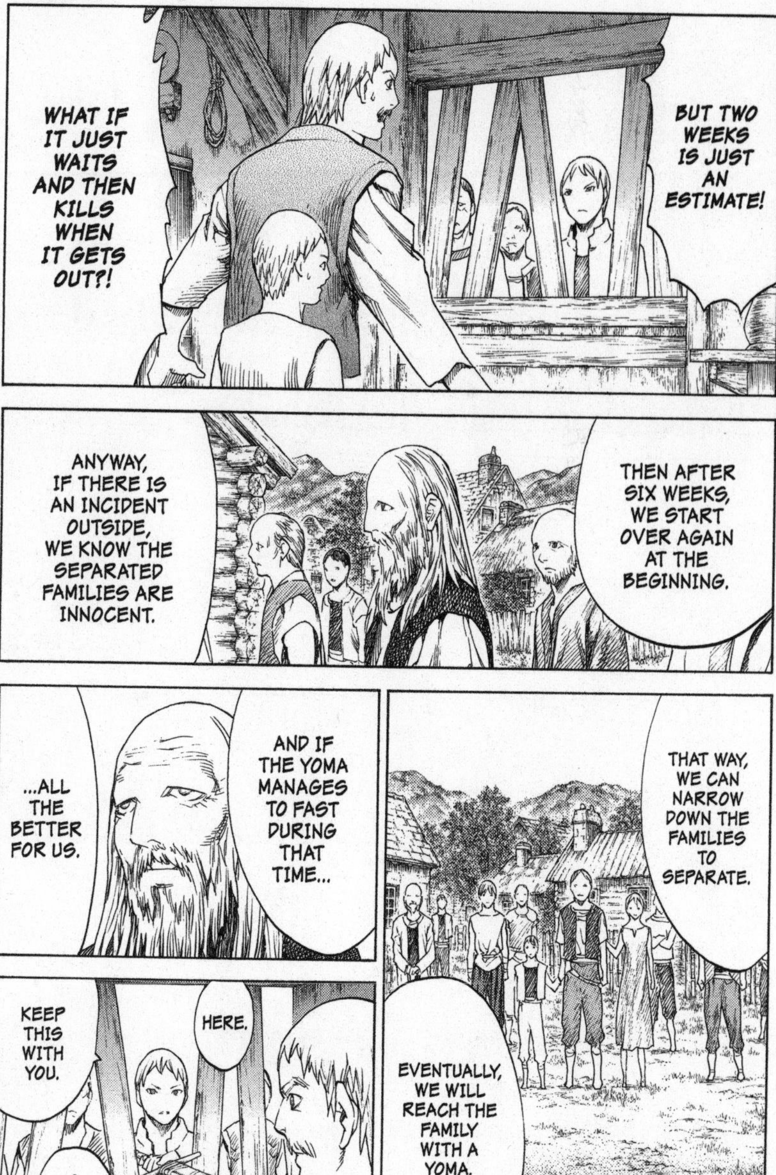

BUT TWO WEEKS IS JUST AN ESTIMATE!
WHAT IF IT JUST WAITS AND THEN KILLS WHEN IT GETS OUT?!
THEN AFTER SIX WEEKS, WE START OVER AGAIN AT THE BEGINNING.
ANYWAY, IF THERE IS AN INCIDENT OUTSIDE, WE KNOW THE SEPARATED FAMILIES ARE INNOCENT.
THAT WAY, WE CAN NARROW DOWN THE FAMILIES TO SEPARATE.
EVENTUALLY, WE WILL REACH THE FAMILY WITH A YOMA.
AND IF THE YOMA MANAGES TO FAST DURING THAT TIME...
...ALL THE BETTER FOR US.
HERE.
KEEP THIS WITH YOU.
!

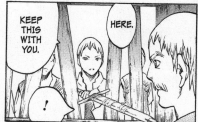

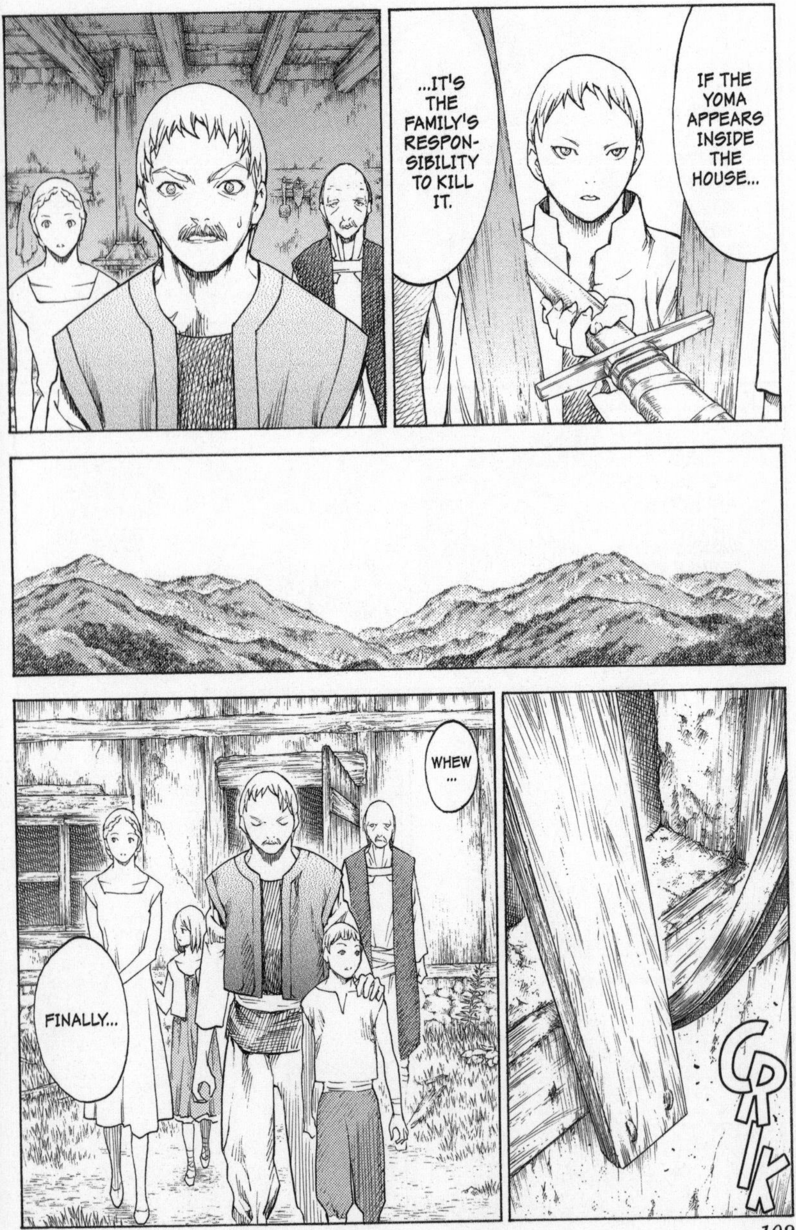
IF THE YOMA APPEARS INSIDE THE HOUSE...
...IT'S THE FAMILY'S RESPON-SIBILITY TO KILL IT.
CRIK
WHEW ...
FINALLY...

READ THIS WAY

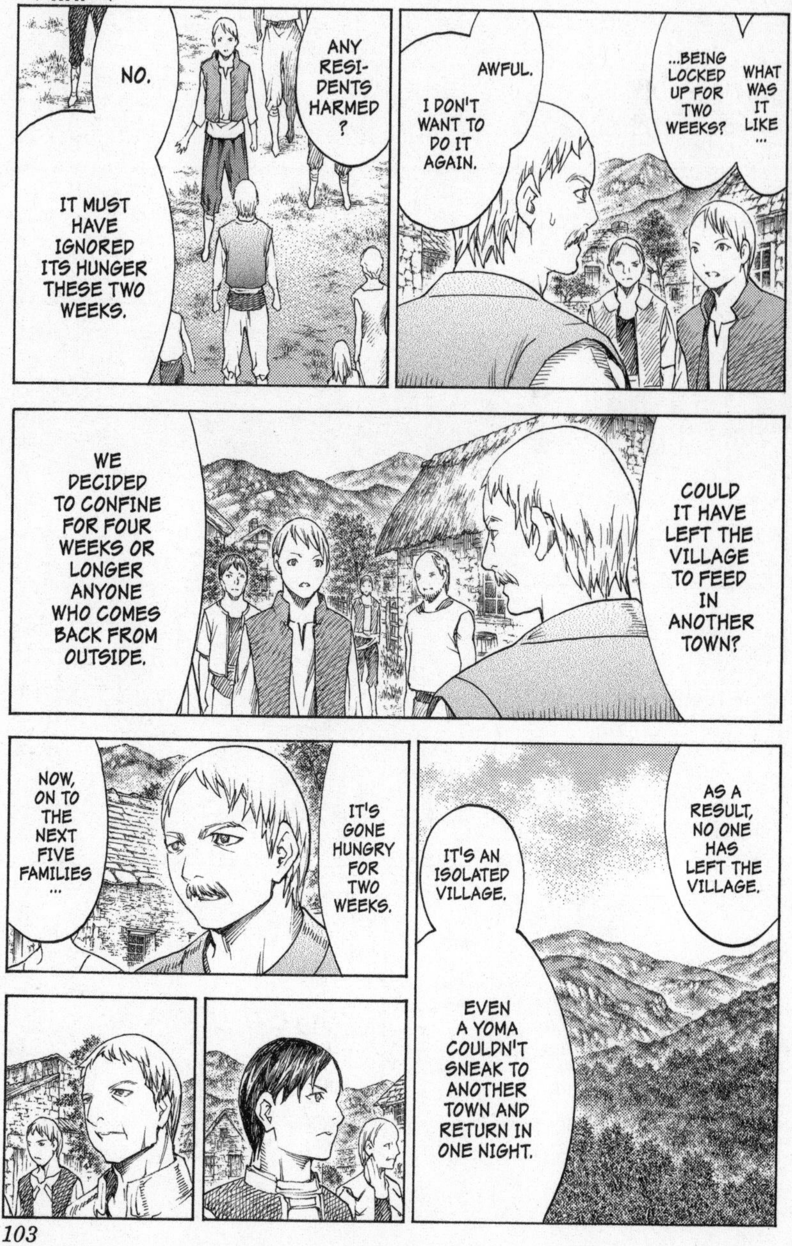
WHAT WAS IT LIKE ...
...BEING LOCKED UP FOR TWO WEEKS?
AWFUL.
I DON'T WANT TO DO IT AGAIN.
ANY RESIDENTS HARMED?
NO.
IT MUST HAVE IGNORED ITS HUNGER THESE TWO WEEKS.
COULD IT HAVE LEFT THE VILLAGE TO FEED IN ANOTHER TOWN?
WE DECIDED TO CONFINE FOR FOUR WEEKS OR LONGER ANYONE WHO COMES BACK FROM OUTSIDE.
AS A RESULT, NO ONE HAS LEFT THE VILLAGE.
IT'S AN ISOLATED VILLAGE.
EVEN A YOMA COULDN'T SNEAK TO ANOTHER TOWN AND RETURN IN ONE NIGHT.
IT'S GONE HUNGRY FOR TWO WEEKS.
NOW, ON TO THE NEXT FIVE FAMILIES ...

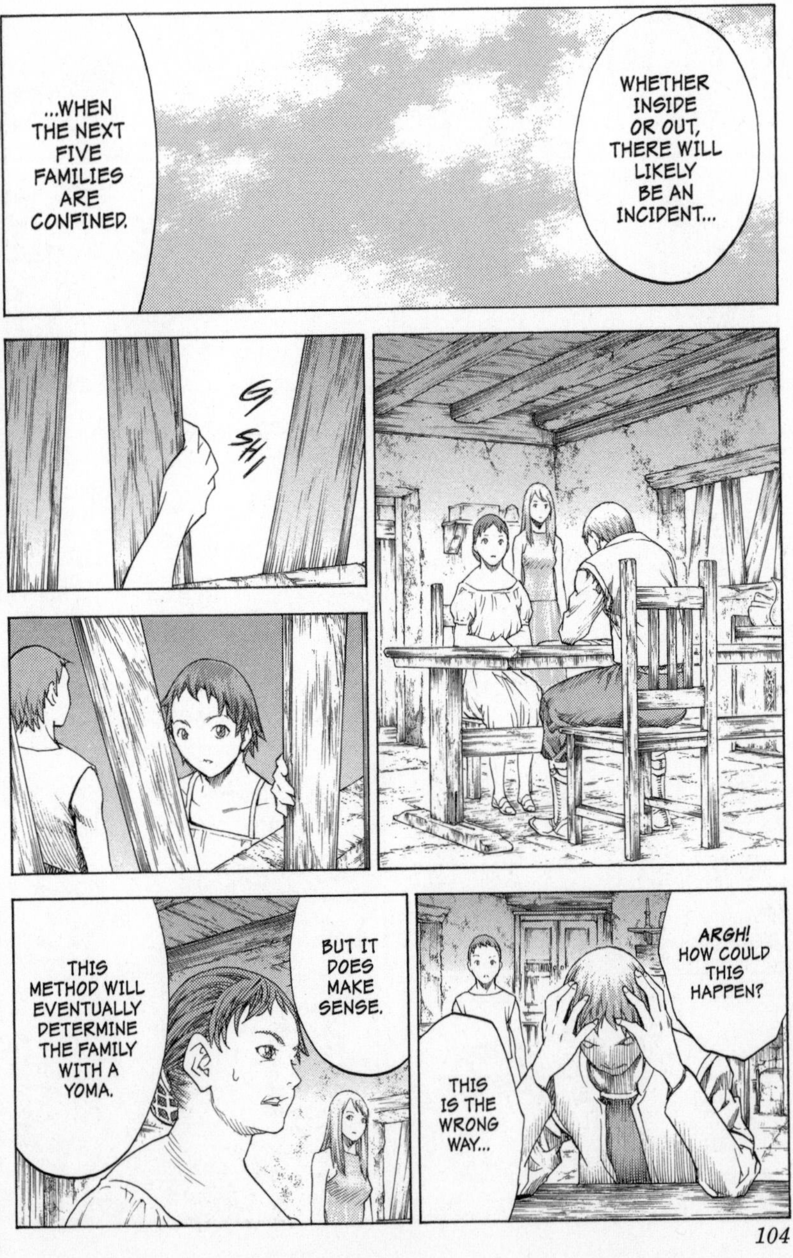
WHETHER INSIDE OR OUT, THERE WILL LIKELY BE AN INCIDENT...
...WHEN THE NEXT FIVE FAMILIES ARE CONFINED.
GI SHI
ARGH! HOW COULD THIS HAPPEN?
THIS IS THE WRONG WAY...
BUT IT DOES MAKE SENSE.
THIS METHOD WILL EVENTUALLY DETERMINE THE FAMILY WITH A YOMA.

READ THIS WAY

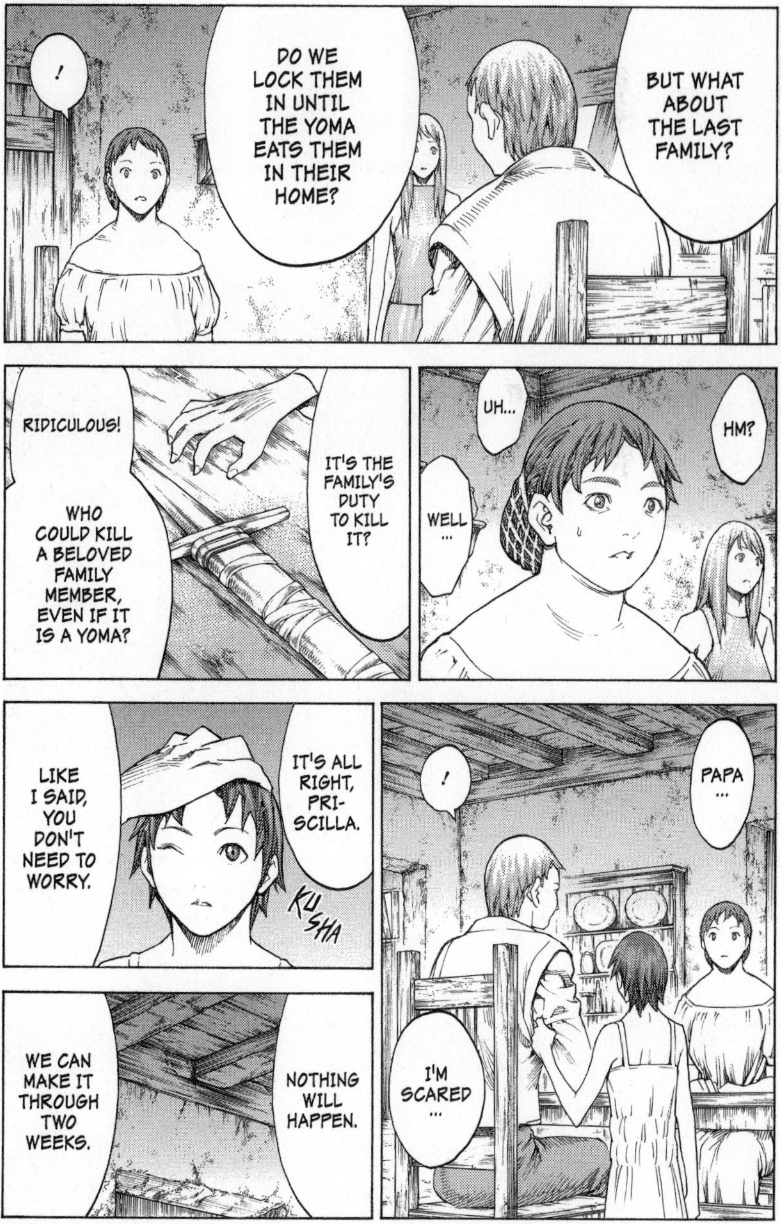

BUT WHAT ABOUT THE LAST FAMILY?
DO WE LOCK THEM IN UNTIL THE YOMA EATS THEM IN THEIR HOME?
!
HM?
UH...
WELL ...
IT'S THE FAMILY'S DUTY TO KILL IT?
RIDICULOUS!
WHO COULD KILL A BELOVED FAMILY MEMBER, EVEN IF IT IS A YOMA?
PAPA ...
!
I'M SCARED ...
IT'S ALL RIGHT, PRI-SCILLA.
LIKE I SAID, YOU DON'T NEED TO WORRY.
KUSHA
NOTHING WILL HAPPEN.
WE CAN MAKE IT THROUGH TWO WEEKS.

MM...

PAPA?

MAMA...?

MAMA...

PAPA...

!

I NEED TO PEE...

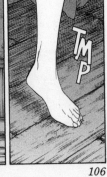

TMP

READ THIS WAY

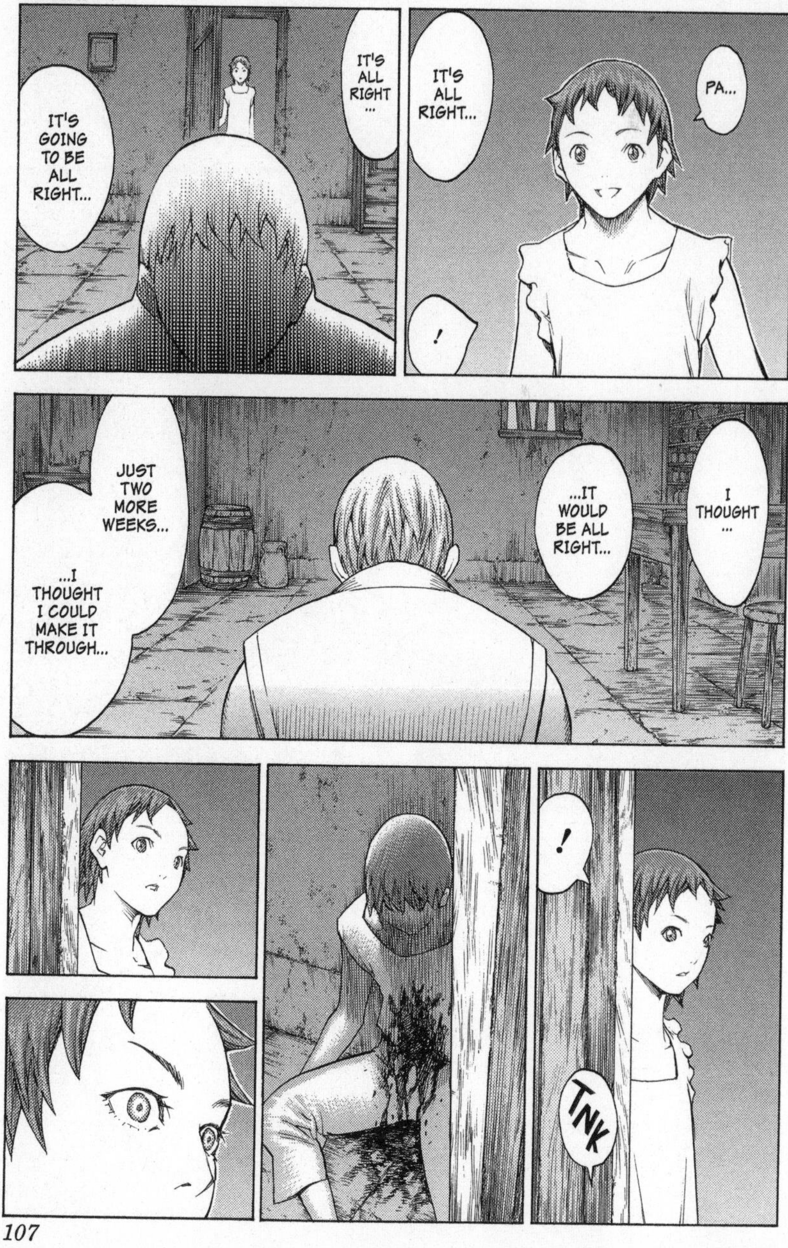
PA...
IT'S ALL RIGHT...
!
IT'S ALL RIGHT ...
IT'S GOING TO BE ALL RIGHT...
I THOUGHT ...
...IT WOULD BE ALL RIGHT...
JUST TWO MORE WEEKS...
...I THOUGHT I COULD MAKE IT THROUGH...
!
TNK

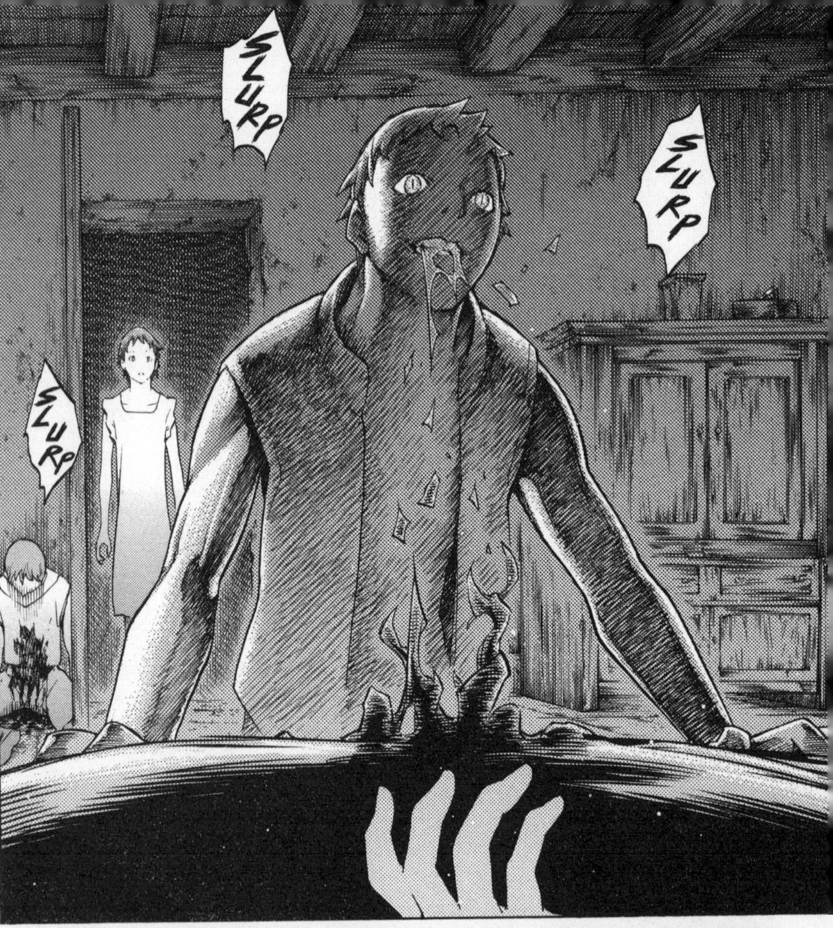
SLURP
SLURP
SLURP
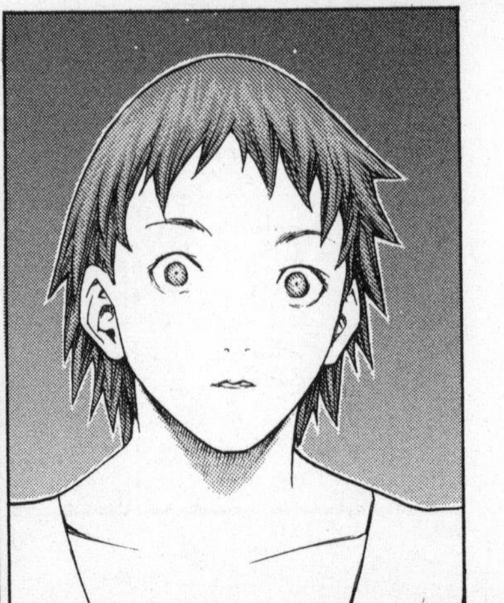
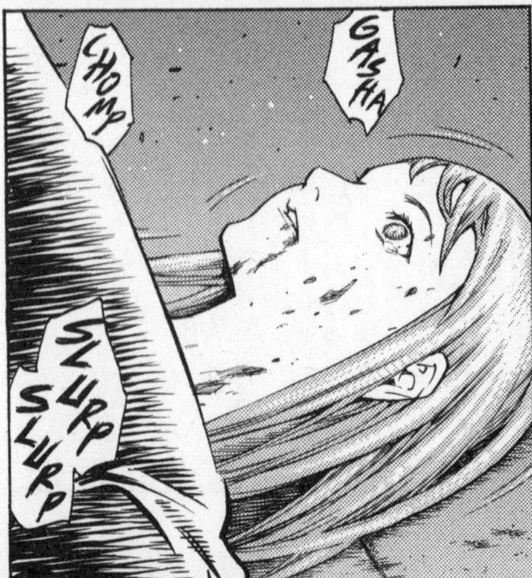
GASHA
CHOMP
SLURP SLURP

READ THIS WAY

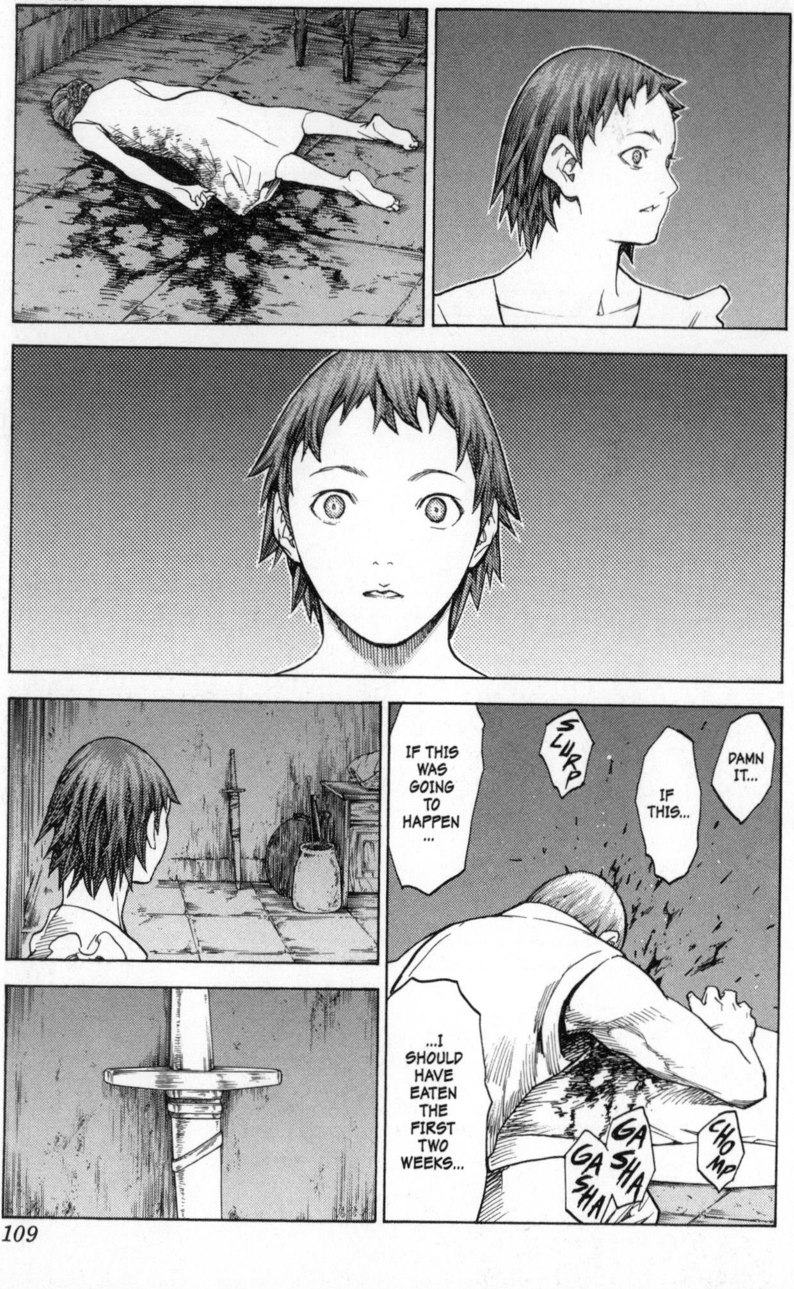
DAMN IT...
IF THIS...
SLURP
IF THIS WAS GOING TO HAPPEN...
...I SHOULD HAVE EATEN THE FIRST TWO WEEKS...
CHOMP
GASHA GASHA
GASHA GASHA

OH,
NO...

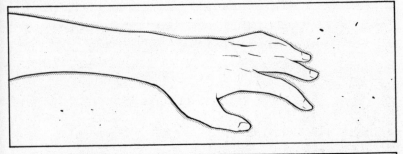

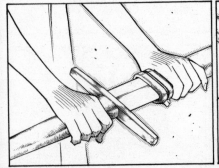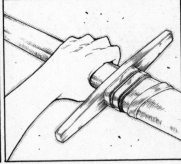

NO
MORE...

READ THIS WAY

SLURP
SLURP
SLURP
SLURP
SLURP
SLURP
SLURP
I DON'T WANT TO REMEMBER ANY MORE...

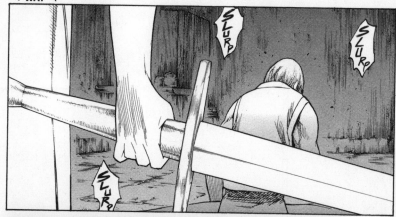

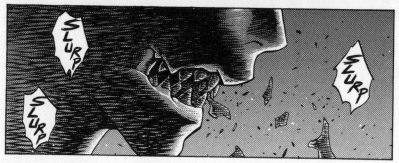

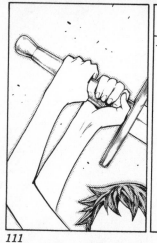

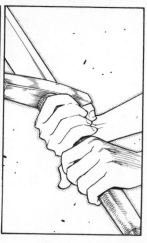

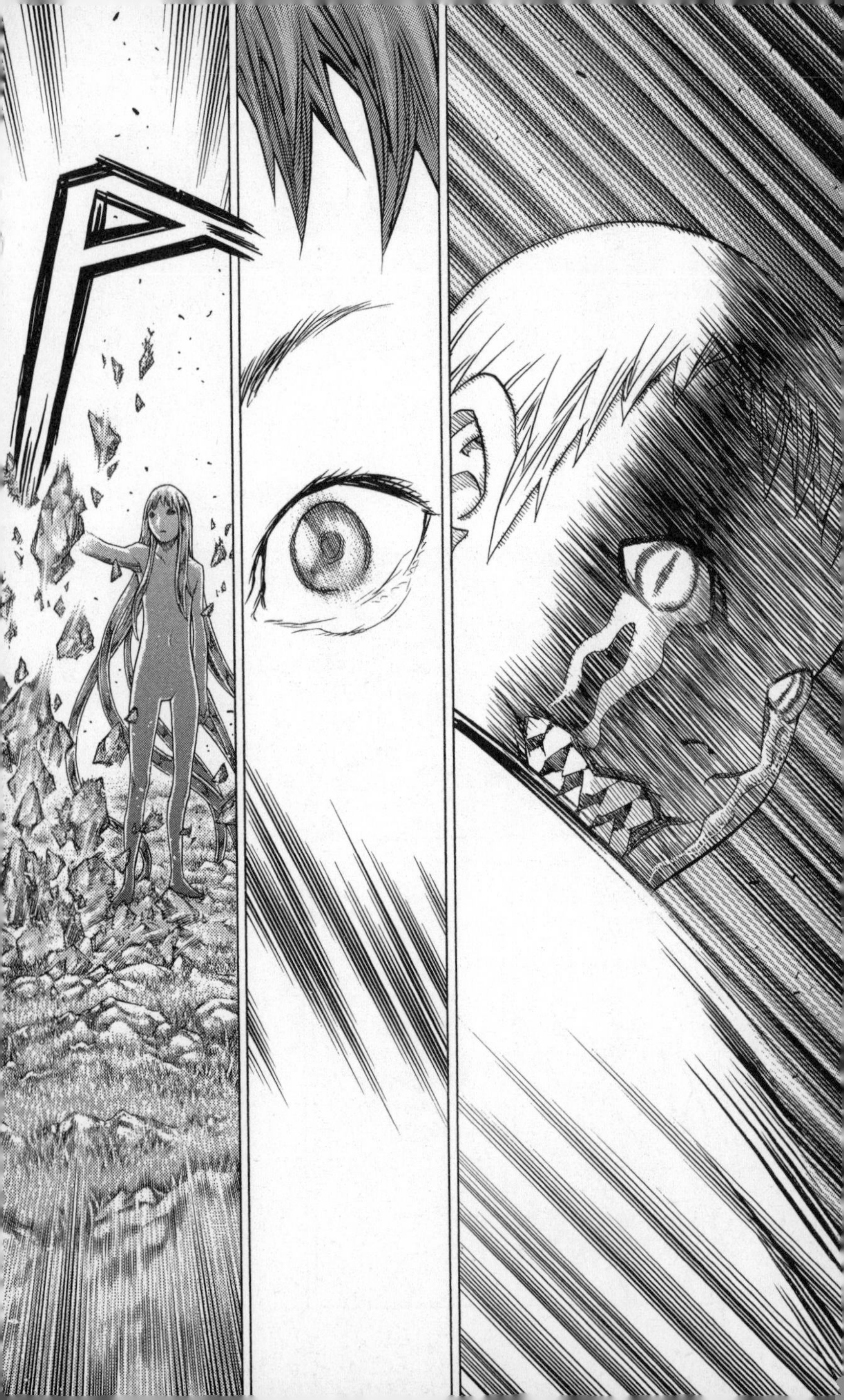

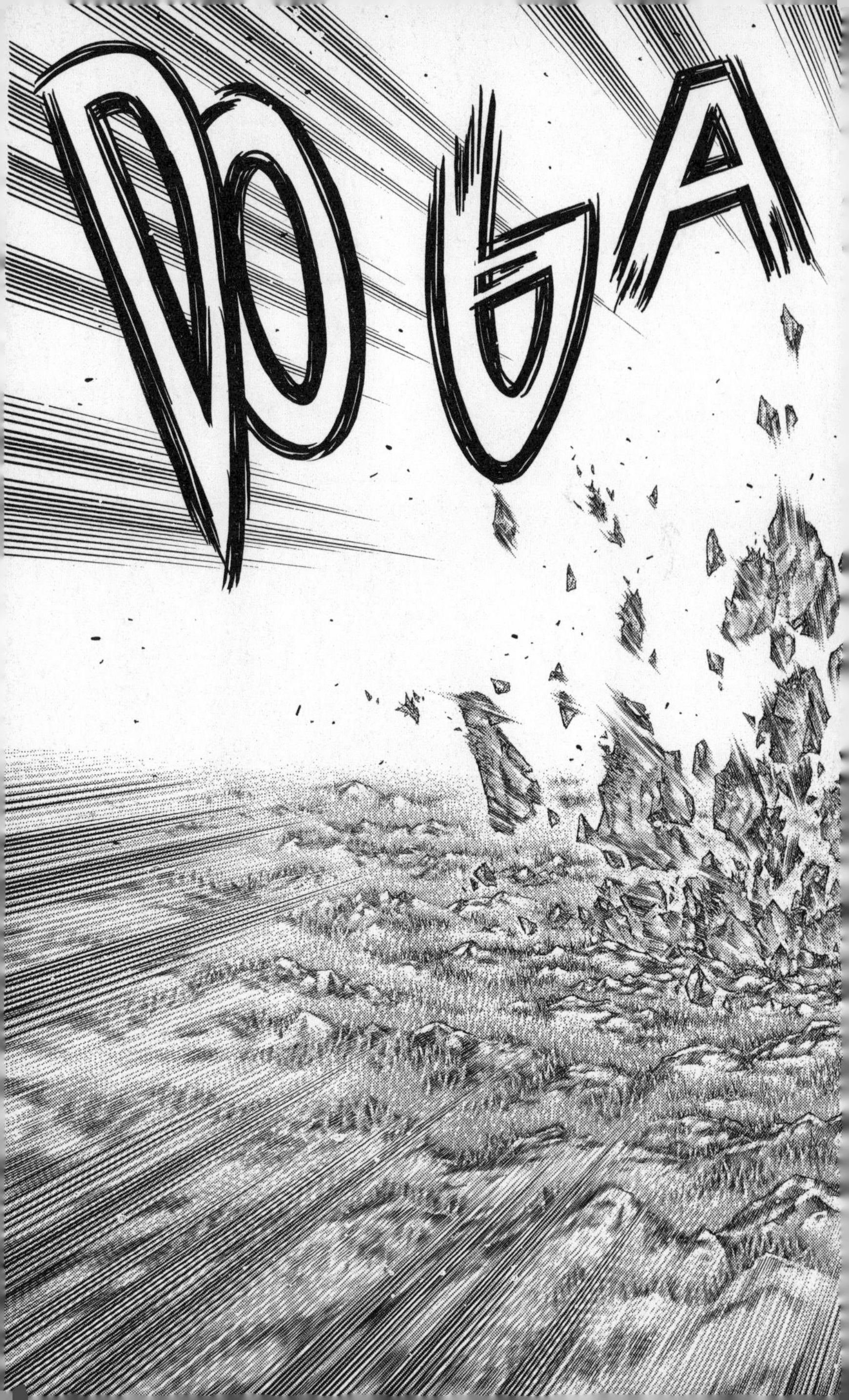
DOGA

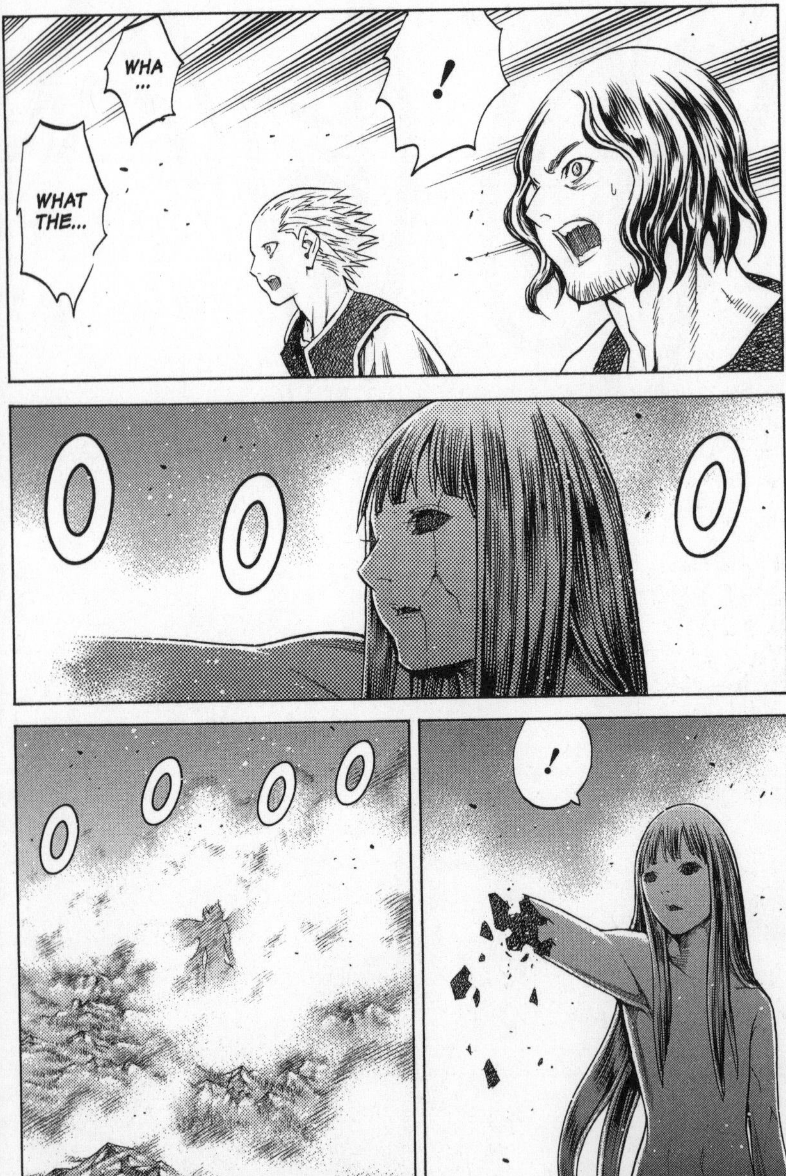
!
WHA ...
WHAT THE...
!

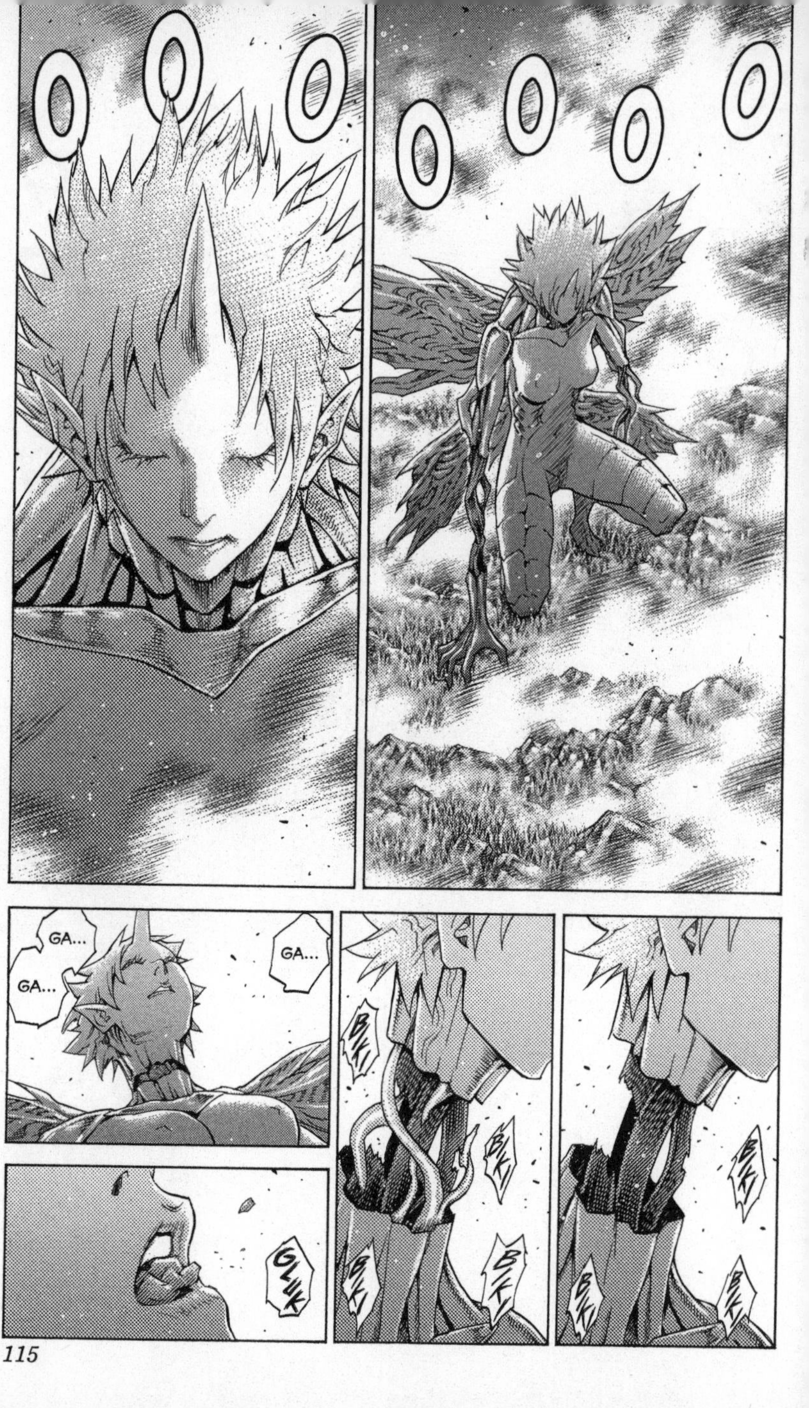
OOOOO
OOO
BIKI
BIKI
BIKI
BIKI
BIKI
BIKI
GA...
GA...
GA...
GLUK

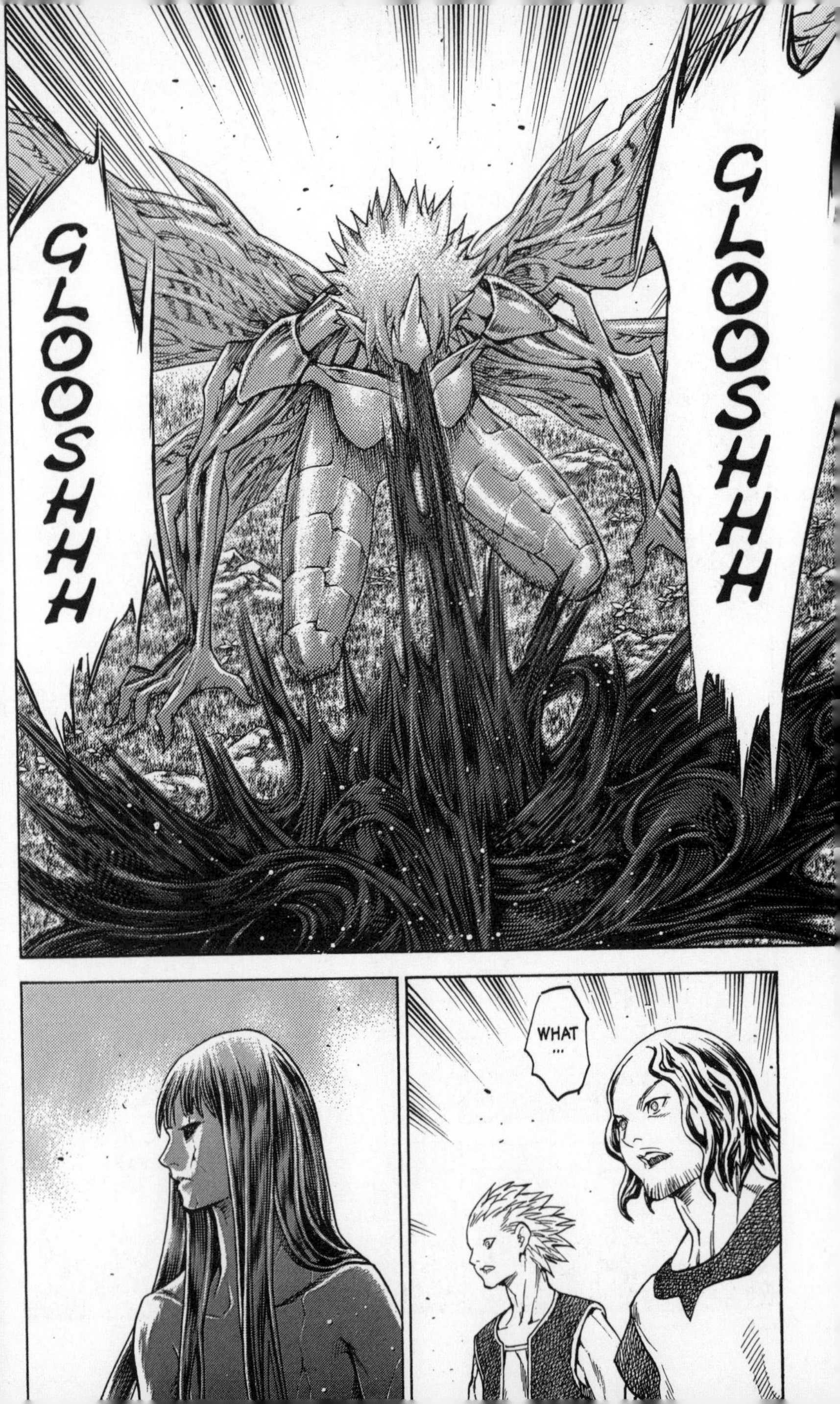
GLOOSHHH
GLOOSHHH
WHAT ...

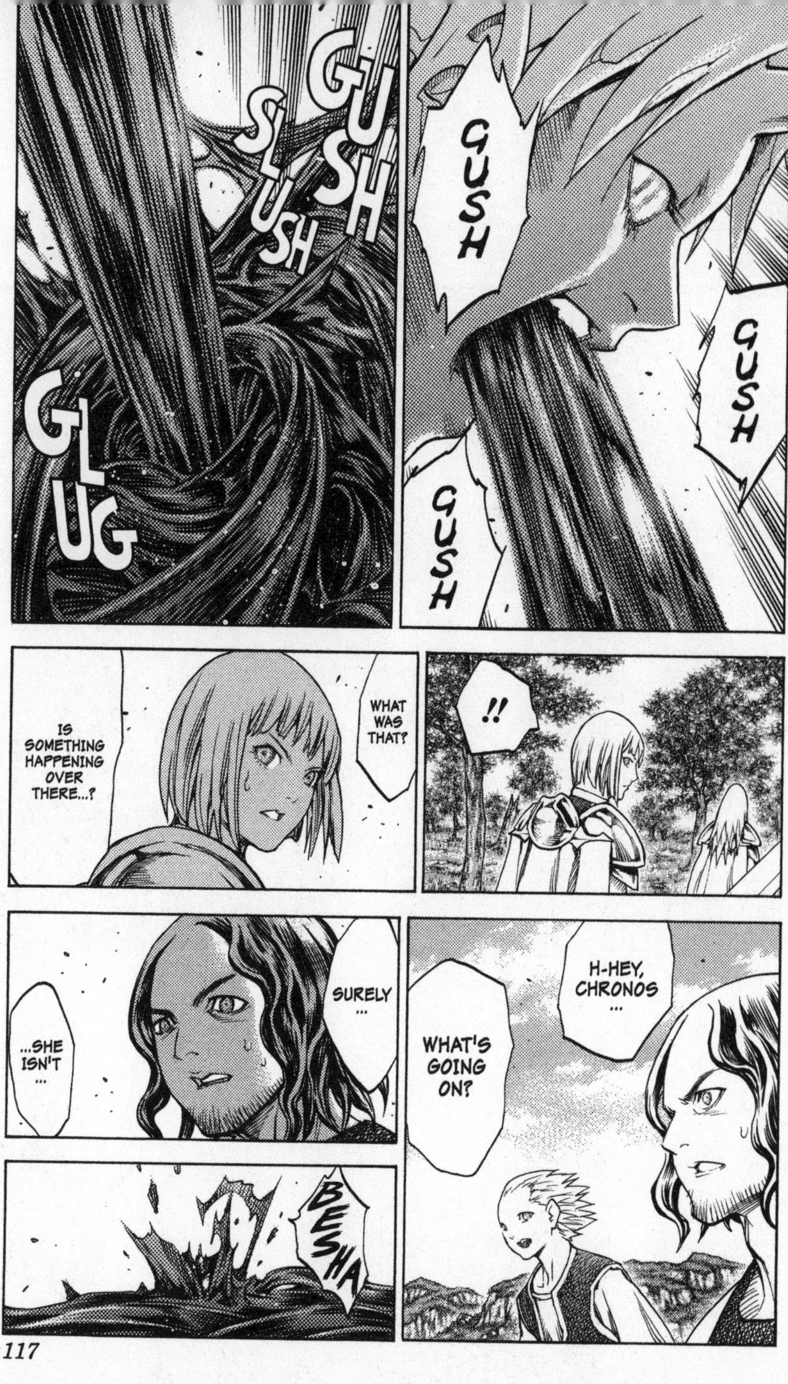
GUSH
GUSH
GUSH
GUSH
SLUSH
GLUG
!!
WHAT WAS THAT?
IS SOMETHING HAPPENING OVER THERE...?
H-HEY, CHRONOS ...
WHAT'S GOING ON?
SURELY ...
...SHE ISN'T ...
BESHA

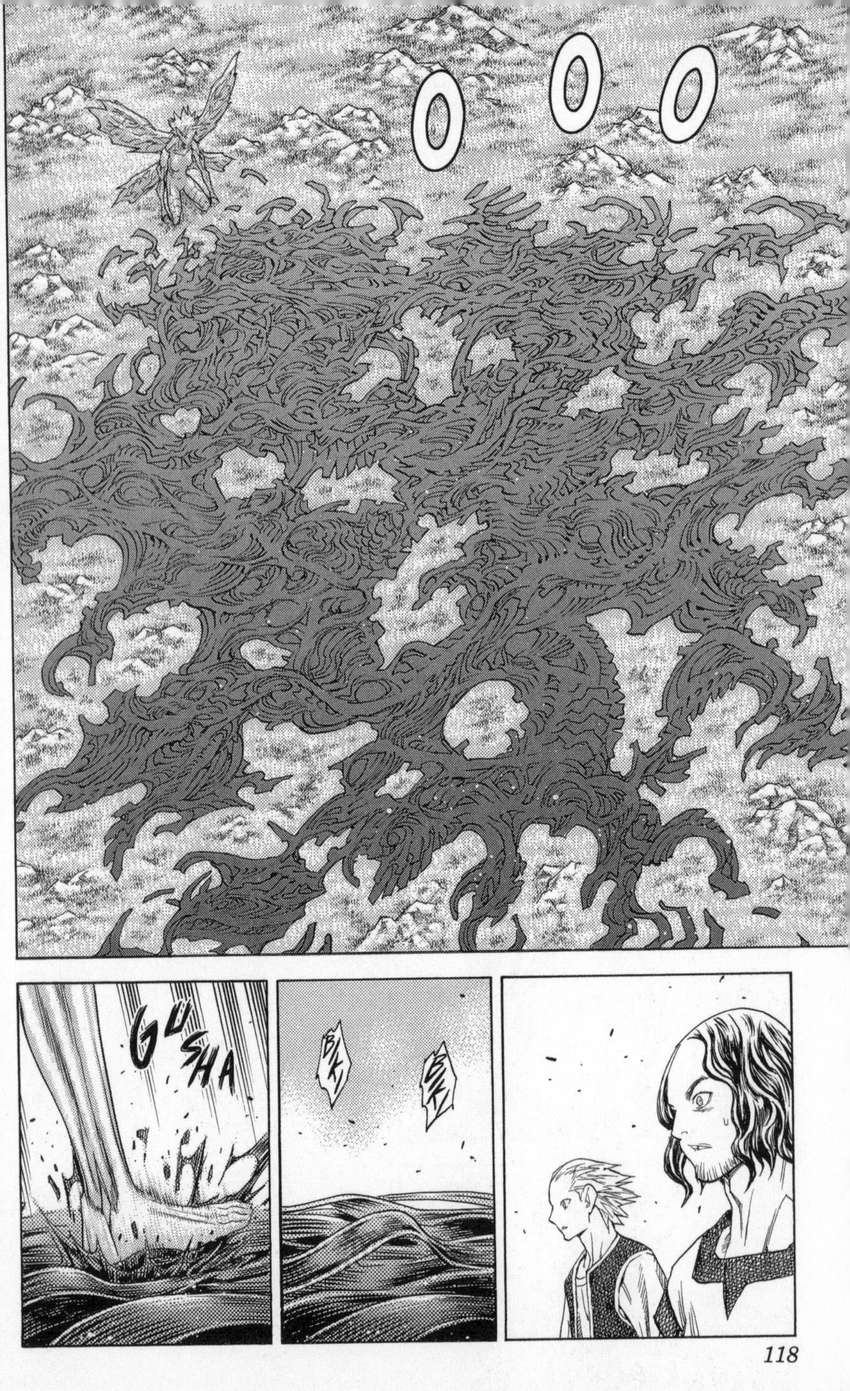
OOO
BIKI
BIKI
GUSHA

READ THIS WAY

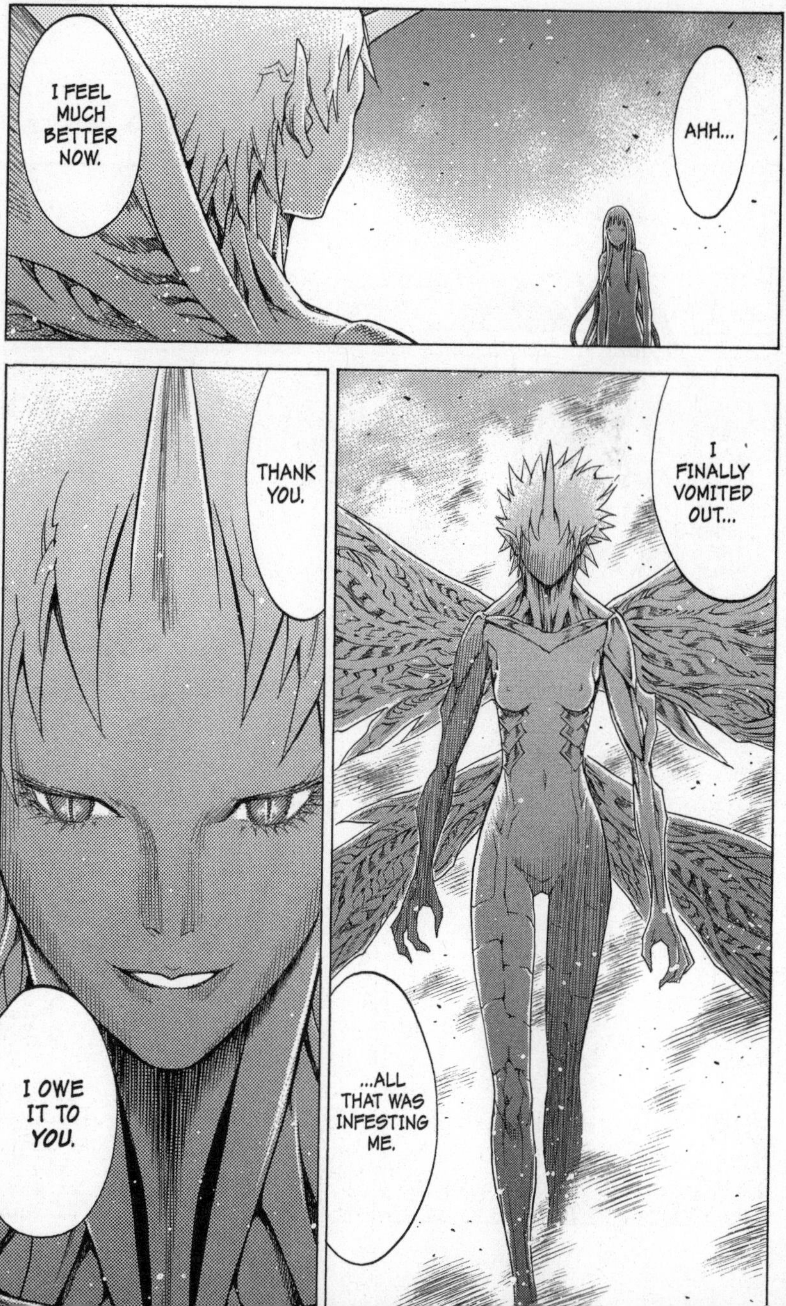
AHH...
I FEEL MUCH BETTER NOW.
I FINALLY VOMITED OUT...
...ALL THAT WAS INFESTING ME.
THANK YOU.
I OWE IT TO YOU.

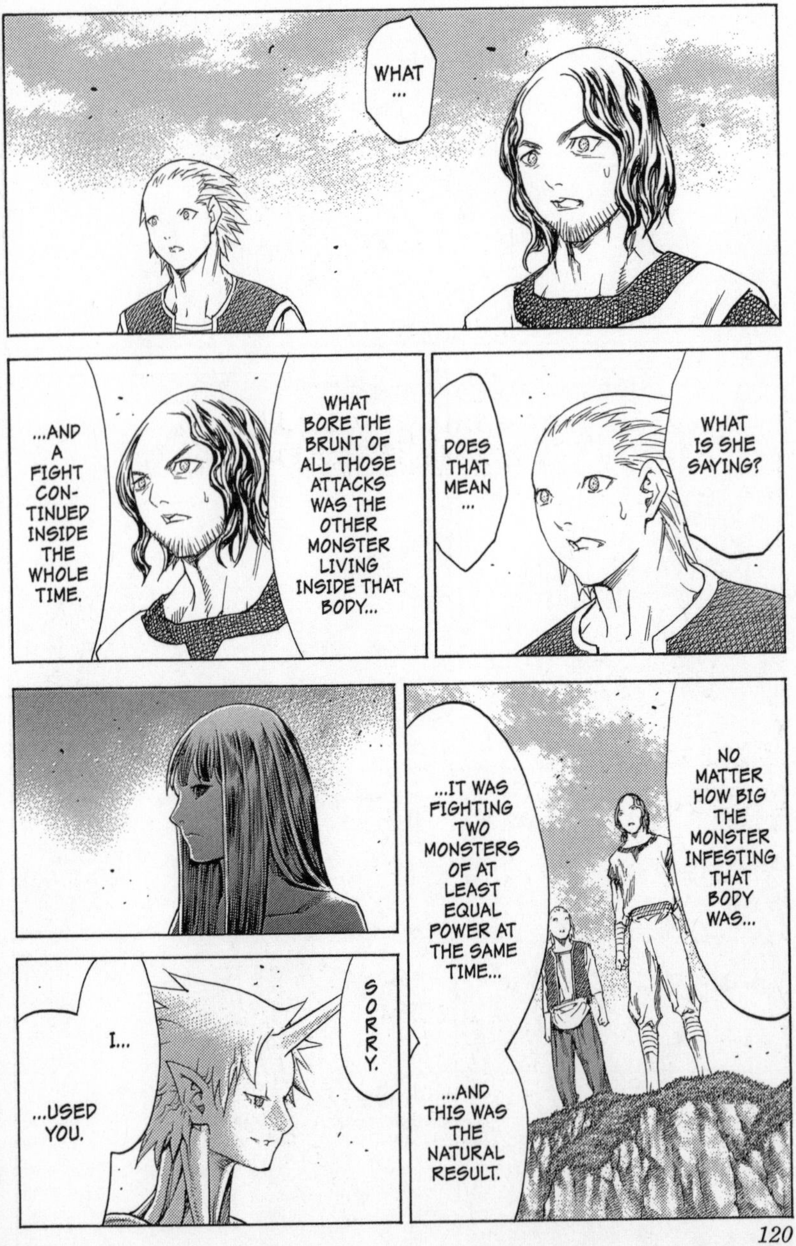
WHAT ...
WHAT IS SHE SAYING?
DOES THAT MEAN ...
WHAT BORE THE BRUNT OF ALL THOSE ATTACKS WAS THE OTHER MONSTER LIVING INSIDE THAT BODY...
...AND A FIGHT CONTINUED INSIDE THE WHOLE TIME.
NO MATTER HOW BIG THE MONSTER INFESTING THAT BODY WAS...
...IT WAS FIGHTING TWO MONSTERS OF AT LEAST EQUAL POWER AT THE SAME TIME...
...AND THIS WAS THE NATURAL RESULT.
SORRY.
I...
...USED YOU.

READ THIS WAY

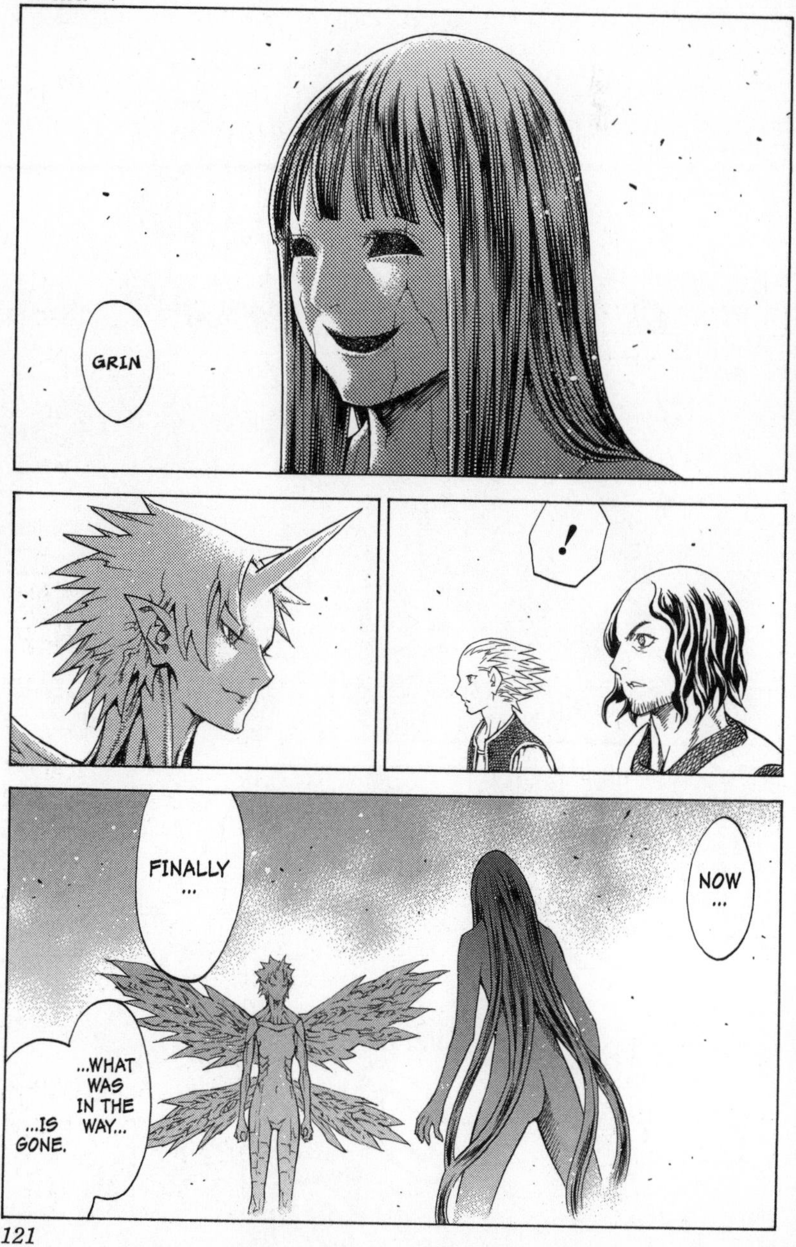
GRIN
!
NOW ...
FINALLY ...
...WHAT WAS IN THE WAY...
...IS GONE.

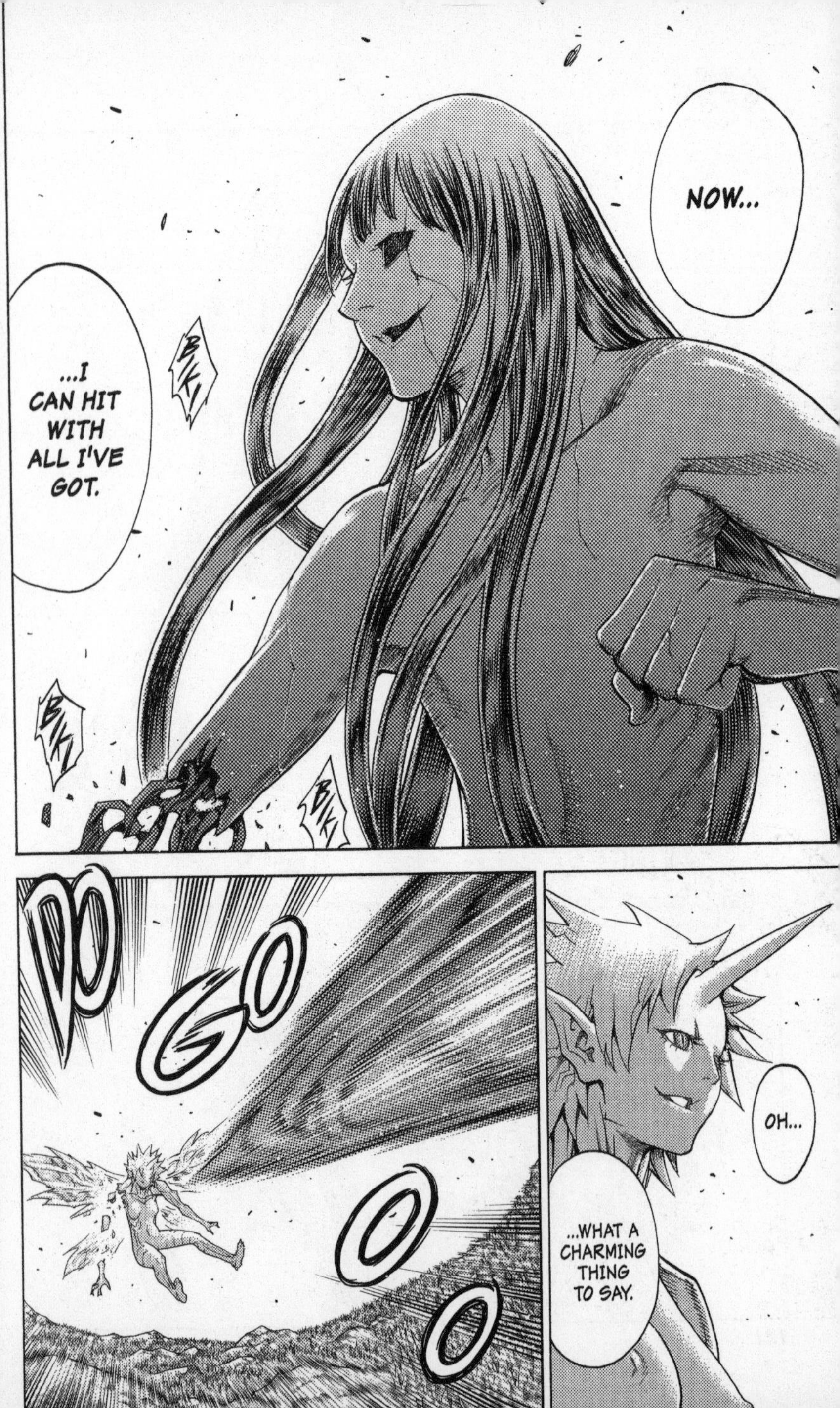
NOW...
...I CAN HIT WITH ALL I'VE GOT.
BIKI
BIKI
BIKI
OH...
...WHAT A CHARMING THING TO SAY.
DOGOOO

READ THIS WAY

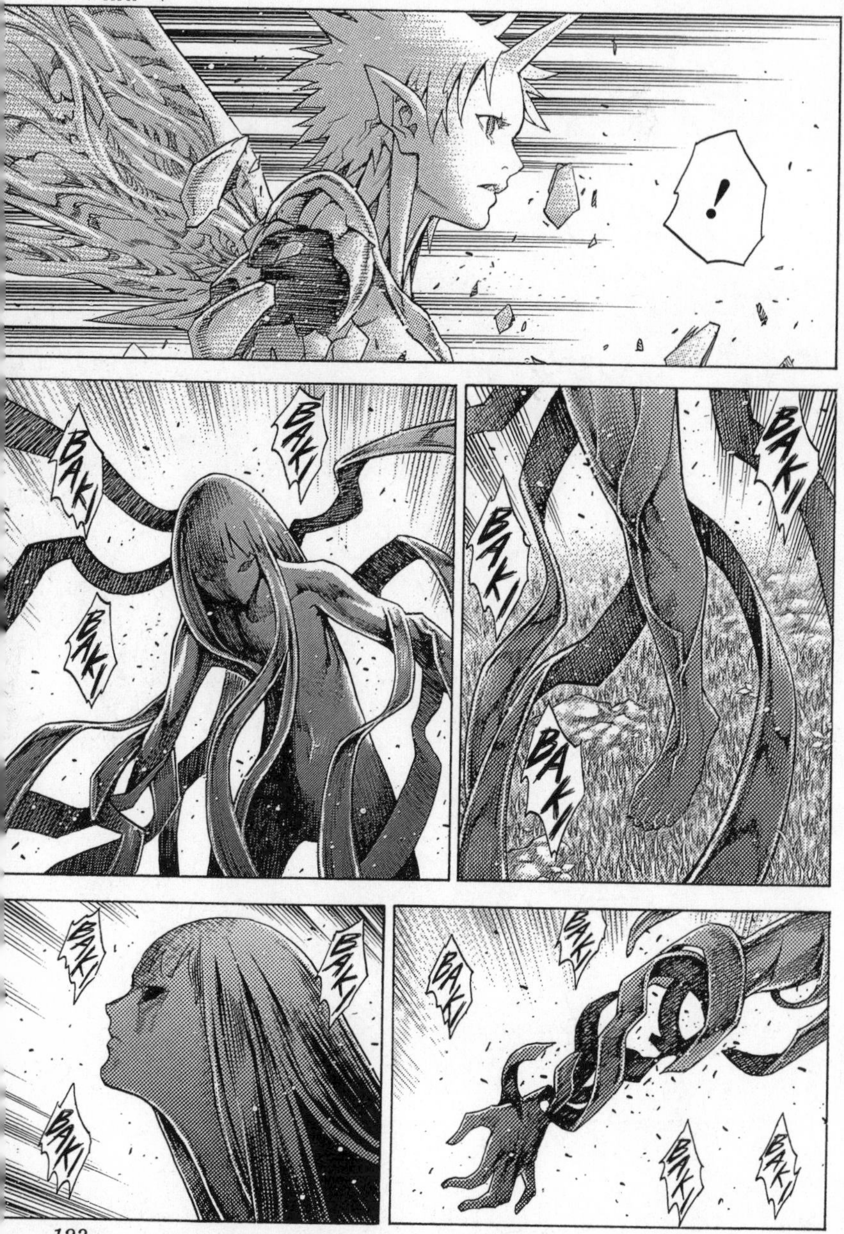
!
BAKI
BAKI
BAKI
BAKI
BAKI
BAKI
BAKI
BAKI
BAKI
BAKI
BAKI
BAKI
BAKI

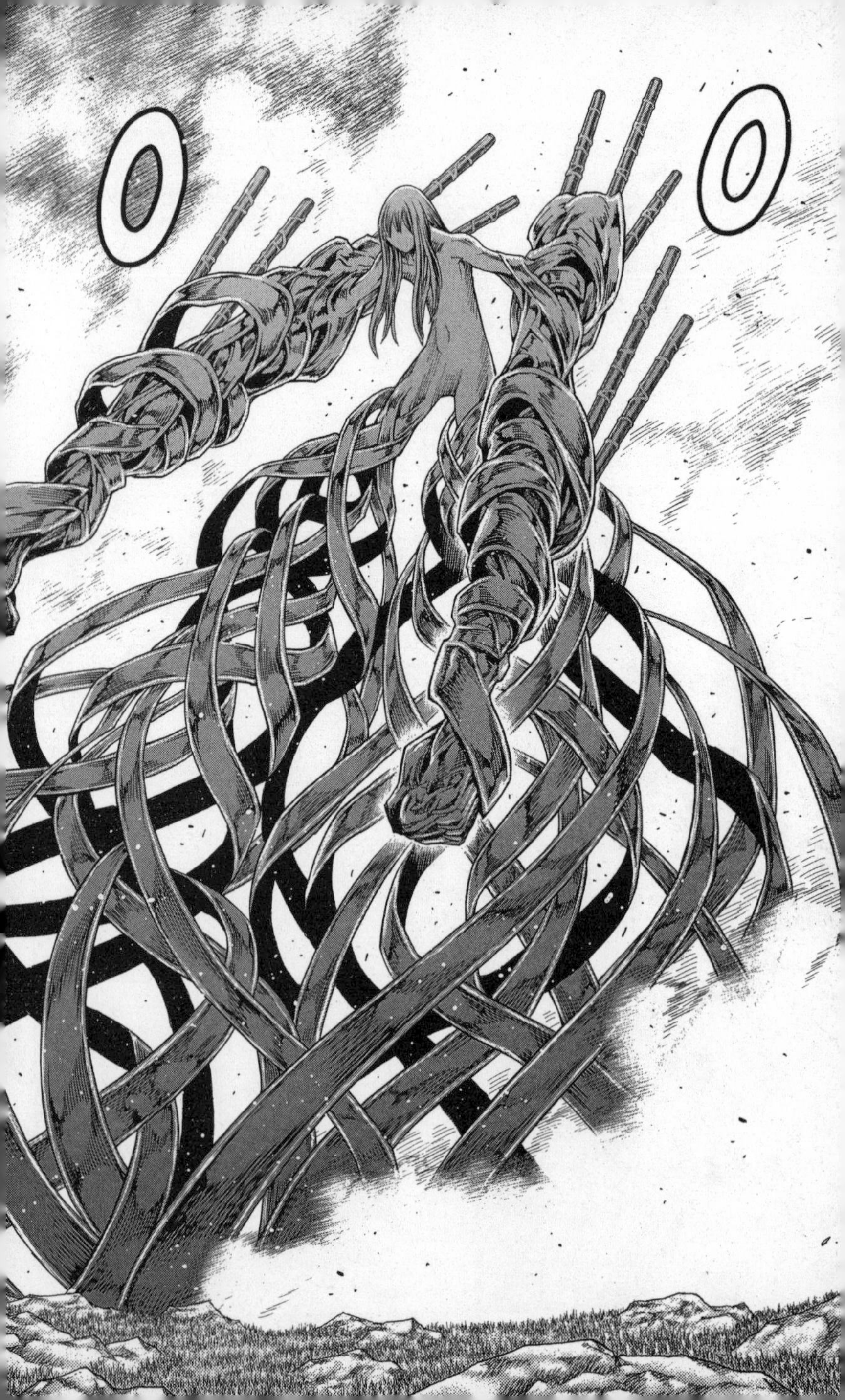
O
O

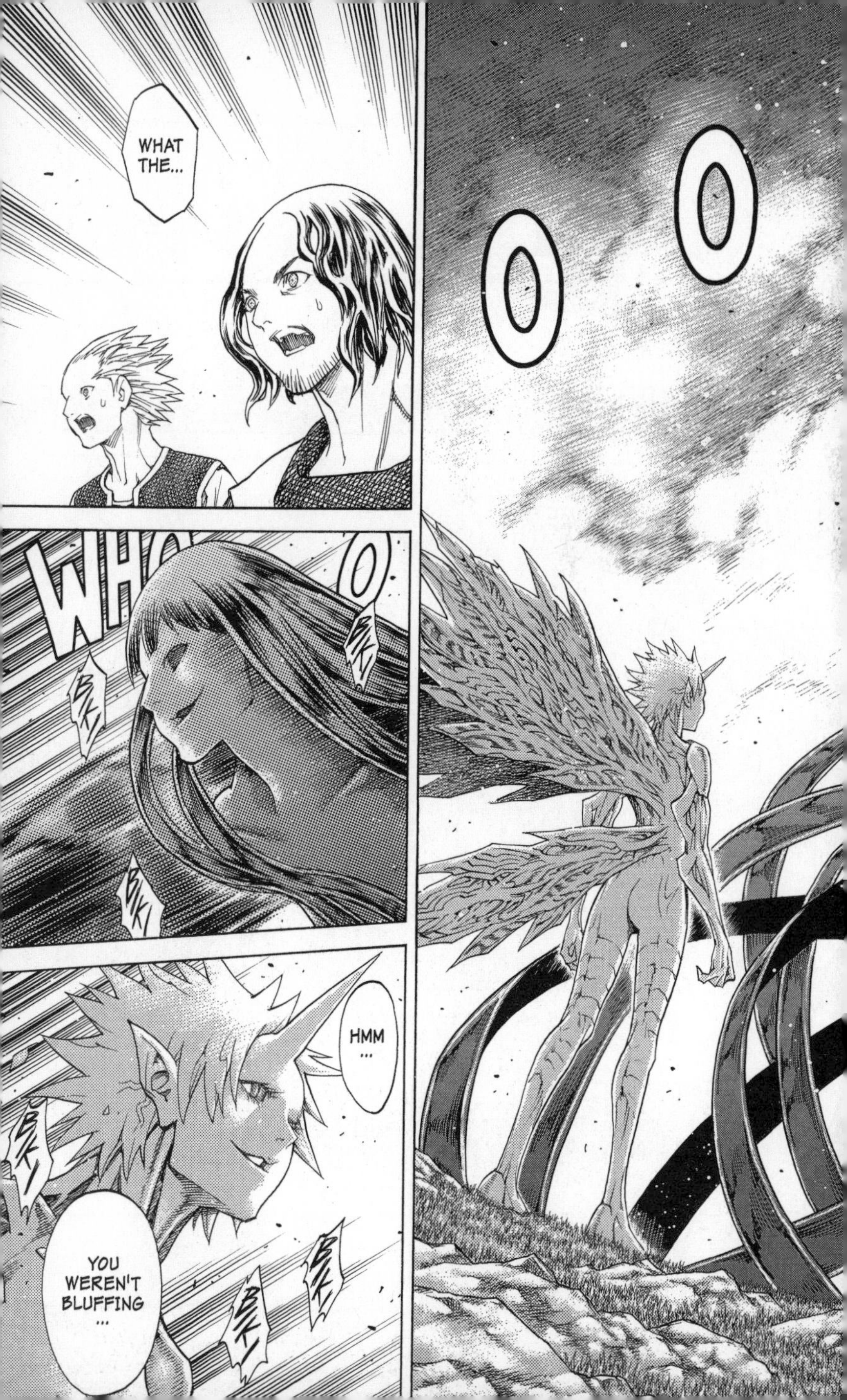
O O
WHAT THE...
WHO
O
BIKI
BIKI
BIKI
HMM ...
BIKI
YOU WEREN'T BLUFFING ...
BIKI
BIKI

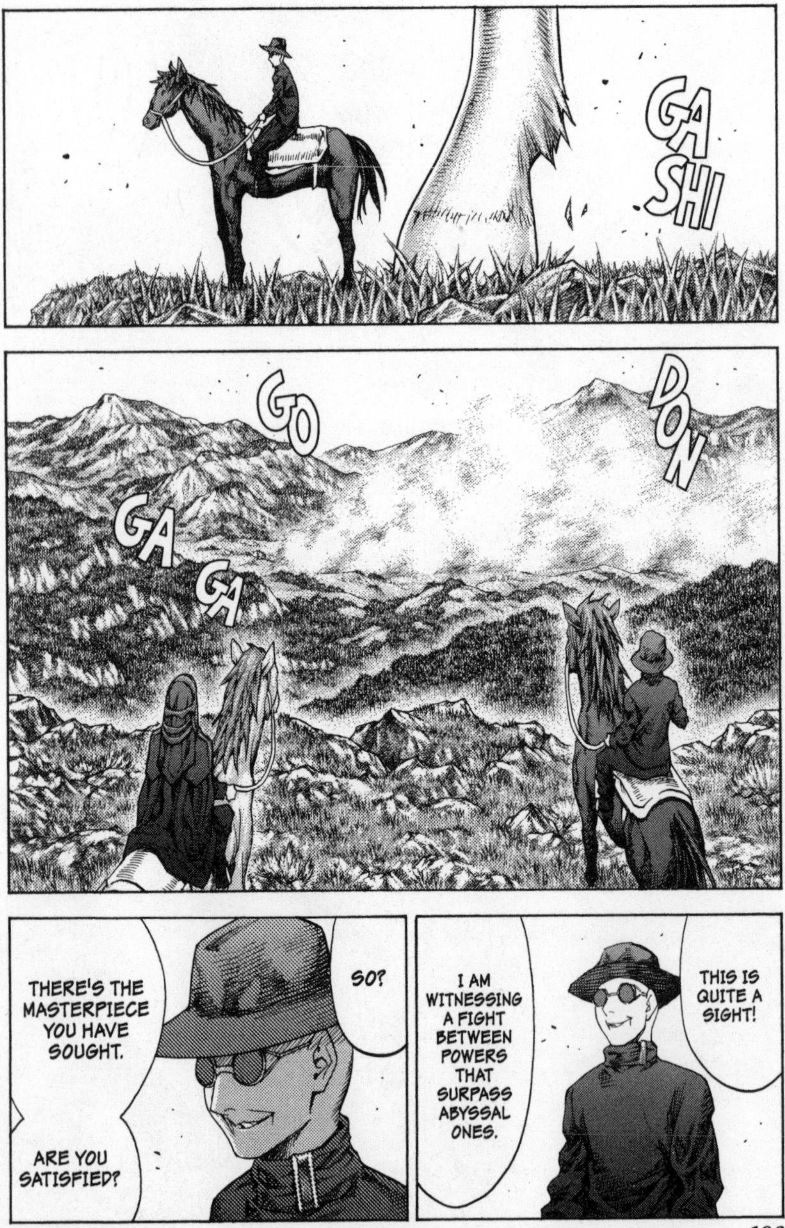
GA
SHI
DON
GO
GA
GA
THIS IS QUITE A SIGHT!
I AM WITNESSING A FIGHT BETWEEN POWERS THAT SURPASS ABYSSAL ONES.
SO?
THERE'S THE MASTERPIECE YOU HAVE SOUGHT.
ARE YOU SATISFIED?

READ THIS WAY

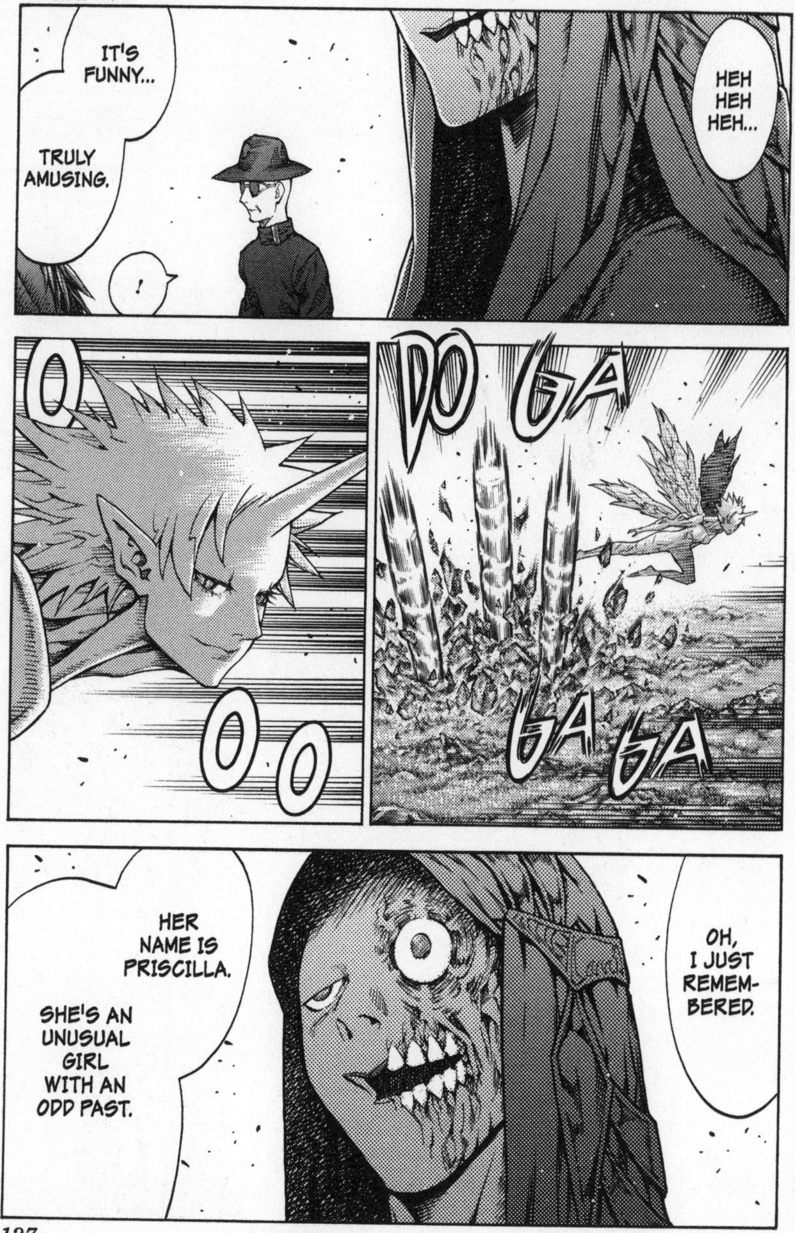
HEH HEH HEH...
IT'S FUNNY...
TRULY AMUSING.
!
DO GA
GA GA
O
O O
OH, I JUST REMEMBERED.
HER NAME IS PRISCILLA.
SHE'S AN UNUSUAL GIRL WITH AN ODD PAST.

クレイモア
Claymore

Scene 136: Army of the Underworld, Part 4

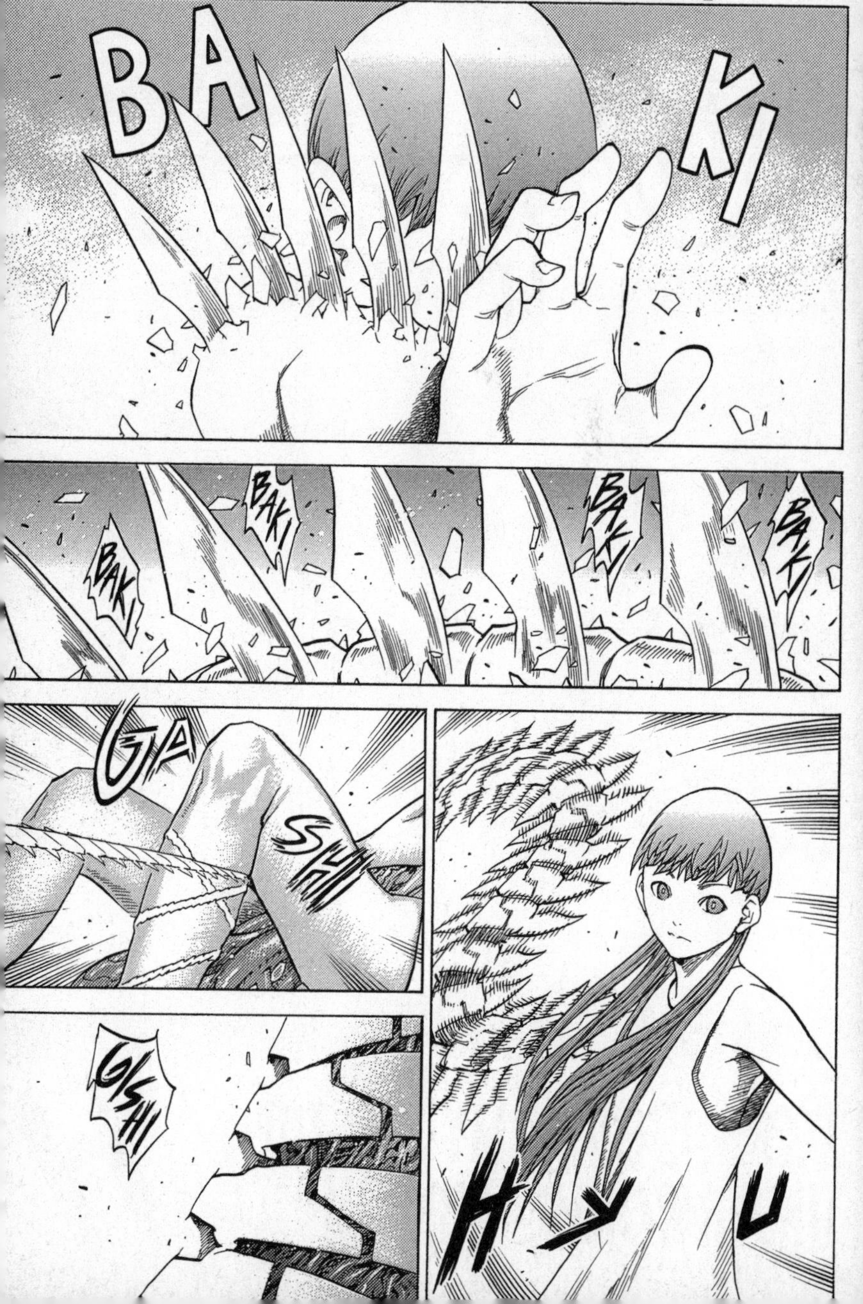
BAKI
BAKI
BAKI
BAKI
BAKI
HYU
GA
SSHI
GISHI

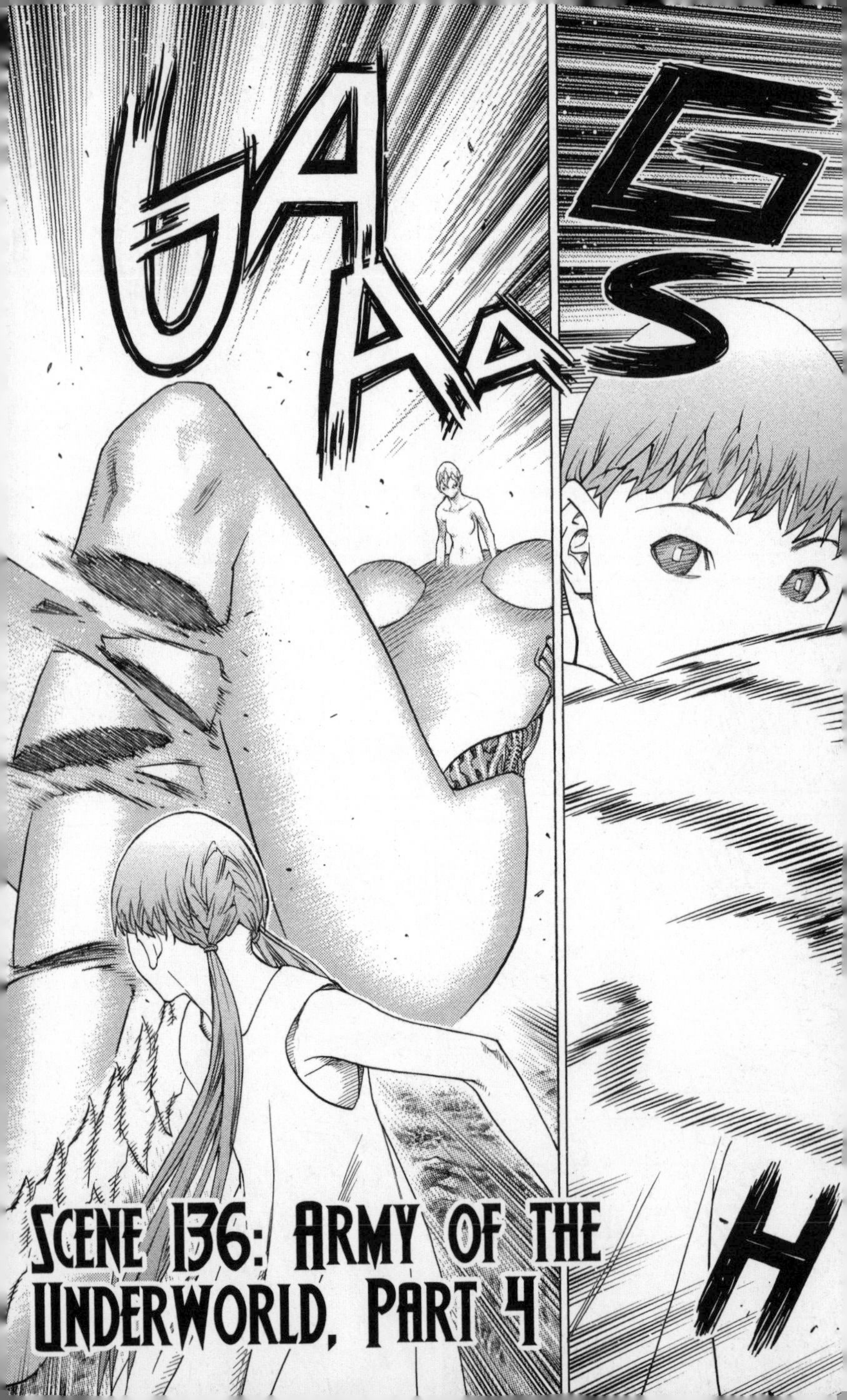
Scene 136: Army of the Underworld, Part 4

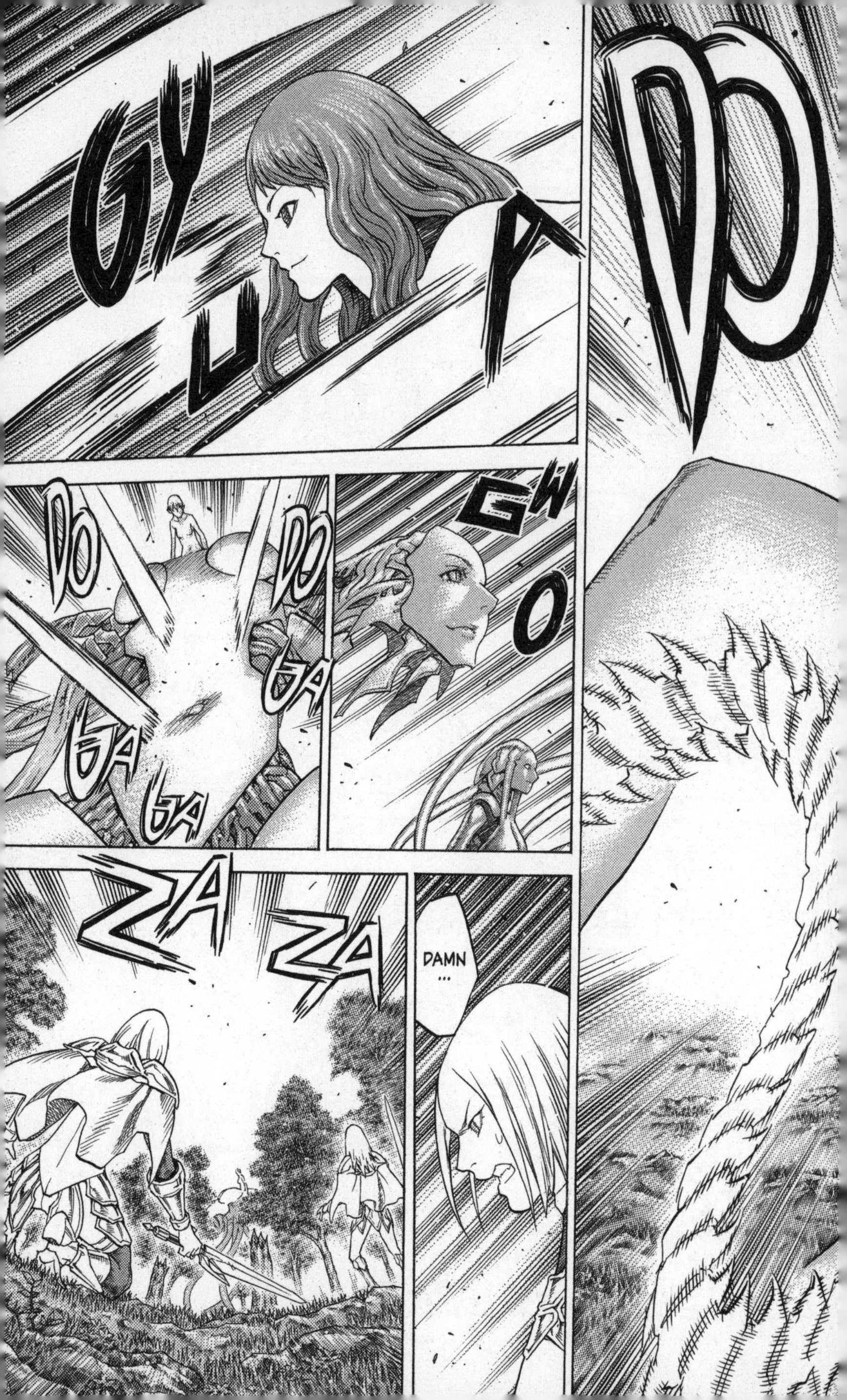
DO
GYUA
GWO
DO
DO
GA
GA
GA
GA
DAMN ...
ZA
ZA

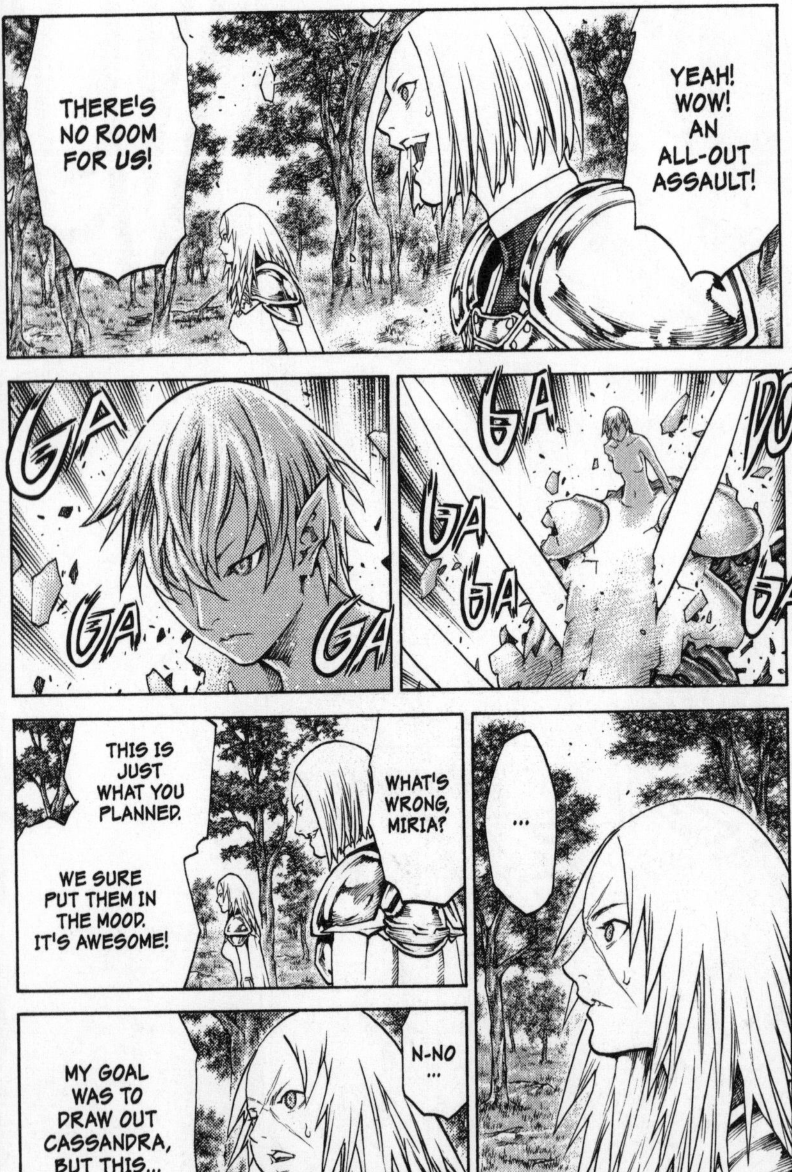
YEAH! WOW! AN ALL-OUT ASSAULT!
THERE'S NO ROOM FOR US!
GA
DO
GA
GA
GA
GA
GA
GA
...
WHAT'S WRONG, MIRIA?
THIS IS JUST WHAT YOU PLANNED.
WE SURE PUT THEM IN THE MOOD. IT'S AWESOME!
N-NO ...
MY GOAL WAS TO DRAW OUT CASSANDRA, BUT THIS...

READ THIS WAY

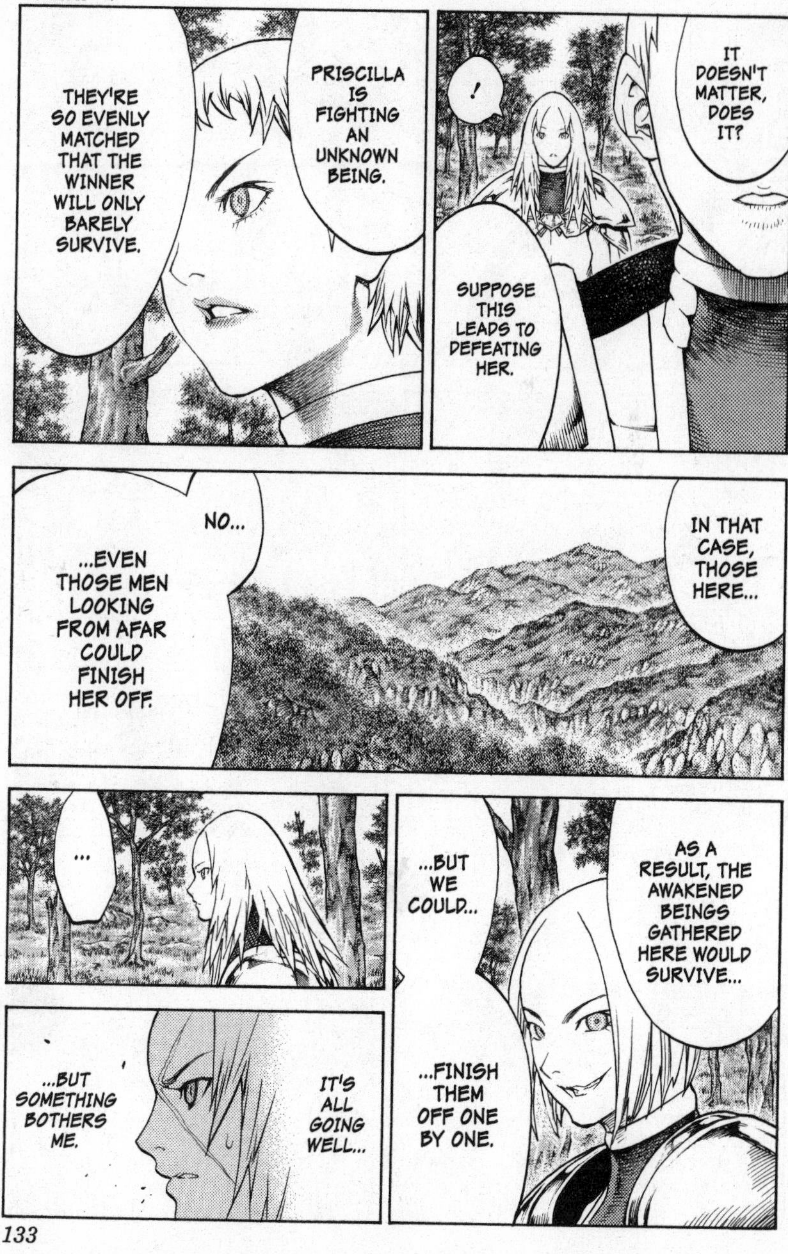
IT DOESN'T MATTER, DOES IT?
!
SUPPOSE THIS LEADS TO DEFEATING HER.
PRISCILLA IS FIGHTING AN UNKNOWN BEING.
THEY'RE SO EVENLY MATCHED THAT THE WINNER WILL ONLY BARELY SURVIVE.
IN THAT CASE, THOSE HERE...
NO...
...EVEN THOSE MEN LOOKING FROM AFAR COULD FINISH HER OFF.
AS A RESULT, THE AWAKENED BEINGS GATHERED HERE WOULD SURVIVE...
...BUT WE COULD...
...FINISH THEM OFF ONE BY ONE.
...
IT'S ALL GOING WELL...
...BUT SOMETHING BOTHERS ME.

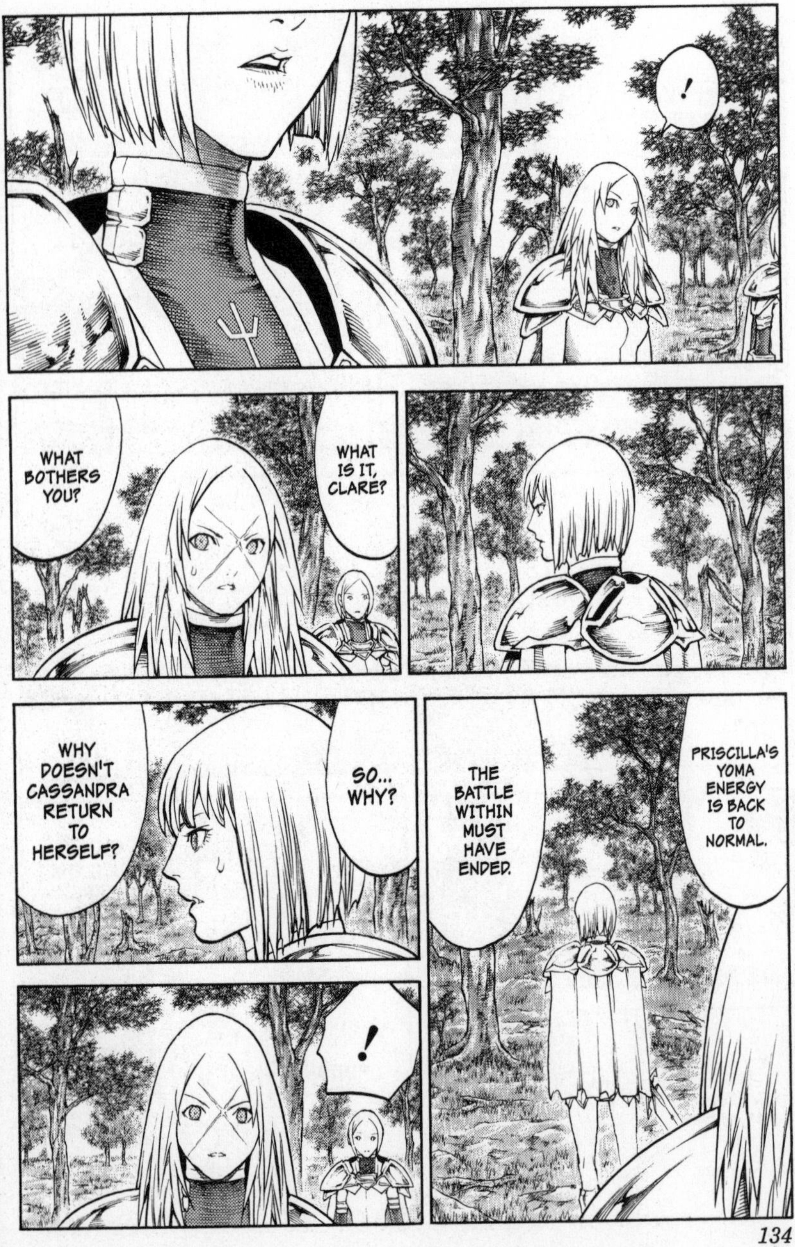
!
WHAT IS IT, CLARE?
WHAT BOTHERS YOU?
PRISCILLA'S YOMA ENERGY IS BACK TO NORMAL.
THE BATTLE WITHIN MUST HAVE ENDED.
SO... WHY?
WHY DOESN'T CASSANDRA RETURN TO HERSELF?
!

READ THIS WAY

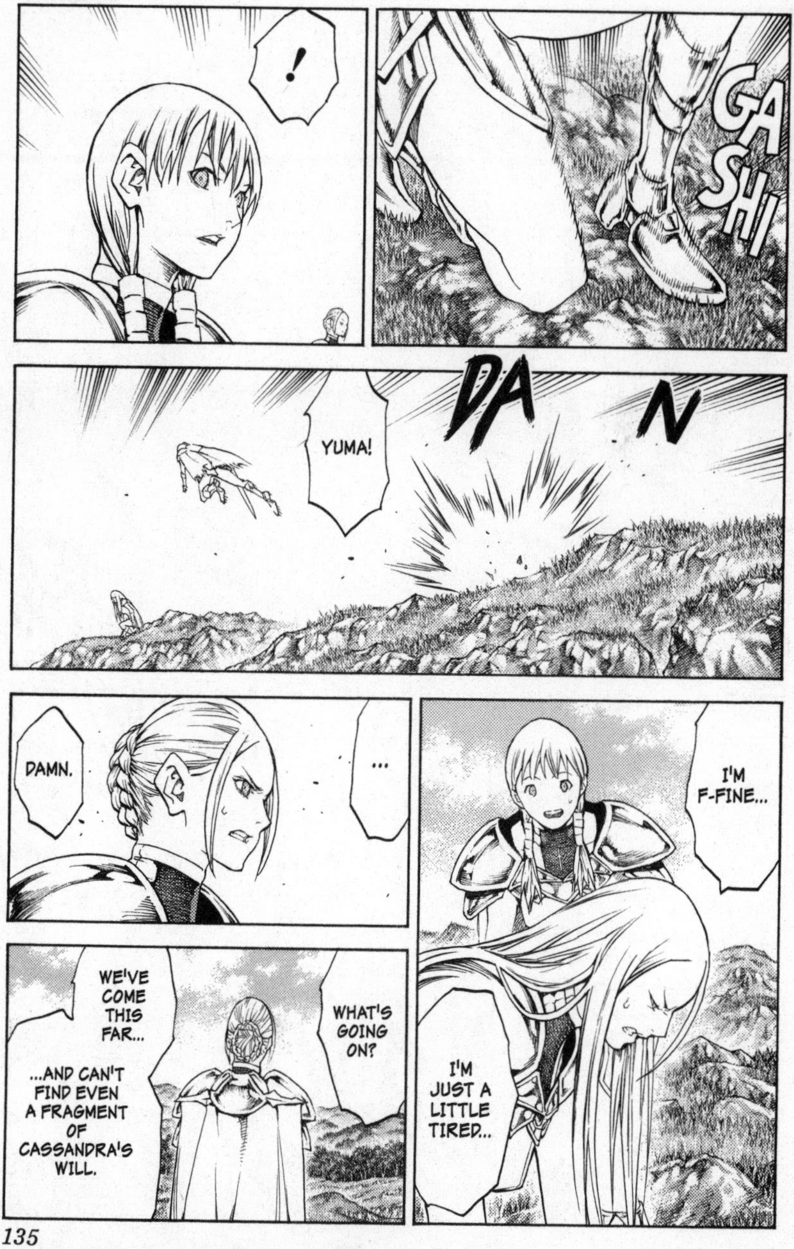

GASHI
!
DAN
YUMA!
I'M F-FINE...
I'M JUST A LITTLE TIRED...
...
DAMN.
WHAT'S GOING ON?
WE'VE COME THIS FAR...
...AND CAN'T FIND EVEN A FRAGMENT OF CASSANDRA'S WILL.

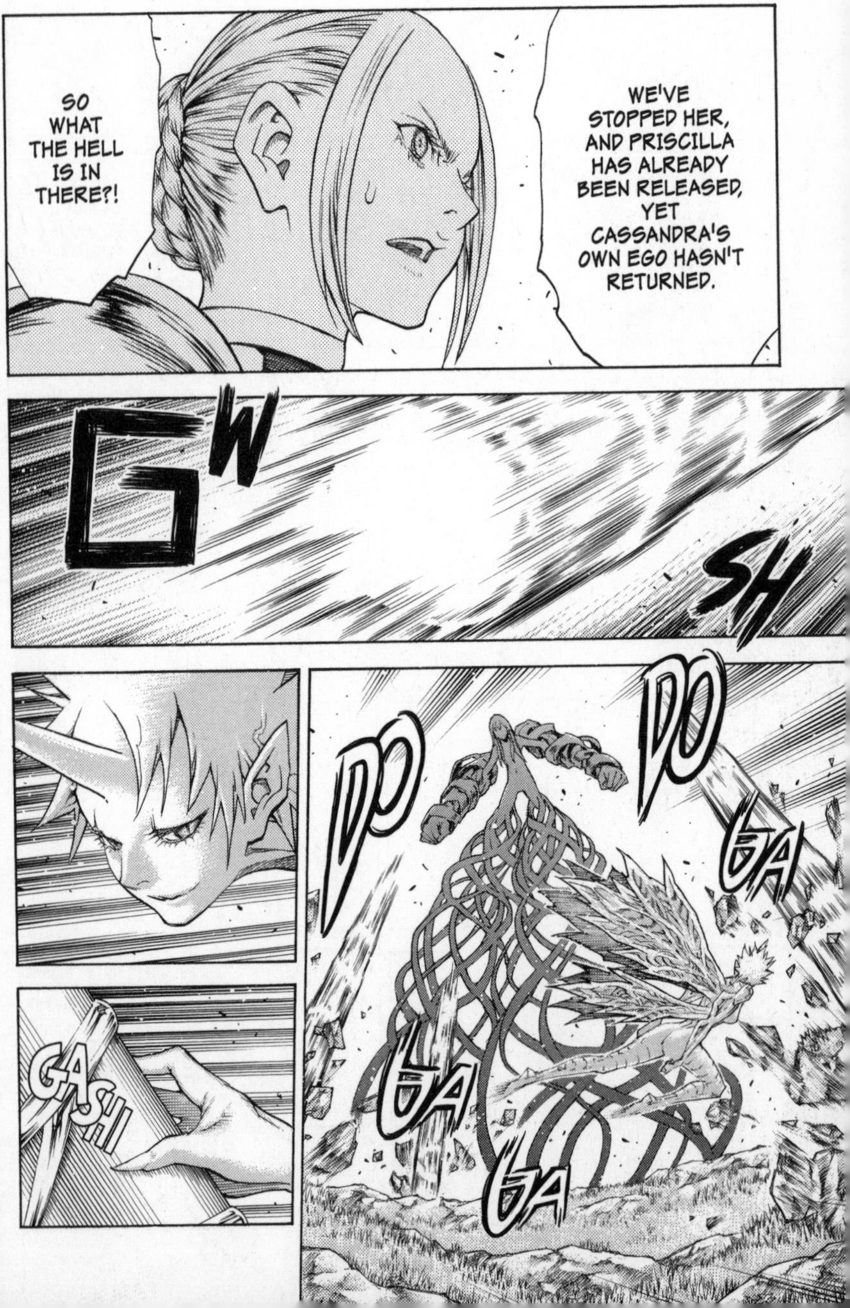
WE'VE STOPPED HER, AND PRISCILLA HAS ALREADY BEEN RELEASED, YET CASSANDRA'S OWN EGO HASN'T RETURNED.
SO WHAT THE HELL IS IN THERE?!
GW
SH
DO
DO
GA
GA
GA
GASHI

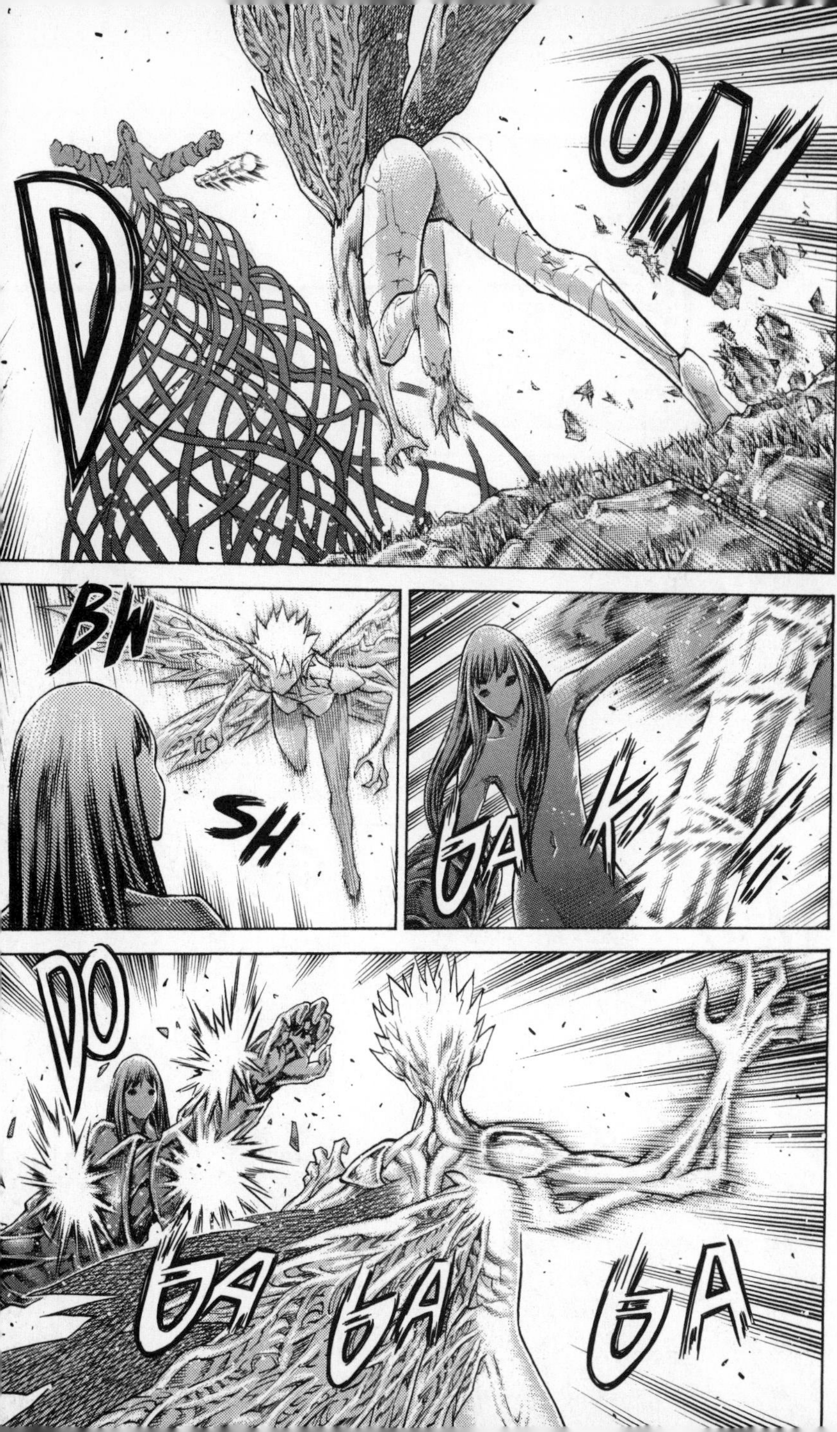
D ON
GA K
BW
SH
DO
GA GA GA

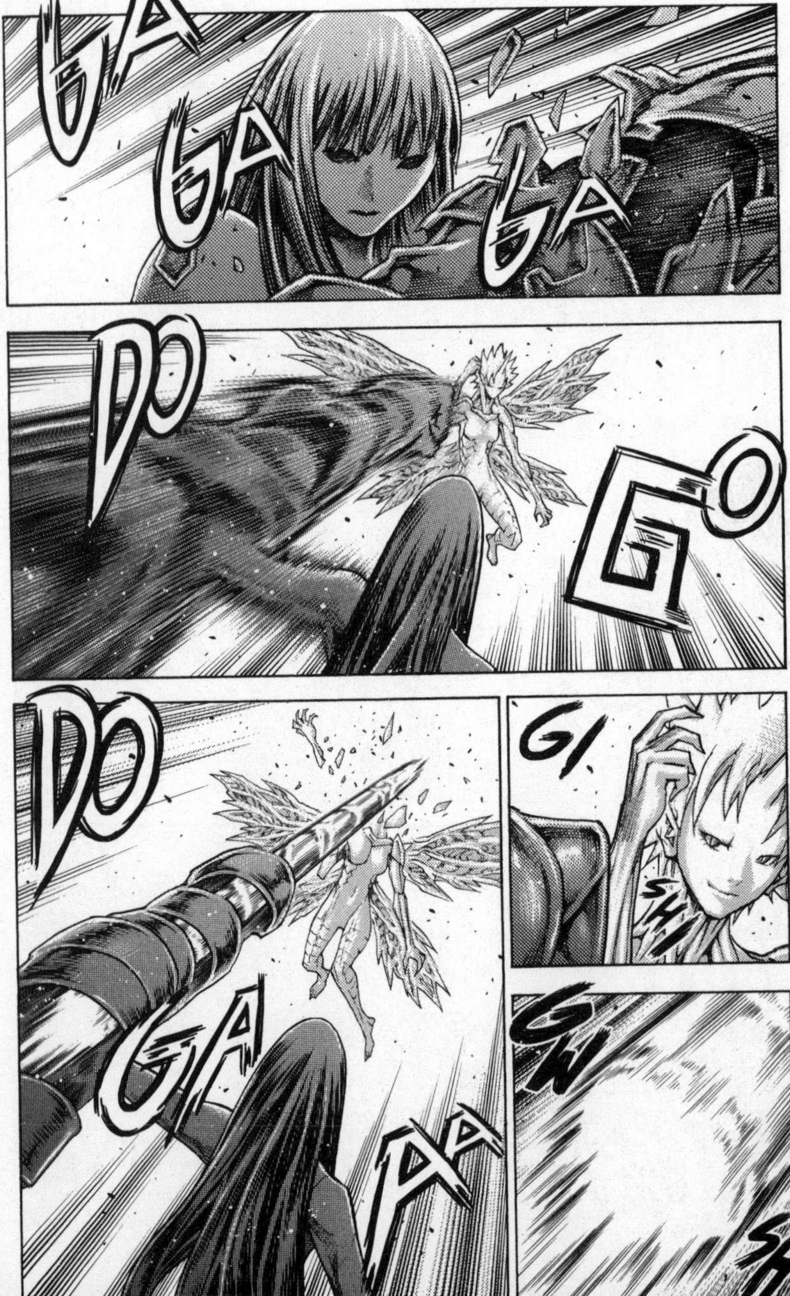
GA
GA
GA
DO
GO
GI
SHI
GW
SH
DO
GA
AA

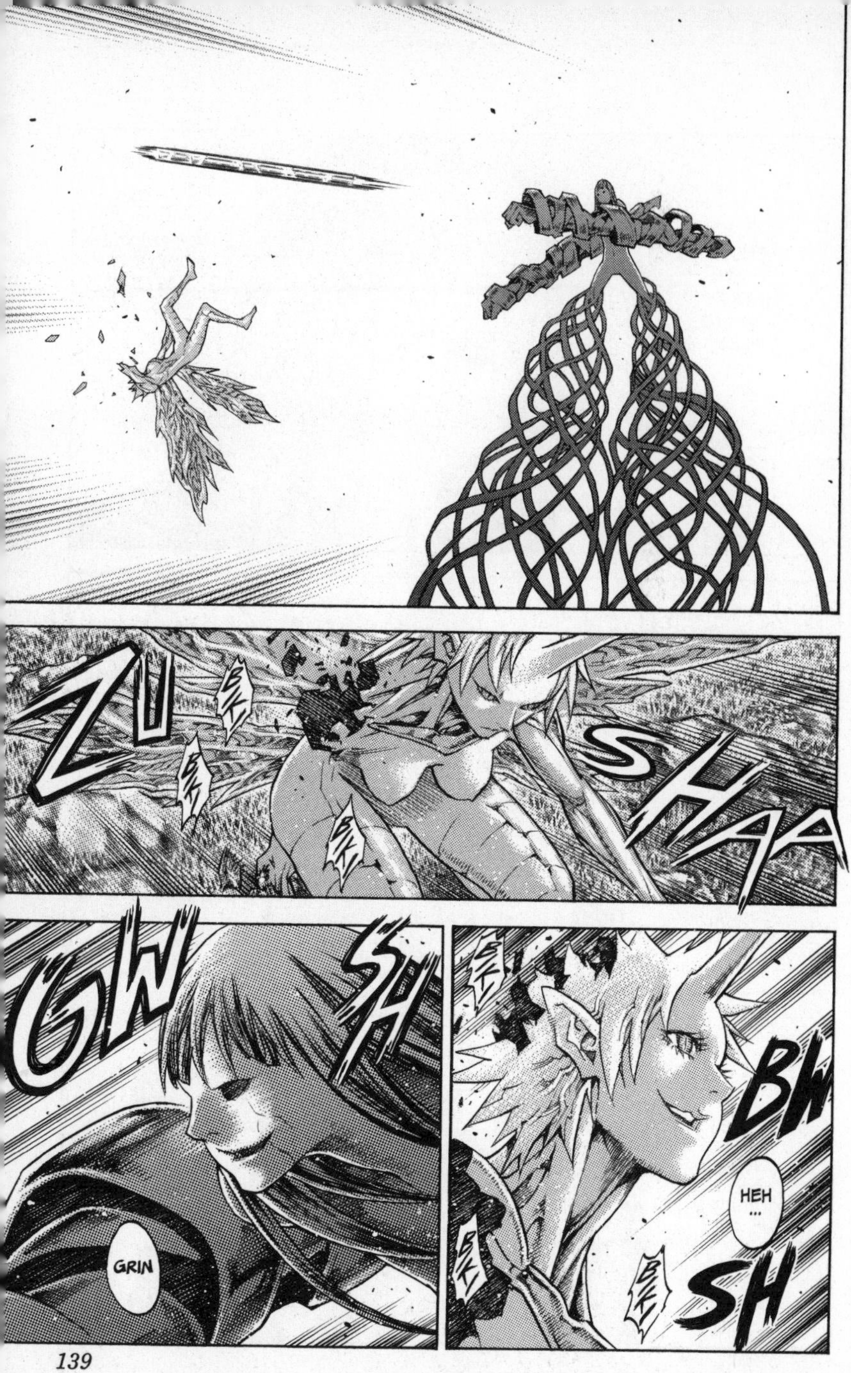
SHAA
BKI
BKI
BKI
ZU
BW
HEH...
SH
BKI
BKI
SH
GW
GRIN

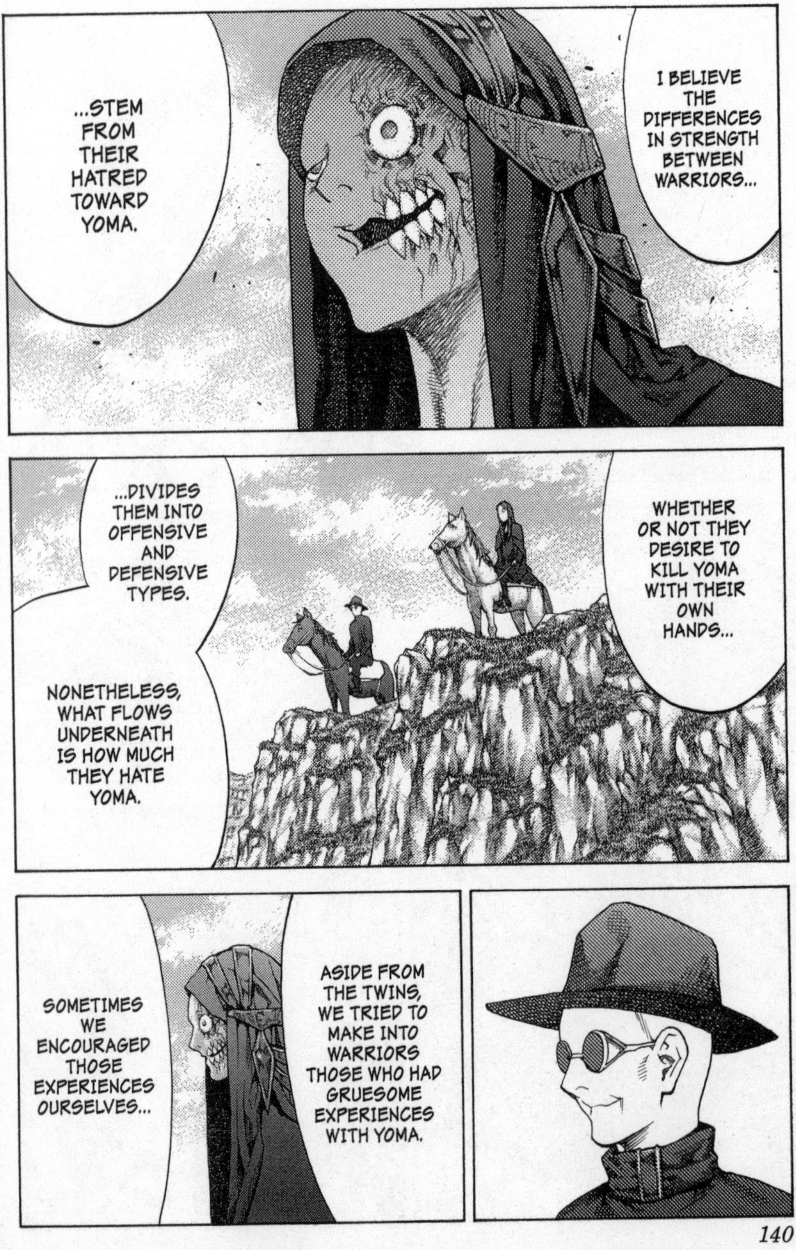
I BELIEVE THE DIFFERENCES IN STRENGTH BETWEEN WARRIORS...
...STEM FROM THEIR HATRED TOWARD YOMA.
WHETHER OR NOT THEY DESIRE TO KILL YOMA WITH THEIR OWN HANDS...
...DIVIDES THEM INTO OFFENSIVE AND DEFENSIVE TYPES.
NONETHELESS, WHAT FLOWS UNDERNEATH IS HOW MUCH THEY HATE YOMA.
ASIDE FROM THE TWINS, WE TRIED TO MAKE INTO WARRIORS THOSE WHO HAD GRUESOME EXPERIENCES WITH YOMA.
SOMETIMES WE ENCOURAGED THOSE EXPERIENCES OURSELVES...

READ THIS WAY

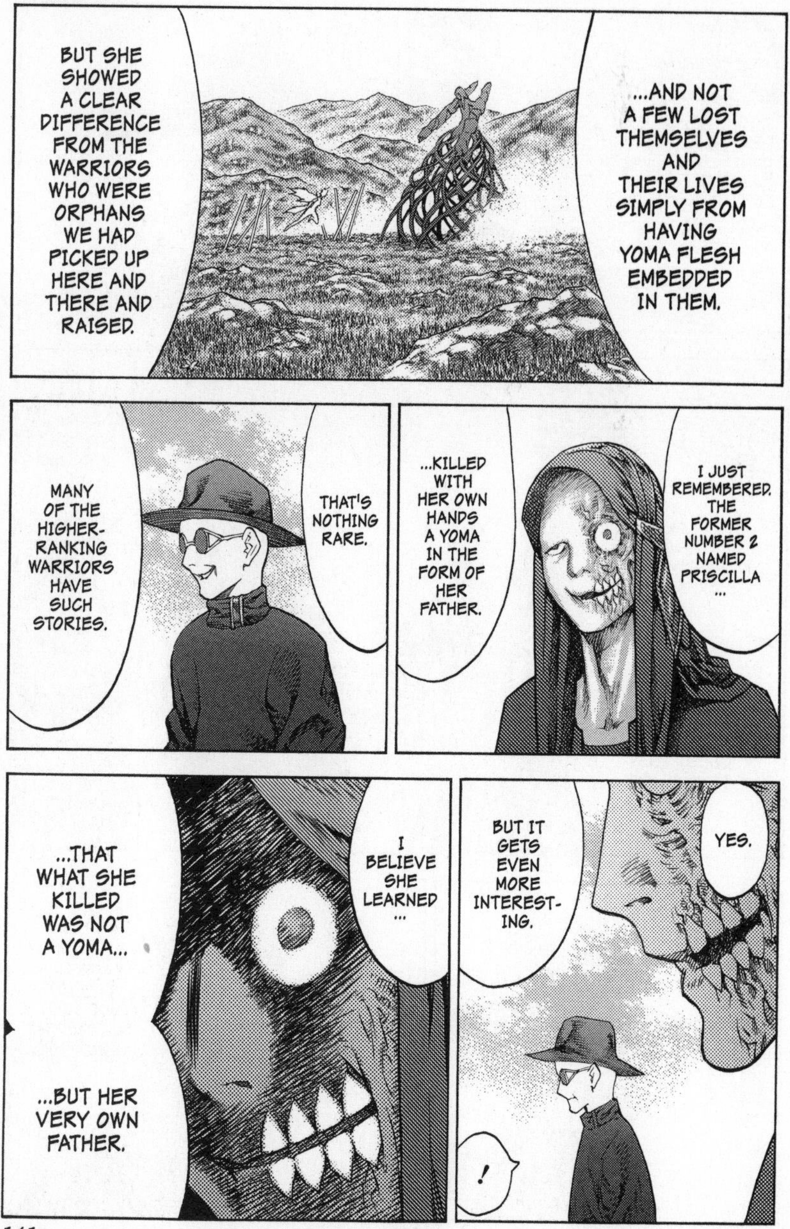
...AND NOT A FEW LOST THEMSELVES AND THEIR LIVES SIMPLY FROM HAVING YOMA FLESH EMBEDDED IN THEM.
BUT SHE SHOWED A CLEAR DIFFERENCE FROM THE WARRIORS WHO WERE ORPHANS WE HAD PICKED UP HERE AND THERE AND RAISED.
I JUST REMEMBERED. THE FORMER NUMBER 2 NAMED PRISCILLA...
...KILLED WITH HER OWN HANDS A YOMA IN THE FORM OF HER FATHER.
THAT'S NOTHING RARE.
MANY OF THE HIGHER-RANKING WARRIORS HAVE SUCH STORIES.
YES.
BUT IT GETS EVEN MORE INTEREST-ING.
!
I BELIEVE SHE LEARNED...
...THAT WHAT SHE KILLED WAS NOT A YOMA...
...BUT HER VERY OWN FATHER.

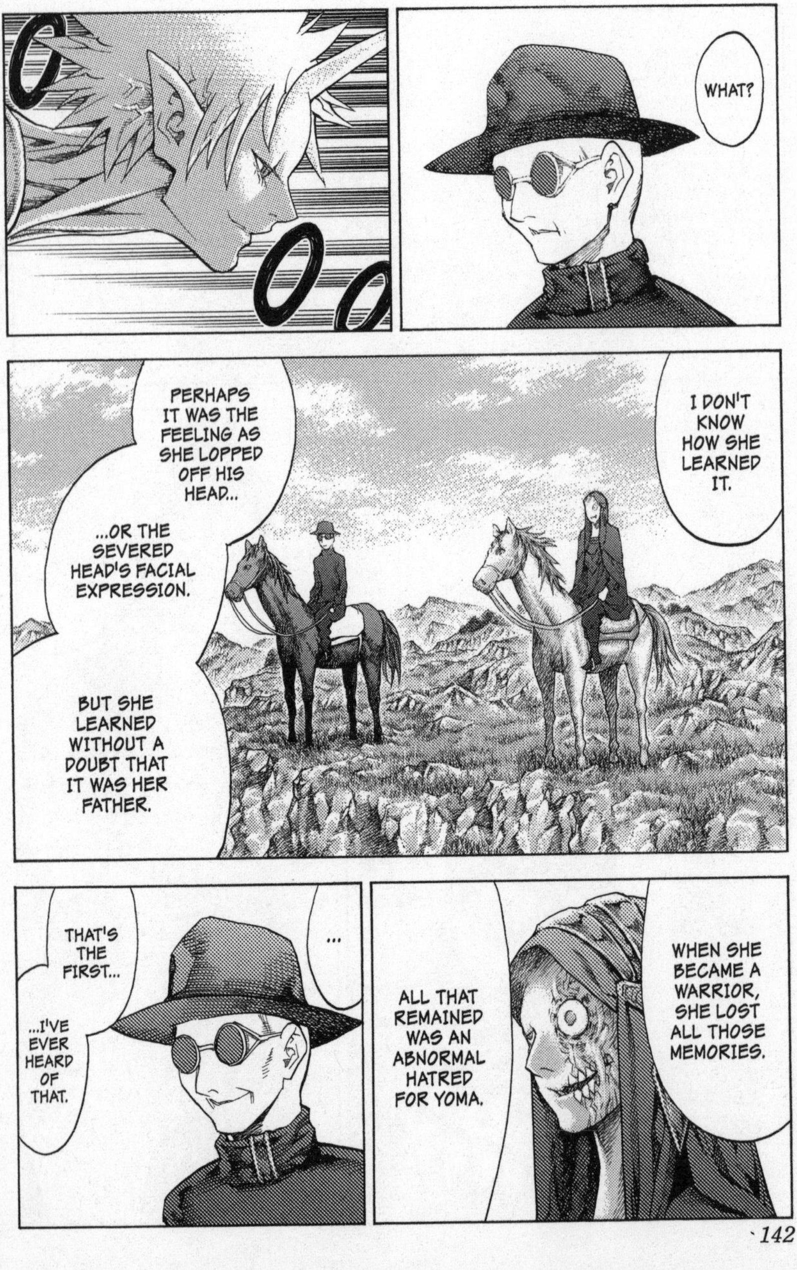
WHAT?
I DON'T KNOW HOW SHE LEARNED IT.
PERHAPS IT WAS THE FEELING AS SHE LOPPED OFF HIS HEAD...
...OR THE SEVERED HEAD'S FACIAL EXPRESSION.
BUT SHE LEARNED WITHOUT A DOUBT THAT IT WAS HER FATHER.
WHEN SHE BECAME A WARRIOR, SHE LOST ALL THOSE MEMORIES.
ALL THAT REMAINED WAS AN ABNORMAL HATRED FOR YOMA.
...
THAT'S THE FIRST...
...I'VE EVER HEARD OF THAT.

THEY HAVE AN EXTREME HATRED FOR YOMA...

...YET THEY CARRY YOMA WITHIN THEIR BODIES.

THE WARRIOR'S HATRED FOR YOMA AND DISGUST FOR HERSELF...

...ARE THE FOUNT OF AN INHUMAN AND TWISTED STRENGTH.

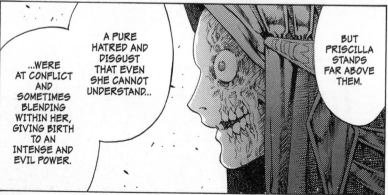

BUT PRISCILLA STANDS FAR ABOVE THEM.

A PURE HATRED AND DISGUST THAT EVEN SHE CANNOT UNDERSTAND...

...WERE AT CONFLICT AND SOMETIMES BLENDING WITHIN HER, GIVING BIRTH TO AN INTENSE AND EVIL POWER.

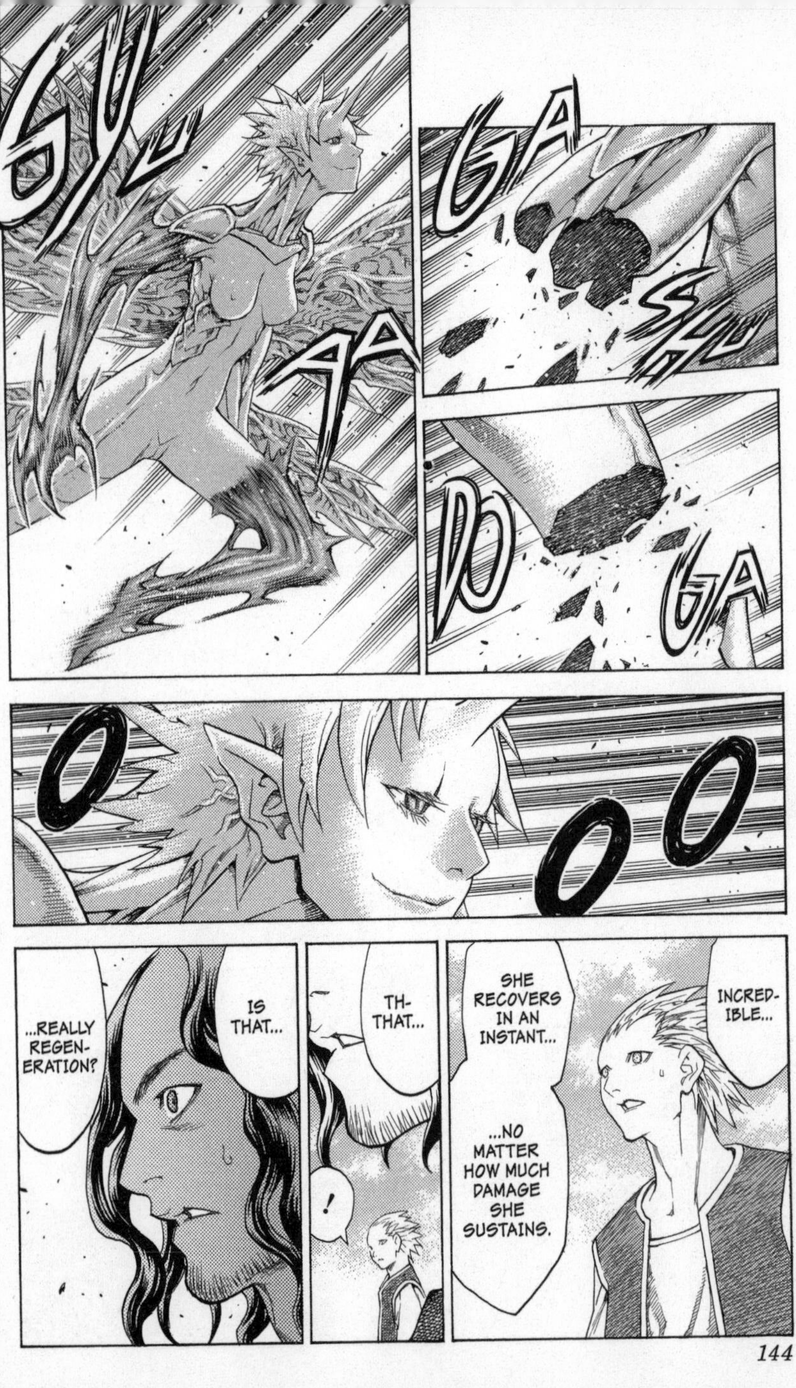
GASHU
DOGA
GYUAA
OOOO
INCRED-IBLE...
SHE RECOVERS IN AN INSTANT...
...NO MATTER HOW MUCH DAMAGE SHE SUSTAINS.
TH-THAT...
!
IS THAT...
...REALLY REGENER-ATION?

READ THIS WAY

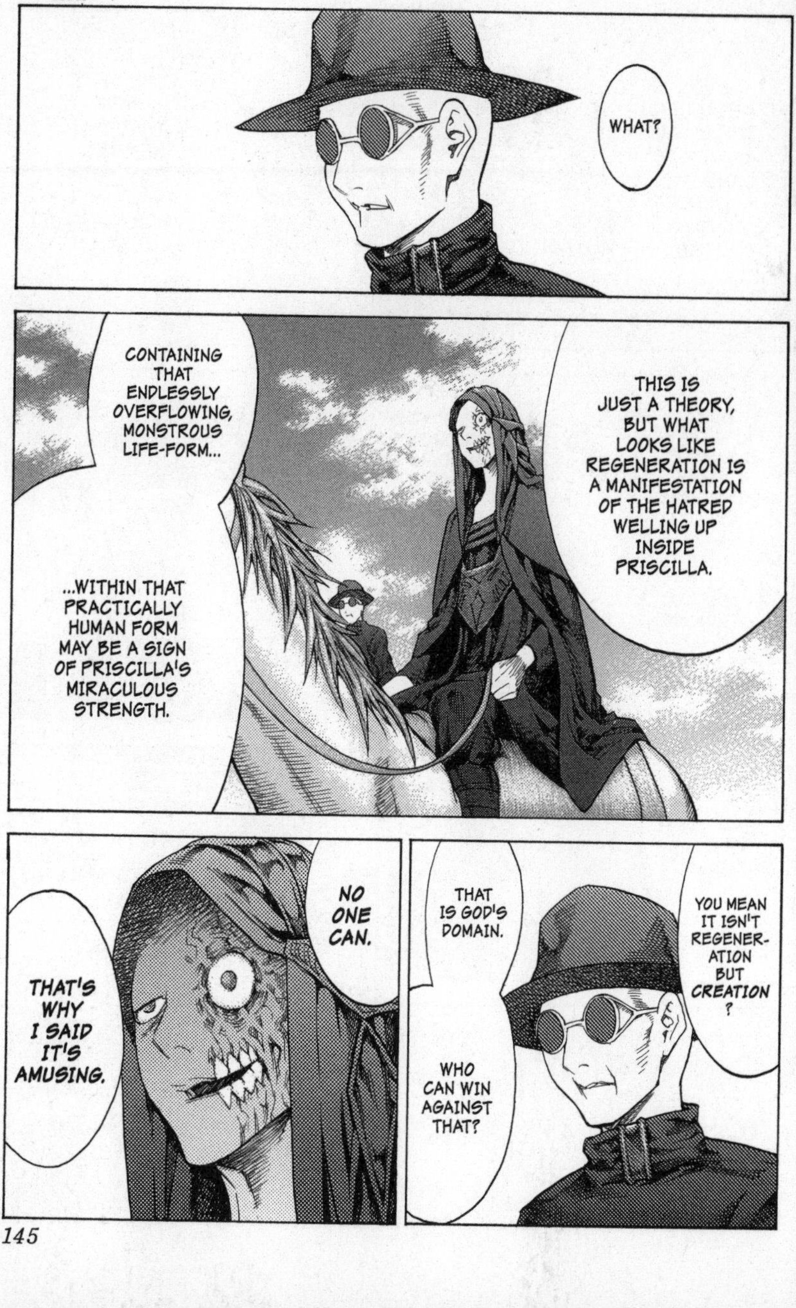
WHAT?
THIS IS JUST A THEORY, BUT WHAT LOOKS LIKE REGENERATION IS A MANIFESTATION OF THE HATRED WELLING UP INSIDE PRISCILLA.
CONTAINING THAT ENDLESSLY OVERFLOWING, MONSTROUS LIFE-FORM...
...WITHIN THAT PRACTICALLY HUMAN FORM MAY BE A SIGN OF PRISCILLA'S MIRACULOUS STRENGTH.
YOU MEAN IT ISN'T REGENER-ATION BUT CREATION?
THAT IS GOD'S DOMAIN.
WHO CAN WIN AGAINST THAT?
NO ONE CAN.
THAT'S WHY I SAID IT'S AMUSING.

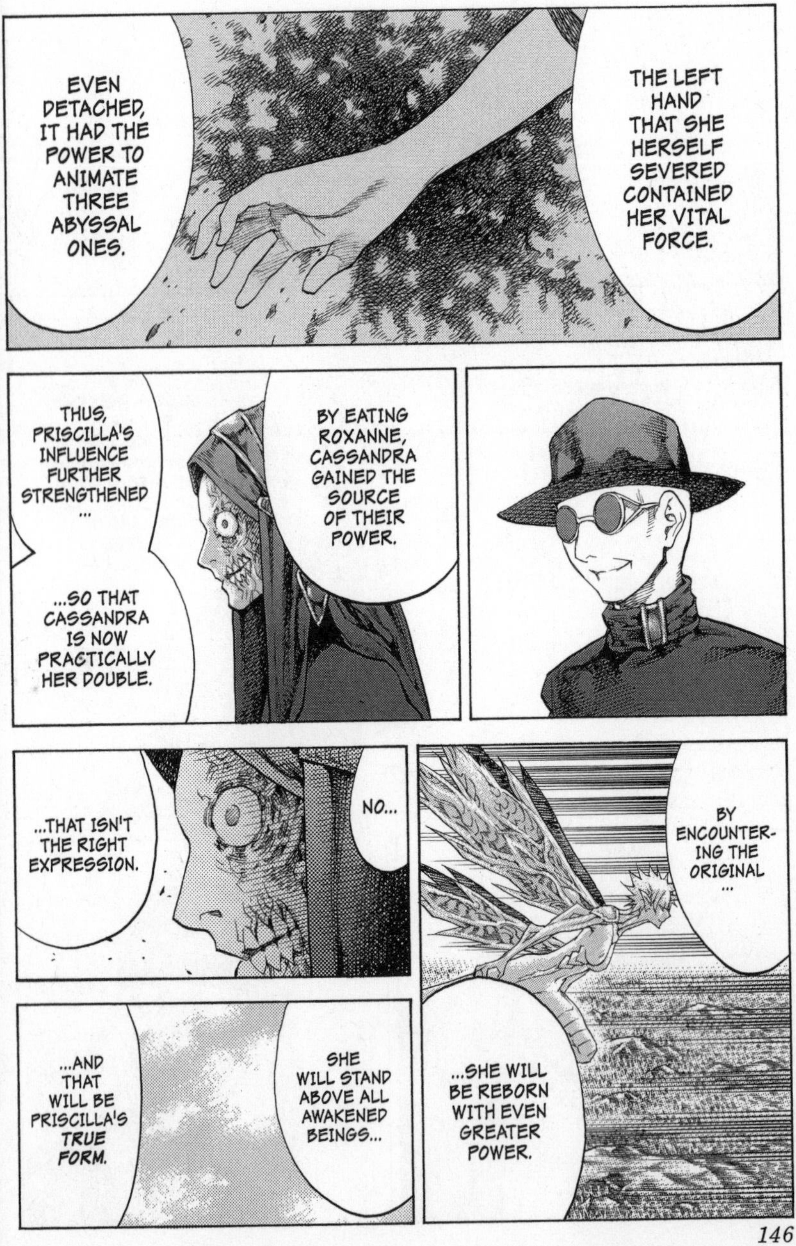
THE LEFT HAND THAT SHE HERSELF SEVERED CONTAINED HER VITAL FORCE.
EVEN DETACHED, IT HAD THE POWER TO ANIMATE THREE ABYSSAL ONES.
BY EATING ROXANNE, CASSANDRA GAINED THE SOURCE OF THEIR POWER.
THUS, PRISCILLA'S INFLUENCE FURTHER STRENGTHENED ...
...SO THAT CASSANDRA IS NOW PRACTICALLY HER DOUBLE.
BY ENCOUNTER-ING THE ORIGINAL ...
...SHE WILL BE REBORN WITH EVEN GREATER POWER.
NO...
...THAT ISN'T THE RIGHT EXPRESSION.
SHE WILL STAND ABOVE ALL AWAKENED BEINGS...
...AND THAT WILL BE PRISCILLA'S *TRUE FORM.*

READ THIS WAY

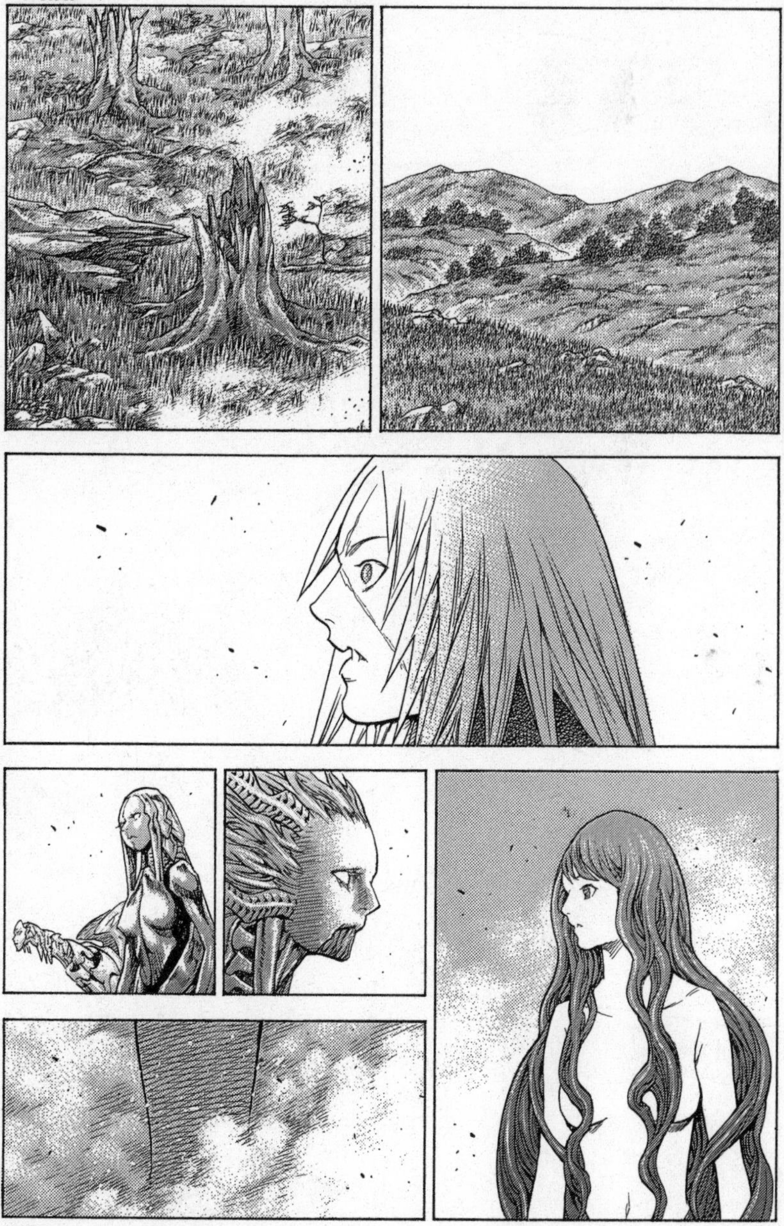

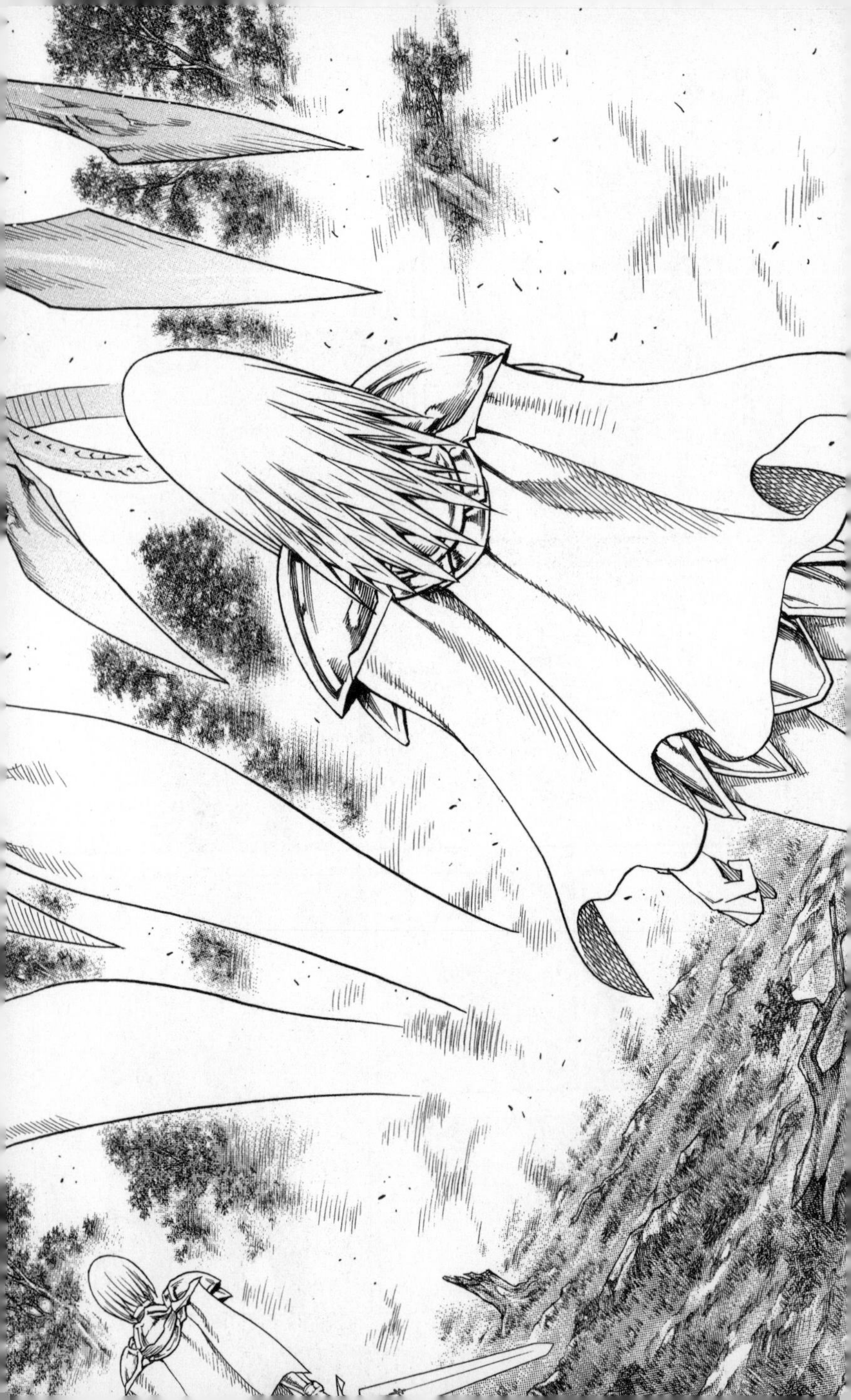

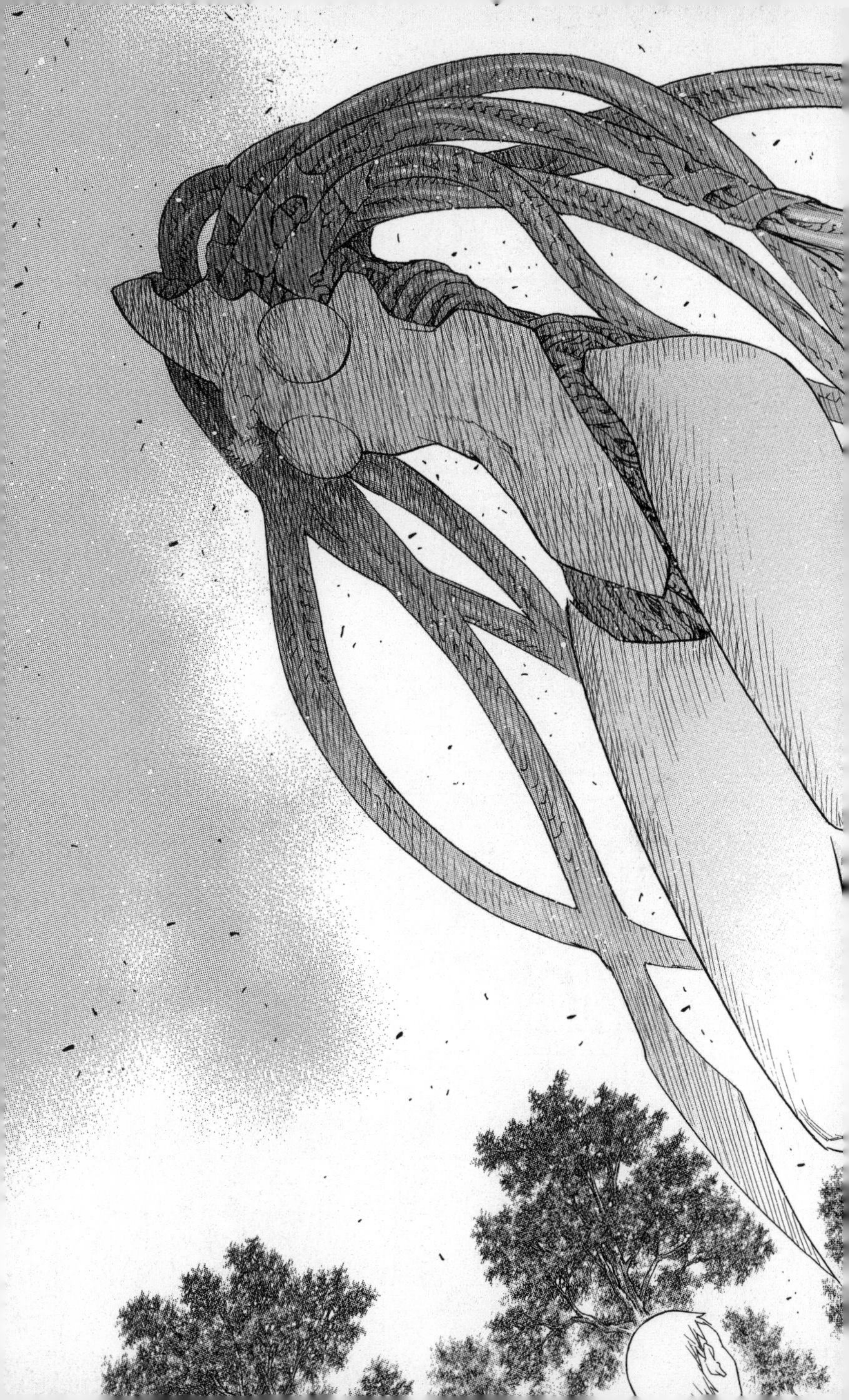

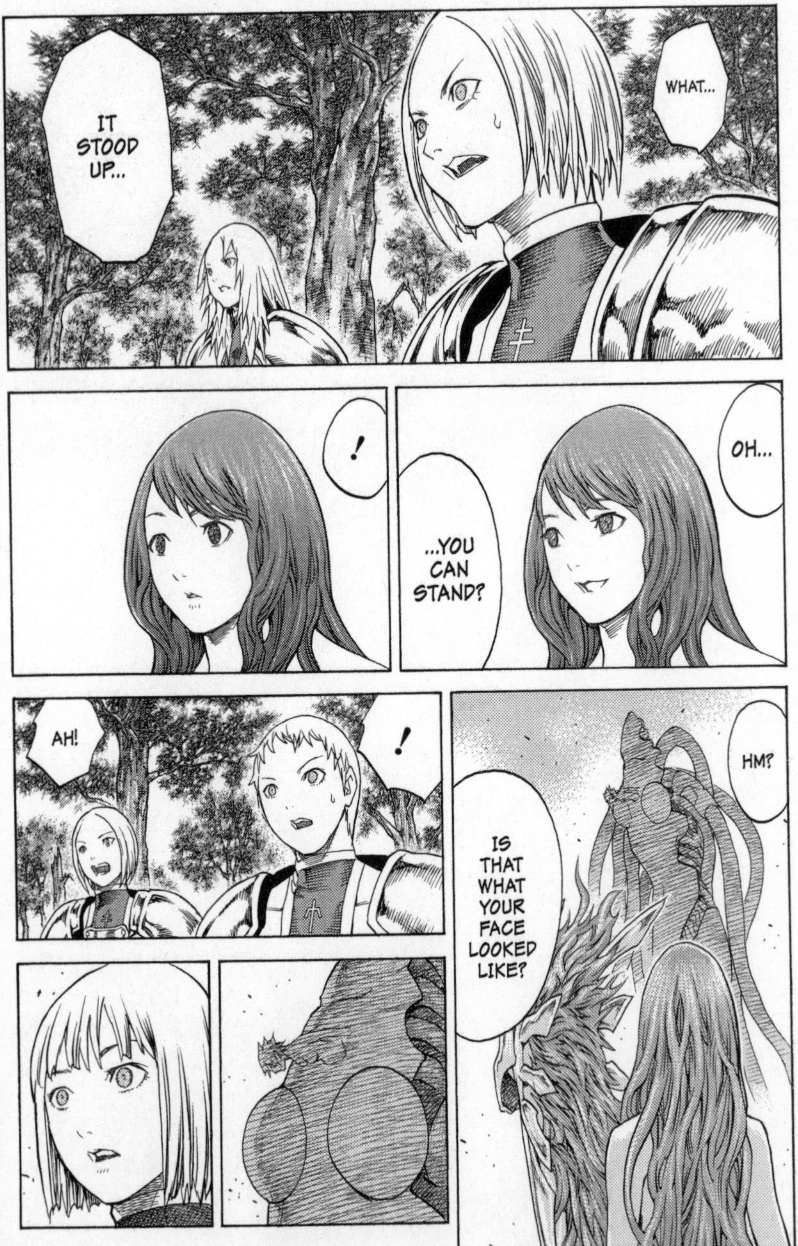
WHAT...
IT STOOD UP...
OH...
...YOU CAN STAND?
!
HM?
IS THAT WHAT YOUR FACE LOOKED LIKE?
!
AH!

BIKI
BIKI
BIKI
BIKI
BIKI
BIKI
BIKI
BIKI
BIKI

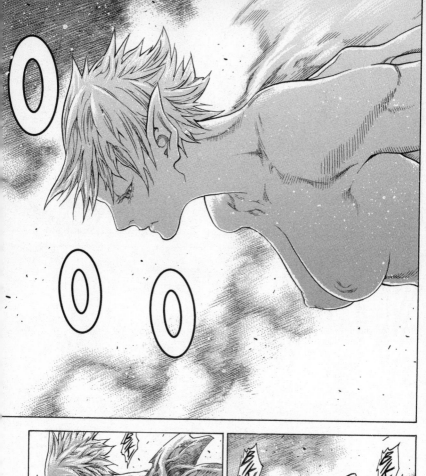

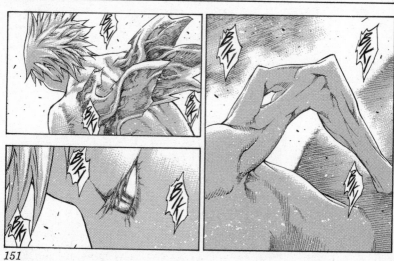

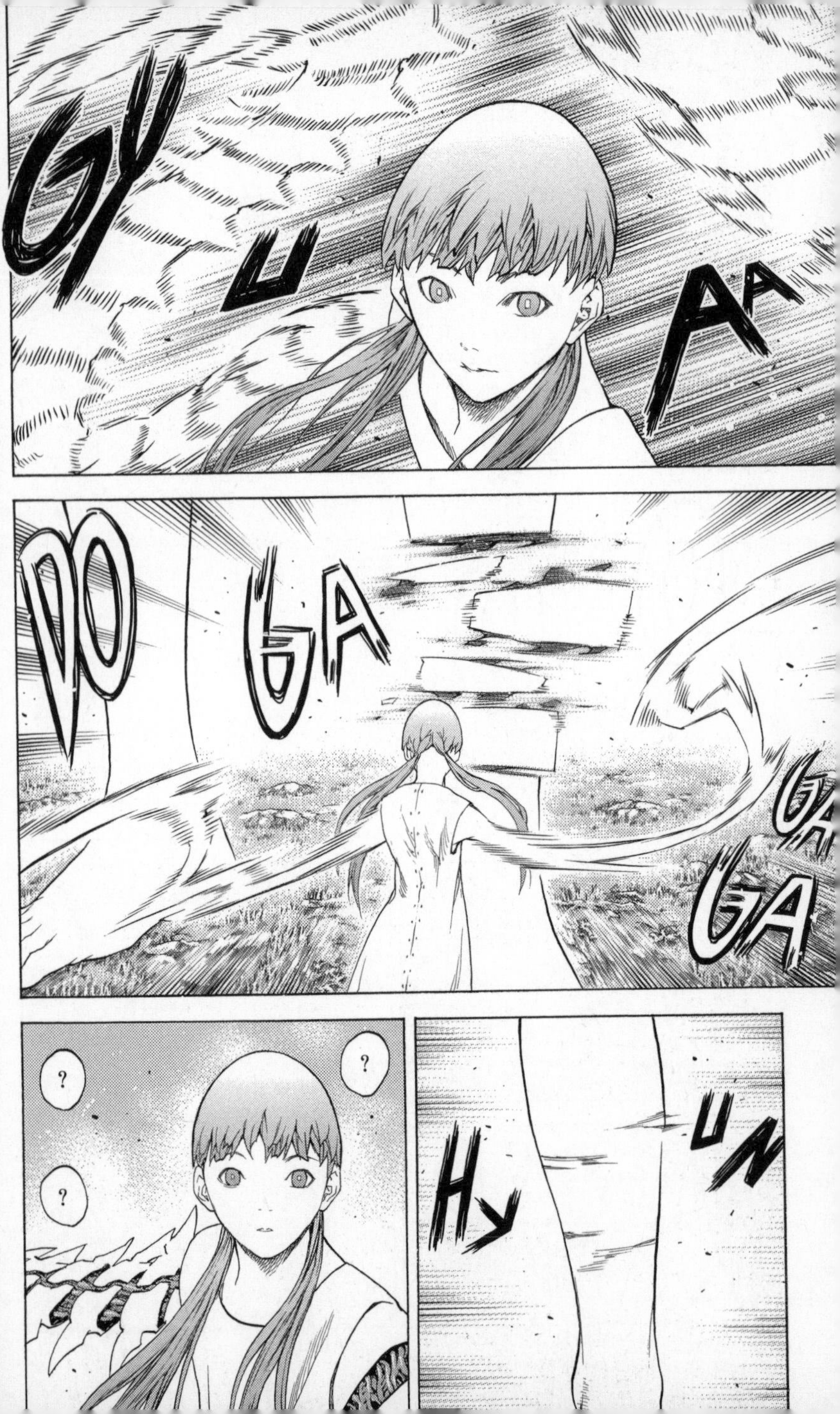
GYUAA
DOGA
GAGA
HYUN
?
?
?

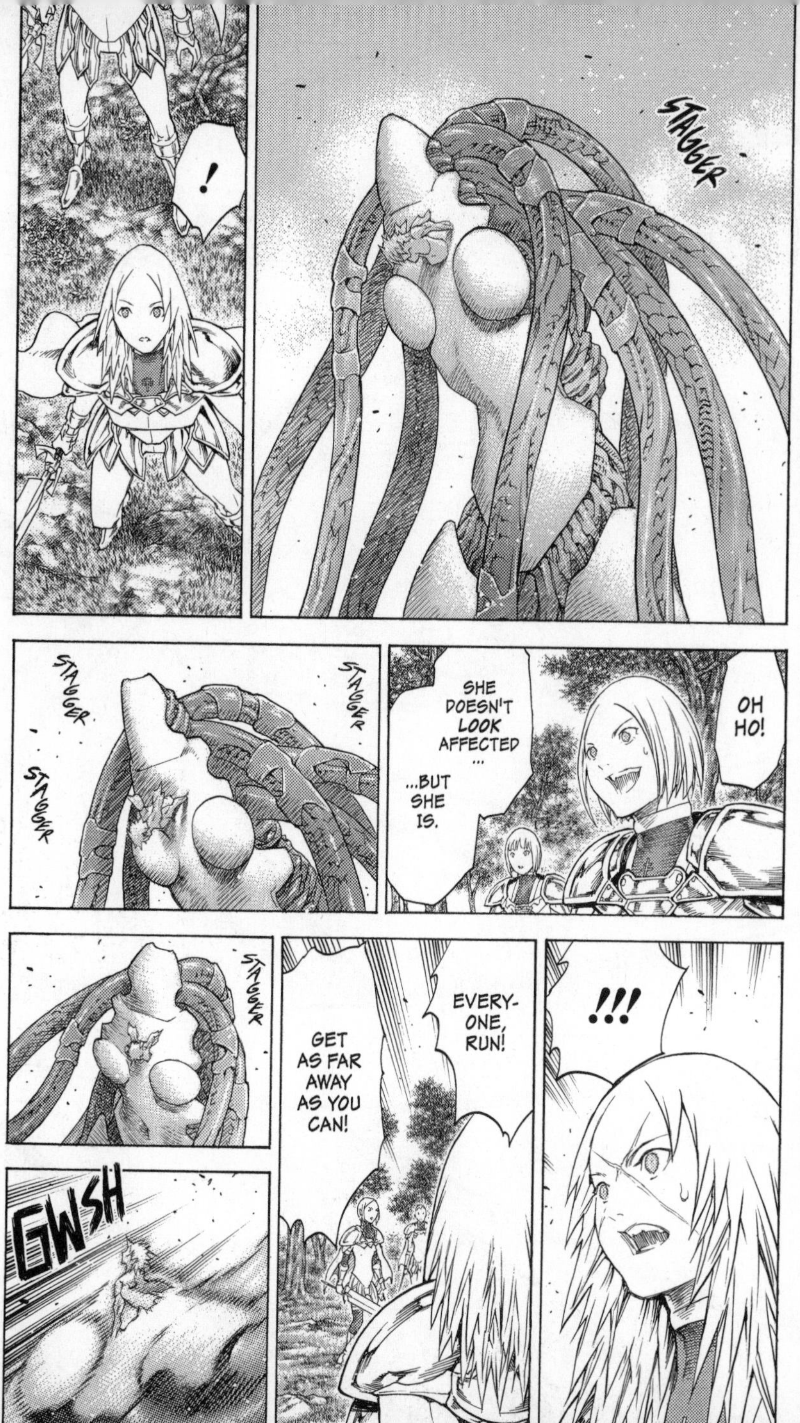
STAGGER
!
OH HO!
SHE DOESN'T LOOK AFFECTED...
...BUT SHE IS.
STAGGER
STAGGER
STAGGER
!!!
EVERY-ONE, RUN!
GET AS FAR AWAY AS YOU CAN!
STAGGER
GWSH

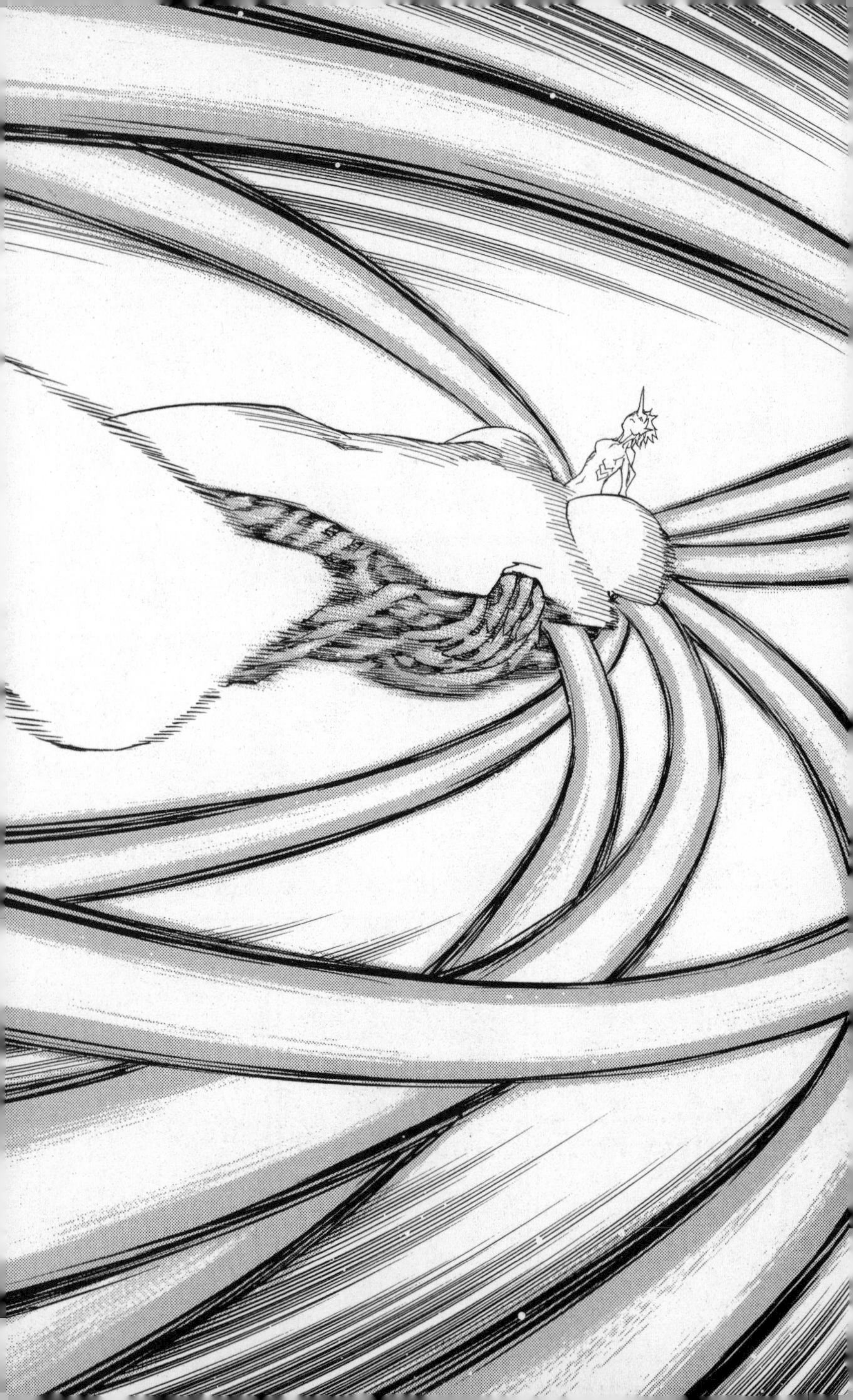

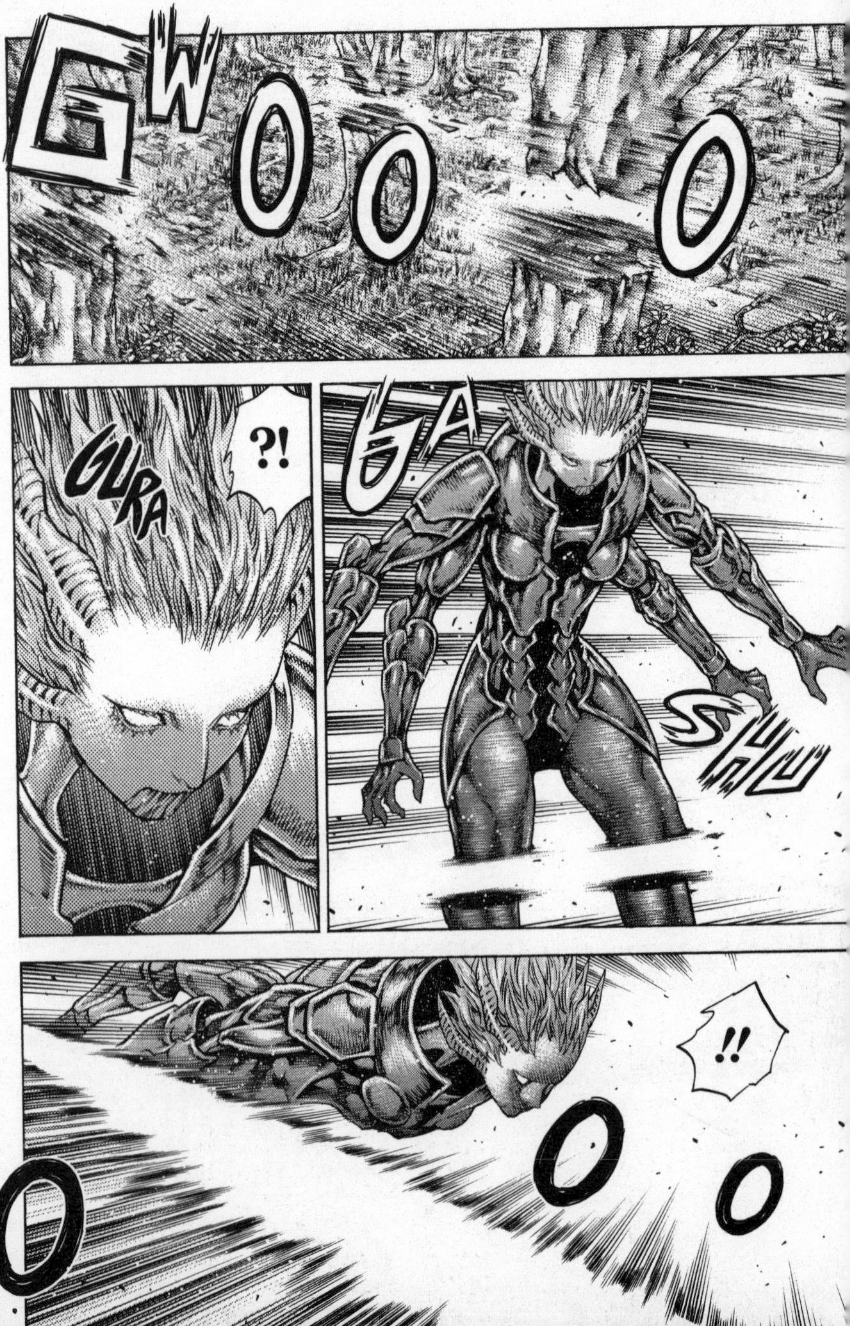
GWOOO
GA
SHU
GURA
?!
!!
OOO

READ THIS WAY

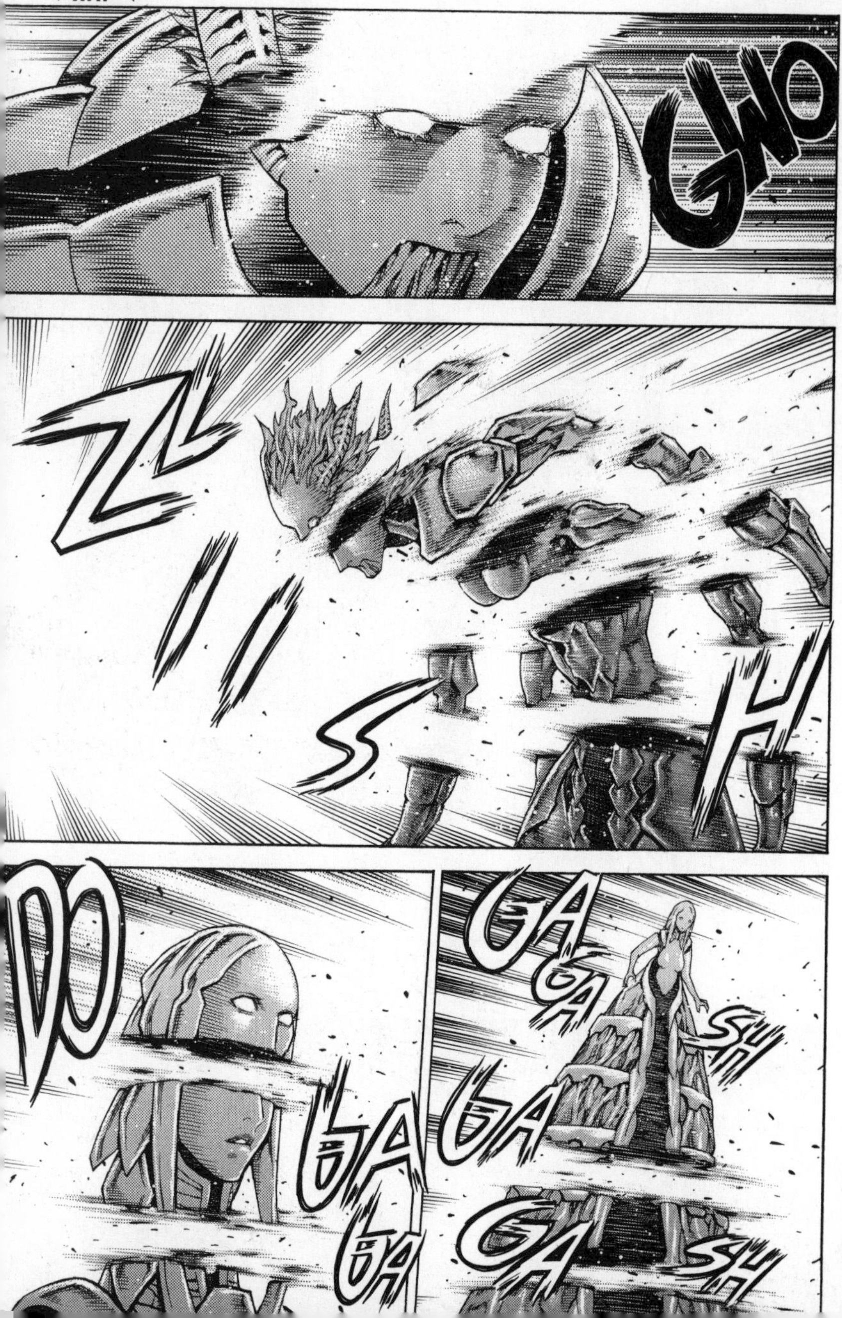
GHO
ZUSH
GAGA
SH
GAGA
SH
DO
BABA

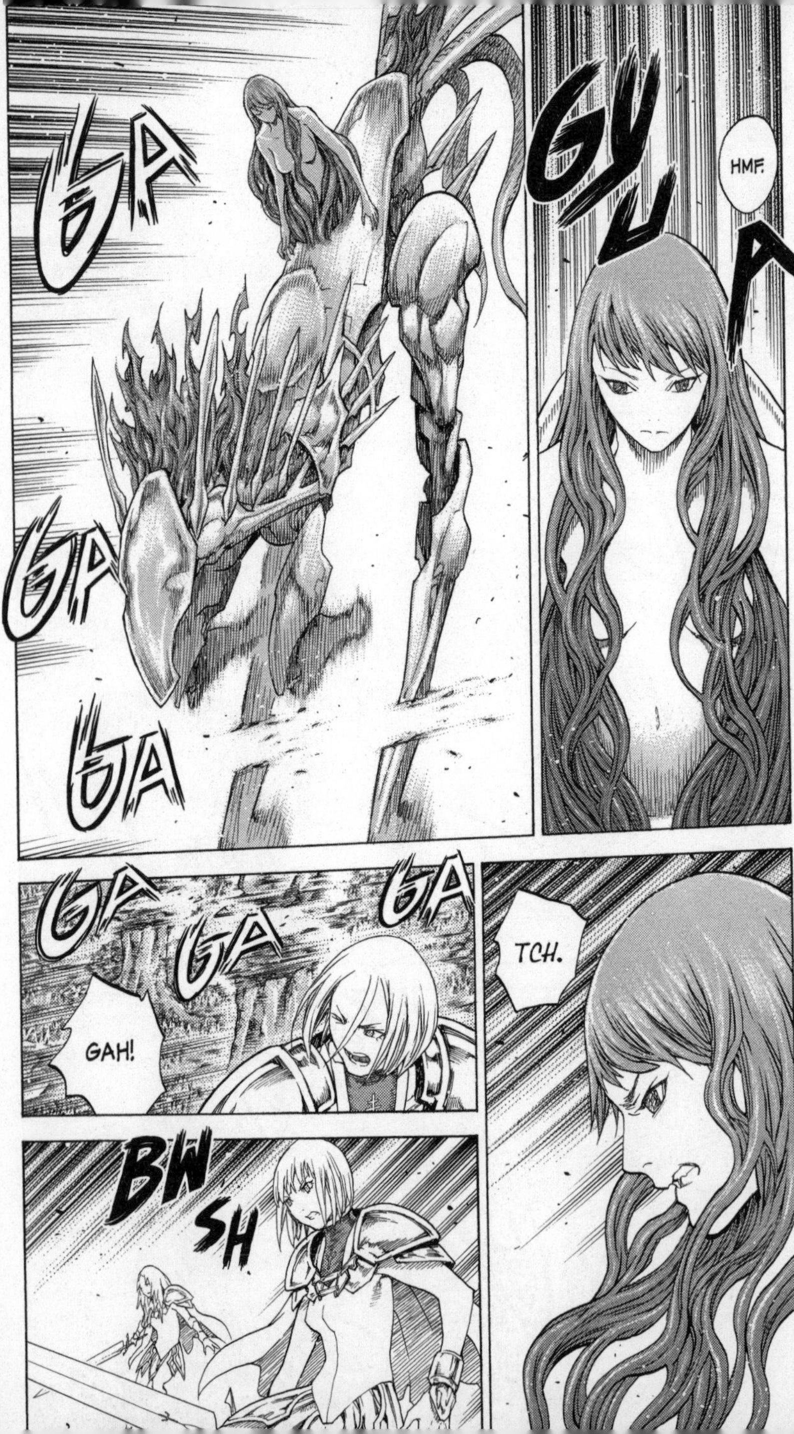
GYUA
HMF.
GA
GA
GA
TCH.
GA
GA
GA
GAH!
BWSH

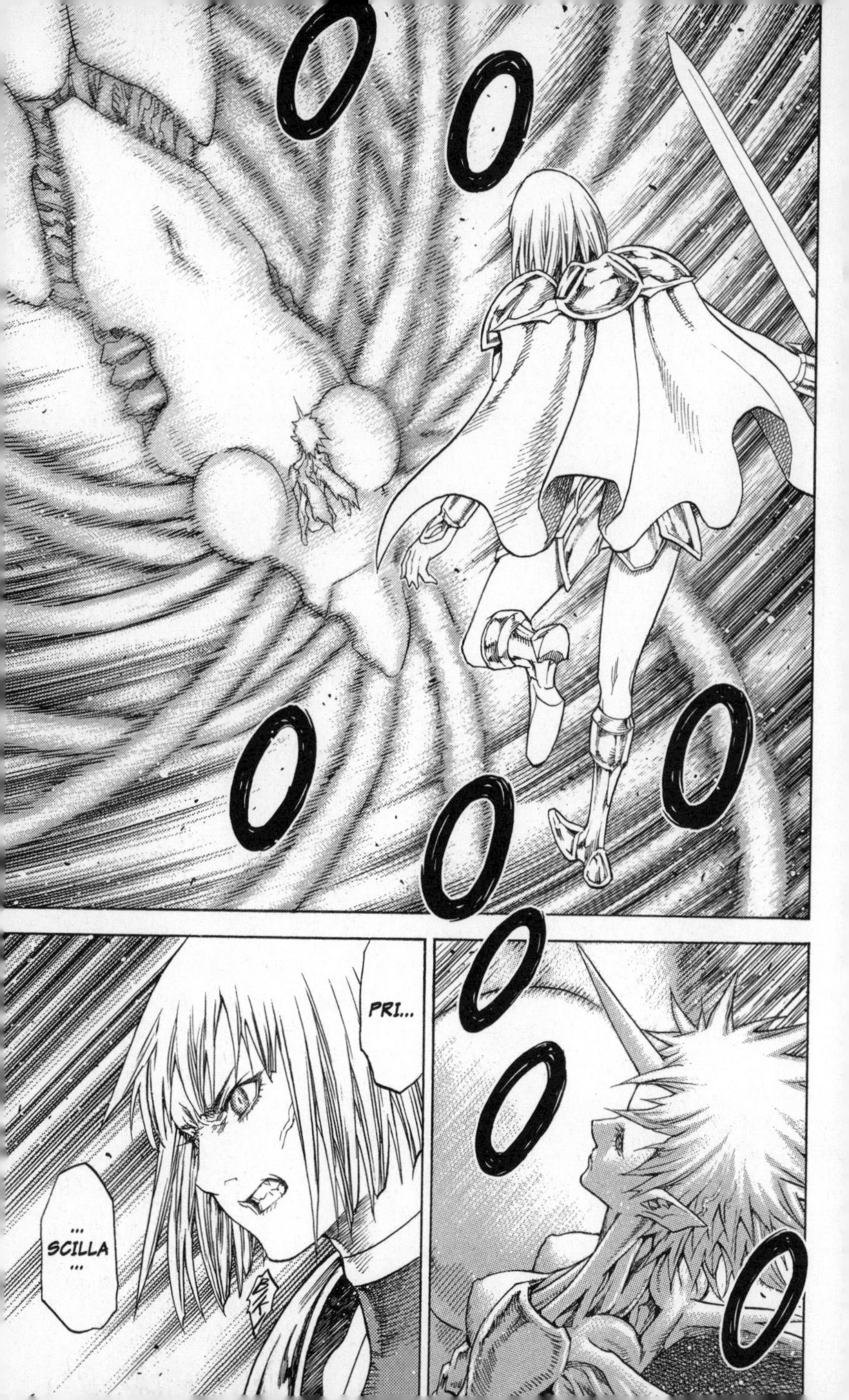
PRI...
...
SCILLA
...

クレイモア

Claymore

Scene 137: Army of the Underworld, Part 5

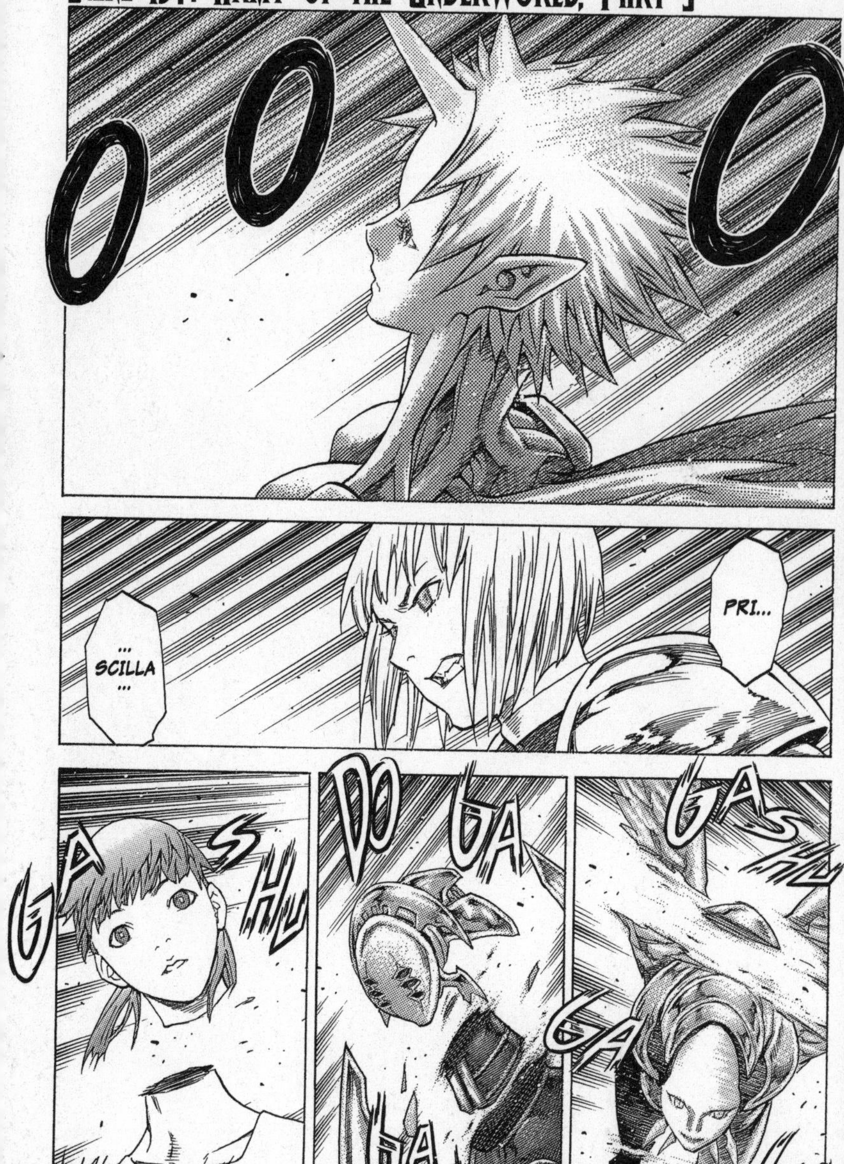
OOO
PRI...
... SCILLA ...
GASHU
GA
GA
DO GA
GA
GA
GASHU

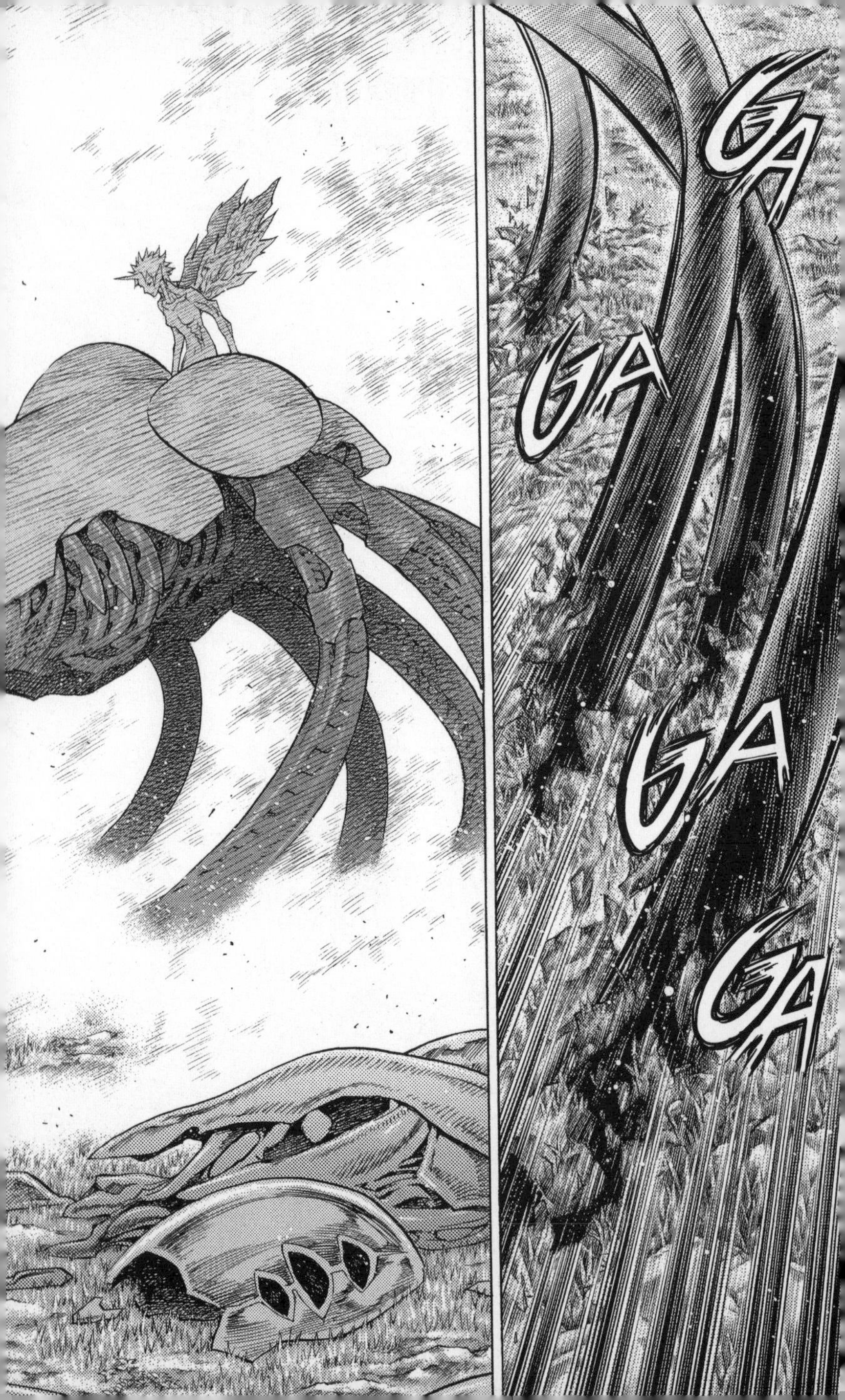
GA
GA
GA
GA

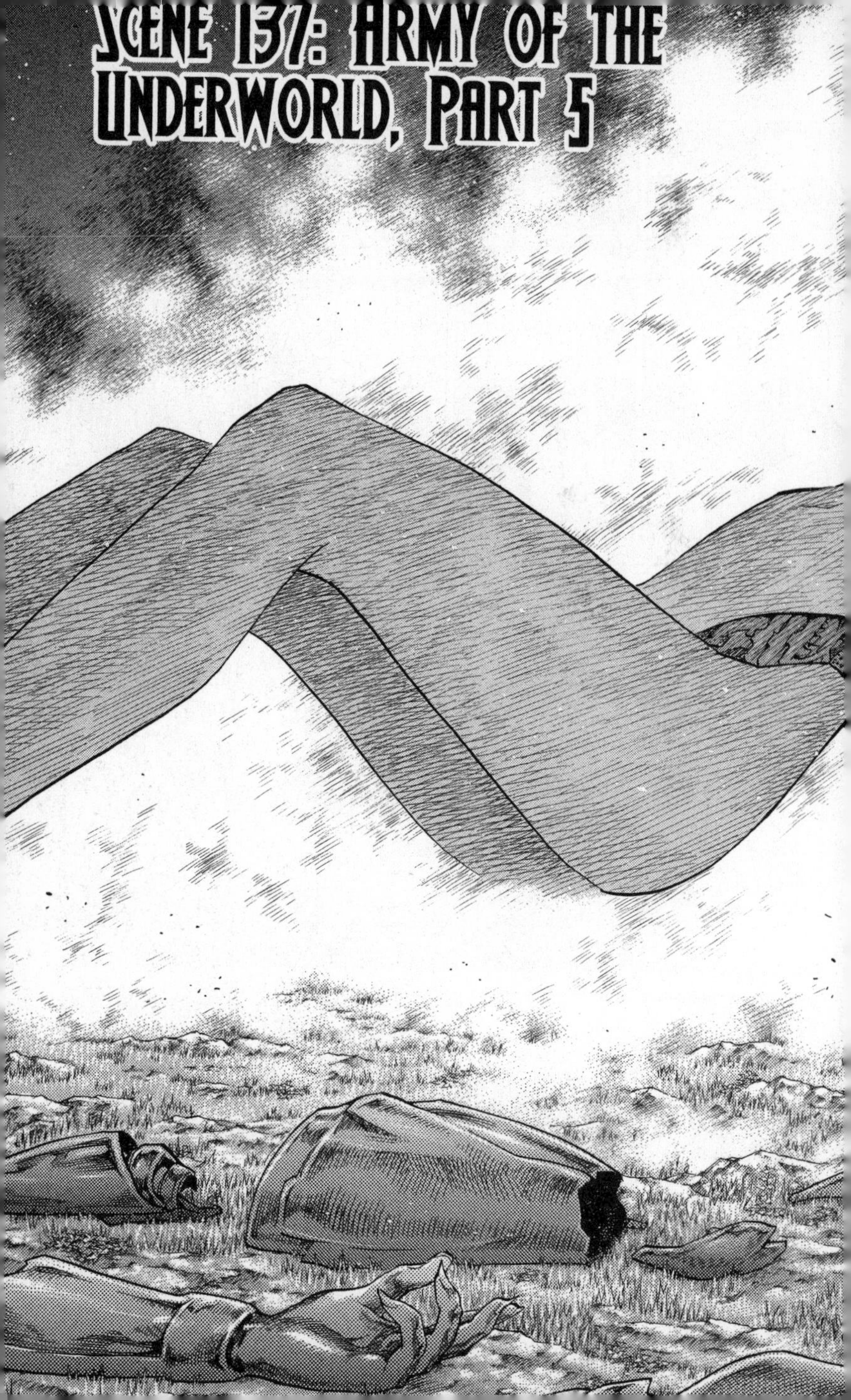
SCENE 137: ARMY OF THE UNDERWORLD, PART 5

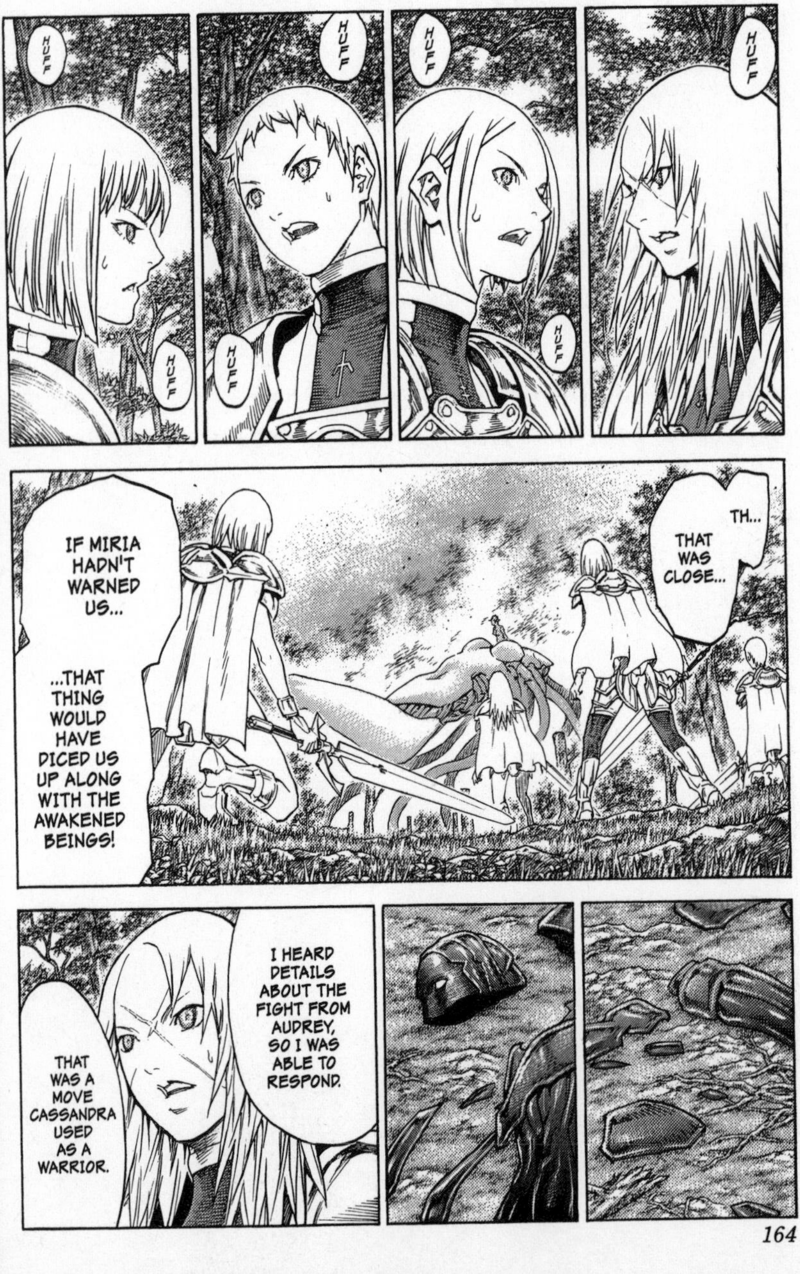

HUFF
HUFF
HUFF
HUFF
HUFF
HUFF
HUFF
TH... THAT WAS CLOSE...
IF MIRIA HADN'T WARNED US...
...THAT THING WOULD HAVE DICED US UP ALONG WITH THE AWAKENED BEINGS!
I HEARD DETAILS ABOUT THE FIGHT FROM AUDREY, SO I WAS ABLE TO RESPOND.
THAT WAS A MOVE CASSANDRA USED AS A WARRIOR.

READ THIS WAY

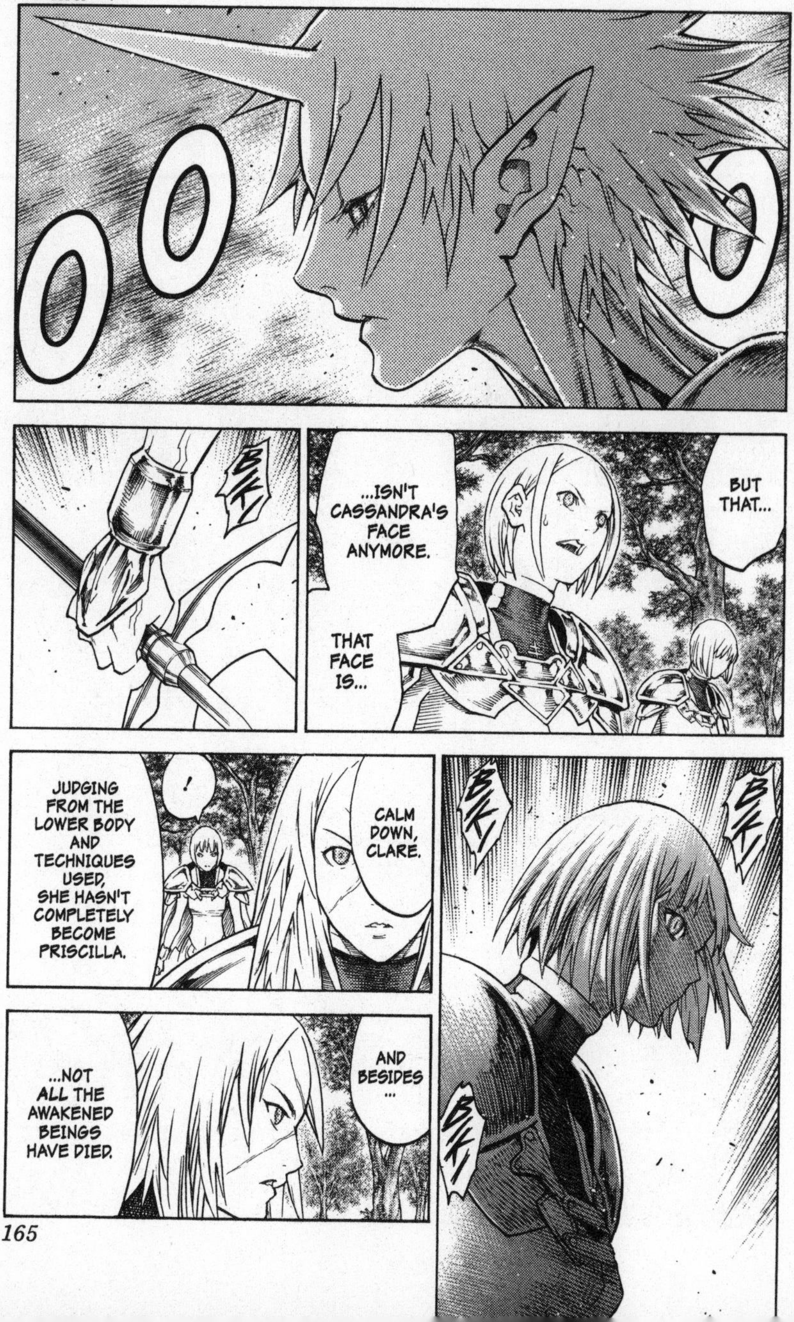
BUT THAT...
...ISN'T CASSANDRA'S FACE ANYMORE.
THAT FACE IS...
BIKI
BIKI
BIKI
BIKI
CALM DOWN, CLARE.
!
JUDGING FROM THE LOWER BODY AND TECHNIQUES USED, SHE HASN'T COMPLETELY BECOME PRISCILLA.
AND BESIDES...
...NOT ALL THE AWAKENED BEINGS HAVE DIED.

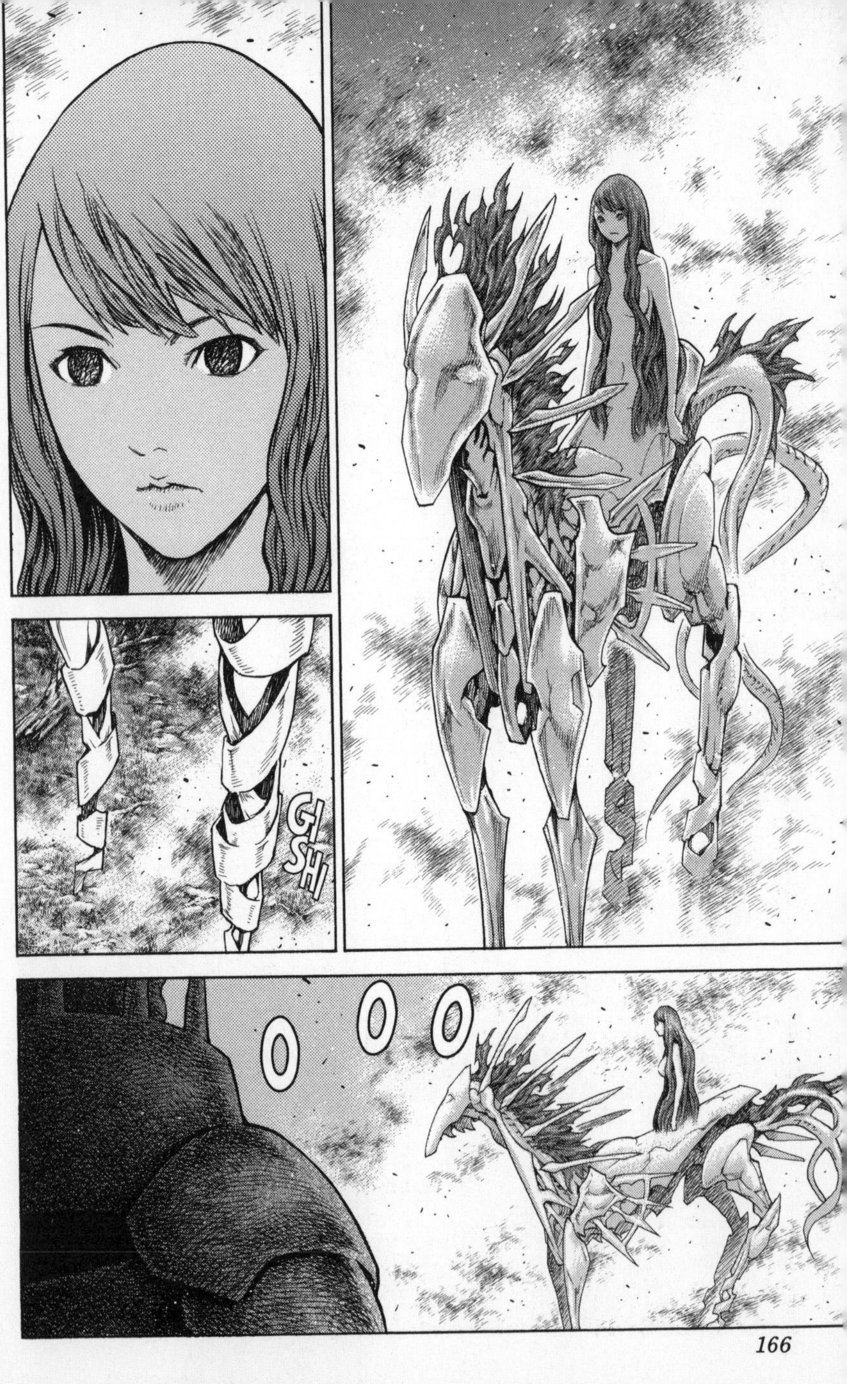
GISHI
OOO

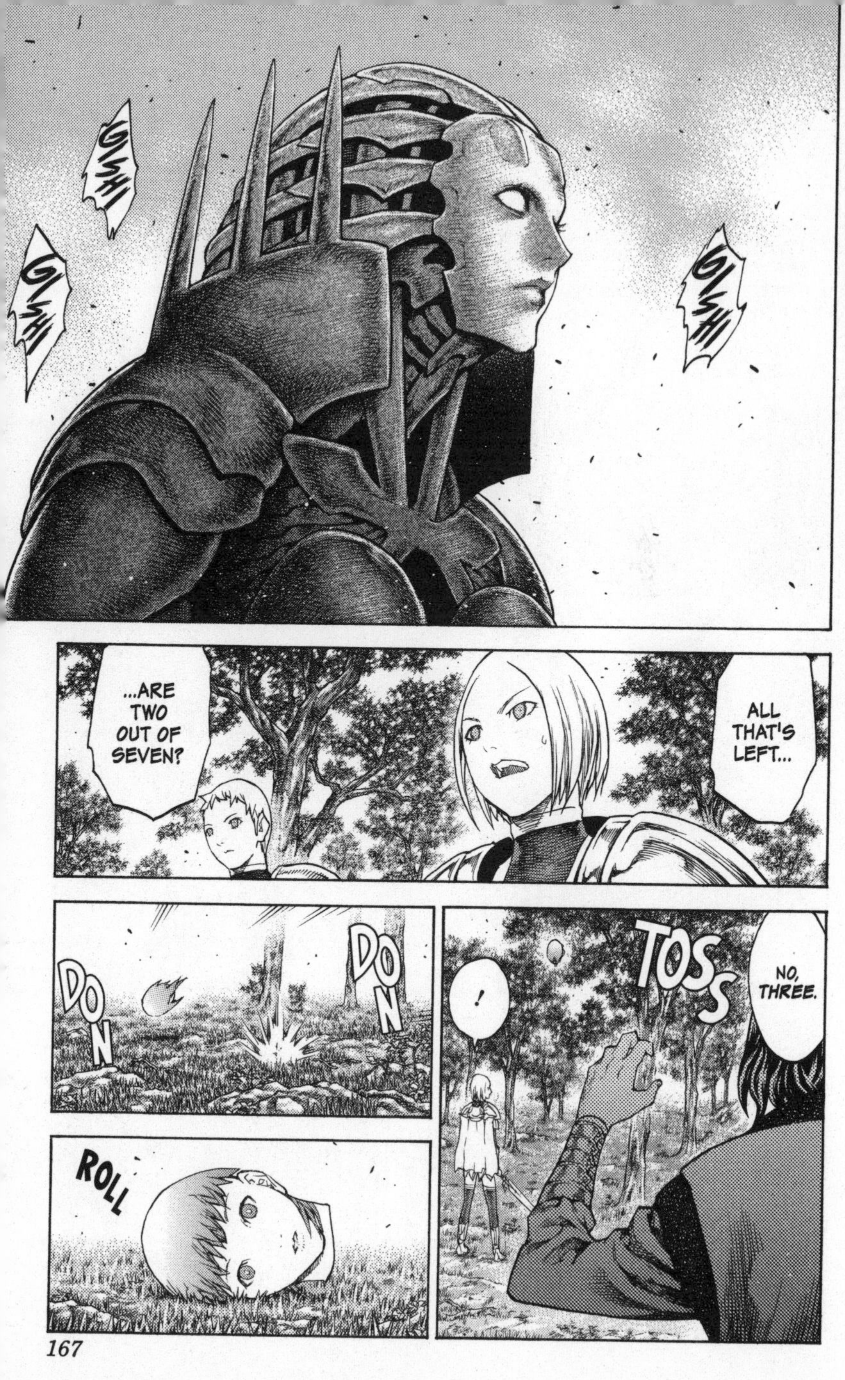
GISHI
GISHI
GISHI
ALL THAT'S LEFT...
...ARE TWO OUT OF SEVEN?
NO, THREE.
TOSS
!
DON
DON
ROLL

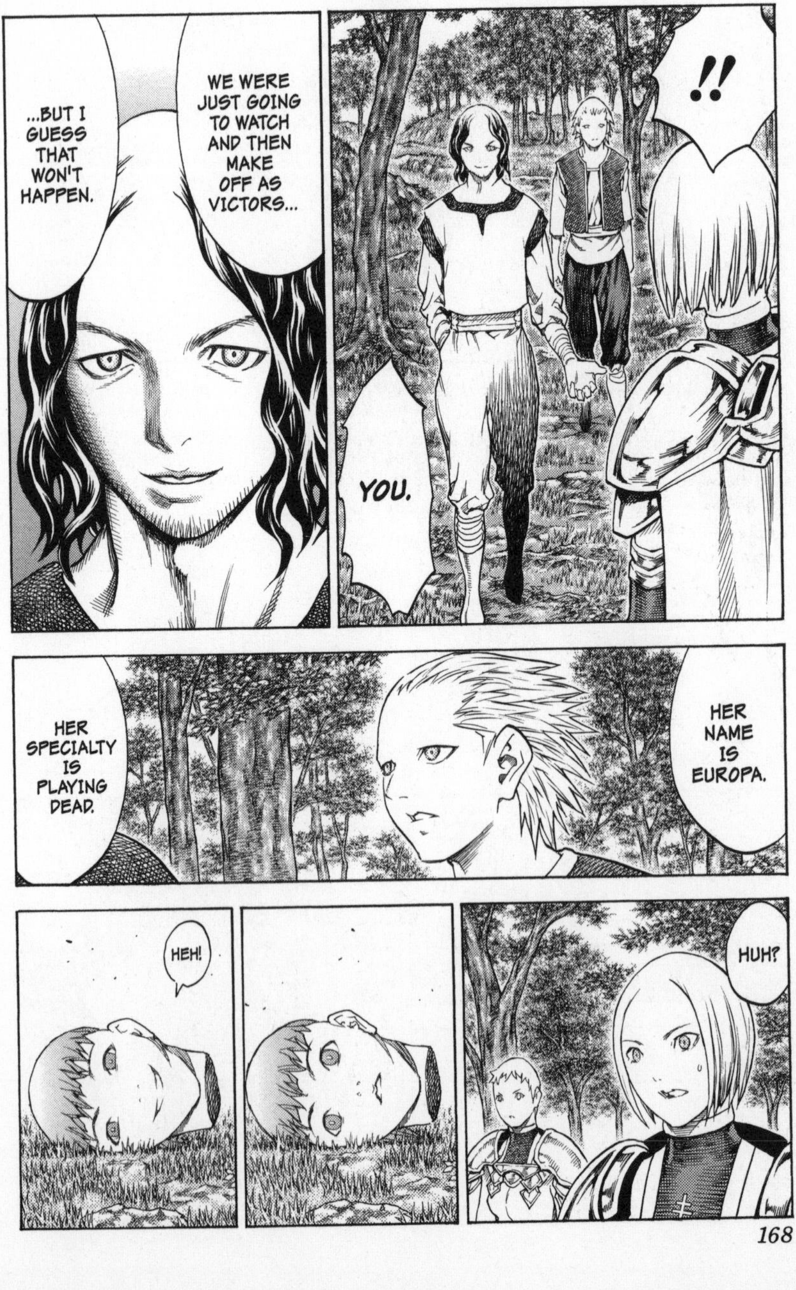
!!
YOU.
WE WERE JUST GOING TO WATCH AND THEN MAKE OFF AS VICTORS...
...BUT I GUESS THAT WON'T HAPPEN.
HER NAME IS EUROPA.
HER SPECIALTY IS PLAYING DEAD.
HUH?
HEH!

READ THIS WAY

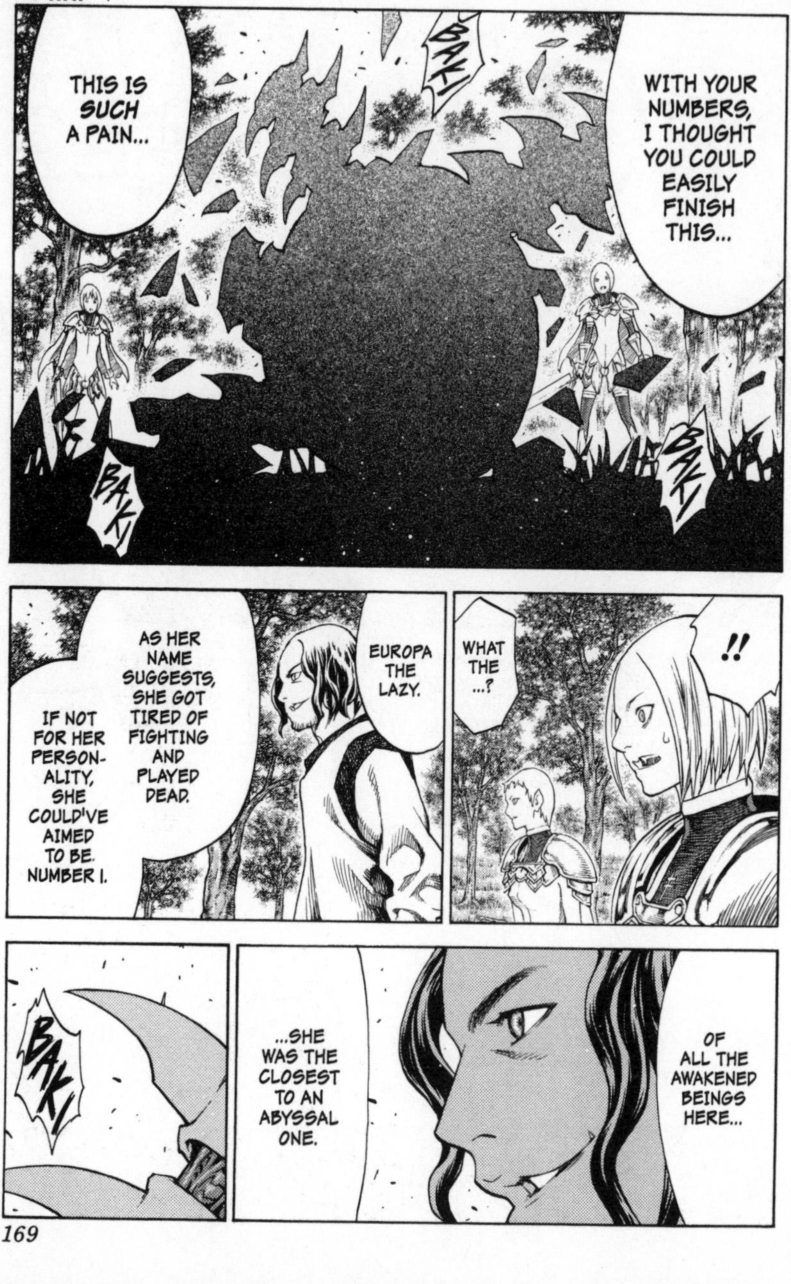

BAKI
WITH YOUR NUMBERS, I THOUGHT YOU COULD EASILY FINISH THIS...
THIS IS SUCH A PAIN...
BAKI
BAKI
!!
WHAT THE ...?
EUROPA THE LAZY.
AS HER NAME SUGGESTS, SHE GOT TIRED OF FIGHTING AND PLAYED DEAD.
IF NOT FOR HER PERSONALITY, SHE COULD'VE AIMED TO BE NUMBER 1.
OF ALL THE AWAKENED BEINGS HERE...
...SHE WAS THE CLOSEST TO AN ABYSSAL ONE.
BAKI

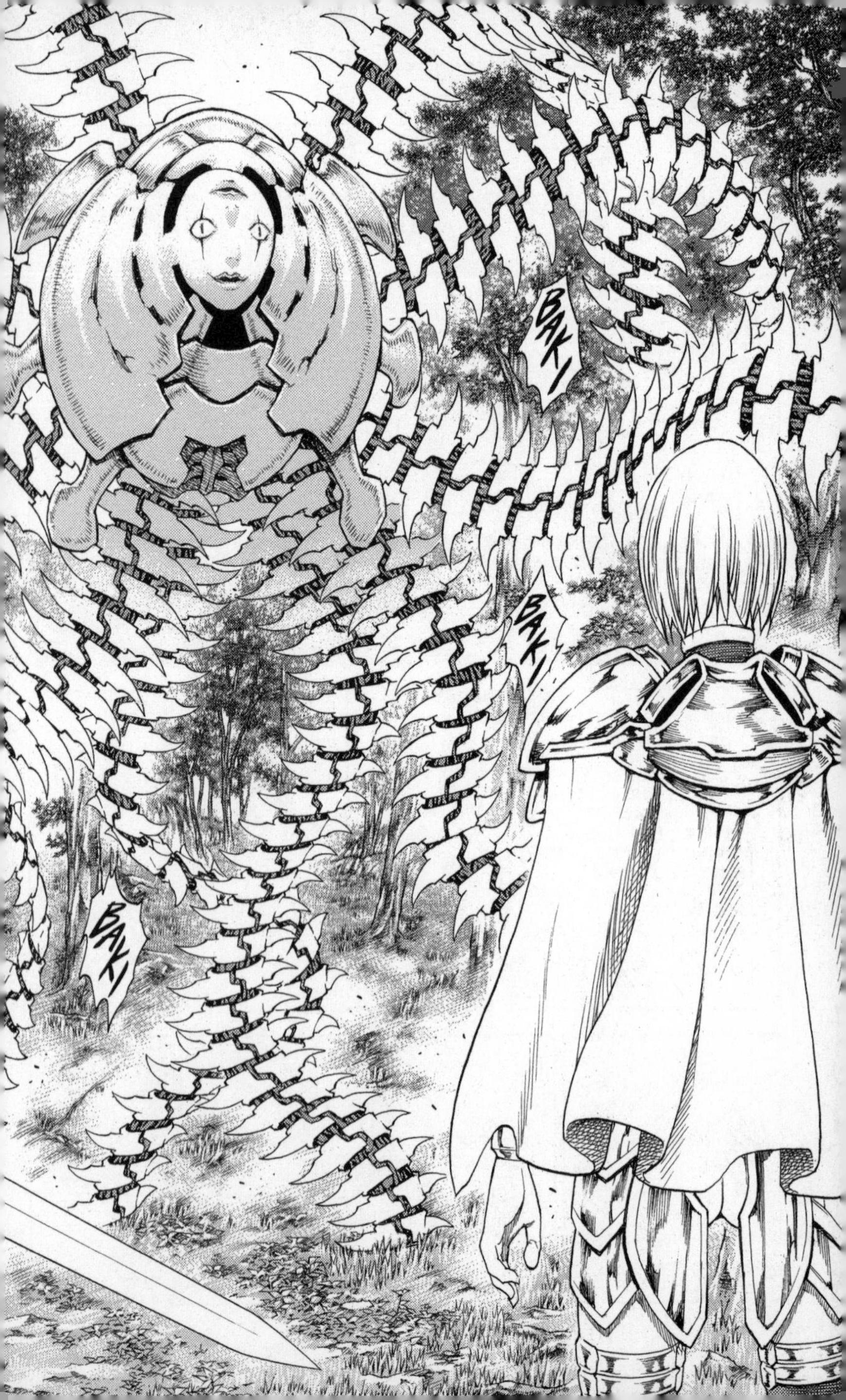
BAKI
BAKI
BAKI

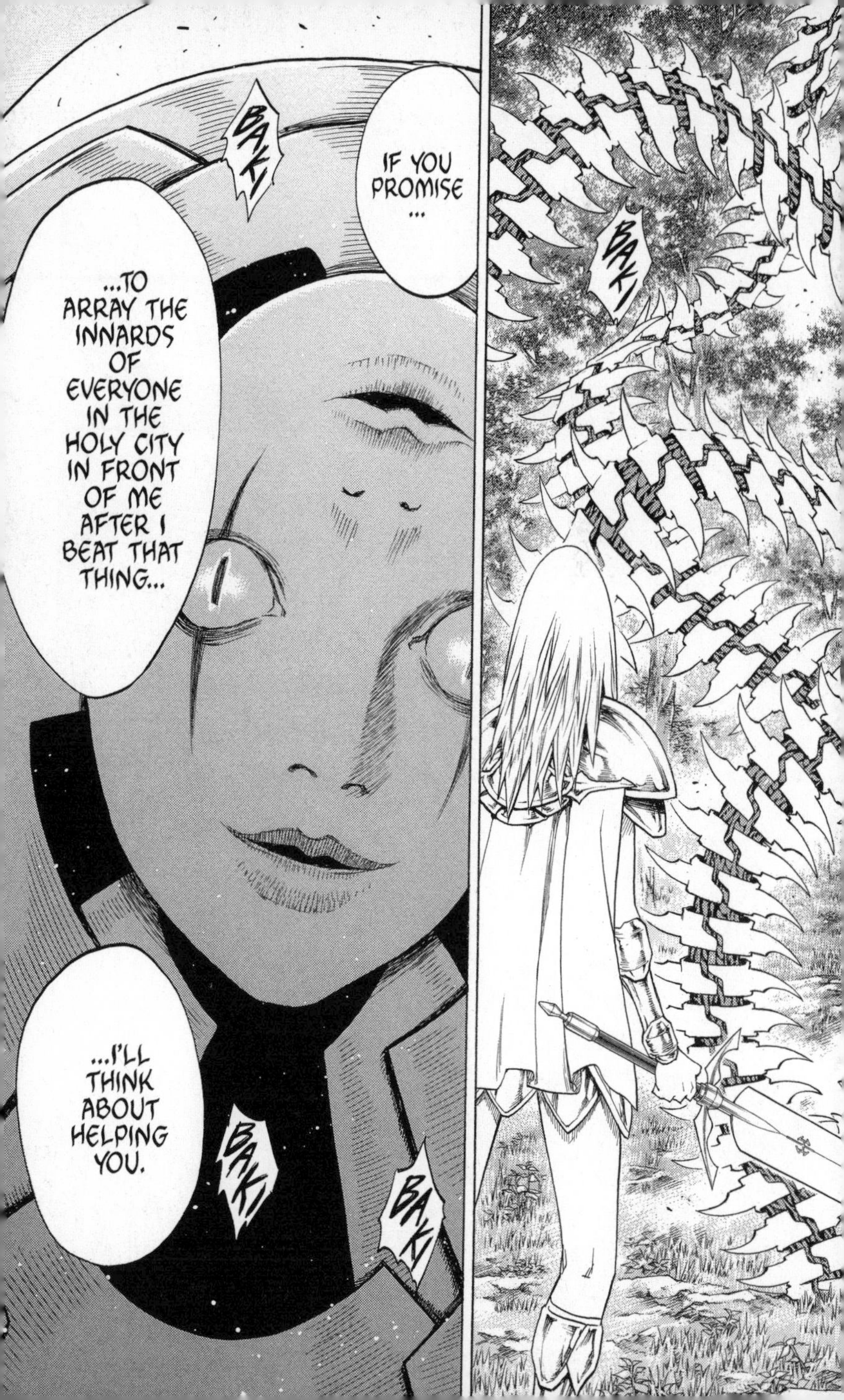
BAKI
IF YOU PROMISE ...
BAKI
...TO ARRAY THE INNARDS OF EVERYONE IN THE HOLY CITY IN FRONT OF ME AFTER I BEAT THAT THING...
...I'LL THINK ABOUT HELPING YOU.
BAKI
BAKI

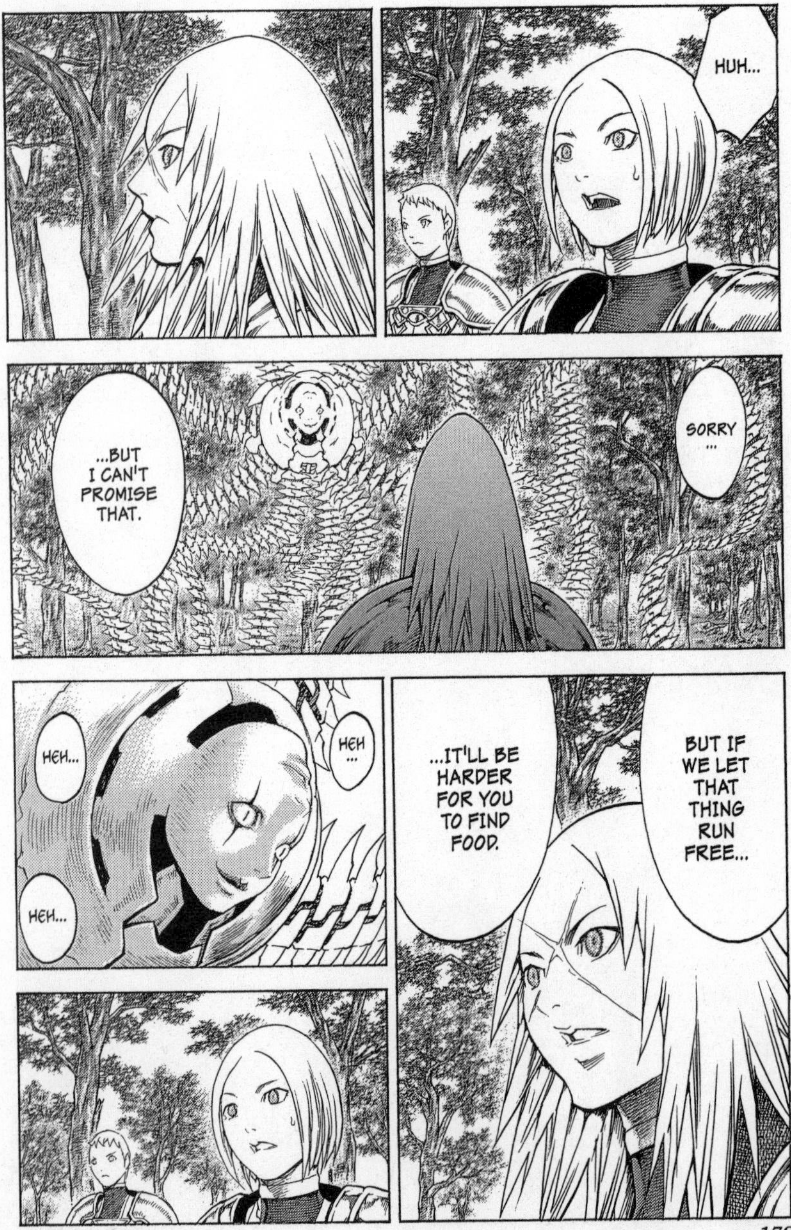
HUH...
SORRY ...
...BUT I CAN'T PROMISE THAT.
BUT IF WE LET THAT THING RUN FREE...
...IT'LL BE HARDER FOR YOU TO FIND FOOD.
HEH ...
HEH...
HEH...

READ THIS WAY

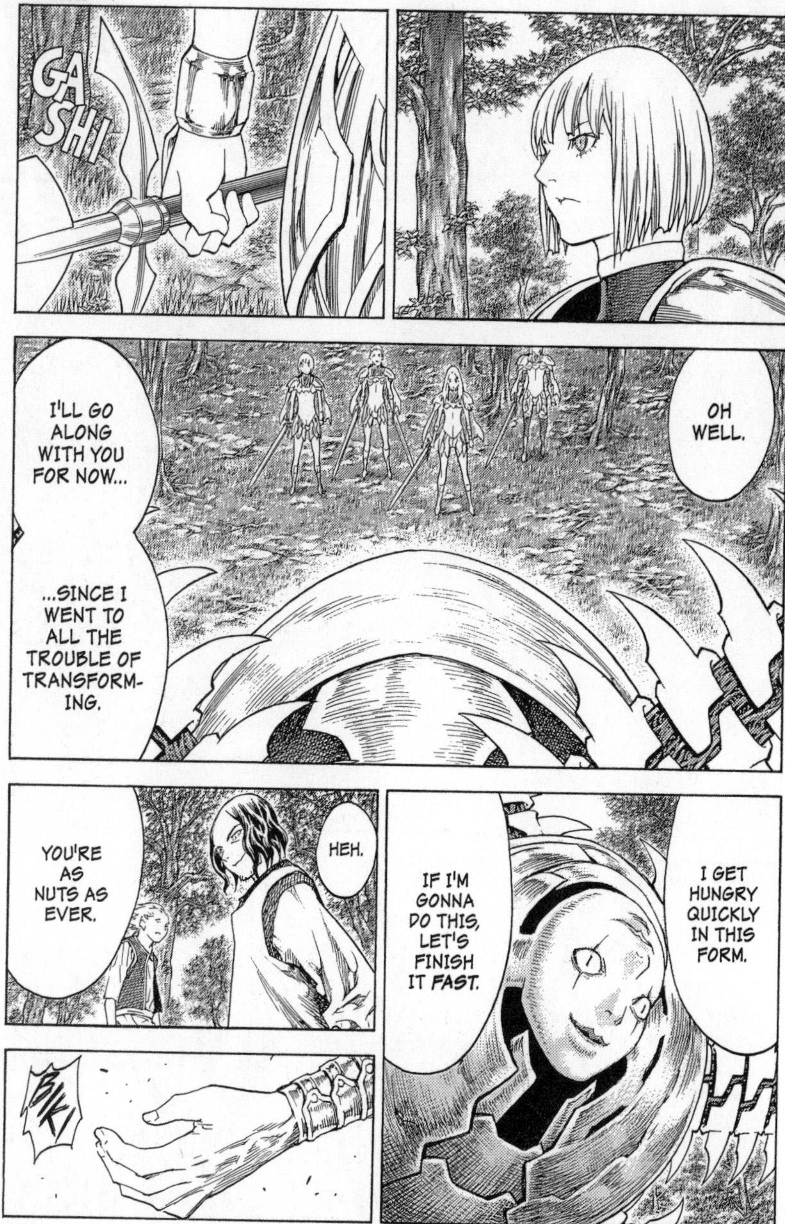
GASHI
OH WELL.
I'LL GO ALONG WITH YOU FOR NOW...
...SINCE I WENT TO ALL THE TROUBLE OF TRANSFORMING.
I GET HUNGRY QUICKLY IN THIS FORM.
IF I'M GONNA DO THIS, LET'S FINISH IT FAST.
HEH.
YOU'RE AS NUTS AS EVER.
BIKI

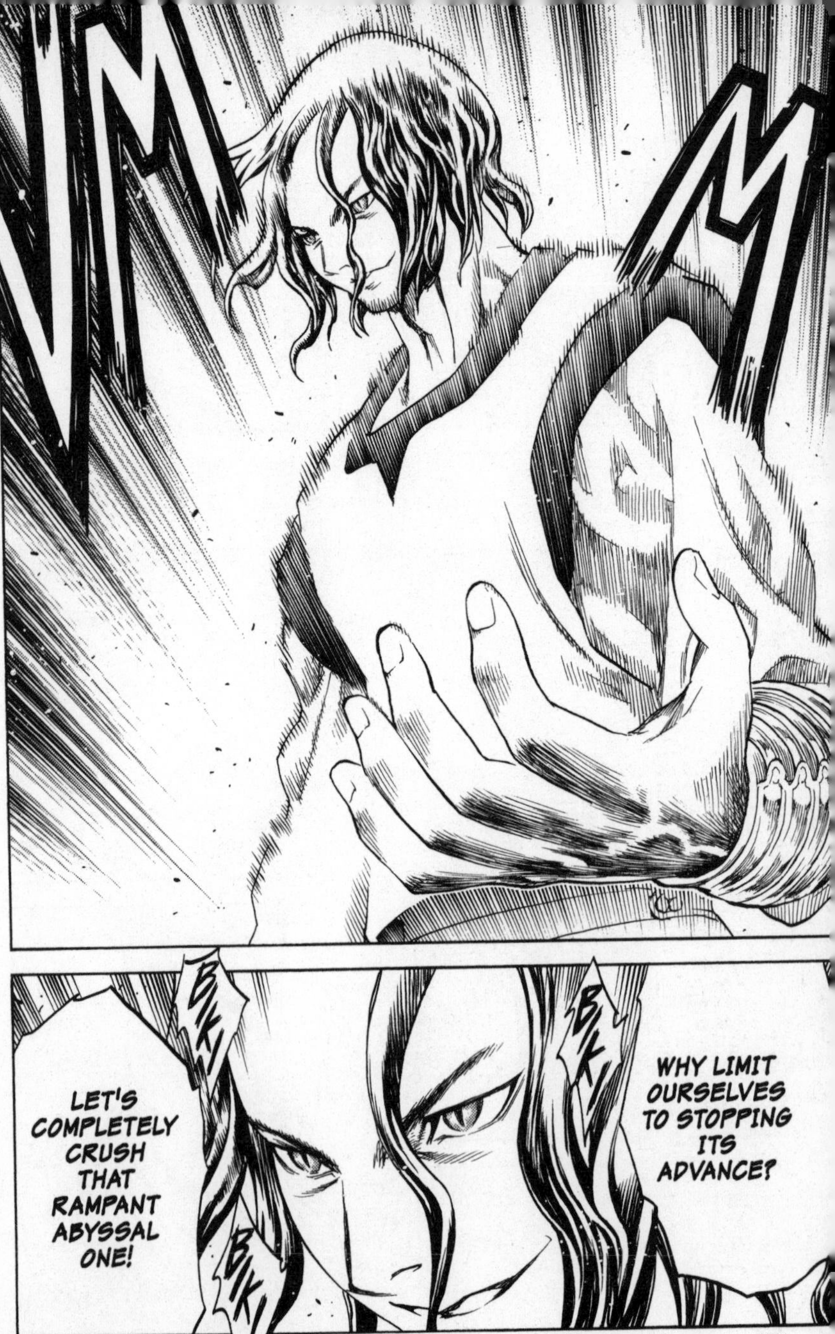
VM
M
BIKI
BIKI
BIKI
WHY LIMIT OURSELVES TO STOPPING ITS ADVANCE?
LET'S COMPLETELY CRUSH THAT RAMPANT ABYSSAL ONE!

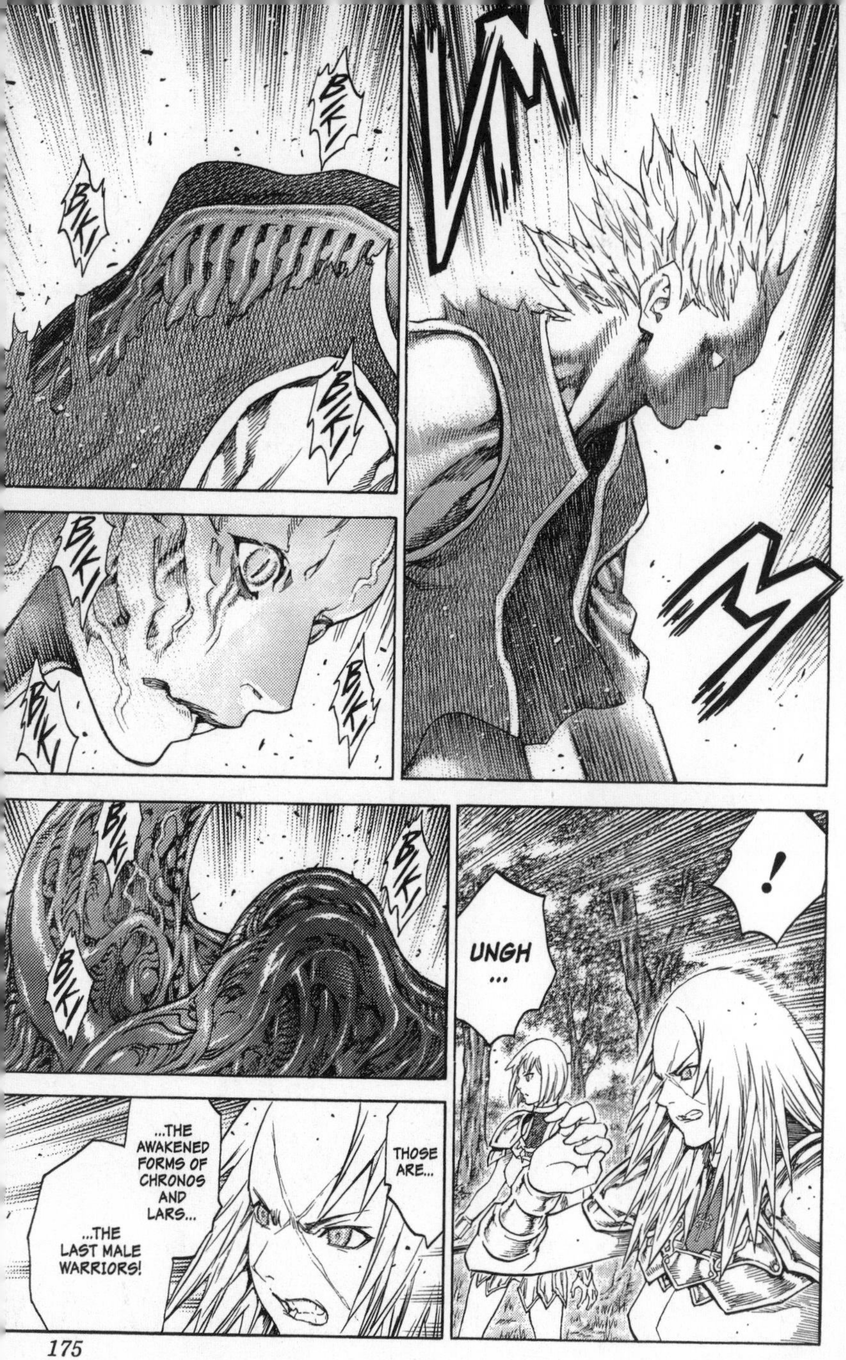
VM
M
BIKI
BIKI
BIKI
BIKI
BIKI
BIKI
!
UNGH ...
BIKI
BIKI
BIKI
THOSE ARE...
...THE AWAKENED FORMS OF CHRONOS AND LARS...
...THE LAST MALE WARRIORS!

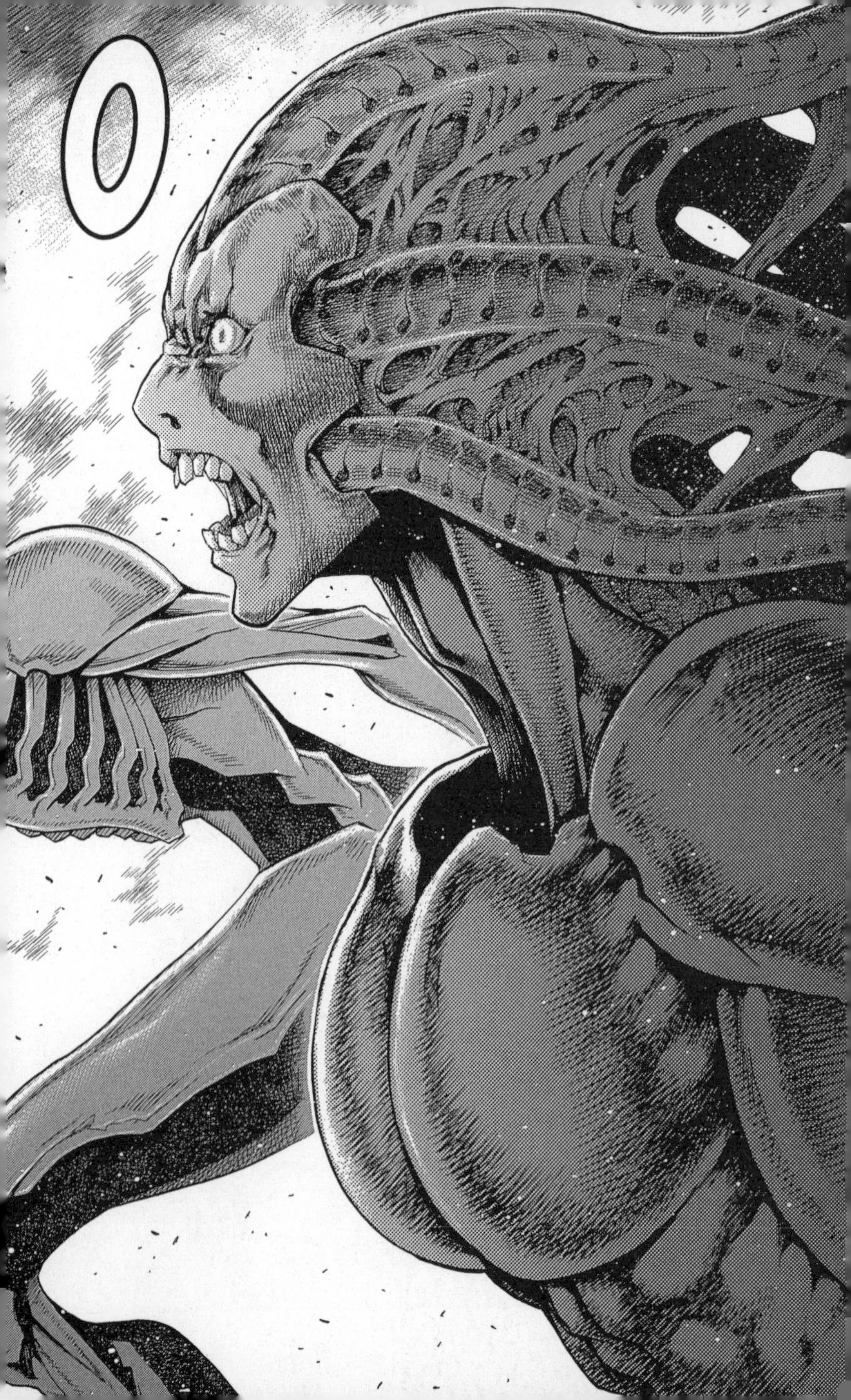
O

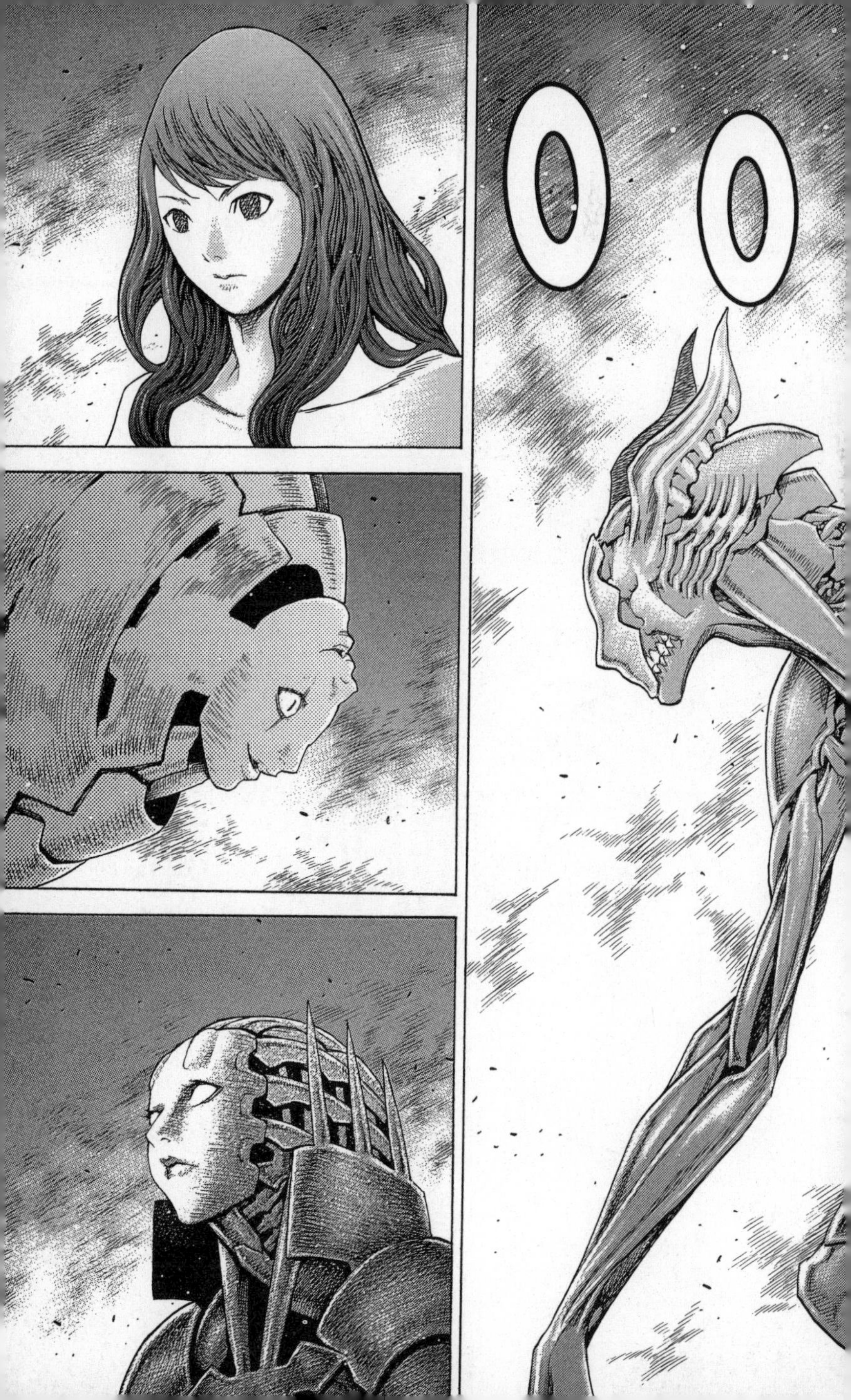

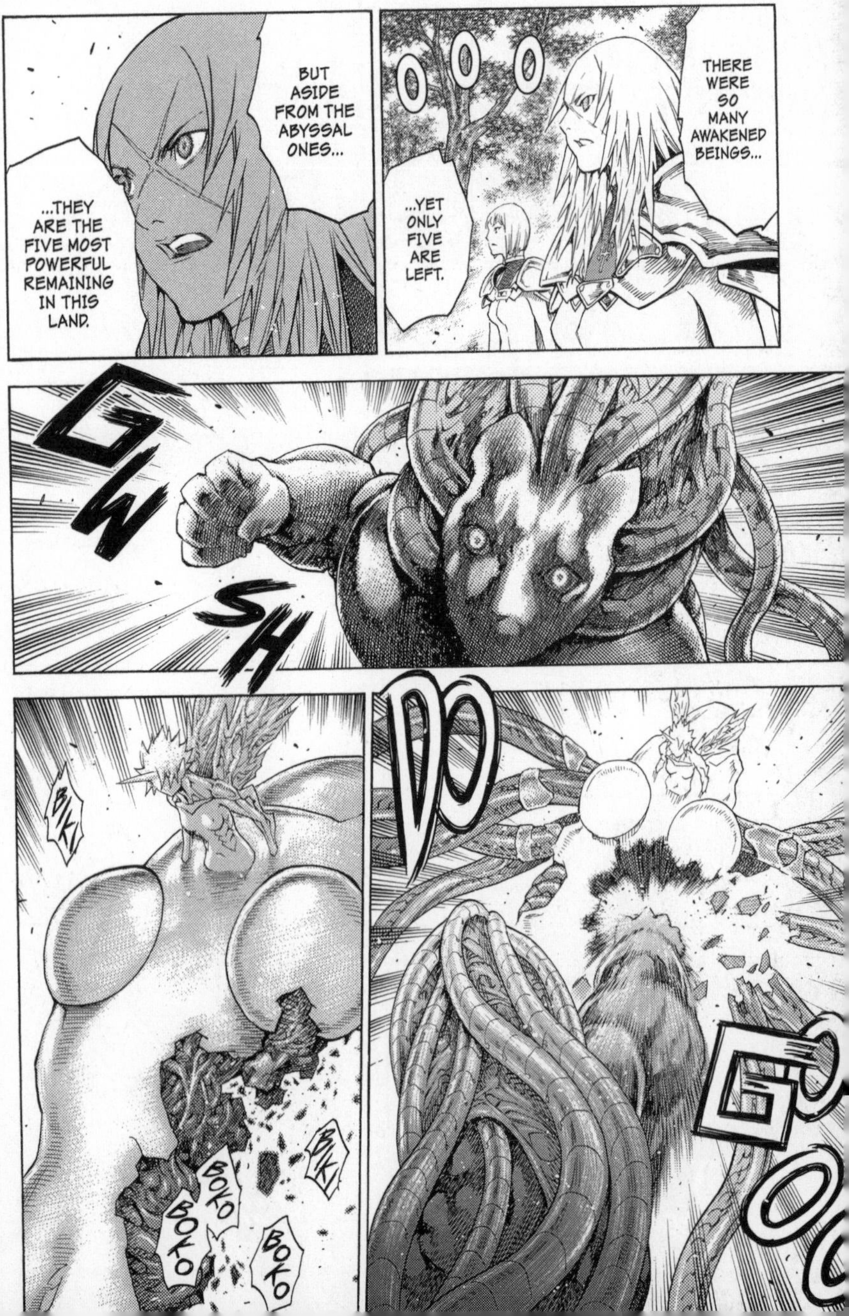
OOO
THERE WERE SO MANY AWAKENED BEINGS...
...YET ONLY FIVE ARE LEFT.
BUT ASIDE FROM THE ABYSSAL ONES...
...THEY ARE THE FIVE MOST POWERFUL REMAINING IN THIS LAND.
GWSH
DO
GOOO
BIKI
BIKI
BOKO
BOKO
BOKO

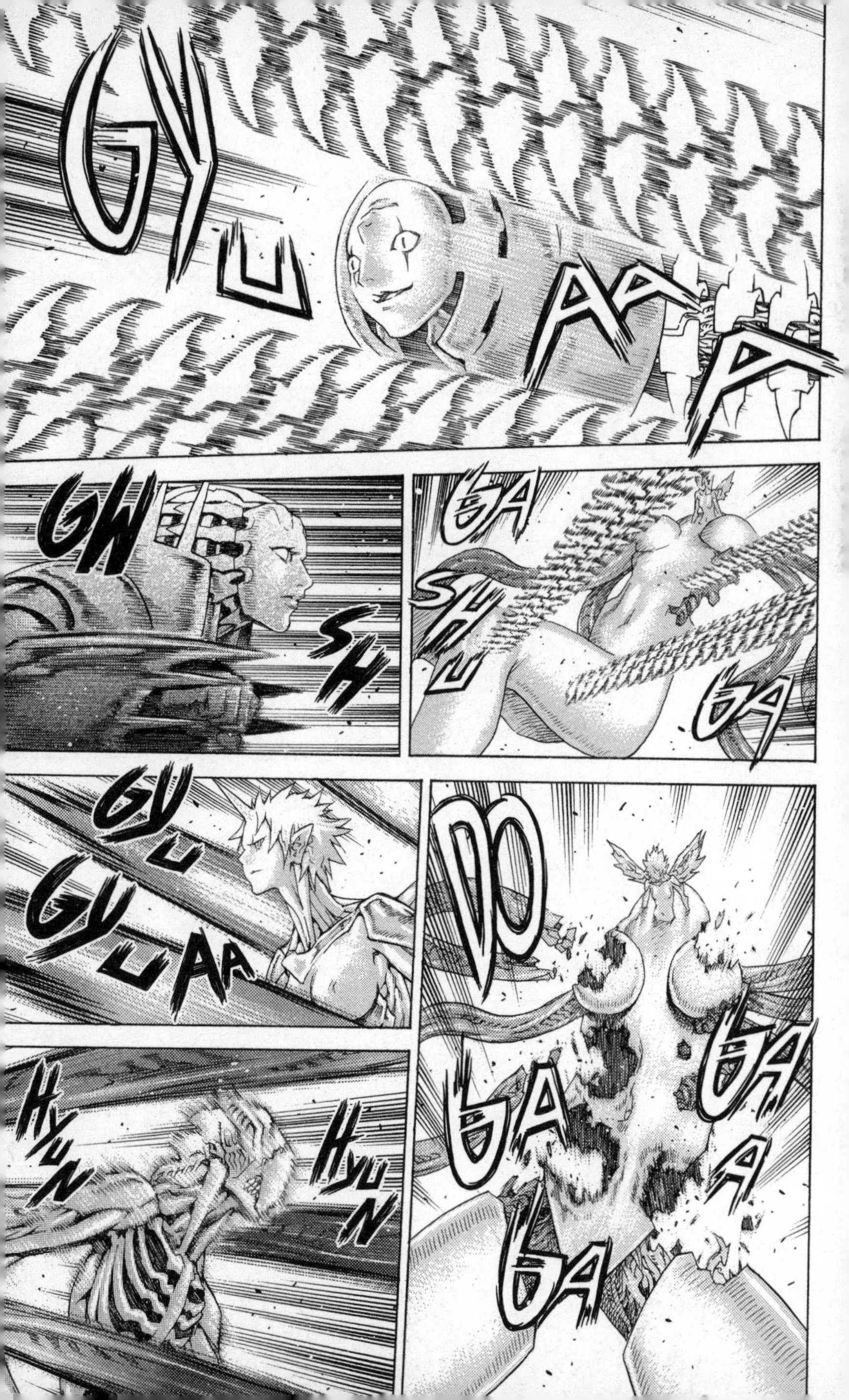
GYUAAP
GA
SHU
GA
GW
SH
DO
GAA
GA
GA
GYU
GYUAA
HYUN
HYUN

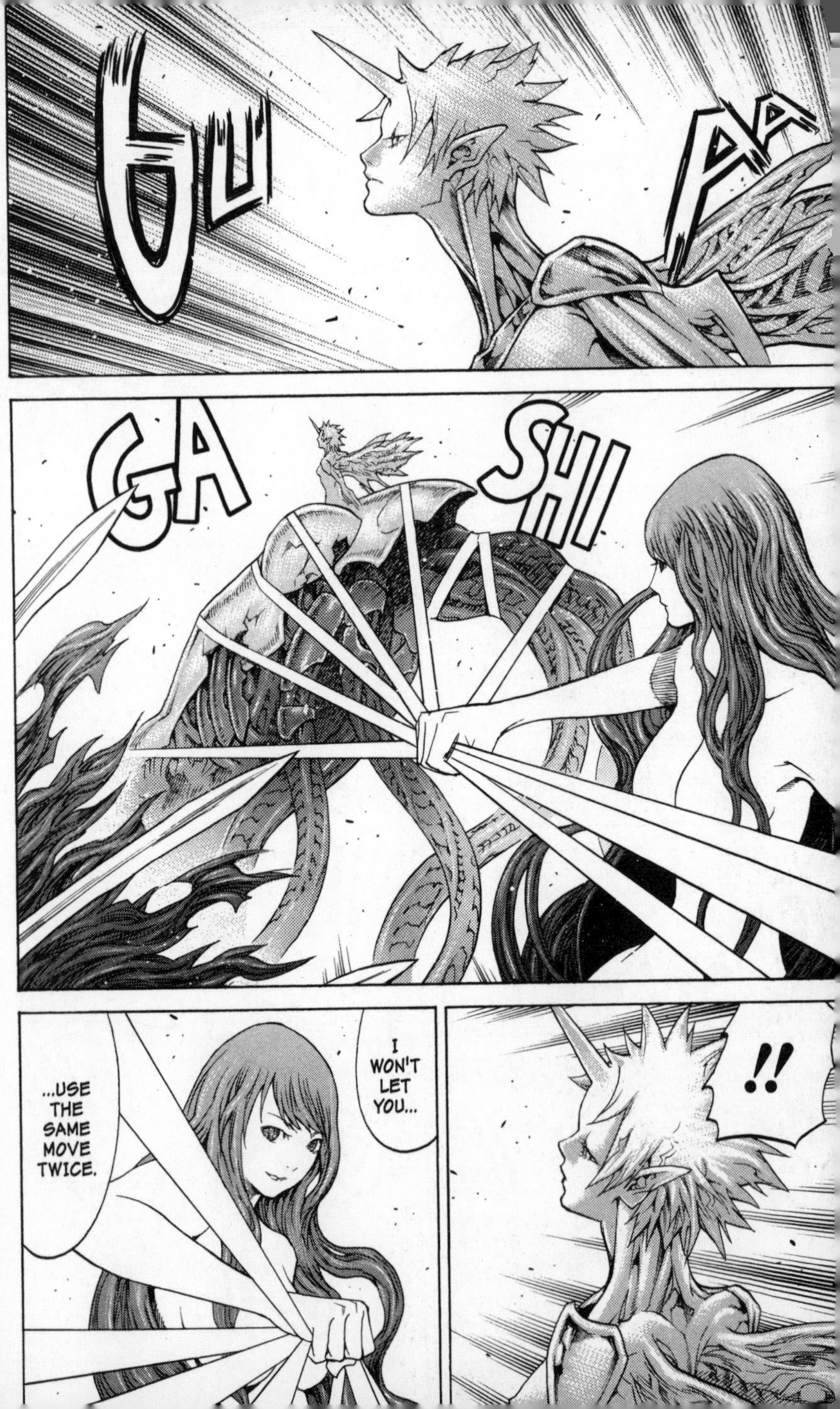
GU
AA
GA
SHI
!!
I WON'T LET YOU...
...USE THE SAME MOVE TWICE.

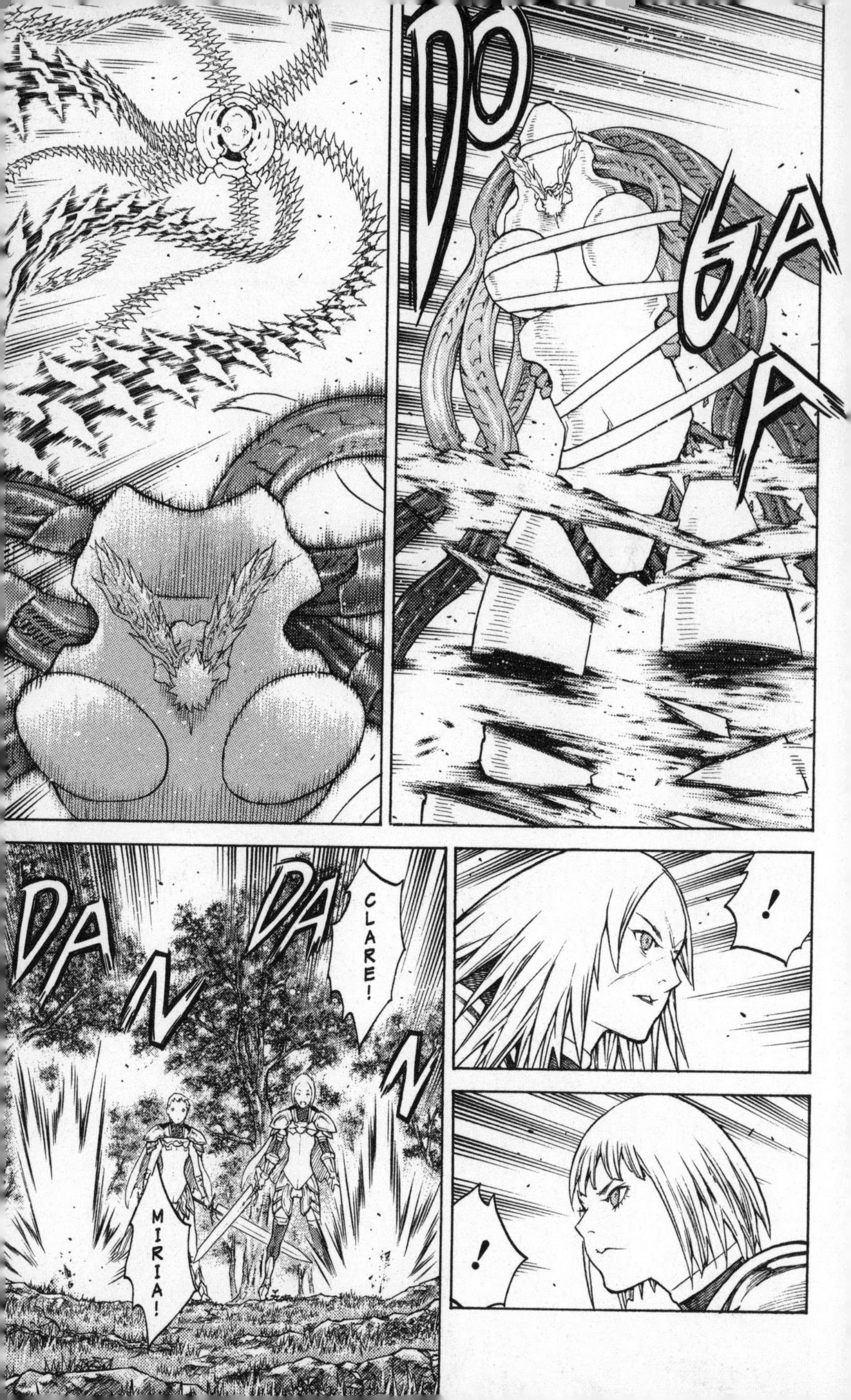

DOGAA
!
!
CLARE!
DADAN
DAN
MIRIA!

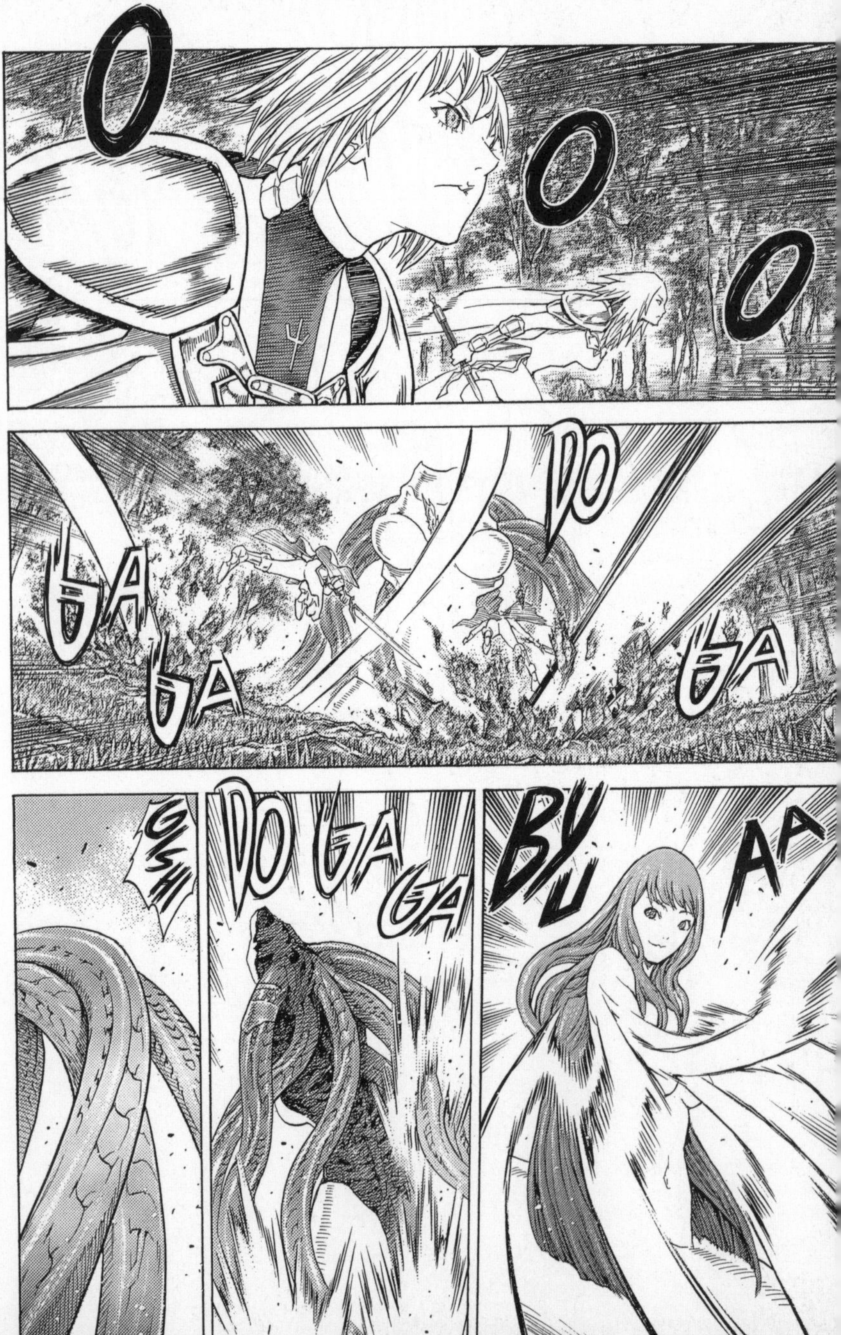
O
O
O
DO
GA
GA
GA
BYU
AA
DO
GA
GA
GSH

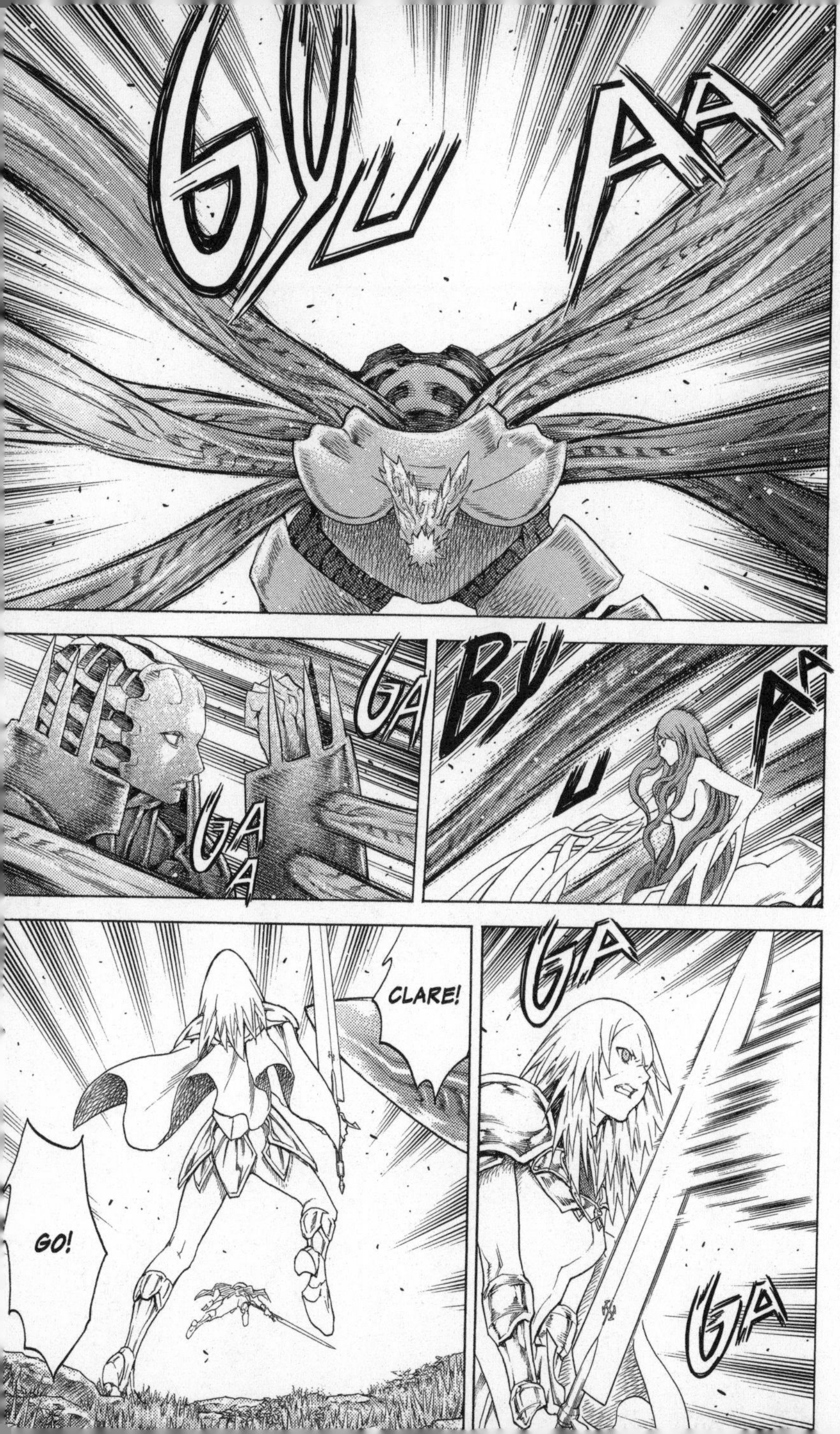
GYU AA
GABYU AA
GAAA
GA
GA
CLARE!
GO!

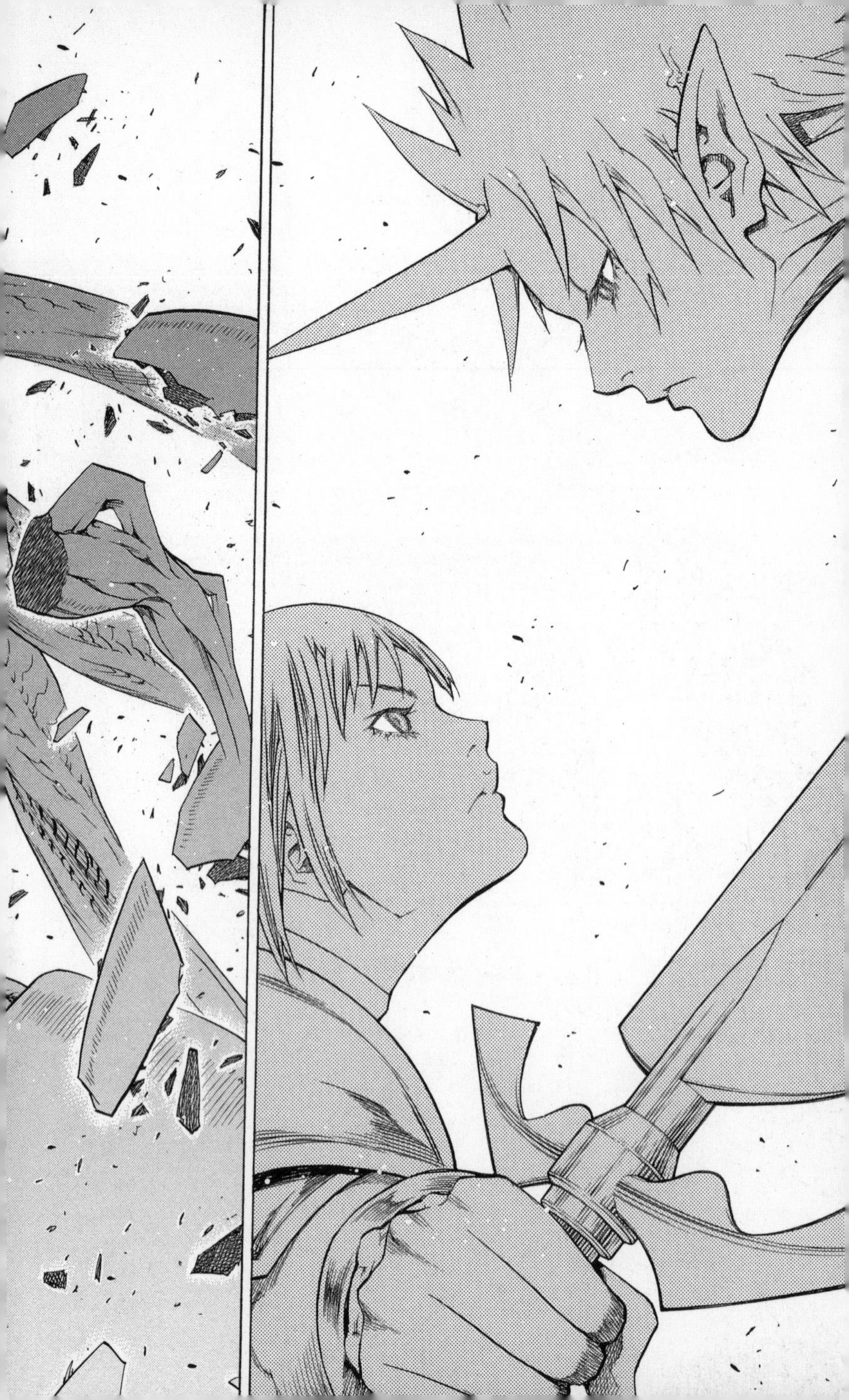

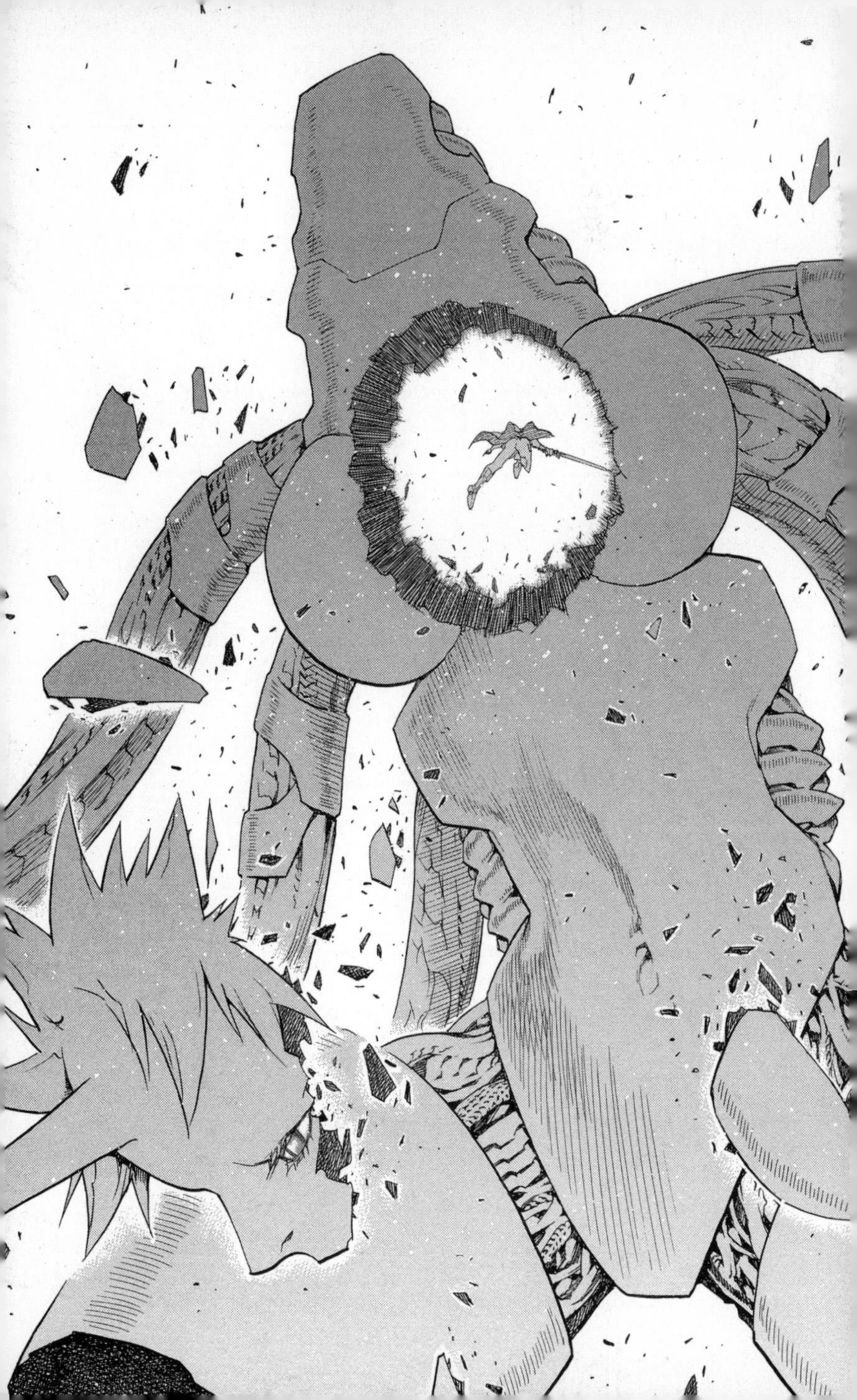

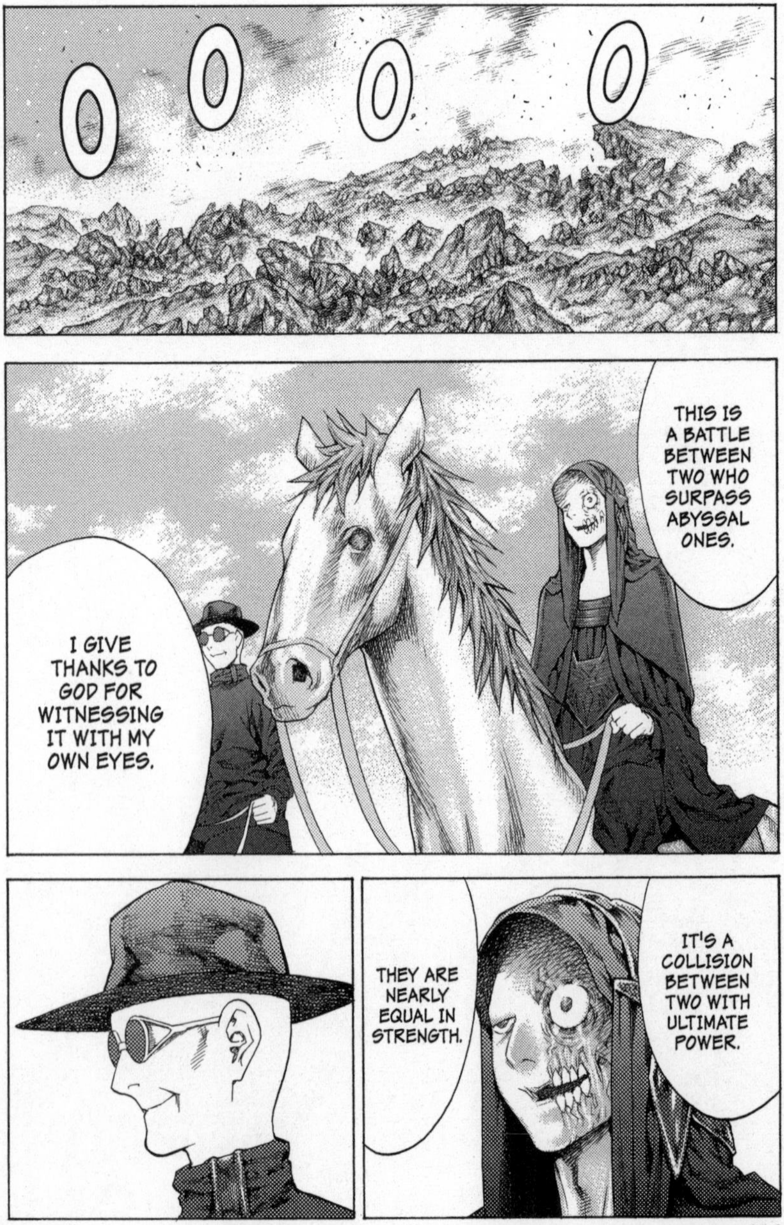
THIS IS A BATTLE BETWEEN TWO WHO SURPASS ABYSSAL ONES.
I GIVE THANKS TO GOD FOR WITNESSING IT WITH MY OWN EYES.
IT'S A COLLISION BETWEEN TWO WITH ULTIMATE POWER.
THEY ARE NEARLY EQUAL IN STRENGTH.

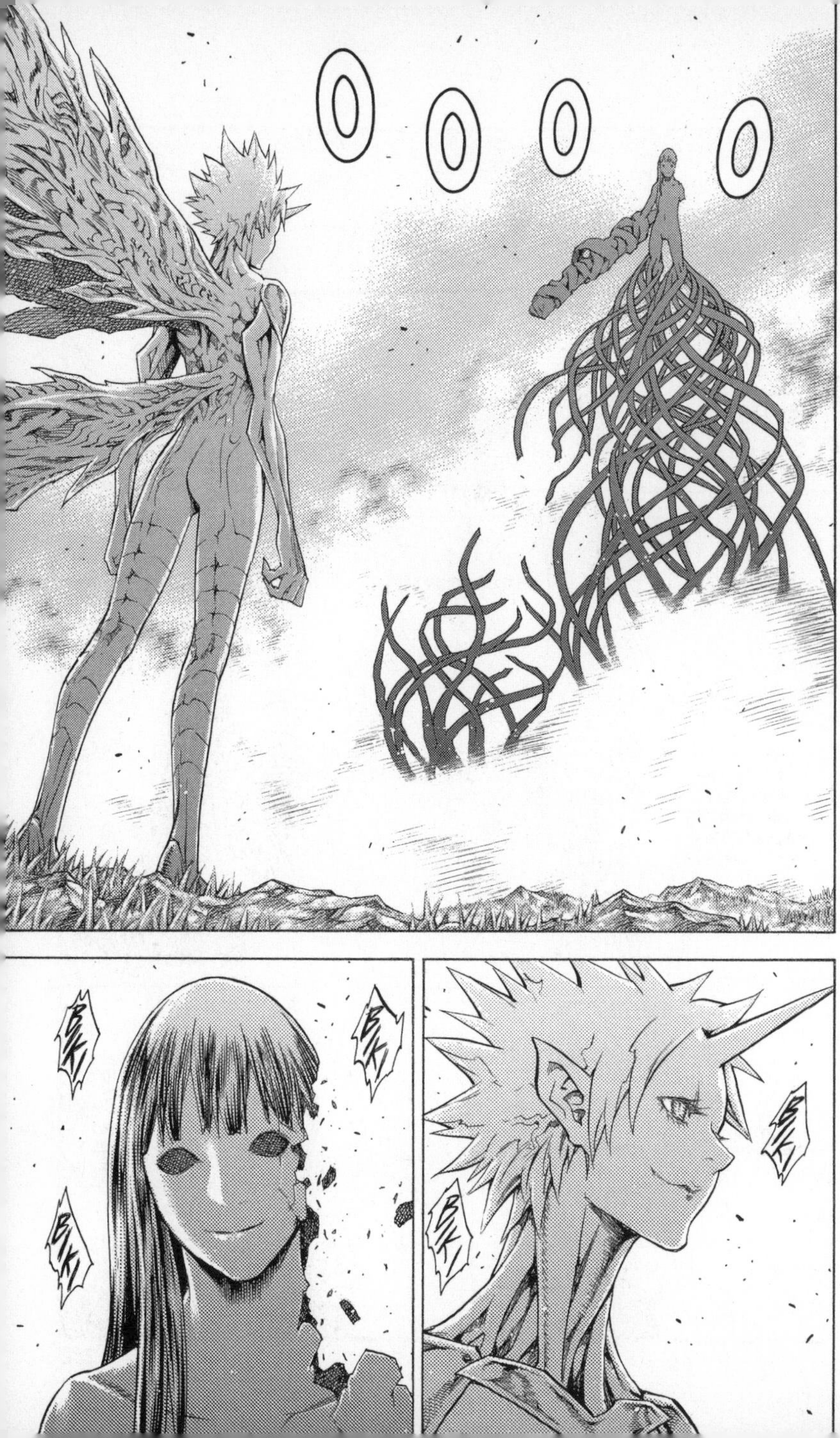
OOOO
BIKI
BIKI
BIKI
BIKI

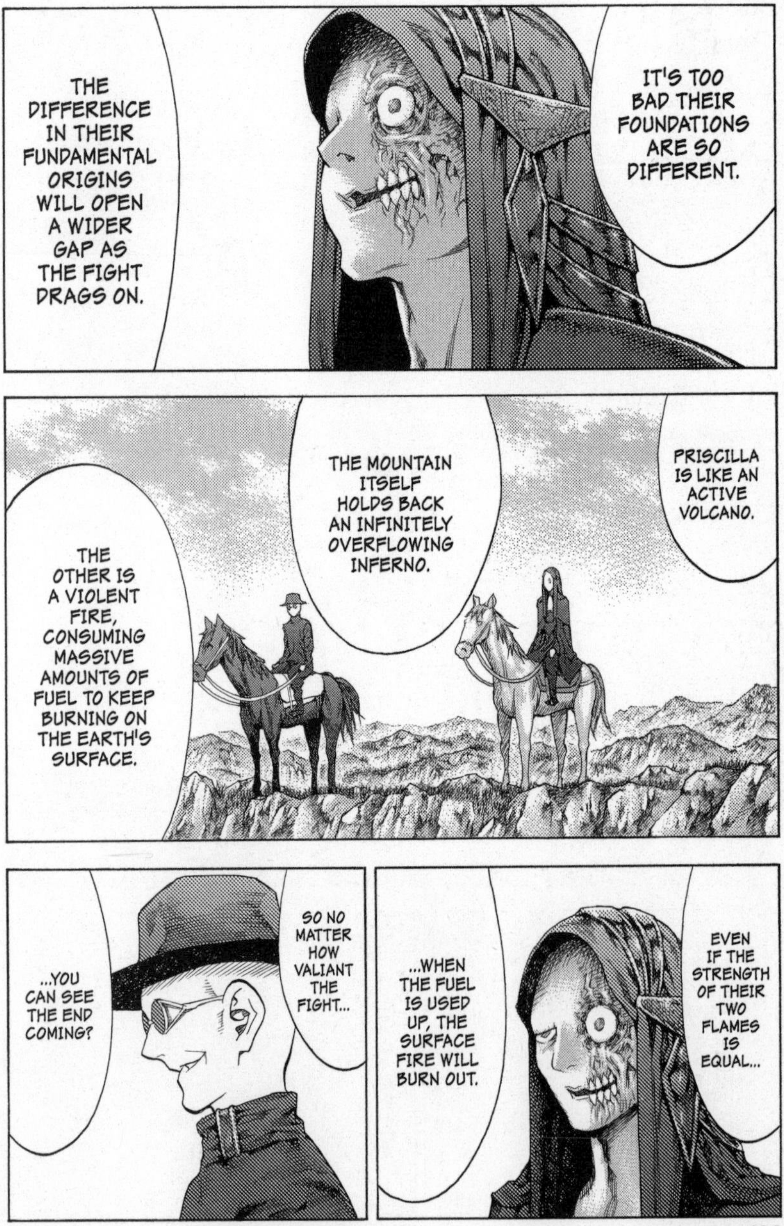
IT'S TOO BAD THEIR FOUNDATIONS ARE SO DIFFERENT.
THE DIFFERENCE IN THEIR FUNDAMENTAL ORIGINS WILL OPEN A WIDER GAP AS THE FIGHT DRAGS ON.
PRISCILLA IS LIKE AN ACTIVE VOLCANO.
THE MOUNTAIN ITSELF HOLDS BACK AN INFINITELY OVERFLOWING INFERNO.
THE OTHER IS A VIOLENT FIRE, CONSUMING MASSIVE AMOUNTS OF FUEL TO KEEP BURNING ON THE EARTH'S SURFACE.
EVEN IF THE STRENGTH OF THEIR TWO FLAMES IS EQUAL...
...WHEN THE FUEL IS USED UP, THE SURFACE FIRE WILL BURN OUT.
SO NO MATTER HOW VALIANT THE FIGHT...
...YOU CAN SEE THE END COMING?

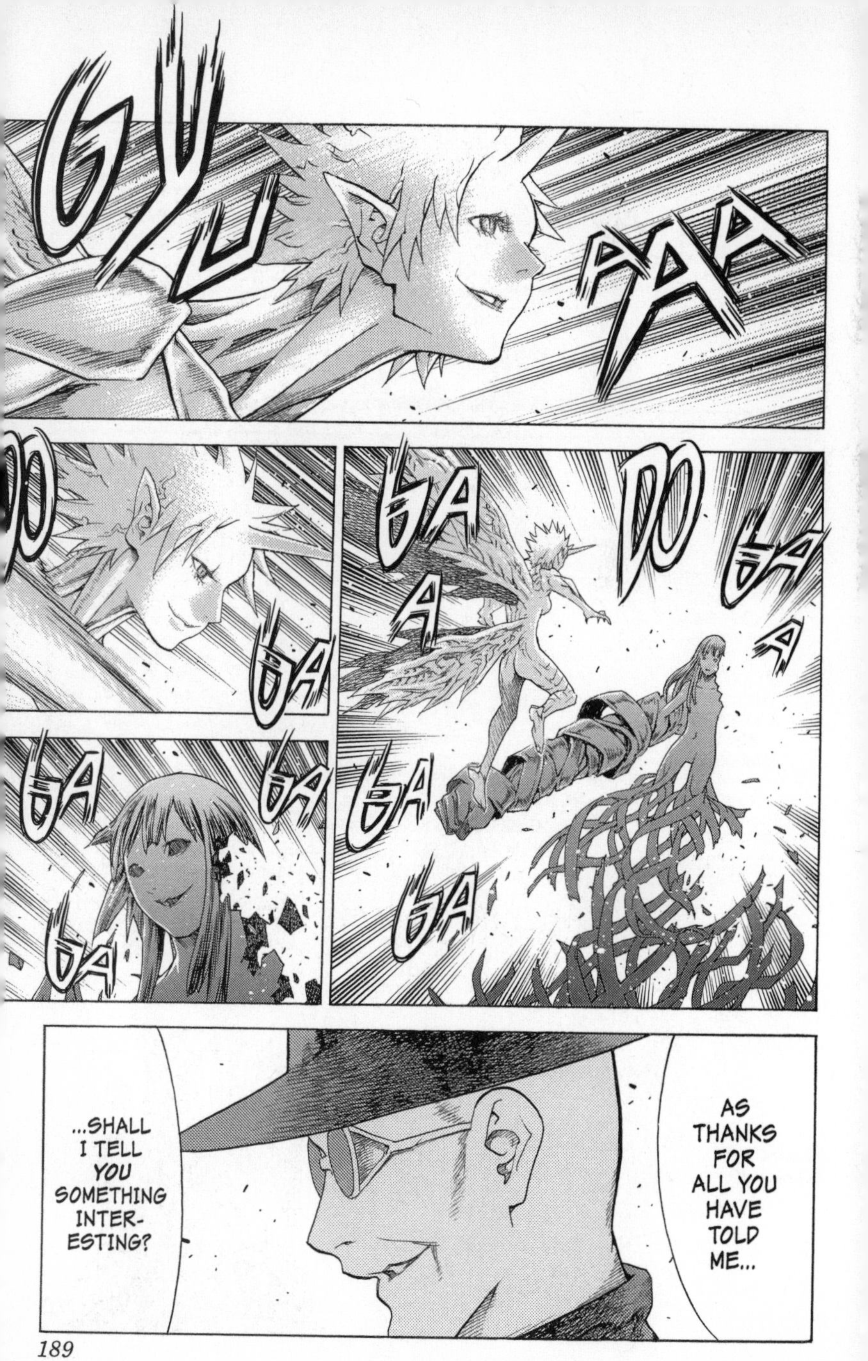
GYUAAA
DO
GAA
GAA
GA
GA
DO
GA
GA
GA
GA
AS THANKS FOR ALL YOU HAVE TOLD ME...
...SHALL I TELL *YOU* SOMETHING INTERESTING?

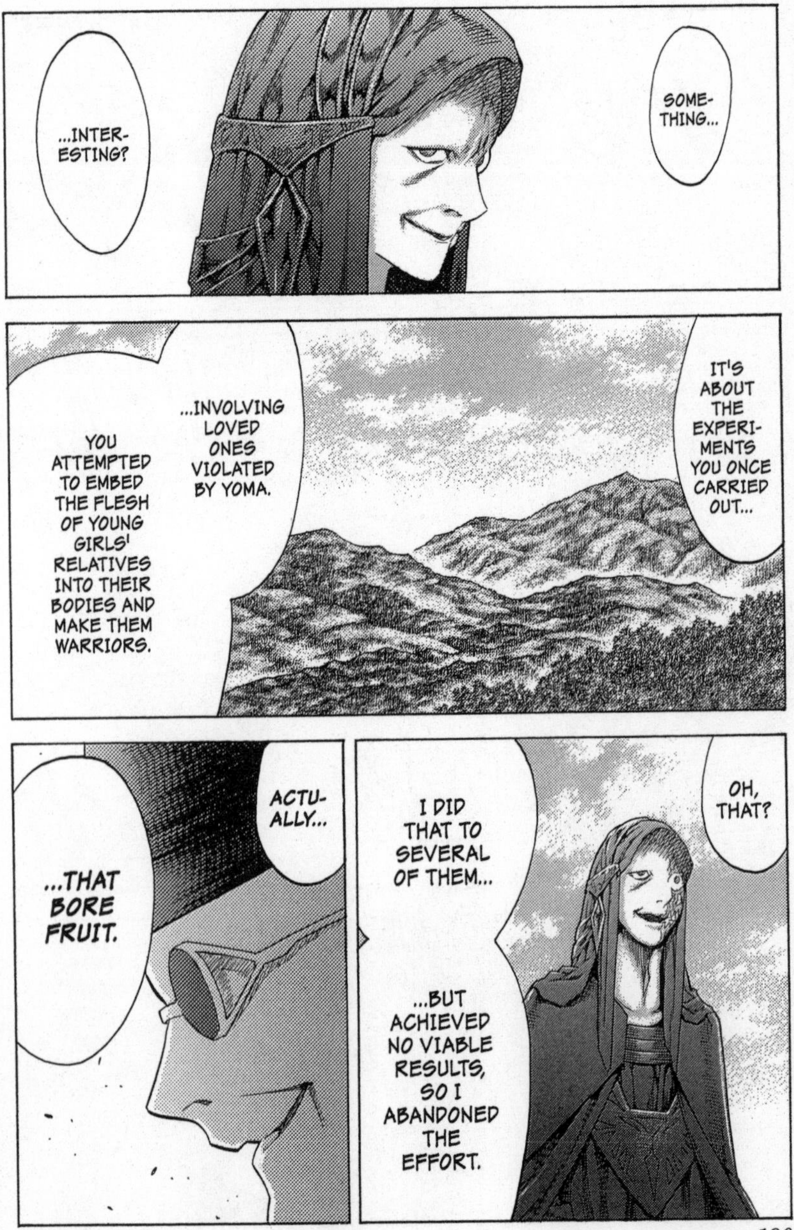
SOME-THING...
...INTER-ESTING?
IT'S ABOUT THE EXPERI-MENTS YOU ONCE CARRIED OUT...
...INVOLVING LOVED ONES VIOLATED BY YOMA.
YOU ATTEMPTED TO EMBED THE FLESH OF YOUNG GIRLS' RELATIVES INTO THEIR BODIES AND MAKE THEM WARRIORS.
OH, THAT?
I DID THAT TO SEVERAL OF THEM...
...BUT ACHIEVED NO VIABLE RESULTS, SO I ABANDONED THE EFFORT.
ACTU-ALLY...
...THAT BORE FRUIT.

READ THIS WAY

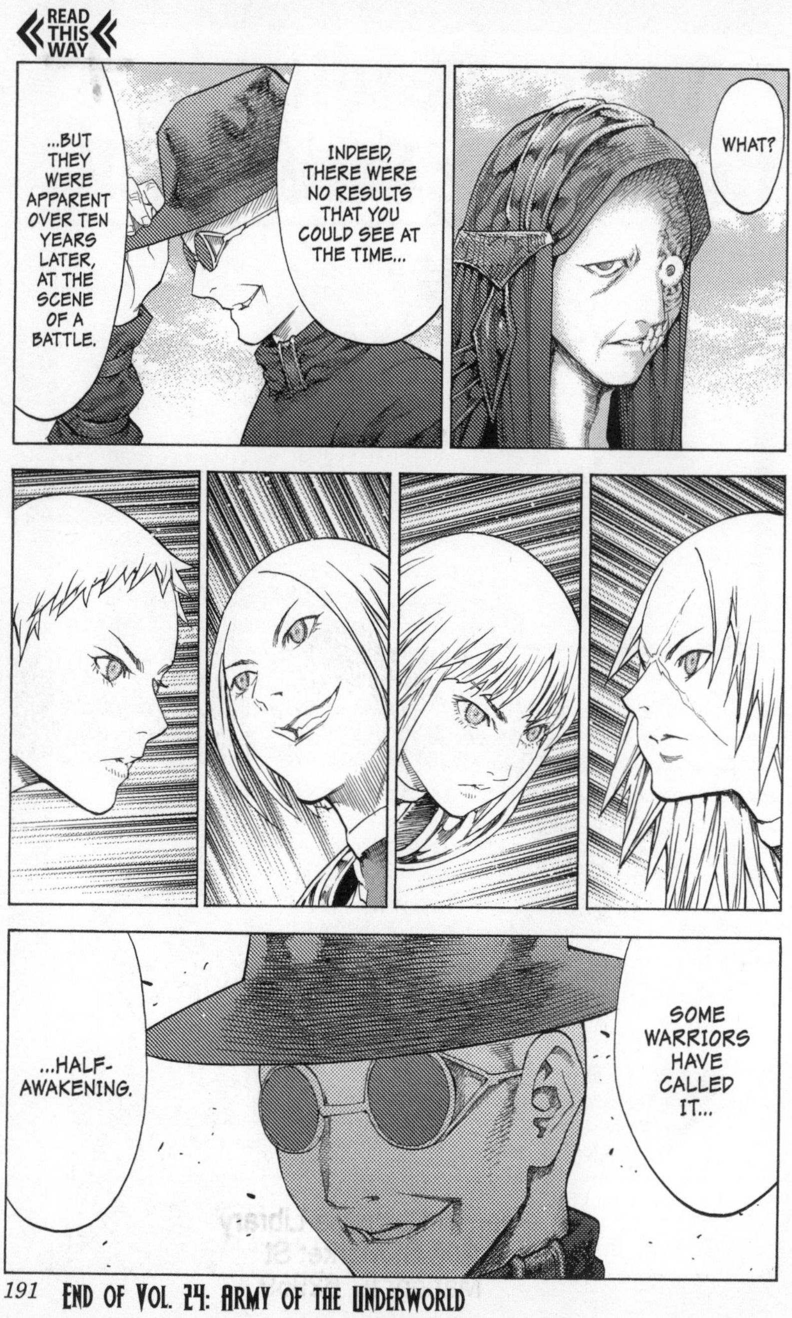
WHAT?
INDEED, THERE WERE NO RESULTS THAT YOU COULD SEE AT THE TIME...
...BUT THEY WERE APPARENT OVER TEN YEARS LATER, AT THE SCENE OF A BATTLE.
SOME WARRIORS HAVE CALLED IT...
...HALF-AWAKENING.

 End of Vol. 24: Army of the Underworld

You're Reading in the Wrong Direction!!

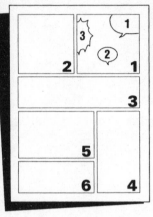

Whoops! Guess what? You're starting at the wrong end of the comic!

...It's true! In keeping with the original Japanese format, **Claymore** is meant to be read from right to left, starting in the upper-right corner.

Unlike English, which is read from left to right, Japanese is read from right to left, meaning that action, sound effects and word-balloon order are completely reversed... something which can make readers unfamiliar with Japanese feel pretty backwards themselves. For this reason, manga or Japanese comics published in the U.S. in English have sometimes been published "flopped"–that is, printed in exact reverse order, as though seen from the other side of a mirror.

By flopping pages, U.S. publishers can avoid confusing readers, but the compromise is not without its downside. For one thing, a character in a flopped manga series who once wore in the original Japanese version a T-shirt emblazoned with "M A Y" (as in "the merry month of") now wears one which reads "Y A M"! Additionally, many manga creators in Japan are themselves unhappy with the process, as some feel the mirror-imaging of their art skews their original intentions.

We are proud to bring you Norihiro Yagi's **Claymore** in the original unflopped format. For now, though, turn to the other side of the book and let the adventure begin...!

—Editor